RELIGIOUS EDUCATION AS PRACTICAL THEOLOGY

ANNUA NUNTIA LOVANIENSIA

XL

Religious Education as Practical Theology

Essays in Honour of
Professor Herman Lombaerts

Edited by

Bert Roebben and Michael Warren

PEETERS
LEUVEN - PARIS - STERLING, VA
2001

Library of Congress Cataloging-in-Publication Data

Religious education as practical theology : essays in honour of professor Herman
Lombaerts / edited by Bert Roebben and Michael Warren.
    p. c. -- (Annua nuntia Lovaniensia ; 40)
    Includes bibliographical references.
    ISBN 9042910321 (alk. paper)
    I. Christian education--Philosophy. I. Lombaerts, H. (Herman), 1935- II. Roebben,
Bert, 1962- III. Warren, Michael, 1935- IV. Series.

BV1464 R45 2001
268--dc21   2001045155

Image on the cover: Gustave van de Woestyne, Christus in de woestijn,
Gent, Museum voor Schone Kunsten.

© Uitgeverij Peeters, Bondgenotenlaan 153, B-3000 Leuven (Belgium)
ISBN 90-429-1032-1
D/2001/0602/54

Contents

Introduction

Some people have a passion for *religious education*. They experience the permanent challenge of inviting others to explore, to explain and to experience their daily life from another angle. This angle has a subversive character, one that transcends ordinary meaning and that engages the ones who are involved in new ways of knowing and loving. These educators display comprehensive religious leadership. In their relationship with others they exemplify what they believe. They invite others to participate in their struggle with a particular living tradition, with the "fides et mores" of that tradition and, through this, with their own narrative identity. In this process they open up the hermeneutic space in which others can confront themselves with their meaning giving framework.

Herman Lombaerts is such an inspired religious educator. He writes: "The contemporary social and cultural sensibility for an 'overflow' of meaning, values and norms in the actual life world, makes young people suspicious for current strategies of incorporation. On the boundaries of the institute [*church or church affiliated school*, note of the editors] religious educators are deliberating over profit and loss. They ask themselves whether the 'fermentation' of their personal commitment to tradition and church will be honoured and respected and will flourish. Profit and loss are delicate issues. But precisely on this issue, the disciples of Jesus have learned to discern what real 'profit' is. The relationship between living faith and the institute lies in the literary mediation: the story, the narrative strategy of faith"[1].

Some people have a passion for religious educational *research*. They are eager to know how young people are responding to a secularising and modernising society. They want to define the educational framework that is needed to make progress. They want to explore, together with the learners, the "powerful learning environment" that is appropriate for them, particularly fitting for them – just because it is their context. They want to find out how young people can become real family

---

1. H. LOMBAERTS, *Religieuze aanspreekbaarheid van jongeren vroeger en nu*, in J. BULCKENS & H. LOMBAERTS (eds.), *Jeugd tussen religieuze aanspreekbaarheid en levensbeschouwelijke onverschilligheid* (Nikè-reeks, 23), Leuven – Amersfoort, Acco, 1990, 11-50, p. 49 [editor's translation].

members of the 'house of learning', with their own space for working out their process of identity formation (instead of being mere house guests, welcomed but only so long as they know they do not have the privileges of family members)[2]. Moreover, these religious education scholars challenge their colleagues in theological schools, institutes and faculties to re-evaluate their theology from the perspective of religious-educational praxis. They stimulate their colleagues – sometimes successful, sometimes fruitless – to re-imagine their theology in a practical-theological way, to take seriously the context in which people struggle with existential and societal issues. Their argumentation is solid: the process of creative and innovative coping of theologians with the ambivalent tension between modern existence and Christian religious tradition, will affect theology as a whole. The hermeneutic-communicative 'Gestalt' of contemporary religious education, the fact that the younger generation will re-discover and re-appropriate Christian faith and other religious traditions in line with their de-traditionalised and modernised life world experience, is an unavoidable challenge for Christian theology[3]. It stimulates questions such as: "Do we understand what we confess? And who is this 'we'?"

Herman Lombaerts is such an inspired religious education scholar. He writes: "Exposing for examination a non-confessional religion (in its ethical and esthetical realm) allows the school to connect with the deeper perplexity and complexity of contemporary life. It creates space for the surprising message of the Christian tradition and other traditions. One may not forget that Jesus of Nazareth integrated his preaching and teaching in his daily association with his disciples, in order to be understood properly: as proclaiming the start of new and unexpected life. Probably this dream of new life will be the strongest covenant between adults and youth in the school of the future – where people learn to manage their communal learning task"[4].

This book is meant to honour Professor Herman Lombaerts by reflecting on his legacy. The contributors were invited to turn their attention to the practical theological implications of contemporary reli-

---

2. M. WARREN, *At This Time, In This Place. The Spirit Embodied in the Local Assembly*, Harrisburg PA, Trinity Press International, 1999, p. 76.

3. B. ROEBBEN, *The Vulnerability of the Postmodern Educator as Locus Theologicus. A Study in Practical Theology*, in *Religious Education* 96 (2001) no. 2, 175-192.

4. H. LOMBAERTS, *Onderwijs en maatschappij: wat brengt ons de toekomst?*, in *Impuls* 25 (1995) no. 4, 55-64, p. 63 [editor's translation].

gious education. They all have in common the passion for an actualised reaffirmation of the contribution of religious education to a modern context. Each author was asked to honour Lombaerts by taking his/her own studies on fundamental issues one step further. Such "conceptual stretching" has been at the heart of Lombaerts' own work. Contributors were asked to reflect upon three key elements which have a central place in his analysis. They form indispensable elements in a solid contemporary religious educational research: the self-agency of the learner, the hermeneutic and communicative interpretation of religious tradition(s) in the teaching of religion, and the contextualisation of theology on the basis of concrete human religious practices. Let us have a closer look at each of them.

(Young) people as organisers of their own religious learning environment

Secularisation has interrupted a particular (c.q. confessional) religious interpretation of the world. Modernisation has confronted the modern human person with processes of de-traditionalisation, individualisation and pluralisation. This cultural-philosophical environment of a secularised and modernised society in the Western world is thoroughly changing the perception, evaluation and boundaries of contemporary religious education. This shift has accelerated the need to concentrate on the subject-in-dialogue-with-others. The full consequences of this turn are, for the moment, not sufficiently integrated in religious educational research or teaching. One thing however is clear: adolescents themselves are actually reorganising the educational field so that their experiences of growing up become dramatically connected to questions of life, worldview and religiosity.

Religious education as a work of interpretation of religion

Interpreting faith traditions is part of a larger task of interpreting religions and philosophies of life. This task is undertaken by learners themselves, as a central feature of the process of religious education. Once started among learners, group discourse arises about what it means to believe. Here, the philosophical idea of hermeneutics acquires a broader meaning: people become involved in a communal search process and they design their own faith discourse. In the "hermeneutic-communicative model"[5] of religious education, young people deal with issues concerning "to believe" in a reflexive learning process (meta-reflection), in dialogue with themselves and others. This process is needed so that real appropriation can take place. Learning does not occur in the mediation of extrinsic contents, but in perceiving and reinterpreting the "strong learning environment" in which one is involved with concrete others in everyday life and with the actual answers of religious traditions in breadth and depth. Learning implies a comprehensive and integrated conversation with fellow learners concerning their religious experiences, religious questions, and with the possible insights found in traditions and cultures.

Religious education as practical theology

The discipline of practical theology attempts to provide insight into the religious praxis of individuals and communities towards institutional and non-institutional ways of being religious. The formal object of practical theology is empirical and/or hermeneutic: religion-related dimensions of human existence are mapped and interpreted against the background of social and cultural shifts in time and space. Practical theology is developing its perspectives in and beyond the field of pastoral theology; the latter is more church- and ministry related. Practical theology aims at clarifying and justifying the broader search for meaning, religion and faith, often taking place outside the institutional religious traditions. Religious educational research is, slowly but surely, positioning itself in this relatively new scholarly tradition. It wants to clarify the daily spiritual choices (in German: "Alltagsreligion") that people are making (as children, adolescents and adults) in order to integrate and articulate these insights in the processes of religious education itself. A former approach, linearly centred in ministry and education to (young) people, is now giving way to an approach in which people are themselves subjects of their religious learning. This new way of naming the work to be done by the practical theologian brings a new set of questions to the more fundamental sub-disciplines of theology, such as dogmatics, ethics, scripture and church/theology history. The conviction of current practical theologians is that the focus on praxis and daily spirituality will cause a re-imagination of theology as a whole.

*

5. Cfr. H. LOMBAERTS, B. ROEBBEN, G. GINNEBERGE, *Godinet: A Flexible Working Tool for a Subject on the Move*, in *Journal of Religious Education* [Australia] 49 (2001) no. 1, 51-58; H. LOMBAERTS & B. ROEBBEN (eds.), *Godsdienst op school in de branding. Een tussentijdse balans* (Cahiers voor Didactiek, 7), Deurne, Wolters Plantyn, 2000.

Herman Lombaerts is internationally renowned as a scholar with a strong commitment to the social and cultural context in which people live and learn, and with a clear conceptual analysis of this context. He has travelled all over the world and has been invited to several places to help in this process of analysis. He has challenged the local people to take further steps of discernment about what needs to be done in the realm of religious education. His provocative thoughts and perspectives regarding analysis, discernment and dialogue are appreciated, as well as his remarkable command of language. In this *Festschrift* we have invited some of Lombaerts' friends abroad to discuss his legacy. We have also asked other distinguished scholars in the field to reflect on his ideas. The result is this book: a thought provoking, streamlined design on the confrontation and relationship between theology and education, against the background of cultural and social shifts. The authors have contributed remarkably to a new set of ideas on the relationship between religious education and practical theology. We are very grateful to them.

Rosemary Crumlin (Melbourne) opens this series of collected essays with a remarkable piece of biographical notes on Herman Lombaerts. She reconstructs his religious educational research career with the images of modern religious art. By recalling situations and encounters with Lombaerts, she gives a good insight into the importance of his work and thought. In the same movement, she opens an important door for a domain of religious learning which was also very precious for Lombaerts, namely, modern art.

Anton Bucher (Salzburg) continues with an issue that is raised not often enough in writings about religious education and youth: that of happiness. The value of his original research is to stimulate consideration by religious educators about the place of delight in any work with young people. This essay contains a theoretical framework with brief overviews of the place of happiness in life, and a presentation of recent empirical research of the author.

Roland Campiche (Lausanne) analyses from a sociological point of view the belief system of young people of the eighties, who are the parents of today. In his findings (related to the situation in Switzerland) he presents the reader a clear picture of the existential ambiguities and the problematic identification with religion of this generation. These people grew up themselves in complexity; how will they now raise their own children?

From the Australian context, Graham Rossiter (Sydney) surveys the current literature on youth's search for spirituality and identity today.

While his focus is on the context of the school, he is concerned with establishing relevant connections with youth ministry, theology and spirituality. These connections are possible when the language used is accessible to contemporary youth and found helpful by them for their ongoing work of identity formation.

In his essay Hans-Georg Ziebertz (Würzburg) defines the place of religious educational research within an empirically oriented approach to theology. His paper provides a helpful overview of different dimensions of this approach: the material and formal object of religious educational research, the different methodologies and the importance of an appropriate perception of data for the improvement of religious education.

Michael Warren (New York) examines the distinctive value of both religious education and catechesis by considering the contexts in which these activities take place. In Warren's view, the local church's commitments, both on the level of religious education and catechesis can provide young people an invitation to enter a new way of being a person in the world: the way of *paideia* (discipleship). Religious educators need to honour the distinctive values of each other's efforts in this work.

Kieran Scott (New York) raises questions about the future and viability of religious education from the perspective of the teacher, or to be more precise, from the side of the act of teaching. He adopts the perspective both of public and religiously affiliated schools in North-America. He defends the thesis that, when theological content is taken into the classroom of the school, it becomes the teaching of religion. The relationship between religious education and practical theology is therefore the central issue for Scott.

In her critical analysis of the *General Directory for Catechesis* (1997), Catherine Dooley (Washington) sets out in detail the fundamental themes of this document that provide the context for religious instruction in the schools. She is especially interested in the main purposes delineated of this school-based instructional process. In comparison with the 1970 directory, she discovers the centrality of the distinction between catechesis and teaching of religion in the 1997 document.

What will be the function and status of religious education in the Europe of tomorrow? That is the starting question for the Italian specialist in comparative research in religious education, Flavio Pajer (Roma). He specifies the role of ethics and world views in a radically secularised social and cultural environment, and examines the degree of commitment of educational policy to this situation in different European countries. He concludes with a suggestion of elements of a multifaith curriculum for universities, built on the knowledge of religious sciences.

Norbert Mette (Paderborn) raises important issues about the relationship in a school context between the confessionalism that may direct the very existence and purpose of the school and the open search for understanding religion as a social and personal phenomenon. By problematising what can often be taken-for-granted ways of actually carrying out religious education, Mette invites readers to enter deeply into hermeneutical questions. He is especially interested in a modern concept of identity formation (*Bildung*), that transcends pre-modern and post-modern aspirations in our society.

Bert Roebben (Tilburg) depicts the situation of the religious education course in Dutch and Flemish secondary schools from the perspective of the "tradition crisis" of churches. The modernisation of religion makes it difficult for institutional religious communities to understand their task in schools properly. And yet, young people are involved in all sorts of quests for meaning. In Roebben's essay elements are brought together for a new concept of religious education that relates this quest with the wisdom of religious traditions. Precisely this tension should be the starting point for the learning process.

The essay of Maureen O'Brien (Pittsburgh) unites in a certain way all the essays of this collection around their underlying theme of theological education. Every essay is at some level a work of theological education, in the sense that they all spell out questions that need to be pressed on those engaged in religious education with the young. O'Brien adopts recent models of adult education to define these questions. Based on her research on the education of lay ministers in North-America, she offers a good tool box for a comparable work in the field of the education of religious educators.

Tjeu van Knippenberg (Tilburg) explores the competencies of pastoral ministers in a modernised social and cultural environment. How will they relate to people, knowing that changes of personal and collective identity go together with changes of religious identity? In his analysis, the dimension of "spiritual guidance" deserves a central place in the pastoral education of ministers, in the dialectical space between training of competencies and education for ministry, and between pastoral counselling and theology. Discovering meanings of people in the narration of their life stories and exploring the theological language in this narration, are the main purposes of a contemporary theological education for ministry.

Herman Lombaerts (Leuven) explains Gustave van de Woestyne's "Christ in the Desert", the picture which is also on the cover of this book. The author depicts the symbolic stratification of this painting, relying on his commitment to the Christian faith tradition. In doing so he gives the reader an idea of how modern religious art stimulates and surprises the act of religious learning in the spectator.

We conclude this series of essays with a bibliography of Herman Lombaerts and a list of contributors.

*

For Herman Lombaerts, the search processes of religious people have their own dynamic and dignity. Practical theology should listen carefully and empathetically to this quest. But Lombaerts is also convinced of the need of solid fundamental research to understand critically its ambiguities and perspectives. When we were preparing a proposal for a research project in 1998, he argued: "Life is powerful enough, people will help it to come to surface. As researchers, we have the task to anticipate meaningfully to this process of emergence". Let us hope that this collection of essays will honour him by being helpful in this process.

We would like to thank Professor Marc Vervenne, the former dean of the Faculty of Theology of the K.U. Leuven, who has stimulated the initial idea to create a streamlined design for this *Festschrift* and who has helped in the funding. We are grateful to Professor Leo Kenis of the same faculty who was willing to accept the manuscript in the series of the "Annua Nuntia Lovaniensia" and to provide it a good context for publication. We thank the publishing house Peeters in Leuven for their competent advice in the typographical aspects of the text. A special word of thanks should be addressed to Rosemary Crumlin, who helped us spontaneously with the difficult task of obtaining copyright for the images of modern art in the book and for the text of Lombaerts on "Christ in the Desert" (images and text published before in "Beyond Belief: Modern Art and the Religious Imagination", Melbourne, National Gallery of Victoria, 1998). We thank the "Museum voor Schone Kunsten" in Gent for the copy of Gustave van de Woestyne's "Christ in the Desert", on the cover of this book. We thank Antoon Bekaert for his contribution in the translation of three of the papers. We would like to thank Jacqueline Aug (Faculty of Theology Tilburg), Joke Maex and Godelieve Ginneberge (Faculty of Theology Leuven) for their consistent help during the crucial moments of finalisation of the manuscript. And finally we are grateful to the authors of this book. For both of us it has been a pleasure to read their papers and to reflect along with them on their mental journey through the ever-amazing scenery of contemporary religious education.

Bert Roebben
Michael Warren

Prologue
Remember the Skin

Rosemary Crumlin

The visual is integral to the way people see in their hearts and come to change attitudes. This essay looks at the way encounters with the visual, and particularly with art has influenced the lives of at least two people.

Melbourne, Australia
Sunday in August 2000

Dear Herman,

When your colleague, Bert Roebben, told me of the book of essays in your honour and invited me to be part of it, it was easy to say 'yes'. And to know the privilege of being asked. You are clearly one of the seminal people in both the theory and practice of Religious Education in the last forty years and our lives have intersected many times for thirty of these years. So in the past month I have sat with the invitation and reflected on some of the most influential moments of our life meetings. Your life has stayed steadily in the academic community of Practical Theology, my journey has been more restless with each shift turning up more questions. From religious education with teenagers to adult education to curating and writing in art and religion to art and the spiritual – ever widening circles.

To tell the story of our meetings I have decided to take my notes, diaries, drawings and letters of these thirty years and to write you some postcards or maybe letters. I wish I had written these at the time. Perhaps hindsight and imagination are an OK lens.

These letters will, as you might expect, move with the visual, then with art and, I hope, with a sense that what happens most to change our lives happens through relationship and what I can only call 'the spaces between'. In particular I think of the space inhabited by the artist and by the creative; it has the annoying habit of seeming random and disorganized at first, then tentative or often brash. It is a space of encounter that is both seductive and dangerous.

Corpus Christi
London, 1972

Dear Herman,

Many thanks for the visit with you which Beatrice Taylor arranged in Brussels – and for the wonderful meal and hospitality. I'm back now with time to reflect on what the newspapers and magazines are labelling 'the crisis at Corpus Christi'[1], and on how much of what is happening here in the conflict between the staff and the hierarchy mirrors the wider international scene in religious education. Both sides are filled with right reason and good intentions.

Pluralism is at the heart of the issue, although on the surface it appears that in resigning their positions the Director, Bert Richards and his staff are over-reacting to Cardinal Heenan's directive to dis-invite particular visiting lecturers including Gregory Baum and Enda McDonagh. But as their statement in the recent *Tablet* (08.01.72) notes: "The totality of today's church contains many theological points of view, which must be reflected in a catechetical institute by a widely representative lecturing staff. The exclusion of men of quality, highly esteemed in the Catholic world, seemed to be the beginning of a narrowing process ... where finally only one point of view would be acceptable".

My own experience in Australia in working on the catechetical source material, *Come Alive*, supports this, although I would probably want to name it more as a difference of belief about the ways in which God speaks and is heard today. On the one hand there are those who hold firmly to the position that revelation ceased with the death of the last Apostle; on the other, that God's word is found also in the history of our times. *Come Alive* stands strongly for the latter and upholds the value of the life experience of the students and their (learned) ability to reflect critically on it. Those who hold firmly to the former position worry that all will indeed be lost. As one critic, I. C. Holford, has commented in a letter to the *Catholic Weekly*: "Unless the present rot is stopped, Catholicism in this land will soon be in grave danger. If our schools turn out not informed Catholics but confused, vacuous slaves of the secular mass-ideologies ... we will be wasting the lives of our

---

1. Corpus Christi was a famous Religious Education Institute in London. Its Director was scripture scholar and writer, Hubert Richards. In 1972 the academic staff resigned over issues of academic freedom.

children, of our priests, of our brothers and nuns, and wasting the incalculable efforts of those living and dead whose labour and devotion built our Australian Church" (17.06.71).

The 'rot' seems to refer to the *Come Alive* material, which includes images, story, poetry and question rather than (dogmatic) question and (dogmatic) answer to be committed to memory for some imagined future use. The anger generated by *Come Alive* gave birth within a couple of weeks to a small booklet, circulated free, entitled *What's wrong with 'Come Alive'?* I fear that the enmity surrounding these questions will not go away.

Herman, I think that a pluralism of understanding in the meaning of Revelation is also a way to understand the issues that so divided the participants in the International Catechetical Congress in Rome last year. One funny moment that I remember happened in the geography of the meeting. On the stage in the illustrious hall of the Lateran University sat the cardinals like carved chessmen or judges in some fantastic court. In the tiered seats were the rest of us – the 'learned' or 'influential' of world catechesis, overwhelmingly male and clerical and white; then came non-European black clerics, a vocal minority; next, a few habited nuns; and, last of all, a sprinkling of lay women, one from the Philippines but the others from the U.S. Speakers had a maximum of five minutes and then a little silver bell was rung (sometimes waking the cardinals on stage). I noticed only the white clerics seemed to obey the bell.

Now to the crux of this letter. Herman, the Bishops Conference of Australia are to set up a National Pastoral Institute of Religious Education in 1973. They have invited me to be a member of the inaugural staff team. Given my present experience in *Come Alive* and now at Corpus Christi as I watch the courage and pain of people like Bert Richards, I have just two questions: "Am I the stuff of martyrs?" and "Should I take courage and say *yes*, knowing how short-lived and fraught catechetical institutes usually are now?"

I look forward to your reply.

National Pastoral Institute
Melbourne, 1982

Dear Herman,

Well, you've come and gone for the second time to the National Pastoral Institute, now in its ninth year and almost longer than the full life
of Corpus Christi in London.

Some of your ideas have become common currency here as has your
language – 'conscientization', 'central subsystem', 'world community',
'discourse', 'dialogical', 'decisive issues', 'the mover: the person who
shapes the historical landscape'. Most influential for me, however, has
been your insistence on experience as the starting point for analysis and
for the future action that then grows out of analysis. This time, as
before, the quality of your presence invited people to reassess their positions and take another step forward towards a global rather than simply
a local awareness. They learned from you that responsibility is to be
understood as communal as well as personal, and that change and influence are possible rather than overwhelming. Not everyone welcomes
such tough mindedness. A colleague of mine in Newcastle, Margaret
Woodward, remembers watching positions being hardened as you challenged some established certainties. But isn't that the way it always is
with change?

Herman, although what you present disturbs some people and ener-
gizes others, it gels well with the underlying philosophy and purpose of
the National Pastoral Institute (NPI). These were expressed in 1973 as
"[embracing] the needs of the whole Church and the promotion of the
nourishment and balanced growth of all in the Church". This sounded
a little high-flying in 1973 when the major concern was understood
(whatever the words) to be catechetical in the earlier sense of preparing
teachers, usually teachers of children, to communicate the truths and
habits of the Faith so that their students could become good Catholic
adult parents and citizens. There were many of the same assumptions
underlying the curriculum at Corpus Christi, which may go some way
to explaining how Cardinal Heenan, who sacked the staff, could at the
same time declare himself in support of its aims and curriculum.

I hope we have gone beyond that limited understanding of religious
education at NPI in that we have consistently stood open to the questions of the adults who come here. As their questions (and our own)
have changed, so has this place. I could go on about change but, as you

noticed both times when you were here, the shift is toward self-directed learning, towards systems analysis of the situation (thanks for your contribution to this), and towards enabling students to understand themselves as adults and so to shift the central focus from child to adult. The effect of all of this has been to keep NPI as a place which initiates and manages change, both in people and in curriculum. You will have noticed on your two visits that most who come here are at mid-life. In the early years, they were predominantly vowed religious, mostly women and while this is changing (near to 40% this year are lay people who are dependent on scholarships to attend), the questions which they bring are now located around issues of gender discrimination in ministry and around insights and questions related to the theologies of liberation. And, of course, the interrelation of these two. It augurs well for the future of lay leadership in the Church.

Herman, do you remember the day we spent at the Melbourne exhibition of works by the Australian artist, Arthur Boyd? No better way, I thought, to introduce you to the landscape of this country, especially that around the Shoalhaven River in New South Wales. Wonderful trees and cliff and a strong river often in flood. Remember our shock as we turned the corner from the first room to be confronted by two crucifixions, both in the river against the background of the rugged hills? One was of a male figure with a rose (the symbol of England) floating in the river below; the other cross held the crucified figure of a woman.

I've since written to the artist, now in England, to express appreciation and wonder and to tell him of our response. I said, too, that if ever it were possible to bring together the greatest religious images of this country since 1945, I would want to include these two paintings. Because they are very fine works they raise key questions which have to do with the person and meaning of Jesus Christ, the notion of redemption and renewal, and the need of our age to be aware of the whole of creation, the earth and woman, as an integral part in possible futures. In other ways our students are raising the same questions, although their articulation of these is not as prophetic as Boyd's. Did you know that these works became the focus of a lot of negative criticism – the image of a woman crucified was so shocking.

Plate 1
Arthur Boyd (1920-1999) *Crucifixion, Shoalhaven 1979-80*

Melbourne,
the day NPI closed (December 1988)

Dear Herman,

1986 was my fourteenth and last year at NPI, hard as that is to believe
– almost all of my midlife years in this one place. Staying so long was
always about change and energy for me, and by the end of 1986 NPI
was offering specialized courses in Adult Education, Leadership and
Youth Ministry as well as Religious Education. Within these areas there
was a lot of enthusiasm to pursue questions around feminist and liberation theology, contemporary approaches to Scripture, media studies,
working with personal story, and creativity. All of this, adult education.
The Youth Ministry course brought young people in for three months,
and younger members to the staff (the principle of 'like to like' is pretty
self-evident in ministry as elsewhere). Clearly it was time for me to go,
so I resigned and went.

But I bring you the sad news that today, two years later, NPI closed.
I was present for the 'funeral rites'. The story of the closing is too long
to tell here but if I were an optimist I would say that perhaps NPI had
done its part and it was time to step aside. However it is very hard not
to express regret at its passing, even though my own life is now elsewhere. So, Herman, know that you and Mike Warren, Connie Loos,
Maria Harris, Virgil Elizondo and Dan Berrigan were in my mind as
I wrote this to each past student last week:

> Thank you for your part in building NPI, and for the laughs and
> struggles of your time. At this moment faces tumble before me, and
> I regret a bit that this page cannot contain a collage of all the draw-
> ings across the years. But I hope it does evoke people you knew, and
> that it causes you to speak with some of them again – even simply to
> share memories as a way of marking the event of the closing.

> You know, the Church is going to miss NPI. Where now will people go
> to take time to reflect, to question and to be back in touch with the call
> to freedom? Where will the sort of leadership training be offered that
> allowed for people to be at ease with their own personal style while still
> being able to work to change it? Where will enthusiasm be nurtured in
> the same way? I do not know. Part of the richness of NPI was its
> poverty. Without large financial resources it was free to respond to indi-
> vidual needs as they emerged. Without massive building programmes it
> was not preoccupied with government grants and forms. Without
> career structures it was able to build a peculiar staff committed to
> scholarship yet believing in a listening style of education.

Can it happen again? I do not know. I hope so. The Church needs
such a place. And it will not find it in teachers' colleges or in universities or even in theologates. Their goals and restraints are different.

Herman, this letter isn't simply about a death. Since leaving NPI I've
been working towards the fulfilment of the dream of bringing together
the best of Australian religious art since 1945. Pretty well all my life has
been a flirtation with art and the visual, and my five years at Art School
in the sixties were like an extended honeymoon with the creative. Then
Come Alive and the fourteen years at NPI followed and in one sense at
least the romance faded, stepped into the shadows and waited. But the
last two years have been filled with art – visits to studios, looking at
paintings, interviewing artists, dancing around galleries both here and in
Europe. These years have also been about seeking sponsorship, research
and writing, and talking with publishers.

But that is over. The exhibition and the book, *Images of Religion in
Australian Art²*, were launched last week at the National Gallery of Victoria. As I watch people moving around the works, talking softly, looking through this beautifully produced book, I know in a different way
the power of images to inspire, confront, raise questions and comfort.
Art, like religious education, is not simple. Nor is it easy. Ultimately it
is complex, unclear, puzzling and occasionally ecstatic.

Oh, and we did get Boyd's Crucifixions! He told me he had never
sold them, but in fact had kept them in case I ever got this exhibition
up. What amazing generosity!

---

2. *Images of Religion in Australian Art*, Sydney, Bay Books, 1988.

Images of Religion in Australian Art

Arthur Boyd, *Moses Leading the People*, 1947 Collection of Maurice and Helen Alter, Melbourne

Plate 2
Poster for the exhibition, *Images of Religion in Australian Art*

Melbourne, 1992

Dear Herman,

I am remembering the journey through Germany which we made in 1989 in search of works for a world exhibition of religious art – the best in this century. So it had to include the German Expressionists centred in Germany from the beginning of the century. People like Beckmann, Ernst, Kokoschka, Kandinsky, Schmidt Rottluff, Barlach and the wonderful Käthe Kollwitz.

What a shot in the arm it was to meet Horst Schwebel at Marburg and to find that whatever I thought, he'd been there first! Then down to Cologne, and that Saturday with Friedhelm Mennekes, the Jesuit parish priest who has set up the ancient St Peter's in Newmarket as a centre of modern art. And the space behind the high altar for a changing feast of contemporary triptychs – Bacon, Droese, Brown, Saura and so on. Here is the modern artist – Christian and not, believer and not – brought right to the heart of the Christian mystery. Works shocking and inspiring, beating with the integrity of true genius.

I returned determined to hold the dream of the exhibition and book; you, brimming over with plans to bring modern art and artist into the theory and practice of practical theology. My plans were unexpectedly put on hold when I agreed to curate an exhibition and edit a book on Australian Aboriginal art[3] to coincide with the meeting of the World Council of Churches in Canberra last year.

Painting, dance and story are integral to Aboriginal culture and are intimately related to the survival of the ancestor spirits who dwell in the land – in its waterholes, hills, trees, animals and birds of the air. Should they die, the people will die. Keeping the relationship right between land and people is done through the painting, dance and story which initiate the Aboriginal people in this responsibility. Such is the way it has been for forty thousand years, long before 'white fellas' (as they call us) came in with flour, sugar and often with Christianity.

Finding great Aboriginal paintings is easy, for the best are born of the necessity to survive in the spiritual sense. But finding great Christian Aboriginal works is near to impossible, as we found[4]. Most are tainted with the cultural and religious limitations of the white missionaries and

---

3. *Aboriginal Art and Spirituality*, Melbourne, Collins Dove, 1991.
4. Frank Brennan sj and co-curator Anthony Knight were parties to the search.

often look like those simple holy cards that are full of kitsch. Most, but not all, as we found when we set out into the desert in search of great works in which the Aboriginal artist 're-thinks' the symbols of Christianity. Not that many non-Aboriginal Christian works rise above the level of the mundane and repetitious in their handling of the Christian story – perhaps one of the reasons why the face of the Church is so boring to many young people.

Back to our story. Across the top end and the desert we journeyed. Vast distances that most Europeans cannot imagine. Thousands and thousands of red-earthed kilometres, seemingly empty of life or spirit. One community after another – Darwin, Daly River, Bathurst Island, and down in a tiny plane to the remote community in Balgo at the edge of the Great Sandy Desert. Hot, hot, hot and sticky – and so dry. And the magic of the works of the Dreaming[5]. In Balgo I sat and watched while women dotted in their stories on canvases spread on the earth and then sang them into life. I learnt that this land breathes its life stories and that the ancestor spirits are reborn in these people.

Eventually we flew into Warmun, a small community at Turkey Creek in Western Australia. The group here and its elders are Catholic; the elders are also guardians of the Dreaming (Law). Two are great artists. George Mung Mung and Hector Sundaloo are old men. They keep the stories and the secrets and are proud to be 'two-way" – both Aboriginal and Christian. Christianity goes well with their traditional beliefs. "We always knew about Ngapuny (God) and the Holy Spirit", Hector said to me one day, "but youse mob had to come and tell us about Jesus and Mary".

They took us to an old shed attached to the school and, in that silent way Aboriginal people have, they left us alone. Tutankhamen's tomb is nothing to this. Tacked up on the walls, standing on the floor, around every space are these amazing paintings, narratives for the most part, which they use for great liturgies. There are crucifixes and nativities, dancing figures and spirits to be carried on shoulders during ceremonies[6]. This was an experience of the sacred that is with me again as I write this. And, standing on an old tin cylinder, is a carved figure of a young woman, pregnant. Her body has been painted with the body designs reserved for young, unmarried Warmun girls. The child in her

5. 'Dreaming' is a term commonly used to describe the sum total of ancestor stories and customs that make up the law and lore by which Aboriginal people guide their lives.
6. Traditionally in this area the boards are carried across the shoulders of the dancing leaders.

womb is a man, a man dancing. Old George Mung Mung said to me in
his high-pitched voice:

> This young woman
> she's a young woman, this one.
> The spirit of the little baby
> comes in a dream
> to his mother.
> Proper little one,
> his mother says.
> The baby grows and
> he might be ready at
> Christmas time.
> He says,
> Mother, I'm ready now.
>
> And the old woman take her away
> and the little one is born
> down in the river here.

This is, I believe, one of the great images of this century. Even in reproduction it has remarkable presence. These Warmun people hold a Christianity that is washed clean.

Plate 3
George Mung Mung (c. 1920-1991) *Mary of Warmun*
(The pregnant Mary), c. 1983

Melbourne, 1998

Herman,

Well, it is finished. I am so pleased that you came for the last week. You – and more than three thousand others – to the last day of the exhibition of some of the greatest religious images of the century. Both the exhibition and the book carry the same title: *Beyond Belief: Modern Art and the Religious Imagination*[7].

The title is about many things but it also describes the Everest-type journey that getting it together has been. Wonderful, depressing, hard, stressful, rich and ecstatic, until here it is – so many works, so many people, so much talk and so much silence. More than twelve hundred people wrote comments, many of them deep, about what happened as they came each time. The power of art.

It is now clear that the biggest group of viewers were in their twenties and thirties. That surprised everyone, including me. Every day they came, but they crowded in at weekends. Young men and women holding hands, a bit scruffy looking some of them as they stood watching or being watched. As R. S. Thomas has written, "They (the paintings) are not asleep ... It is not they are being looked at, but we"[8].

Why did they come? I do not know for sure. Most of the works were truly great but it wasn't simply that. Some of the works were explicitly Christian, but it wasn't that. I suspect, though I cannot be certain, that together these works somehow spoke into the journey towards learning and justice that so many young people seek and do not often find (they say) in Church.

One work in particular always had people around it, looking. Old and young. I saw a young man with a child on his shoulders alongside a bent gnarled woman, both with tears in their eyes. People have stopped me in the street – strangers whose names I do not know – with "I remember the skin". "I remember the skin".

'The skin' is Daniel Goldstein's *Icarian II/Incline* 1993 made of leather, sweat, wood, copper, felt and plexiglass. It is one of a whole series, *Reliquaries*, on which he has been working since 1991. Each beautiful case contains a skin, the leather cover from a piece of equipment

7. *Beyond Belief. Modern Art and the Religious Imagination*, Melbourne, National Gallery of Victoria, 1998.
    8. R.S. THOMAS, *Collected Poems 1945-1990*, London, Phoenix, 1995, p. 455.

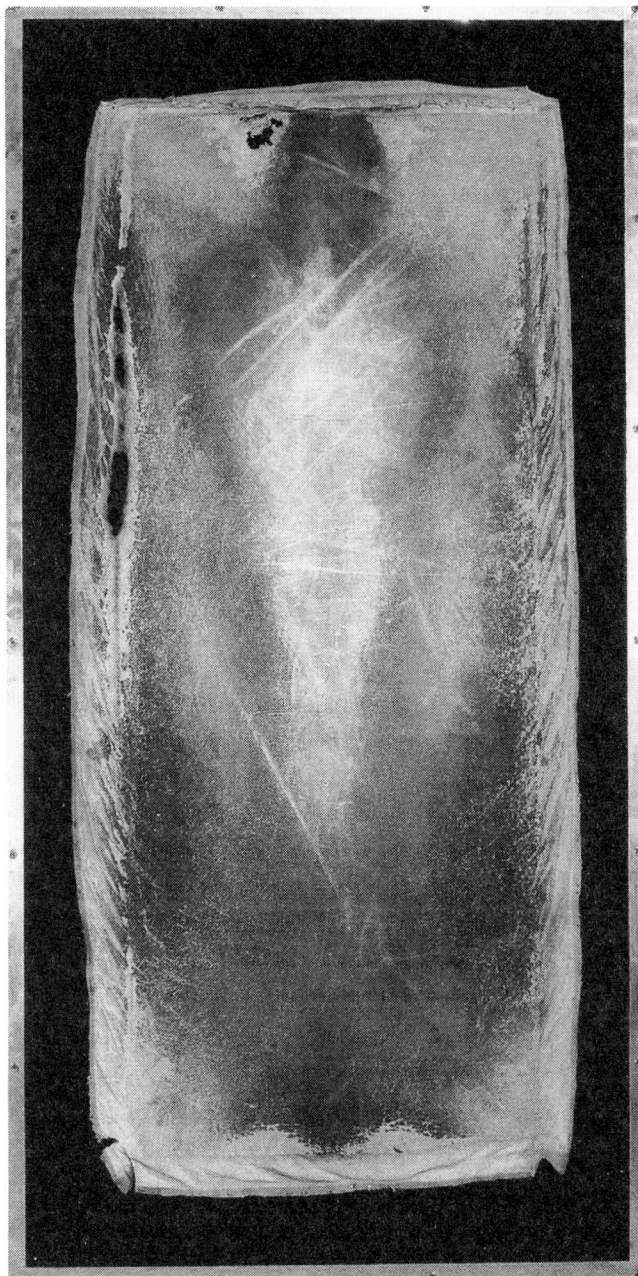

Plate 4
Daniel Goldstein (b. 1950) *Icarian II/Incline*, 1993

in a San Francisco gymnasium (or sports room) frequented by young
gay men. They came before the advent of HIV/AIDS to this place, for
social reasons and to keep their bodies beautiful. Many have since died.
Others, often HIV-positive, still come. Goldstein removed the skins
from the equipment (this one is from an Incline), spread them out, and
realized that the constant contact with human bodies, the vapours and
the sweat and dirt from the hands had impregnated the skin with
images. This work, *Icarian II*, is redolent also of the young Greek
Icarus, who flew so close to the sun that the wax of his wings melted
and he fell to earth.

But then, Herman, you saw all this – and the way the original shone
with the ghostly image of the suffering Christ. It is a work that is both
key and challenge; it opens the door and beckons into darkness or
light.

Back to 2000

Herman,

   That's about it for this skipping across the years; that's about it for
the opening of some doors labelled 'Art' and others labelled 'Religion
and Art'. You are the expert in the door that carries the label, 'Religious
Education and Art', but opening that reveals some darknesses. This
Church we both love does have a pretty bad record over the past couple
of centuries about its willingness to listen to the artist. Dogmatism, certainty and narrowness are antithetical to what breathes life and openness
and sight. I think Christianity is born of these last three.
   You, of all people, know this and it is write large in your life.

Sincerely, and in admiration,

Rosemary.

Happiness of the Children: A Task for the Pedagogics of Religion?

Anton Bucher

Introduction: The Discrimination of Happiness

It is one of the most profound human desires to be or to become happy. It is a "desire that never becomes obsolete"[1]. No matter how central the theme of happiness may be – not only in the life of most people, but in all cultures – Christianity and religious education have always been ambivalent toward it. Although Jesus Christ, for Dorothee Sölle "the happiest man"[2], brought us glad tidings and with his unconventional practice made many outsiders, sick or socially stigmatized people happy, during many centuries it was proclaimed that a Christian was not born to be happy on earth. Augustine (354-430) was very influential with his statement that a person's life is "full of evil", and consequentially had to be pitied and mourned for. Only the Grace of the Savior could redeem "from the hell of our unhappy lives", instilling the hope of heaven, "where there is no evil", but "full, certain and eternal happiness to glorify God"[3].

For centuries, the Church put all its hope on happiness in the afterlife, to be gained by living a virtuous, conformist life, which could be endangered by sin. Undoubtedly, the numerous images of heavenly happiness that continually changed in the course of time, have comforted countless people and helped them to bear the pains of life (poverty, serfdom, sicknesses, etc.)[4]. On the other hand, the critics of religion have rightly denounced such images of happiness being abused to legitimize structures of injustice on earth and to keep humankind in a state of alienation: "The abolition of religion as of imaginary happi-

1. "Eine Sehnsucht, die nicht altert". L. Marcuse, *Philosophie des Glücks. Von Hiob bis Freud*, Zürich, Diogenes, 1996, p. 11.
2. D. Sölle, *Phantasie und Gehorsam. Überlegungen zu einer künftigen christlichen Ethik*, Stuttgart – Berlin, Kreuz, 1968, p. 63.
3. Augustine, *De Civitate Dei*, XXII, 22.
4. B. Lang & C. Mc Dannell, *Der Himmel. Eine Kulturgeschichte des ewigen Lebens*, Frankfurt am Main, Suhrkamp, 1990.

ness of the people", Marx wrote in his *Kritik der Hegelschen Recht-sphilosophie* (Critic of the philosophy of right of Hegel), "means the promotion of their real happiness (…). The critic of religion is therefore in germ the critic of the vale of tears, of which religion is the shrine"[5].

It is necessary to learn from critics, also in theology and church. "No falling back behind Marx"[6]. Never again Christianity as "solace of the hereafter, deformation of consciousness, adornment with flowers of the chains instead of breaking them"[7]. But even then it also took quite a time before (practical) theology rehabilitated earthly happiness. Until the middle of 20th century, manuals of faith[8] took over the first passage from Deharbe's Catechism (first edition in 1854): "We are on earth to recognize God, to love him, to serve him and in this way to come into heaven – the place of eternal, complete bliss"[9]. In the commentary we can read: "No human person is created for bliss on earth, let us not forget that"[10]. First, earthly happiness perishes. Second, people are created by God, who would have belied his nature, if he had destined them for a happiness which can be found outside him. Although the American Founding Fathers three generations before (1776) had already claimed for the human person the fundamental right to pursue happiness, the Catholic Church clung to the priority of supernatural salvation after life over earthly happiness. It was the so-called *Théologie Nouvelle* that for the first time tried to overcome the fatal distinction between happiness and salvation: "in striving for authentic happiness, in endeavoring to provide favorable life circumstances and in the experience that life is truly bound to succeed, it becomes clear that salvation already comes into history and – by the mediation of human action – can be experienced in many anticipations of salvation in life, whereby it refers to a final fulfillment beyond"[11].

5. "Die Aufhebung der Religion als des illusorischen Glücks des Volkes, ist die Forderung seines wirklichen Glücks (…). Die Kritik der Religion ist also im Keim die Kritik des Jammertales, dessen Heiligenschein die Religion ist". K. MARX & F. ENGELS, *Studienausgabe, Band I: Philosophie*, Frankfurt am Main, Fischer, 1990, p. 21.

6. H. KÜNG, *Existiert Gott?*, München, Piper, 1978, p. 288.

7. *Ibid.*, p. 289.

8. E.g. *Katechismus der katholischen Religion, neubearbeitet und herausgegeben auf Befehl und mit Gutheißung des bischöflichen Ordinariates Chur*, 1938, p. 1.

9. "Wir sind auf Erden, um Gott zu erkennen, ihn zu lieben, ihm zu dienen und dadurch in den Himmel – den Ort ewiger, vollkommener Glückseligkeit – zu kommen". J. DEHARBE, *Gründliche und leichtfassliche Erklärung des Katholischen Katechismus, I. Band: Lehre von dem Glauben*, Paderborn, Schöningh, 1888, p. 3.

10. *Ibid.*, p. 6.

11. "Im Streben nach authentischem Glück, im Bemühen um die Schaffung glückender Lebensumstände und in der Erfahrung, daß das Leben wahrhaft glückt, wird deutlich,

For practical theology, especially for the pedagogics of religion, this results in the endeavor to contribute to a successful life and to the endorsement of happiness, especially that of the children, as one of its objectives. Happiness is not a subject explicitly thematized by the new pedagogics of religion. In the bibliography of the year 1998, the issue appears once, whereas in the Constitution of Western Germany it occurs 14 times[12]. Articles such as *Ist der Religionsunterricht eine Anstiftung zum Glück?* (Is religious education an instigation to happiness?)[13] are exceptions confirming the rule. Do past reserves with respect to happiness and joy still have their after effect in religious education? For centuries, religious education, to the extent that it was oriented by the doctrine of the original sin, aimed at "mutilating childhood; only by breaking the originally evil nature of the child, was it possible to turn the human being again into the image of God"[14]. If practical theology in general, and pedagogics of religions in particular, aim at contributing to human happiness, it is necessary to take into account the theories of happiness (section 1). Of further relevance is the information available in the psychology of happiness concerning favoring happiness of children (section 2). It is also necessary to examine whether religiosity is favorable or unfavorable to human happiness, especially that of children (section 3). In section 4 we will try to concretize how religious education might contribute to the happiness of children and adolescents.

1. What Is Happiness?

Theories of happiness are torn between subjective experiences of happiness and claims of objective validity. Classical and theological doctrines of happiness[15] tried to objectively determine happiness and to

---

daß Gottes Heil jetzt schon in die Geschichte tritt und – vermittelt durch das Handeln des Menschen – in vielfältigen Antizipationen heilen Lebens als beglückend erfahren wird, dabei freilich zugleich über sich hinaus auf eine endgültige Erfüllung verweist". G. GRESHAKE, Art. *Glück*, in *Lexikon für Theologie und Kirche*, Vol. 4, Freiburg – Basel – Wien, Herder, 1995, col. 759 ff.

12. *Religionspädagogische Jahresbibliographie* 13 (1998) 283.

13. F.W. NIEHL, *Ist der Religionsunterricht eine Anstiftung zum Glück?*, in *Katechetische Blätter* 122 (1997) 64-71.

14. H.J. EWERS, *Die Literatur der versehrten Kindheit*, in R. CORDES (ed.), *Welt der Kinder – Kinder der Welt. Kindheitsbilder in der Kinder- und Erwachsenenliteratur*, Schwerte, Viktor Verlag, 1989, p. 87.

15. E.g. M. FORSCHNER, *Über das Glück des Menschen*, Darmstadt, Wissenschaftliche Buchgesellschaft, 1993.

point the way to a "beatitudo objectiva". Aristotle did not fail to remark that happiness was a disputed concept[16], that the poor determine it to be riches, the sick as health, some as desire, others as prestige and honor. He proposed a concept of happiness with objective-normative validity: the really happy person is the one who acts according to perfect virtue and is sufficiently provided with external goods, not for a determined period but for all his/her life[17]. Happiness is not fortuitous (in Greek: *eutychia*) or a matter of luck, but a long-lasting state (in Greek: *eudaimonia*). Happiness is the result of intelligent and virtuous activity. This activity is elsewhere defined by Aristotle as activity executed for its own sake[18]. It brings about lust, which motivates new activity[19]. This means that Aristotle anticipated the psychology of intrinsic motivation. He further stated that friendships, at least the ones not oriented towards personal utility or lust, but those whereby friends are loved for their own sake, stimulate happiness.

This activity-theoretical approach to happiness is a milestone in the history of western ideas. It could be demonstrated how this approach still affects actual (psychological) concepts of happiness, as for instance the Flow concept of Csikszentmihalyi[20]. But it certainly was not the only concept in Antiquity. Augustine states that the Roman scholar Varro had gathered no less than 288 different definitions of happiness[21]. This abundance of concepts of happiness did not prevent the Church Father himself from determining happiness in an objective way as to be reserved for the bliss given by God in heaven to glorify and praise him.

Objective determinations of happiness are nowadays obsolete and this not only because of the social changes usually called individualization and pluralism. Kant has stated that happiness can be very different in different persons and therefore could never become a principle of moral judgment and action, susceptible to generalization[22]. He did not conclude therefore that the human being had no right to happiness; it is rather so that "there is an obligation to look for one's happiness"[23]. But he opposed the eudaimonistic viewpoint, according to which

---

16. ARISTOTLE, *Nicomachean Ethics*, 1095 a, 20ff.
17. *Ibid.*, 1101 a, 14ff.
18. *Ibid.*, 1097 a, 31ff.
19. *Ibid.*, 1175 a, 20ff.
20. M. CSIKSZENTMIHALYI, *Flow – das Geheimnis des Glücks*, Stuttgart, Klett-Cotta, 1998[6], p. 13.
21. AUGUSTINE, *De Civitate Dei*, XIX, 1.
22. I. KANT, *Kritik der Praktischen Vernunft*, A 47.
23. *Ibid.*, A 167.

happiness is the principle of morals. The theory of happiness had to be distinguished from morality. Modern philosophy mostly clung to the subjectivity of happiness emphasized by Kant, although there were exceptions. Herbert Marcuse, for instance, required the "objectivity of happiness" to be directed by reason and went so far as to determine the happiness really experienced by the human person under the actual conditions of existence as untrue[24]. Schneider criticized this as an unheard of process[25]. It is indeed arrogant to deny happiness to, for instance, a bourgeois family gathered around the Christmas tree and singing. It is more acceptable to define happiness like the analytical philosopher Wright, as "first person judgment". "First person judgments are not true or false. They express a subject's valuation of his own circumstances. They are genuine value judgments, and yet in an important sense of 'judgments' they are no judgments. Ultimately, a man [*sic*] himself is judge of his own happiness. By this I mean that any third person judgment which may be passed on his happiness, depends for its truth-value on how he himself values his circumstances of life"[26].

"Other people can only be called happy if they *could* say it of themselves"[27]. Judgments about the happiness of the others made in their absence are not only erroneous, but are mere power claims that cannot be justified because they are not respectful of subjective self-understanding. Everyone is the judge of his own happiness. People can be happy in situations, where others might not. A grandmother can experience profound happiness when kneeling down for a whole hour in church and reciting the rosary. Her fifteen years old niece, however, might panic at the very thought. For the empirical analysis of the concept of happiness this means that self-experience as felt by the subject itself has priority over judgment by the others, however expert they might be.

Against a subjective determination of happiness some might usually object that people can feel happy even when they act amorally[28], for instance – if one is a sadist – by humiliating and hurting people. The

24. H. MARCUSE, *Zur Kritik des Hedonismus*, in ID., *Kultur und Gesellschaft I*, Frankfurt am Main, Suhrkamp, 1965, p. 129 and p. 159.

25. W. SCHNEIDER, *Glück, was ist das? Versuch, etwas zu beschreiben, was jeder haben will*, München, Piper, 1978, p. 34.

26. G.H. VON WRIGHT, *The Varieties of Goodness*, London, Routledge and Kegan, 1963, p. 99.

27. M. SEEL, *Freie Weltbegegnung*, in H. STEINFATH (ed.), *Was ist ein gutes Leben? Philosophische Reflexionen*, Frankfurt am Main, Suhrkamp – Routledge, 1998, p. 296.

28. J. SCHUMMER (ed.), *Glück und Ethik*, Würzburg, Köningshausen & Neumann, 1998; J. ANNAS, *The Morality of Happiness*, New York – Oxford, Oxford University Press, 1993.

objection remains serious, even if sadism is a perversion. The relationship between morals and happiness has to be elucidated to the extent
that happiness becomes a normative option, for instance in pedagogy:
education oriented toward happiness, but in what sense? Such an option
must be oriented towards the happiness of all, whereby limitations have
to be set on happiness claims reducing the possibilities of happiness of
others.

A further argument against a subjective theory of happiness is formulated by Seel: let us imagine someone, "who passes his life in bed in a
clinic, treated with drugs that give him a permanent feeling of happiness. Even if the only words he could say were 'I am happy', we would
find it very difficult to call this happiness and even to believe that this
person is happy"[29]. The situation of that person stands in too great a
contrast with the representation of what happiness is to most of our
contemporaries. But it is precisely this argument that speaks for the subjectivity of happiness, because there is no other possibility to judge
other people's happiness, except from the standpoint of our necessarily
subjective every day theory of happiness. *For him/herself,* the person
described, lying in the clinic and full of drugs, may be happy. It is
thinkable to imagine more perfect beings than us mortal human beings,
though capable of conceiving and shaping the world (for Seel the constitutive elements of a good, happy life)[30] considering us unhappy in
principle, although we feel ourselves happy most of the time and can
give reasons in support of such feelings.

For most people "being happy" is a "subjective experience"[31]. This has
important consequences for philosophy and theology. Both cannot pretend to have discovered what *the* happiness is or *the* good, happy life is.
They have no right to prescribe or enforce such a thing. Were they to do
so, they could be blamed for paternalism, as did Kant in his writing
*Über den Gemeinspruch: das mag in der Theorie richtig sein, taugt aber
nicht für die Praxis* (Concerning the saying: this might be true in theory,
but is not suitable in practice). It would be "the greatest possible despo-
tism" to keep adult people as "infants", who in their judgments on what
is beneficial for them and makes them happy, should be submitted to
the judgment of others[32]. Religions and philosophies, but also educa-

---

29. M. SEEL, *Freie Weltbegegnung* (n. 27), p. 292.
30. *Ibid.,* p. 280.
31. J. SCHUMMER, *Glück und Ethik. Neue Ansätze zur Rehabilitierung der Glücks-
philosophie,* in ID. (ed.), *Glück und Ethik* (n. 28), p. 14.
32. I. KANT, *Kritik der Praktischen Vernunft,* A 237.

tionalists may give advice about what has the potential to make life succeed from their point of view, but they cannot impose prescriptions, as Christianity did over the centuries.

The tension between subjective and objective conceptions of happiness in the domain of religious pedagogics is truly fascinating. Many children like to play "Age of Empires" on their computer and say they are happy when creating a new world. Adults, who in their youth had a mere tape recorder, find it very difficult to admit that the preferred activities of their children have a certain relevance for their feeling happy. There still are parents who think that it is favorable to the happiness of the children to be socialized in church, at least initially, although the children themselves are bored at Corpus Christi or even at a mass for children. Before exposing how to deal with these situations, we first have to analyze how happy children are and what makes them happy, and therefore examine the findings of recent intensive studies about happiness[33].

2. How Happy Are Children and What Makes Them So?

The European history of ideas judged the happiness of children very differently. For Aristotle, the initiator of the still authoritative activity theory of happiness, children cannot be happy, because they lack intelligence[34]. For Augustine, on the contrary, who preferred to be dead rather than becoming a child again[35], they could not be happy because of original sin and because of "the disciplines that the educator should hand out to his beloved son to keep him from growing up licentiously, as says the Holy Scripture"[36]. Rousseau, on the other hand, who described childhood as "l'âge de la gaité", criticized education as "barbarian" if it disturbs the immediate happiness of the children in favor of a future which is unknown in principle[37]. The Romantic period tied in with this conception and promoted the identification of childhood with the happiest period in life. "I tolerate a man to be sad, but not a child", Jean Paul wrote[38]. That children have the right to be happy became common sense in reform pedagogics and was adopted in the declaration of children's rights of the United Nations.

---

33. R. VEENHOVEN, *Bibliography on Happiness. 2472 Contemporary Studies on Subjective Appreciation of Life*, Rotterdam, Erasmus University, 1993.
34. ARISTOTLE, *Nicomachean Ethics*, 1099 b, 32.
35. AUGUSTINE, *Bekenntnisse*, Zürich, 1950, p. 40.
36. AUGUSTINE, *De Civitate Dei*, XXII, 22.
37. J.-J. ROUSSEAU, *Emil oder über die Erziehung*, Paderborn, Schöningh, 1981, p. 55.
38. JEAN PAUL, *Levana*, Langensalza, Hermann Beyer & Söhne, 1910, p. 74 (§45).

It looks as if the dream of Jean-Jacques Rousseau, that children deserve to have a happy childhood, has come true in many ways. An extensive survey of children by the author of the present paper, including 1319 school children in Salzburg, was focused on the experience of happiness and indicated that an overwhelming majority of children evaluated their life until then as happy, even very happy.

Evaluation of childhood, N = 1319 pupils in Salzburg, %

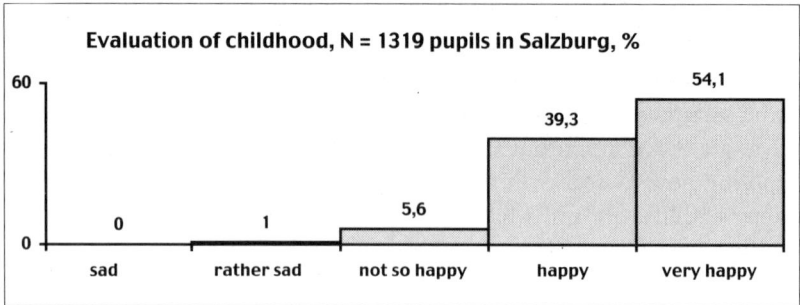

This result is all the more remarkable, given the fact that in actual discourse children often exhibit a catastrophic mood. Actual children would appear to be generally unhappy[39], stressed, overloaded and confused by the media, they would no longer appear to have space and half of them have had to cope with the divorce of their parents. In opposition to earlier periods, they would no longer appear to be able to experience real childhood[40].

The objection might be raised that children have judged their childhood in an unauthentic way. Alternatively, children living in apartment blocks, with only one parent and without brothers or sisters, might not know what a really happy childhood (for instance, in the countryside, with many brothers and sisters and pet animals) might be. It could be objected that children always live in *their* world and only know this one. The objections demonstrate how the evaluation of the experiences of children in particular, and of happiness of other people in general, depends on subjective concepts of happiness. However, not only a majority of children, but also – at least in the industrial nations, less in Africa – a majority of adults estimate themselves to be happy[41].

After consulting several thousands of studies about happiness and well-being, Veenhoven concluded: "Like health, happiness would

39. H. SMITH, *Unhappy Children – Reasons and Remedies*, London, Routledge, 1995.
40. M. WINN, *Children Without Childhood*, New York, Pantheons Books, 1983.
41. P. AUS MAYRING, *Psychologie des Glücks*, Stuttgart, Kohlhammer, 1991, pp. 35ff.

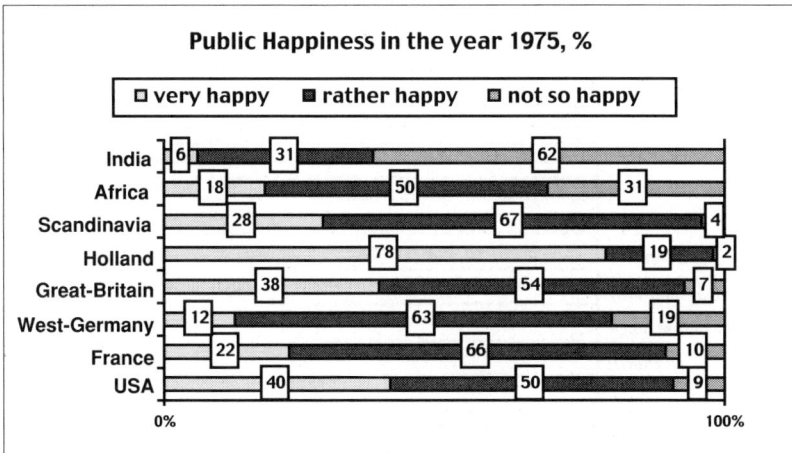

Public Happiness in the year 1975, %

□ very happy ■ rather happy ▨ not so happy

	very happy	rather happy	not so happy
India	6	31	62
Africa	18	50	31
Scandinavia	28	67	4
Holland	78	19	2
Great-Britain	38	54	7
West-Germany	12	63	19
France	22	66	10
USA	40	50	9

0%   100%

seem to be a normal condition" or "happiness is the rule"[42]. Already one of the first studies in the psychology of happiness, that of Hellmann in the year 1930, emphasized – without giving empirical evidence – that there is "more happiness than usually thought, because sadness can be found everywhere, whereas great happiness is silent and hides"[43]. We effectively take happiness and well-being for granted; we become alarmed when problems enter our lives. Schwarz and Clore were able to provide empirical evidence "that people are more motivated to seek explanations for negative than for positive moods, and we suggested that this might be primarily due to the fact that most people experience negative moods as deviating from their usually positive feelings"[44].

Where are children particularly happy? Everything on earth having its time, happiness too has its time, and even its places. The relevance for happiness of different situations has been measured by the method of face expression scales, which is very well adapted to children and has been methodologically assessed.

As can be seen on the chart, children are happiest in nature and in the presence of animals, with their friends and in their play areas. They

42. R. VEENHOVEN, *Questions on Happiness: Classical Topics, Modern Answers, Blind Spots*, in F. STARK et al. (eds.), *Subjective Well-Being. An Interdisciplinary Perspective*, Oxford, Pergamon Press, 1991, pp. 14 and 24.

43. K. HELLMANN, *Psychologie des Glücks*, Wien, Lanyi-Verlagsbuchhandlung, 1930, p. 13.

44. F. SCHWARZ & G.L. CLORE, *Mood, Misattribution, and Judgments of Well-being*, in *Journal of Personality and Social Psychology* 45 (1983) 513-523, p. 521.

Spheres of happiness for children, average, N = 1319

nature / animals	4,63
friends / free space	4,57
family / home	4,44
leisure	4,19
TV / PC	3,96
in the city	3,59
hanging around lazily	3,52
helping at home	3,11
church	3,04
school	2,85
dentist	2,24

1   unhappy –   3   5   very happy

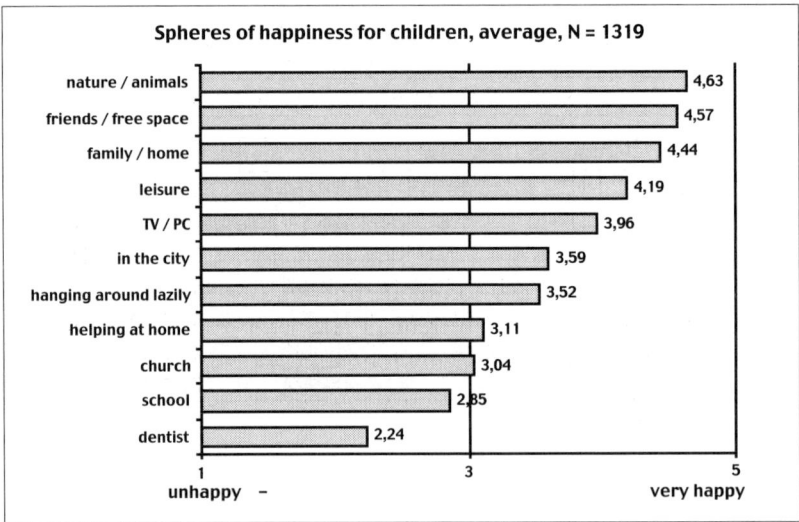

are very happy amidst their family and at home. More concrete than dry data are their stories:

> "*Saturday afternoon, they drove me to a riding school. First, I greet friends, thereafter I ask what horse I shall ride. Then I clean the horses hooves. The riding hour was over too soon. After a riding hour, I am happy. This happiness lasts for the rest of the day.*" (girl, 11)

> "*Skiing has made me very happy. You get acquainted with many other children. Karate has also made me happy. I saw an old friend. But the most pleasant thing to do is being and playing together with friends.*" (girl, 12)

> "*In my life, the things that make me very happy are my family, my friends and sports. What makes me happiest is the fact that I am alive and have such a nice family. I love my family very much.*" (girl, 13).

Less happy are those interviewed at the dentist, in school – except in the pauses, when three-quarters of the children feel happy – and finally in church: every third child associates it with a happy situation, 38% with an emotionally neutral situation and 28% with a sad situation. The reasons for this are explained in section 3.

At first sight, the results confirm the Romantic conception that children are particularly happy in the countryside, in nature, but less so in urban contexts. But this has to be differentiated:

Children who grew up on farms, evaluate the city as making them significantly less happy than those who actually live in urban environments. Children have a tendency to value the environment in

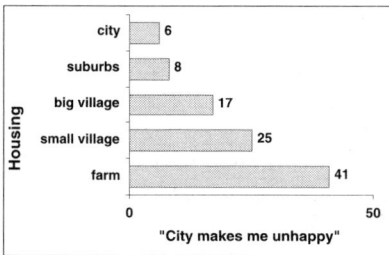

"City makes me unhappy"

Housing	
city	6
suburbs	8
big village	17
small village	25
farm	41

which they actually live as bringing them happiness. This is reminiscent the two-process model of the psychologists Brandstätter and Renner: people tend to fit their judgments of happiness to their actual situation, insofar it cannot be changed[45]. Children who prefer to live in a green environment, but who grow up in high-rise blocks knowing that this will remain so in the future, look for the positive aspects in their actual environment, maybe the cellar or other places where they can do whatever they want when they are not pedagogically supervised.

When do certain situations in the living environment of children become relevant for their feeling happy? When they give them the opportunity to be active. Pet animals are felt to be relevant for children's happiness to the extent that the children can be busy with them (the correlation coefficient r is .48 and is very significant). The same is valid for the computer games that many educators criticize; children who play very frequently, feel very happy.

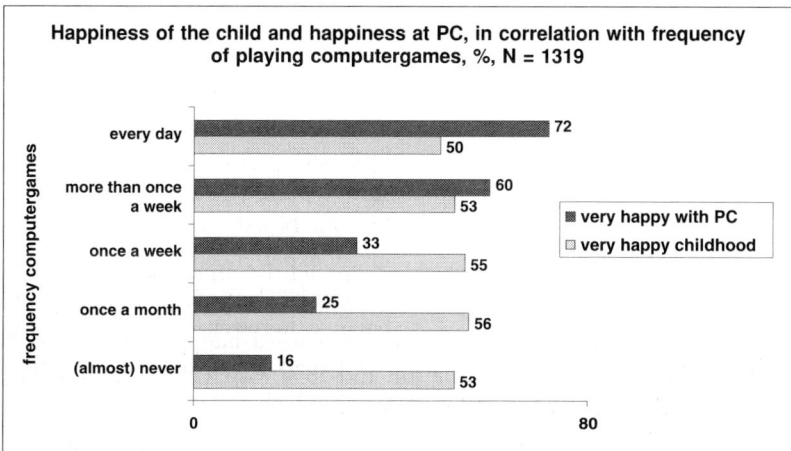

Happiness of the child and happiness at PC, in correlation with frequency of playing computergames, %, N = 1319

■ very happy with PC
□ very happy childhood

45. J. BRANDSTÄTTER & G. RENNER, *Coping with Discrepancies between Aspirations and Achievements in Adult Development. A Dual-process Model*, in L. MONTADA *et al.* (eds.), *Life-crises and Experiences of Adult Development*, Hillsdale NJ, Erlbaum, 1992, 301-319.

As the chart shows, there is a significantly positive correlation (r = 0.48) between the frequency of playing computer games and the experience of happiness at that game, but no correlation with the evaluated childhood happiness. This means that children sitting frequently before the screen, evaluate their childhood as equally happy compared with children who don't. Pessimistic statements such as "computer kids are less happy than girls on horse back or than adolescents in a youth movement" are not correct; they reveal rather the subjective conceptions of happiness or the projections of the people who judge.

What makes children happy? It is obvious that the theory of happiness elaborated for the first time by the philosopher who denied that children had the capacity to be happy, namely Aristotle, is the most accurate. According to him, happiness results from activity, and this insight is also at the center of the popular Flow theory of the Hungarian psychologist of happiness, M. Csikszentmihalyi[46]. He analyzed why people passionately dedicate themselves to climbing, playing chess and dancing. He established first of all that they seek the activity itself and experience it to be all the more pleasant, the more their capacities and the degree of difficulty they are faced with are in balance; then "flow" is manifesting itself, a "flowing" in which the active person not only forgets time, but also himself and becomes totally wrapped up in the activity.

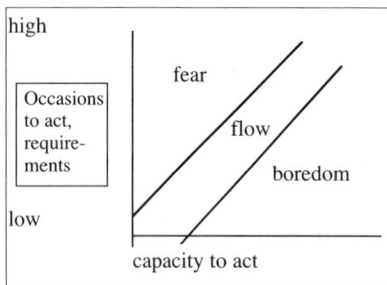

Csikszentmihalyi described this flow or happiness channel as follows. A chess player who always loses the game, will lose all pleasure; a player who always wins, will become bored. Happiness is particularly experienced when a new difficulty level is overcome and the balance between capacity and the requirements of the situation is lifted to a higher level. The happiness experienced in such a situation is described by an eleven years old school girl as follows:

"When I was still small, I wanted to learn to ride a bike. My father put me on the bike and I began to cycle. He kept me up straight. In a street

46. M. CSIKSZENTMIHALYI, *Flow – das Geheimnis des Glücks* (n. 20); see also ID., *Das Flow-Erlebnis: Jenseits von Angst und Langeweile: Im Tun aufgehen*, Stuttgart, Klett-Cotta, 1996[6].

with a slight incline, he let me loose and I went on without being aware that he had done so. Suddenly, my father cried: "you can do it". Then I realized I was riding alone. That was the happiest experience of my life."

This example introduces another factor of happiness for children: praise. It presupposes an achievement having been performed, a challenge being overcome, otherwise it is seen through as being mere words. That happiness – for children as for adults – results from activity, can also be shown by the fact that it is negatively correlated with boredom. Finally we give a synthesis of the results of the multiple regression analysis of the characteristic "global childhood happiness evaluation", before treating the question if and to what extent religiosity makes people, particularly children, happier.

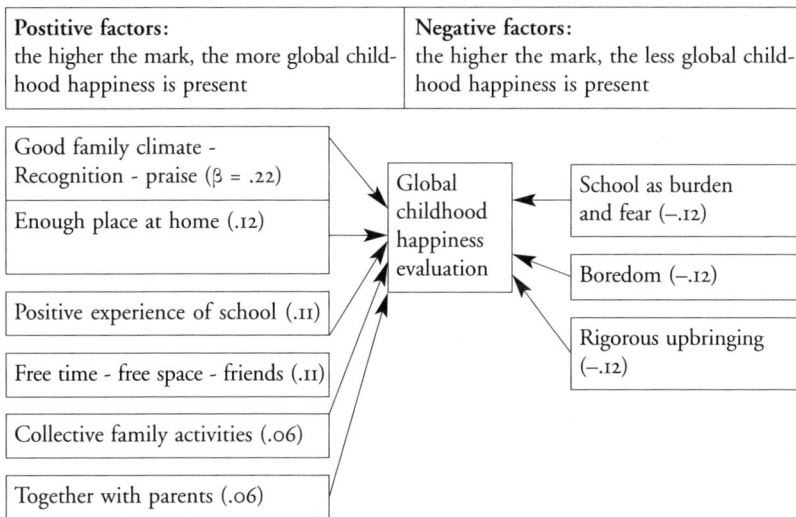

Postitive factors: the higher the mark, the more global childhood happiness is present	Negative factors: the higher the mark, the less global childhood happiness is present

Good family climate - Recognition - praise (β = .22)		School as burden and fear (–.12)
Enough place at home (.12)	Global childhood happiness evaluation	
		Boredom (–.12)
Positive experience of school (.11)		
		Rigorous upbringing (–.12)
Free time - free space - friends (.11)		
Collective family activities (.06)		
Together with parents (.06)		

3. Does Religion Make People, Particularly Children, Happy?

In 1974 the well-known opinion researcher E. Noelle-Neumann published her survey *Lebensfreude – kein Thema für die Kirche?* (Joy of living – not a theme for the church?). She gave an account of interviews with 2000 individuals in the Federal Republic of Germany, in which the interviewers also estimated how happy the respondents were (corner of the mouth up or down, relaxed or contorted posture, open or evasive glance). The interviewees were divided into three groups: "working cheerfully", "rather cheerfully", "not cheerfully", and afterwards the number of persons who stood close to or far from the church in each group was evaluated: "People close to the church look less happy"[47]. The researcher explained this by the "mystical" suffering mentality the church used to adopt and expressed the wish that church leaders should pay more attention to happiness and joy.

The sociologist also reported a deviating result in her analysis. Younger people, under the age of 30, more often worked happier when standing close to the church. She gave no explanation for this observation. Does religious education or socialization endorse the importance of joy? The relationship between religiosity and well-being seems not as unequivocal as is suggested by Christian tradition with its age-long depreciation of happiness. This is also assessed by empirical studies, especially in the field of psychology of religion, focused on the relationship between religiosity and well-being. They raise difficult theoretical and methodological questions, especially the question as to how one should conceptualize and measure religiosity[48]. According to Allport[49], the differentiation between extrinsic and intrinsic religiosity was very popular at the end of the fifties[50]. Extrinsic religiosity refers to religious acts performed in view of another aim, for instance church attendance in order to seek alliance with a social group or to fulfill the obligation to go to Sunday mass. Intrinsic religiosity on the other hand is adopted for its own sake and concerns one's global existence: "I try hard to carry my religion over into all my other dealings in life". This intrinsic aspect calls up associations with the Flow concept of Csikszentmihalyi. It is not surprising therefore that intrinsic religiosity has a positive correlation with happiness, but also with psychic well-being and health, especially at an older age, when the effects of religiosity on well-being are significant. Religiosity "provides companionship and friends of similar age and interests a supportive environment to buffer stressful life changes, an atmosphere of acceptance, hope and forgiveness ... and a common world view and philosophy of life"[51].

47. E. NOELLE-NEUMANN, *Lebensfreude – kein Thema für die Kirche? Fragen zu einem Test über Bewegungs- und Mienenspiel von Katholiken*, in *Herder Korrespondenz* 28 (1974) 41-47, p. 44.

48. S. HUBER, *Dimensionen der Religiosität. Skalen, Meßmodelle und Ergebnisse einer empirisch orientierten Religionspsychologie*, Fribourg, Huber, 1996.

49. G.W. ALLPORT, *The Individual and his Religion*, New York, McMillan, 1950.

50. G.W. ALLPORT & J.M. ROSS, *Personal Religious Orientation and Prejudice*, in *Journal of Personality and Social Psychology* 5 (1967) 432-443.

51. H. KÖNIG, *Religion and Mental Health in Later Life*, in J.F. SCHUMAKER (ed.), *Religion and Mental Health*, New York – Oxford, Oxford University Press, 1992, p. 180.

Does religiosity also enhance the well-being of children? Insofar as All-port is right when he states that the religiosity of children is extrinsic – they would primarily pray in order to make material desires come true – this can hardly be the case. But it is very questionable if extrinsic and intrinsic religiosity exhibit a sequence with respect to developmental psychology. Spilka has shown that children – viewed consistently over the different age groups – also prefer items to intrinsic religiosity[52]. The state of affairs is very unsatisfactory here: the relationship between religiosity and well-being has predominantly been analyzed in adults[53], especially in gerontological settings, but rarely in children and adolescents.

The above-mentioned study of happiness offers some empirical indications. To be in church is associated with a happy face only for 34% of the interviewees, half of them being acolytes, who not only attended mass, but were active in the rites, and thus intrinsically motivated. To swing the thurible, ring the bell, bring the offerings to the altar – this too can make people happy and speaks up for an activity-theoretical conception of happiness and well-being. We find some empirical indications in a large-scale study on the acceptance of religious education in the Federal Republic of Germany, involving more than 5000 pupils who were asked to answer religious and personal self-evaluations, such as happy – unhappy, free – unfree, faithful – not faithful, religious – not religious. The four characteristics correlate as follows:

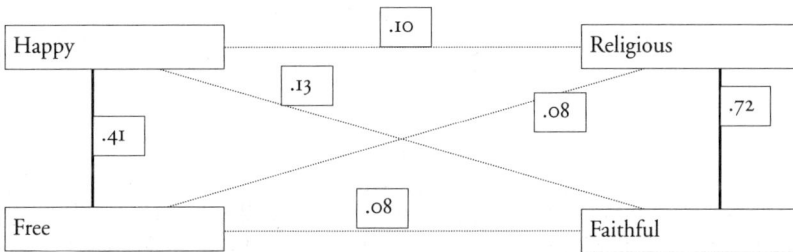

As could be expected, there is a highly significant correlation of the personal evaluation as "religious" with "faithful", but also with the subjective appreciation of feeling oneself close to church, which is not

52. B. SPILKA et al., The Psychology of Religion. An Empirical Approach, Englewood Cliffs, Prentice Hall, 1985.
53. F.K. WILLITS & D.M. CRIDER, Religion and Well-being. Men and Women in the Middle Years, in Review of Religious Research 29 (1988) 281-294.

represented in the chart[54]. With the subjective evaluation of happiness there is no correlation at all (the correlation "happy" – "faithful" not even being 2% variance), which means that when pupils understand themselves as faithful and religious, they feel as happy as those who evaluate themselves as not faithful and not religious. To be happy is correlated with the feeling of determining one's life in a free way – a correlation that since Enlightenment is part of the *habitus* of the modern human person.

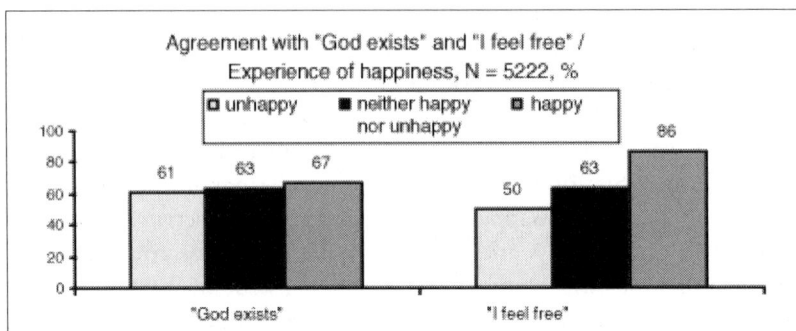

Whether pupils feel themselves happy or not, the quotas of those who stated their belief in God were nearly equal. This is not the case when considering the personal evaluation as "free": this evaluation scores significantly higher in those who feel happy.

As opposed to the hypothesis of the critics of religion that religiosity enhances the dependence of people, this does not correlate with the experience of freedom, which means that pupils, whether they understand themselves to be religious or not, feel equally free.

Summarizing, it may be said that, whereas in adults, more specifically older persons, there is a positive effect of religiosity on happiness and well-being[55], this item needs further study in children and adolescents. The empirical data at our disposal from the studies performed in Salzburg as well as in the Federal Republic of Germany, seem to indicate that the self-evaluation of religiosity does not significantly correlate with

54. A. BUCHER, *Stimmt die Entkoppelungsthese? Zum Verhältnis allgemeiner und kirchlicher Religiosität in einer Stichprobe von 2700 Schuljugendlichen in Österreich*, in C. FRIESL & R. POLAK (ed.), *Die Suche nach der religiösen Aura*, Graz, Zeitpunkt, 1999, 224-230.

55. Cfr. the meta-analysis of R.A. WITTER *et al.*, *Religion and Subjective Well-being in Adulthood. A Quantitative Synthesis*, in *Review of Religious Research* 26 (1985) 332-342.

the subjective self-evaluation of happiness, at least not with respect to one's consent to Christian faith. A possible explanation for this is that happiness in general results from activity. When this is not provided for in religious settings – and this is the case for more and more adolescents –, the happiness potential of religiosity is not able to unfold itself.

With respect to the age-long depreciation of happiness on the part of the church, this result can also be interpreted in a positive way. Adolescents, to the extent that they understand themselves as religious, are not less happy and less free than their secularized contemporaries.

4. How Can Pedagogics of Religion Contribute to the Happiness of Children?

Religious education has all too often made children unhappy, not only via boring religious instruction and repressive educational methods, but also by rejecting the claim to earthly happiness as something reprehensible and bearing horrible consequences, such as the torments of hell. Indeed, theology has overcome the traditional distinction between salvation and (earthly) happiness, and values the latter as a significant foreshadowing of final salvation, when God becomes all in all. Theology has reckoned with the objection of Nietzsche: "They should look more like redeemed persons – the redeemed"[56]. In any event, this rehabilitation of happiness only took place when many contemporaries no longer looked for happiness in the church or in faith, but in opposition with the church, and more and more "etsi ecclesia non daretur" (as if church did not exist). "Everything that brings joy to us young people, is bad according to church", an adolescent pupil told me recently.

Religious education not only recognizes a successful and happy life as an important objective – religious education as support for humanization[57] –, but also immediate happiness and joy, as Jesus procured with his words, and still more with his deeds. Countless teachers of religion try to convey to their pupils not so much knowledge about faith, but the experience of what the Gospel is about: joy and happiness. And indeed: an actual study about the acceptance of religious education in the Federal Republic of Germany, involving more than 7000 pupils,

---

56. F. NIETZSCHE, *Werke in drei Bänden*, München, Hanser, 1954, Vol. II, p. 1200.
57. A. EXELER, *Religiöse Erziehung als Hilfe zur Menschwerdung*, München, Kösel, 1982.

shows that this acceptance is very high in primary school[58]. Primary school pupils associate activities such as " listening to biblical stories", "celebrating", "singing" and even "praying" with a happy facial expression. While it is true that very high satisfaction clearly decreases with increasing age, the pedagogy of religion succeeds in its central domain, religious education, in giving thousands of young people a time and place for happiness.

The pedagogy of religion can contribute to the happiness of young people, to the extent that it succeeds in inciting them to *activity*, especially to activity in common. This is possible not only in an activity-oriented religious education, but also in catechetical settings, for instance while preparing for the First Communion, when children not only have to amass the corresponding knowledge, but also have to celebrate together, to bake bread together, etc. Also when preparing for confirmation, when the group for instance stays in the countryside and experiences adventure and has fun.

Religious education can also contribute to happiness and joy as regards content, when these experiences are not rejected as un-Christian and marginalized, but are given the place they rightly deserve. This requires authenticity. Nothing is more implausible than a gruff, mostly older priest preaching about happiness and joy. Ceremonials, celebrated for their own sake, are also favorable to happiness, as for instance the singing practiced in Taizé, enchanting the audience until they are taken up in rhythm and melody. Meditation too can fill people with profound contentment, although – or because –they let go themselves. "Judaism and Christianity are originally religions of joy and cheerful living together and thankfulness"[59]. It depends upon us to return to these origins[60].

58. A. BUCHER, *Religionsunterricht zwischen Lernfach und Lebenshilfe*, Stuttgart, Kohlhammer, 2000.
59. "Judentum und Christentum sind ursprünglich Religionen der Freude und des fröhlichen Zusammenlebens und der Dankbarkeit". U. GERBER, *Glück haben – Glück machen? Entwürfe für ein sinnerfülltes Leben*, Stuttgart, Kreuz, 1991, p. 131.
60. Translation from German by Antoon Bekaert.

Youth of the Eighties, Parents of 2000
Sociological Observations

Roland Campiche

This essay will focus on the generation of the eighties, or, to be more precise, on young people who were between 19 and 29 years old in that decade. As I recall, the eighties were the years of easy money, rapidly gained, rapidly spent. But they were also marked by great change, particularly characterized by a loss of points of reference, the unexpected consequence of the fall of the Berlin wall. The eighties were also the years of AIDS. The myth of longevity and of staying eternally young and free, collapsed. Death claimed its place again. The individual was confronted once again with social insecurity and the fragility of life.

This period is characterized by abundance and insecurity. It is not surprising therefore to see two contrasted representations of the religiosity of youth being elaborated side by side. The first one sees in the consumerism of youth the *Ersatz* of transcendence[1], the other qualifies the religiosity of youth as a religiosity of the "maybe"[2]. Before trying to sketch a profile of the young people in question, let us focus on two parameters, capable of enlightening our comprehension of the issue at stake: of which values are these young people the inheritors and in what socio-cultural environment do they live?

1. Inherited Religion

The hypothesis that young people of the eighties come from a generation of parents without religious tradition, or even without religion, is contradicted by observations established all over Europe[3] and even all

1. P. ZEUGIN & D. GROS, *Jugendkultur in der Schweiz, Nationales Forschungsprogramm 21: Kulturelle Vielfalt und nationale Identität*, Basel, Nationalfonds, 1991.
2. F. CHAMPION & Y. LAMBERT, *Les "12-15 ans" et la religion*, in Y. LAMBERT & G. MICHELAT (eds.), *Crépuscule des religions chez les jeunes?*, Paris, L'Harmattan, 1992, 65-92.
3. G. DAVIE & D. HERVIEU-LÉGER (eds.), *Identités religieuses en Europe*, Paris, La Découverte, 1996.

over the western world[4]. The common point between the generations coming of age in the sixties and in the eighties is that both had to live in a period of profound religious change. The so-called "baby-boomer" or postwar generation has created a religion, or rather a spirituality at its convenience on the basis of religious reminiscences. This generation consequently could profit from a determined capacity to criticize the beliefs of established religions.

The postwar generation did not take over the religious heritage from its parents without conditions. Faithful to its ideal of personal autonomy, moreover, it withdrew from transmitting its own religious experience out of respect for the free will of its children. These considerations, of course, are more programmatic than real, but they give a good description of the climate of religious transmission at the end of the century. They also compel us to give a more precise description of the religious bearing of the parents concerned.

The generation of the "baby-boomers" has inaugurated the era of religion without institution, of spirituality without a church. The term spirituality has replaced the concepts of religion and faith in current language as well as in ecclesiastic vocabulary. This shift is not innocent because spirituality points toward a form of personal religiosity in which experience and emotion play a dominant role. This form seems to be an alternative for a religious system based on dogmas and tradition[5].

Self-realization, a central issue in the claims of the postwar generation, together with experience and utility – a conviction has to be profitable if it wants to meet public response – will outline a new religious configuration. This configuration is characterized by a flexible relationship with tradition, of which only the aspects fitting in with personal or collective experience are taken over, whereas other aspects are modified in order to correspond with determined modern aspirations, such as the equality of men and women. The invocation of a god mother or father and the feminization of the divinity fit in with that attitude. Reading the founding texts, referring simultaneously to the inner experience of the authors and to the actual experience of the readers is another example.

The distance people experience with regard to religious institutions, a phenomenon observed all over Europe, renders well the crisis of author-

---

4. W.C. ROOF, J.W. CARROLL, D.A. ROOZEN (eds.), *The Post-War Generation and Establishment Religion. Cross Cultural Perspectives*, Boulder – San Francisco – Oxford, Westview Press, 1995.

5. W.C. ROOF, *A Generation of Seekers*, New York, Harper Collins, 1995, pp. 30, 64, 78, 130.

ity manifest in all domains. The contestation of hierarchy and its cleri-calism, however, does not result in an iconoclastic will to do away with religious organizations. Even if they are less frequented, their presence is needed, because their competencies in matters of giving sense, of ethical reflection remain recognized, as well as their know-how in celebrating the rites of passage. Faced with the development of a free-choice reli-gion, the churches present themselves as "stations" at which services are solicited, on the condition that they are not imposed.

Against this background of socio-cultural change affecting the status of religious institutions and the role of religion in western societies, a plural and complex religious landscape emerges. Beside "exclusive Chris-tians", remaining attached to the traditional belief, you find "inclusive Christians", integrating in their system of beliefs propositions coming from different religious traditions, without provoking a feeling of incommensurability. Believing is important, even if one rejects the reli-gious tradition of one's ancestors. "Non-Christian religious" people thus way form a category of believers very present in our western societies. Atheism, being the case of a minority, is to be conceived as religious rel-ativism rather than as anti-religious militancy[6].

Individual and collective religious experience is expressed in different dimensions, the unity and regulation of which are not assured. This is illustrative in another way of the difficulty facing religious organizations on controlling modalities of membership and the forms of adhesion expressing a common religious identity. In this way, the religious can be structured:

- around an identity dimension referring to symbols, rites and practices distinguishing on a local level those who participate in it and those who do not;
- around an ethical dimension which, based upon the recognition of common values, results in norms of universal conduct, giving prior-ity to the individual consciousness of the faithful over the particular-ity of the group;
- around a cultural dimension corresponding with contents and doc-trines expressing a world view and the historical reference of the group;
- around an emotional dimension assembling the faithful through lived, practiced, affective experiences in an instantaneous community,

6. R.J. CAMPICHE, *Individualisation du croire et recomposition de la religion*, in *Archives de sciences sociales des religions* 81 (1993) 117-131.

not aiming at participating in a believing memory, i.e., without fitting in with a particular tradition[7].

On the basis of these remarks we are able to understand the transformation of the religious domain that took place in the period concerned and of which the "baby-boomers" generation provided the actors or spectators. In fact, secularization, a term frequently used to describe a dimension of the socio-cultural change typical of these decades, is not similar to a disappearance or a loss of religion, but to a readjustment of the individual and collective modalities of believing. These processes reveal the insufficiencies of a modernity "incapable of meeting the expectations it gave rise to and the every-day condition of which is insecurity resulting from the endless search for the means to satisfy our expectations"[8].

The individualization of faith, to be considered the paradigm of all the phenomena described, bears testimony to the profound change having affected religion, modifying the authority which constituted its consistency and the obligations (for instance Sunday mass attendance) favoring the constitution of a moral community[9]. The plurality of belief options and ethical orientations contributed to the expansion of the range of possibilities, while at the same time rendering more difficult and fragile the construction of a religious identity. The insecure socio-cultural status of religion made it less attractive, reducing at the same time the prejudices linked with its monopolist claims.

This is the religious heritage of the generation of the eighties.

2. Experimentation, Youth Cultures and Social Change

The disruption of the sequences marking access to adulthood has been accompanied by a transformation of the standards of reference. We have passed from an identification model based on the mechanisms of familial, professional, social transmission to an experimentation model linked with the process of individualization typical of contemporary society (see below). One prefers to experiment with statuses, roles and values rather than taking them over. From school orientation to marital life, experiment prevails over the reproduction of heritage, even if the margin for making

---

7. D. HERVIEU-LÉGER, *La religion des Européens: modernité, religion, sécularisation*, in G. DAVIE & D. HERVIEU-LÉGER (eds.), *Identités religieuses en Europe* (n. 3), 9-23, p. 21.
8. *Ibid.*, p. 19.
9. D. MARTIN, *Remise en question de la théorie de la sécularisation*, in *ibid.*, 25-42.

choices is smaller than it seems. This development results from a conjunction of factors: extension of studies, increase of the aspirations of social mobility, precocious sexuality, difficult access to a stable employment…

Due to the segmentation of the different life spheres and to the liberation of life styles, the distance between the group of origin, especially the family, and the actual life environment increases. The role of the peer group and the socio-cultural environment marked by the media is accentuated. The mechanisms of socialization by transmission of and identification with a family tradition are affected by these evolutions.

As to the experimentation model: identity as well as the corresponding status of everyone is formed along an iterative process of trial and error, through different affective, cultural and social experiences. The point is to achieve self-determination satisfactory for the person concerned and credible in the eyes of society. Becoming adult by taking up as quickly as possible the corresponding roles, the prevailing model at the beginning of the sixties is replaced by a more complex and diffuse process, because the objective is less to be recognized as an adult than to stay young as long as possible. In other words, "one is socially young at an ever older age"[10].

In spite of appearances, young people do not constitute a homogeneous population. In this sense, there is no youth culture, but youth cultures. Young people, however, share a similar situation: they have a provisional social status. Although this is not enough to confer upon them a strong identity, it presents a determined number of common features which are not without relevance for our description of the religious attitudes and conducts of the ten groups of young people between 19 and 29 years old.

The first feature concerns leisure time. As O. Galland writes, "Young people present a marked particularity expressing itself through the overbalanced practice of six forms of leisure activities: going out, sports, reading (even if in the adolescent group the decrease was the most spectacular), television and video (television being the most popular activity in the adolescent group), listening to music and finally amateur literary and artistic practices"[11].

10. "On est socialement jeune de plus en plus vieux". R. HUDON & B. FOURNIER (eds.), *Jeunesse et politique: conceptions de la politique en Amérique du Nord et en Europe*, Paris, Les Presses de l'Université Laval – L'Harmattan – Sainte-Foy, 1994, p. 38.

11. O. GALLAND, *La jeunesse en France, un nouvel âge de la vie*, in A. CAVALLI & O. GALLAND (eds.), *L'allongement de la jeunesse. Observatoire du changement social en Europe occidentale*, Poitiers, Actes Sud, 1993, 19-39, p. 37.

The second feature concerns sociality, the importance of encounters with the peers constituting a quasi-autonomous institution of socialization[12].

The third feature is the absence of generation conflicts, recently confirmed by a poll in Switzerland[13]. The identity of young people seems not to be constructed against their parents but elsewhere (see the second feature). Moreover, in certain domains such as computer sciences, the dependence relationship has switched, giving rise to unheard of tensions[14].

The fourth feature refers to the values of hedonism and solidarity, between which young people hesitate, although there is no real contradiction between these issues. Their propensity for entertainment, however, does not exclude their concern for solidarity[15].

The fifth feature refers to the societal context in which our groups move. Finally, adolescent are left to their own devices at building out and forming their identity. They design their own life style, because their parents' demands in this regard have diminished.

Following the poet Paul Chamberland[16], who could talk about a "peuple heureux et somnambule de la publicité" ("happy and somnambulant people of publicity"), we could call the generation of the nineties, "the pub(licity) generation", a generation integrating in daily life the publicity message inviting it to consume by way of television in particular. Moreover, for the great majority of young people, consumption precedes production, and even for a part of them, remaining without employment, it constitutes the only link with the economic world[17].

12. O. GALLAND, *La jeunesse en France* (n. 11), p. 38; G. CREMER & P. WAHLER, *Grandir dans deux mondes: être jeune en Allemagne aujourd'hui*, in *ibid.*, 57-70; V. DUBSKY, *La jeunesse face aux transformations de la société tchèque*, in *ibid.*, 165-180.

13. M.-H. MIAUTON & A. REYMOND, *La jeunesse en Suisse vue par les leaders et les jeunes* (M.I.S. Trend – Institut pour l'étude des marchés et les sondages d'opinion), Lausanne, Sophia, 1996, p. 11.

14. U. BOËTHIUS, *Youth, the Media and Moral Panics*, in J. FORNÄS & G. BOLIN (eds.), *Youth Culture in Late Modernity*, London, Sage, 1995, 39-57, p. 49; B. REIMER, *The Media in Public and Private Spheres*, in *ibid.*, 58-71, p. 68. – Should this be interpreted as the premises of a new type of generation conflict? The hypothesis is plausible.

15. B. REIMER, *Youth and Modern Lifestyles*, in *ibid.*, 120-144, p. 140.

16. Quoted by R. LEMIEUX, *Histoires de vie et postmodernité religieuse*, in R. LEMIEUX & M. MILOT (eds.), *Les croyances des Québecois* (Les cahiers de la recherche en sciences de la religion, 11), Québec, Université Laval, 1992, 187-234, p. 215.

17. Interested in the way Swedish adolescents create their own style, H. GANETZ, *The Shop, the Home and Feminity as a Masquerade*, in J. FORNÄS & G. BOLIN (eds.), *Youth Culture in Late Modernity* (n. 14), 72-99 (quoting M. Nava), emphasizes the role of consumption in the formation of identity: "Consumption is more than a simple economic activity: it is dream and solace, communication and confrontation, image and identity". The relationships with consumption vary with the individuals.

Consumption, as has already been analyzed by Baudrillard, allows one to distinguish oneself, to differentiate oneself within the uniformizing mass society. With this statement, we tie in with another of the great evolutions or features of modern society, individualization, not to be confused with individualism, which is nowadays strongly correlated and equated with egoism and withdrawing into oneself. Individualization means the process originated by the fragmentation of our societies and the ongoing emancipation of activity spheres from a unique normative body. It implies that each individual must in his own way manage the differentiated rules of conduct he is confronted with in the different spheres of his existence. It is also up to him to find an arrangement between the obligations and rights conferred upon him by his citizenship and the constraints of a market economy that incites him to optimize his assets. Perception and valorization of individuality constitute a fundamental feature of our societies. They affect the ways of socialization, as we have explained above, and therefore are an important key for understanding and interpreting the time of experimentation this new life age represents.

The last great evolution, to which we pay a particular attention, concerns the relationships between the genders. The proclamation of the equality of men and women all over Europe did not wipe out at once the differentiated representations of gender roles nor several centuries of asymmetrical relationships.

The management by young women of the gap between the equality norm and everyday reality constitutes an important parameter in the formation of feminine identity. This is a heterogeneous and complex process dependent upon numerous factors. The fact that the mothers of these young women, due to their professional activity in particular, exert less control upon their daughters or require less contributions to the housekeeping, has certainly enhanced their margin of autonomy, in this way making that margin similar to that of the male population. The changes linked with the socialization modes, however, did not fundamentally modify the constraints inherent to the roles of the sexes[18]. For instance, a young Swedish woman is confronted today with four opposite requirements affecting the formation of her adult identity:
– ideological equality of the sexes and segregation existing in practice;
– the tension between her professional career and motherhood;

18. S. HOLSTEIN-BECK, *Consistency and Change in the Lifeworld of Young Women*, in J. FORNÄS & G. BOLIN (eds.), *Youth Culture in Late Modernity* (n. 14), 100-119.

– the necessity of self-affirmation in accordance with the male model
and at the same time remaining feminine;
– the obligation to develop her personal autonomy and the cultivation
of a femininity oriented toward sociality[19].

Consumption and mass production, individualization of conducts
and attitudes, differentiated formation of the identity of the sexes: three
evolutions outlining the context of social change wherein our ten groups
move and explain the concomitant similarity and heterogeneity of the
entering into adult age. We finally have to analyze the features of the
religiosity of young people in connection with the religious heritage
transmitted to them and the social change they were subjected to.

3. Religious Socialization and Confessional Identification[20]

Were young people of the eighties able to identify with a confessional
tradition? A simple look at the families they came from tends to reveal
that their parents generally shared the same confession. Opposite to
that, only a small majority of both Catholic parents regularly attended
mass on Sundays when the young generation was between 12 to 15 years
old. For the Protestants, a similar conduct is only seen with one fifth of
both parents. Even if this information corresponds with the representation the concerned actually imagined of the passed religious conducts of
their parents, it gives an indication about the existence of a link between
the generation of the parents and religious organizations. This link is
attested furthermore by the fact that an overwhelming majority of the
"young" generation have been baptized and confirmed. That this
"young" generation has been socialized in a confessional tradition is
verified moreover by the conduct of the ones concerned themselves.
Their participation in religious cult between the age of 12 and 15 years is
indeed high.

19. S. HOLSTEIN-BECK, *Consistency and Change* (n. 18), pp. 114ff.

20. For the presentation of the religiosity of young people of 19 to 29 years old in the
eighties, we refer in the following paragraphs, to the data of a survey in Switzerland
1988/1989; cfr. R.J. CAMPICHE, A. DUBACH *et al.* (eds.), *Croire en Suisse(s)*, Lausanne,
L'Age d'Homme, 1992. The generation of the eighties was represented by 300 persons in
1315 inquiries, 151 Catholics, 132 Protestants and 16 others or without confession; this
repartition is in tune with reality, because the persons of Catholic denomination constitute a relative majority. The following commentaries exclusively concern the 283 persons
who identify themselves, at least in name, with Catholicism or Protestantism.

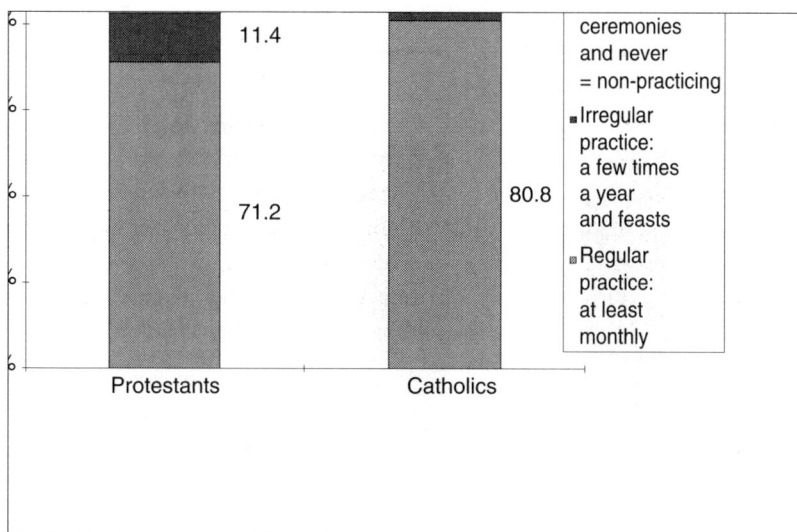

Chart 1: Religious practice between 12 and 15 years of the generation of the eighties, in function of declared confession

Generally speaking, therefore, the generation of the eighties has apparently been socialized within a religious tradition, particularly the group of the Catholics. It should be noted, moreover, that one third of the members of this generation took part in the activities of a religious youth movement (in connection with this conduct, the gap between Catholics and Protestants is greater than concerning the practice of Sunday mass: 35.8% against 31.1%). It can be expected, therefore, that they affirm their confessional specificity and know the differences between religious Christian traditions.

This hypothesis, however, does not hold up to analysis. The idiosyncrasy of the confessions is little perceived at a cognitive level. The doctrinal divergences between Catholics and Protestants are blurred by tolerance. A residual confessional identification with affective and family coloring remains. But let us have a look at the evidence.

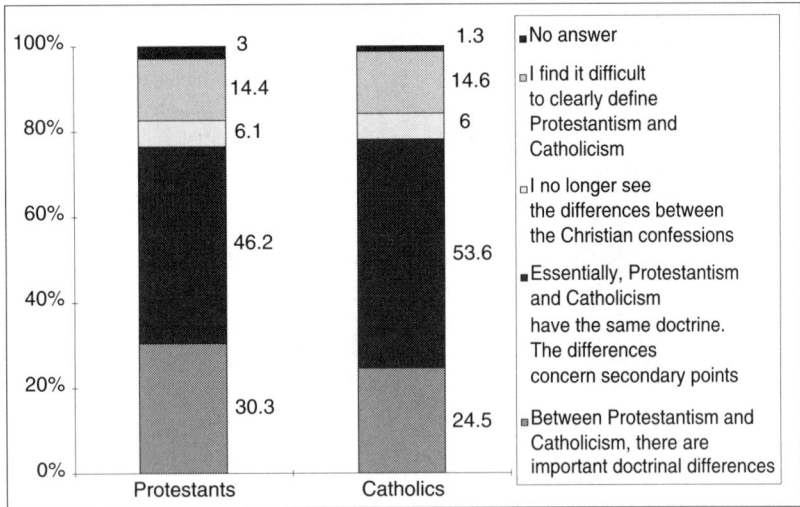

Chart 2: Doctrinal differences perceived by the generation of the eighties, in function of declared confession

A majority of the population minimizes the doctrinal differences between Catholics and Protestants. This attitude is illustrative of the actual state of religious knowledge transmitted by the family, religious organizations, the media and the school. It highlights the effects of the plurality of orientations inside the religious organizations, in particular the effect of the ecumenical orientation looking for ways and means of an inter-confessional rapprochement. This attitude finally reflects the barely differentiated profile of religious organizations within Swiss society, where they compete rather softly with each other. It should be noted furthermore that young Protestants perceive the importance of the doctrinal divergences separating Catholicism and Protestantism in less significant numbers than their elders. This is a sign of the progress of tolerance within this confessional group. This progress is character-ized yet in another way, namely by the judgment passed on the differ-ent Christian traditions by the young generation:

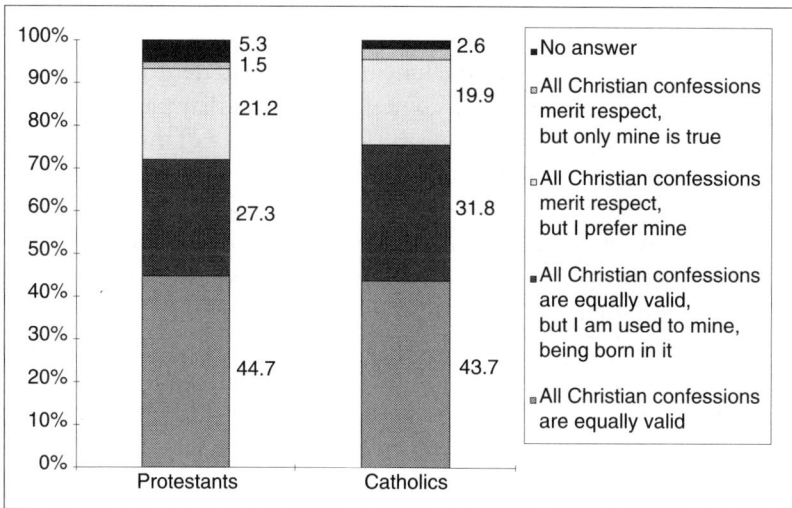

Chart 3: Opinions on the Christian confessions of the generation of the eighties, in function of declared confession

A relative majority of young people support religious indifferentiation. It should also be noted that when young people do not choose this type of answer, they choose more frequently than their elders the position referring to habit and point less toward an affective link with a religious tradition. It can be concluded that the process of unlinking or detachment from a confessional tradition is accelerating. Is the rapprochement of the two religious traditions in Switzerland profiting from that distance? Not necessarily. Even if on the Catholic part this wish may be that of the majority, the perplexity expressing itself through the answer "I hesitate" concerns more than half the generation of the eighties. The latter position, even if not prevailing, constitutes an attitude characteristic of many young people in the area of religion. This position seems to signify that they did not yet made their choice or that they remain undecided when they are confronted with a religious domain that becomes more and more complex not only because of ambient cultural pluralism, but even because of the pluralism within the religious organizations themselves.

4. Values and Belonging to a Generation

Young Catholics and Protestants tend to minimize the sense and importance of confessional attachment. Their attitude exemplifies the tendency of relativization of the confessional circles that is more marked in Catholicism than in Protestantism. The persistence of this habit compels us to further investigate the differentiation effect in the domain of values, beliefs and practices.

Let us begin with values and state that Catholics and Protestants do not differ in the way they rank the different domains of existence and attach value to them.

In family life, for instance, the couple and the children rank first with very similar scores for both confessions (about two thirds).

Further, we can find leisure activities valorized with identical scores for Catholics and Protestants (46%), whereas work is very positively valued by a more significant group of Protestants (33.1%) than of Catholics (27.2%).

To conclude from these data that young people are the bearers of a culture other than that of the rest of the population would be wrong. The deviations from the average calculated on the basis of a scale of importance varying from 1 to 7 are indeed weak. Opposite to that, young people seem to bear testimony to an evolution in attitudes that took place over the second half of this century. This is particularly manifest with respect to work, where differences in attitude between the generation of the 56 to 75 year olds and the generation we are focusing on in this article are spectacular. Indeed, more than half of the older generation declare work to be very important (55.0%).

With regard to values, young people indicate the direction of the changes that took place, for instance the relativization of the value "work" and the affirmation of the importance of leisure. Their position however, must, not mask the influence of the period effect. Indeed, certain attitudes are not at all influenced by the age of the persons who adopt them. The three examples which follow will allow us to understand this last remark:

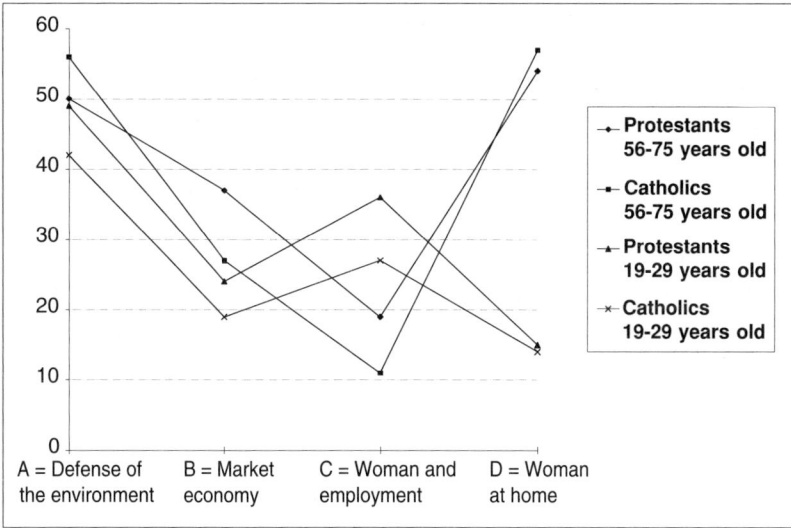

Chart 4: Favorable opinions (totally agreed) concerning some societal problems, in function of age and declared confession

Legend of the items:

A = If we want to save the environment, we will need to change our life styles fundamentally and reduce our personal comfort

B = The state is not allowed to limit the freedom of economics

C = For a woman, professional accomplishment is at least as important as having children

D = It is preferable for everyone in the family that a man dedicates himself to a professional life and that a woman stays at home to take care of the children

Belonging to the "young" generation has a determined coincidence on the representation of the role of women in society. Deviations concerning the role of the sexes between the generation of grandparents and that of the grandchildren are telling, in particular in the Catholic group. On the other hand, the ideological gap between left and right concerning the role of the state in the economic domain carries on through all generations. But the period effect is the most striking when it comes to adopting an attitude with regard to the environment. Ecological consciousness is a societal phenomenon. This fact would certainly become more pregnant still if favorable, but mitigated opinions of the type "rather agreed" were taken into account. Through these considerations we discover the variables linked with the fluctuations in the opinions on the subject of values. At this level, the variable "confession" plays a minor role or even no role at all. Is this also the case when one diminishes the scope in order to focus on the religious domain in the proper sense?

Let us first look at the world of beliefs.

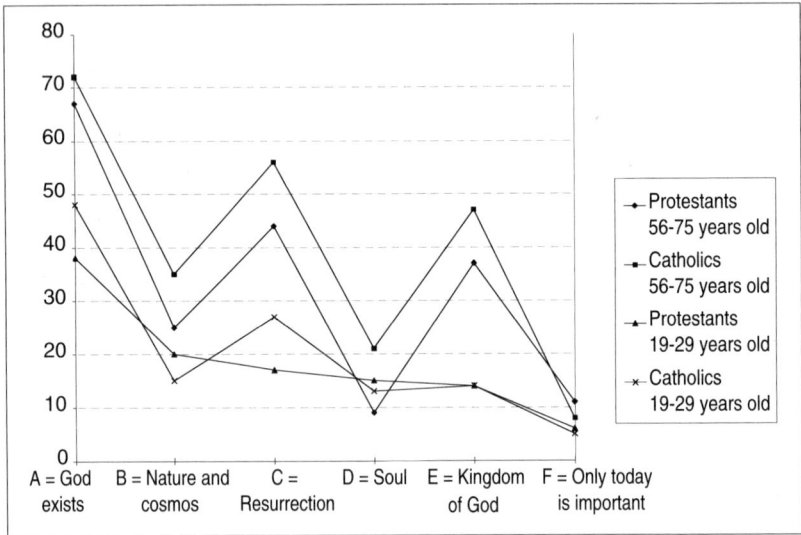

Chart 5: Religious beliefs, in function of age and declared confession (totally agreed)

Legend of the items:

A = God exists, He has revealed Himself in Jesus Christ

B = Transcendent power is residing in the eternal cycle that unites the human person, nature and the cosmos

C = The resurrection of Christ gives meaning to my death

D = The soul is reincarnated in another life

E = The Kingdom of God announced by Jesus Christ is the future of humankind

F = Only today is important

These data tend to show that the variable "confession" lies not at the basis of differentiated attitudes between Catholics and Protestants. When the very high participation in the cult of young Catholics during childhood is taken into account, it could be expected that they would resume their affirmations of Christian belief more often than Protestants. It should be noted that the gaps between Protestants and Catholics concerning these affirmations are of the same order as the ones we observe between the members of both confessions belonging to the generation of the elders. Notice should be taken however of the convergence of the percentages of the answers stemming from young people with regard to reincarnation or the theme of the future. Young Catholics thus seem less marked than their grandparents by the propensity to include in their system of beliefs, heterodox propositions with respect to Christian tradition, which has been qualified by certain researchers as popular Catholicism[21].

Moreover, if attention is paid to the data expressing the rejection of these affirmations, it appears that either the scores are identical or Protestants show the tendency of taking their distance with regard to the belief contents not fitting in with Christian tradition more often.

In other words, Protestants adopt more mitigated positions than Catholics but do not break with their tradition nor choose in larger proportionality for another religious tradition. It should be noted that in both groups there is a weak representation of those who express their disagreement with the different affirmations of their beliefs, in particular the ones attached to Christian tradition.

As was the case with values, young people exhibit a greater propensity than their elders to express their hesitations or their ignorance about these propositions. The choice of the answer "I hesitate" or "I don't know" varies with the cases between a few percentages and two fifths of the polls in the generation of the eighties. A fraction of them hesitate, but this religion of the "maybe" only concerns a minority.

The differences of attitude between Catholics and Protestants might be caused by a differentiated access of the individuals concerned to the school system. However, this is not the case. Young Protestants and young Catholics are almost identically distributed between the different school levels. This repartition on the contrary has effects on the choices of values and belief affirmations. Apprentices, for instance, seem to be more conservative than university students concerning the status of women and the intervention of the State in the economic domain. These same apprentices, without restriction, adhere to the Christian faith in a higher percentage than students. They are also more numerous in accepting non-Christian affirmations concerning death and future, but without these becoming majority positions. These few notes emphasize the implications of the interaction between religion and culture for understanding the recomposition of the religious domain.

When we pass from the analysis comparing the beliefs one by one to the analysis of the belief systems of young people of 17-26 years old, and confront them with the belief systems of their elders, we must observe today a tendency toward polarization on more marked positions. Whereas many members of the "baby-boomer" generation (see above,

---

21. M. KRÜGGELER, *Les îles des bienheureux. Les croyances religieuses en Suisse*, in R.J. CAMPICHE, A. DUBACH *et al.* (eds.), *Croire en Suisse(s)* (n. 20), 87-113, p. 107.

paragraph 1) are to be found in the "inclusive Christian" type, integrating, besides Christian affirmations, other beliefs fitting in with other religious traditions, the generation of the eighties is less prone to make that choice, preferring either an exclusively Christian position or a body of beliefs fitting in with another line or agnosticism, as can be seen on the following chart:

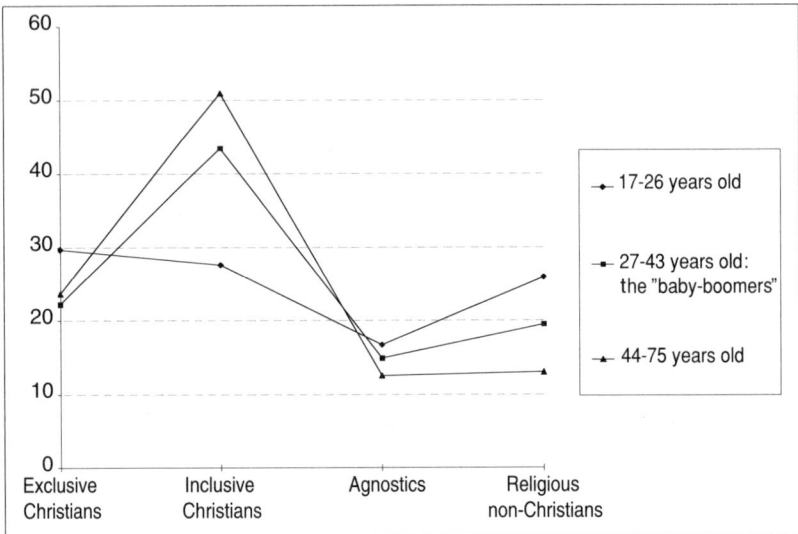

Chart 6: Types of believers in function of the generation they belong to[22]

5. Religion and Society

What image of the relationship between religion and society, or more precisely of the role of the churches within Swiss society does the generation of the eighties exhibit? In order to explore this issue, we subjected the surveys to a nightmare scenario. This scenario invited the interviewees to evaluate the social, political, economic, religious effects of the disappearance of the Swiss Protestant and Catholic churches. For this chapter, I will merely highlight the societal functions carrying a broad consensus. How are the churches seen by the young generation?

22. At variance with the other charts in this text, the repartition takes into account the "baby-boomer" generation and not first and foremost the generation of the eighties.

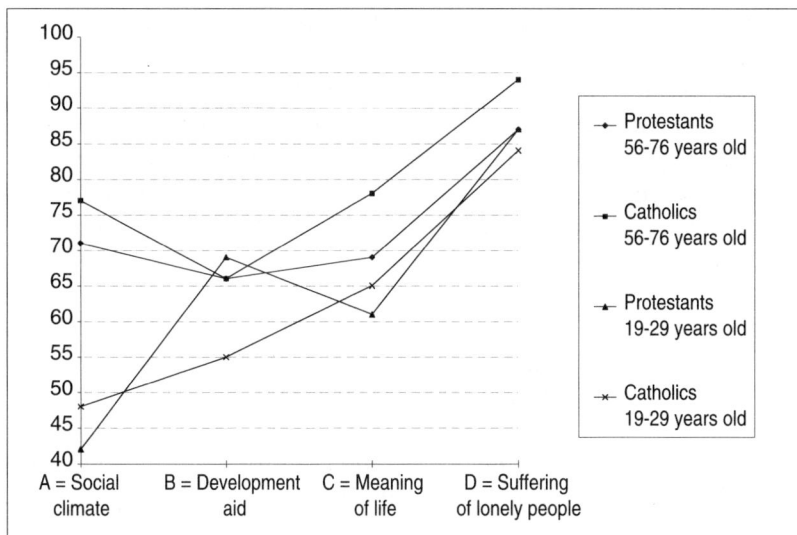

Chart 7: Socio-political role of churches, in function of the age and declared confession

Legend of items:

If the Protestant and Catholic church would disappear,

A = ... the social climate would be more tense

B = ... development aid would diminish

C = ... many people would no longer find the meaning of life anymore

D = ... lonely people (disabled people, elderly) would suffer more from their situation

From the positions figuring on a list of possible consequences if the churches would disappear (a list encompassing large areas of society), four functions emerge: the function of charity, the ideological function, the function of redressing inequalities, the function of integration. The churches are not granted a global function, that of constituting the "sacred canopy" covering social life as a whole. They are granted partial functions instead. The institutional role of the churches is in this way defined and so is the concept of secularization.

The generation of the eighties largely supports the first three functions. There is more skepticism, however, concerning the fourth. Is this reserve due to their age, their lack of social experience? The hypothesis is fragile, because the percentage of the people hesitating does not justify it. It also can be put forward that their attitude in this matter attests to the continued erosion of the societal position of religious organizations. They would be more and more confined to a partial role presenting a charity pole and an ethical pole. The hypothesis is convincing.

Whatever the case may be, the identification with a confession is not the cause of a differentiation of attitudes. This is particularly clear when comparing the attitudes of the members of the two generations concerned. The young generation seems to be reliant on the period effect. The religious institutions remain recognized, but this recognition is conditional and limited.

6. Relativization of the Christian Tradition and Recomposition of Religion

Within the generation of the eighties, declaring oneself Protestant or Catholic does not lead to a specifically confessional religiosity nor to a particular code of ethics. Even when no alternative religiosity clearly emerges, we should not underestimate the attraction of non-Christian religions. The polarization of the above-mentioned choices between beliefs (see paragraph 4) could well signify the end of Christian domination on the religious scene and the consolidation of a pluralization that not only reinforces the relativization of belief affirmations, but even erodes the status of the established religious organizations.

Considered correctly, the religious conducts and attitudes of the generation of the eighties reveal in the first place the erosion of institutional religiosity. They do not seem to be the privileged agents of the transformation of this religiosity. The compared practice rates of the different generations are illustrative of this evolution.

Three sequences attesting the slow dissolution of the social bond represented by cult practice become apparent. The first concerns regular church practice. This sequence has the same evolution for both confessions; we see a decrease of 16.4% if one compares the conducts of the generation of the eighties with those of their grandparents.

The confrontation of the data concerning the three generations allows us to discover that the break occurred between the middle generation, that of the parents, and the old generation, that of the grandparents. This points toward a relative stabilization of regular practice.

The second sequence concerns occasional church practice. After a minimal increase, it again tends to decrease: the sign of a certain polarization of religious conducts.

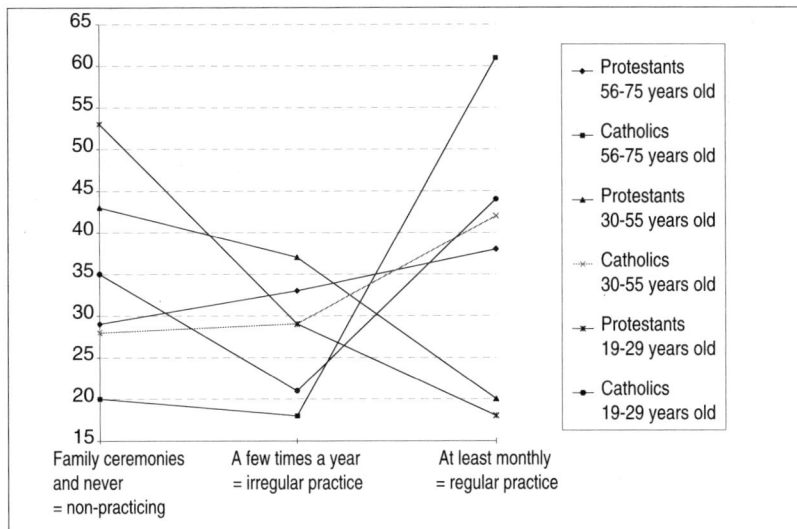

Chart 8: Practice of religious services, in function of age and declared confession

The third sequence, related with non-practice, shows that the social bond with religious institutions is more affected among Protestants than among Catholics. The comparison of the conducts of the Catholic generation of the eighties with their elders allows us to put forward the hypothesis of a asynchronous evolution of the change. The break with the Catholic organization, signified by non-practice, is less advanced, but goes on at a more rapid pace in Catholicism than in Protestantism.

In general, the practice rates taken into consideration reveal the erosion of institutional religiosity, but not the erosion of belief. The extremely weak percentages of the rejection of belief affirmations, whether concerning transcendence, death or the future, draw attention to a characteristic feature of contemporary religiosity. The fact of believing seems to be more important than the content of that belief. To put it in another way: within modern society, religious belief remains a possibility to ward off the insecurity of the present, but it is a "layered" belief. A belief not forming a system – has this ever been the case? – but composite. With a precise interrogation corresponds a religious answer that was chosen by the individual within a large range.

The process of relativization of Christian tradition seems to be going on, but it has not finished yet. The religious socialization of the young Christian generation concerned can give an explanation of this state of affairs. On the other hand, everything is possible in the future. The young generation, tolerant and oriented toward consumerism, seems to be little inclined to take up a particular religious tradition. A religious *habitus*: yes; a confessional tradition: no. Barring a change in the social climate, the religious scene will be structured in a pluralist way, leading to a transformation of the societal status of the established churches[23].

23. Translation from French by Antoon Bekaert. A German version of this paper, entitled *Jugendreligiosität in den achtziger Jahren*, has been published in E. HALTER & D. WUNDERLIN (eds.), *Volksfrömmigkeit in der Schweiz*, Zürich, OZV Offizin Zürich-Verlags-AG, 1999, 146-165.

Reasons for Living
Religious Education and Young People's Search for Spirituality and Identity

Graham Rossiter

In September 1998, the Australian Bishops' Committee for Justice, Development and Peace released the Report, *Young People and the Future*. It resulted from a two-year consultation with Catholic youth. One of three areas of special concern for participants was "identity and the search for meaning"[1].

Though not as tangible an issue as unemployment or drug and alcohol abuse, the need for young people to find ways of making meaning in their lives and to develop an authentic sense of self is fundamental to their moral and spiritual wellbeing. Hence it should be central to any strategies that hope to address the full range of concerns in the Report (and indeed the issues noted in other research reports on the views, attitudes and behaviour of contemporary youth). Where young people are strong and somewhat secure in their sense of purpose, and sure of who they are, they will be better able to cope with and respond creatively to the psychological pressures of life in modern Western societies.

In a changing social, economic and familial landscape, most of the support networks for meaning and identity that functioned for past generations no longer have the same plausibility and force. For many young people, the beliefs about life's meaning drawn from religious convictions and from the Church do not seem to have the same cogency they apparently had in the past. In an environment awash with ways to make meaning and finding the 'true self', there is an urgent need for the churches to find strategies that will resonate with young people in their search for meaning, values and identity. As suggested in the title for this essay, the focus needs to be on *reasons for living*.

---

1. The other areas were unemployment, and drug and alcohol abuse: AUSTRALIAN CATHOLIC BISHOPS' CONFERENCE, *Young People and the Future*, Melbourne, John Garratt Publishing, 1998.

This essay will examine a number of issues related to the search for spirituality and identity; implications will be proposed for the theory and practice of religious education – specifically in the school context. The discussion will also be pertinent to thinking about youth ministry and practical theology – as well as to theology generally – because the perceived *relevance* of theology, ministry and religious education depends on how well they can make meaningful connections with the questions that contemporary youth ask about identity and a spiritual dimension to life. The challenge is to find ways of making the Church's 2000-year heritage of wisdom articulate with young people's perceived life world.

What emerges in this essay is an argument that religious education and theology need to be expressed with a language and focus that are more in tune with the contemporary search for meaning which is such a prominent concern of western cultures – especially for youth. If not, and if the principal focus appears to be 'institutional mainte-nance' or some other theme like 'integrity of doctrine' or 'spiritual/moral authority' etc. then many youth and adults will not bother looking to the Church for the spiritual guidance and support they need.

While some attention will be given to research findings, the essay will be more concerned with interpretations that could be the starting points for research on spirituality and identity development in young people.

Only a brief summary will be given of some issues related to *spirituality*, acknowledging where they are discussed in more detail in the literature – specifically in a forthcoming book on religious educa-tion by Crawford and Rossiter. More attention will be given to ques-tions about *identity*. Brief lists of key issues for religious education will be inserted to help focus the later discussion of implications for religious education. These two first sections will be followed by an exploration of why and how religious education and theology need to take on more of a 'language of meaning' to become more relevant to youth, and people generally. Section three will provide the reader with general remarks on an identity concept that is useful for RE. Section four will focus on school related RE. I will conclude this essay with some comments on relationships with the hermeneutic-communicative model for RE proposed by Herman Lombaerts and his colleagues.

1. Young People and Spirituality

There is a sizeable literature on the spirituality of young people, even though this is not a concept that many youth would readily apply to themselves[2]. For many of them, but not all, spirituality may have a presumed association with religion; the word 'spiritual', however, often has more currency.

I do not want to enter the debate about the definition of spirituality. The only points I wish to make as far as youth are concerned are firstly, that spirituality needs to be wider in connotation than that of the words 'religious' and 'transcendent' – while acknowledging that both of these concepts may often be important aspects of the spirituality of young people. Secondly, the questioning and searching for meaning, values and identity, and the consideration of contemporary spiritual and moral issues are central to the spirituality of youth. To take this second point seriously is fundamentally important for the contemporary relevance of religious education and theology.

A large number of reports and surveys about young people's search for meaning have been published in the last twenty years[3]. Now, more than at any time in history, has the wellbeing of our young been under so much scrutiny. Ranging from surveys commissioned by advertising agencies targeting particular markets, to research projects undertaken by universities, government agencies, churches and institutions in the care of the young, the studies have investigated the lives of young people – looking at their habits, development, aspirations, beliefs, favourite movies and use of personal products etc.

With so many research findings on youth available, one might wonder why the community has not been more effective in addressing the problems of youth, or why advocacy on behalf of young people has not brought about more change. Part of the reason has been the general inability of the community and its leaders to comprehend the *complexity* of the life situations confronting contemporary young people and to wisely address issues across a broad front. An emphasis on one particu-

2. M.L. CRAWFORD & G.M. ROSSITER, *The Spirituality of Today's Young People. Implications for Religious Education in Church-related Schools*, in *Religious Education Journal of Australia* 9 (1993) 2, 1-8; R. BEST (ed.), *Education, Spirituality and the Whole Child*, London, Cassell, 1996.

3. I am indebted to my colleague Mrs Marisa Crawford for the material in this section.

lar finding – for example the high suicide rate for youth – creates anxiety, but gives only a partial insight into the complex psychological world of young people and the intricate mosaic of influences on their spirituality and identity.

Key issues / principles for religious education
1. What is needed is a holistic understanding of the factors and issues that affect youth spirituality; an understanding which holds in creative tension the apparently contradictory aspects of young people's life world.
2. Hopefully, this understanding will inform the work of religious educators – as regards the orientation and content of the curriculum, and the method of teaching.

Some youth surveys both in Australia and other countries highlight the younger generation's ability to cope phlegmatically with rapid change that has more disruptive effects on the lives of adults. Teenagers have been identified as:

> (...) kids, unfazed by the pace of change and the technologies that give adults anxiety attacks. These 'screenagers' are flexible and adaptable. They have learned to thrive on chaos, uncertainty and insecurity in ways their parents never have[4].

However, a greater number of surveys paint a bleaker picture. While it is true that youth are more accustomed to change and are more comfortable with new technology, these surveys claim there is a deep-seated malaise that seems to cut across the whole spectrum of youth. For example:

> Young people are deeply cynical, alienated, pessimistic, disillusioned and disengaged. Many are confused, and angry, uncertain of what the future holds and what society expects of them. While they may continue to work within 'the system' they no longer believe in it or are they willing to serve it. From this perspective, the suicidal, the depressed, the drug-addicted and the delinquent represent the tip of an iceberg of psychological pain and distress that includes a substantial proportion, perhaps even a majority of young people today[5].

The Catholic Bishops' Report (1998, p. 15) noted that:

> Many young people talk of lacking purpose and meaning in life. They often lack helpful role models, feeling that the world in which

---

4. R. ECKERSLEY, *Portraits of Youth*, in *Futures* 29 (1997) 3, 243-249, esp. p. 243.
5. *Ibid.*, p. 244.

they live bears little or no resemblance to that from which their parents emerged[6].

At first sight the findings seem to be contradictory: one view seems optimistic, the other more pessimistic. However, these apparently opposite characteristics may hold true for some young people at different stages of their lives, depending on their life experience. The perspective of a young person living in a rural area, or on the fringes of society, will be markedly different from that of one from a comfortable, economically stable supportive background who sees that life offers a variety of favourable options.

Eckersley draws attention to the urgency of taking action with respect to youth.

> There is evidence that the developed world has passed a threshold, a point beyond which economic growth (as currently defined and derived) ceases to improve quality of life. Trends in suicide, depression and other psychological disorders suggest that young people, in particular, are paying a high price for progress. This situation poses a formidable challenge to education. The task of education is not just to prepare students for the future, but to equip them to create a future they want to live in. This includes nurturing a sense of social and spiritual connectedness that transcends the individual and the material"[7].

Key issues / principles for religious education
Educators' understanding of young people's spirituality needs to hold in tension the apparently contradictory aspects:
confidence – anxiety;
coping with chaos – despair over meaning;
individualism – need for group membership;
self-centredness – altruism and a sensitivity to justice issues;
not ready for commitment – a need for committed role models;
radically different from parents – similar values to parents;
apparently carefree lifestyle – insecurity about life;
materialistic lifestyle – maintaining a sense of the transcendent;
etc.

---

6. AUSTRALIAN CATHOLIC BISHOPS' CONFERENCE, *Young People* (n. 1), p. 15.
7. R. ECKERSLEY, *Wealth, Health and Youth. The Impacts and Implications of Progress*, Occasional paper, National Centre for Epidemiology and Population Health, Australian National University, Canberra, 2000. Quoted in T. WALLACE, *Values and Spirituality. Enriching Curriculum Development and Teaching/Learning Processes for a New Millennium*, in *Journal of Christian Education* 43 (2000) no. 1, 41-49.

A survey conducted by a new, independent market research company, Oracle, called this generation of young people the 'DIY generation' – meaning that they adopt a do-it-yourself approach to life[8]. They pick and choose their lifestyle, code of ethics, and baseline morality from a variety of sources. This reflects other findings that show how youth do not necessarily subscribe to a set of identifiable values; rather they prefer to shop around for a custom made set of values and beliefs which they feel may more closely fit their identity and needs.

At the heart of this need to 'do-it-yourself' is the importance young people place on being an individual. Individuality is a worthwhile goal in life; it is revered by youth and it has very significant effects on their behaviour and values. But excessive individualism carries with it adverse psychological consequences.

One of the major cultural problems with individualism is that it may appear to young people to be one of the few things left for them to believe in. In his paper, *Portraits of Youth*, Richard Eckersley quotes American psychologist Martin Seligman:

> One necessary condition for meaning is the attachment to something larger than the self; and the larger that entity, the more meaning you can derive. To the extent that it is now difficult for young people to take seriously their relationship to God, to care about their relationship to the country, or to be part of a large and abiding family, meaning in life will be very difficult to find. The self, to put it another way, is a very poor site for meaning[9].

Young people can feel caught in a bind. The culture glorifies individualism; the commercial world does everything it can to make individualism a marketable commodity. However, excessive individualism can be the agent of a pathological 'aloneness', the cause of erosion of sense of community, and a heavy pressure on young people to have to work out their meaning and purpose by themselves.

While a sense of meaning and purpose ultimately needs to be appropriated and developed by the individual, it may be expecting too much of the human condition to have individuals construct this meaning entirely by themselves, without the support of some community frame of reference.

Other aspects of the spirituality of youth relevant to the discussion here are considered in the material on the website: wwwdev.acu.edu.au/mre/spirituality_identity. They include, among other topics: seeking community, making choices, and having options; relationship with the churches;

---

8. C. BYE, *Generation X is 'dead'*, in *The Sun Herald* (June 21, 1998) 17.
9. R. ECKERSLEY, *Portraits of Youth* (n. 4), p. 246.

the secular spirituality of youth, their search for meaning[10]; the influence of Relativism, Privatisation of beliefs and Secularisation; the role of film and television in young people's search for meaning, values and purpose[11]; the trauma of living in the twentieth century.

Key principles/issues

1. The important values in individualism and personal autonomy for young people need to be affirmed.

2. Problems flowing from excessive individualism need to be understood and explored educationally.

* Divisiveness, narcissism, selfishness and alienation can flow from excessive individualism;

* A feeling that individuals are all alone and totally responsible for constructing their own meaning and purpose in life can be overwhelming and can lead to despair;

* Individualism can be tempered by community, responsibility, a sense of the transcendent, and a commitment to social justice;

* The commercial world tends to commodify individuality and to seduce people towards a 'retail' identity[12].

---

2. Identity Issues for Religious Education

Commonly the aims for religious education include the development of religious identity. Identity is central to thinking about culture and ethnicity; thus identity development is relevant to education, although the educational role is not always clearly specified. Identity is also prominent in psychological theories such as those of Erikson and Kegan. While no doubt identity is a human property of fundamental importance, like spirituality, it is difficult to define and the processes through which it is formed are complex and difficult to analyse. I assume that spirituality makes an important contribution to identity (and vice versa). What follows will look into some identity issues that I find of interest to reflect on their implications for school religious education.

10. M.L. CRAWFORD & G.M. ROSSITER, *The Secular Spirituality of Youth. Implications for Religious Education*, in *British Journal of Religious Education* 18 (1996) 133-143.

11. G.M. ROSSITER, *Science, Film and Television. An Introductory Study of the Alternative Religious Stories that Shape the Spirituality of Children and Adolescents*, in *International Journal of Children's Spirituality* 1 (1996) 52-67; ID., *The Shaping Influence of Film and Television on Young People's Spirituality. Implications for Moral and Religious Education, Part 2*, in *International Journal of Children's Spirituality* 2 (1997) 21-35; G.M. ROSSITER, *The Shaping Influence of Film and Television* (n. 10).

12. G.M. ROSSITER, *The Shaping Influence of Film and Television on the Spirituality and Identity of Children and Adolescents. An Educational Response, Part 3*, in *International Journal of Children's Spirituality* 4 (1999) 207-224.

Specification of the Meaning of Identity

The reason identity is fundamentally important for individuals and education, and why it is difficult to analyse, is because its meaning emerges from efforts to answer the fundamental questions: "Who am I?" and "Who are we?" The questions have simple answers: "I am a named historical person." And profound ones: "How I understand myself has always been something of a mystery and I will probably continue to plumb the depths of my spirit until the day of my death." Identity can be both a given, physical, unchanging entity while at the same time a life long process of change. At some psychological level, people may spend all of their lives reflecting on and articulating for themselves partial answers to questions about their needs, moods, beliefs, purpose, motivations and values.

Individuals can be thought of as having multiple component identities which blend to constitute a distinct individual. Each identity relates to some aspect of their lives or to some membership which contributes to a description of the individual. Each identity is like a lens for viewing the individual; it highlights who they are and where they stand. This list is not definitive; its aim is to show how there are different and interrelated aspects of identity.

Type of identity	Aspect of life to which it relates.
Personal	Who the named individual is.
Gender	Male or female.
Sexual identity	Heterosexual or homosexual.
Moral	The core values and moral code that show what the individual is like as a person.
Personality	How the individual appears to friends and acquaintances; how the individual 'presents' to others.
Age	The age group with which the individual identifies.
Family	Identification with a particular family or families.
Spiritual	How individuals see themselves as spiritual; how they perceive and relate to a spiritual/moral dimension to life.
Religious	How religion enters into their sense of themselves as spiritual; how they are linked with an organised religion; how religion enters into their lives.
Psychological	What and how individuals think about their own psychological functioning; their understanding of their complex blend of needs, interests, attitudes, values and patterns of behaviour; their understanding of why they behave and live as they do.

Ideals, passions, commitments	Particular ideals, passions, interests and commitments that occupy the individual and which give a picture of the direction they are taking in their lives
Ethnic	The extent to which indivuals identify with a particular ethnic group or groups as a description of who they are.
Cultural	The extent to which individuals refer to a particular cultural group or cultural style in their lives
Regional and national identities	Whether regional and national identities are prominent in the individual's makeup.
Historical	How personal and social history help define the individual.
Dress	The styles and degrees of emphasis in styles with which dress enters into the life of the individual; and how important dress is to self-perception.
Work	The extent to which work/employment figures in the individual's sense of self.
Sport	How sport and sporting groups figure in sense of self.
Leisure	How the type and extent of leisure pursuits describe the individual.
Retail	How the purchase and use of consumer goods enter into the identity of individuals.
Conflictual	How an understanding of the identity of the self and the identities of others is related to conflict with others; how identity can lead to hatred of other individuals or groups.
Etc.	

While a preliminary list like this helps show the complexity of the concept identity, it does not necessarily help educators who seek an understanding of identity that yields useful implications for education. In what follows, I will examine some issues with the aim of working towards such an educational understanding that might help clarify a role for religious education in fostering identity development in young people.

My preliminary assumption would be that the identity components "Moral, spiritual, religious, psychological, and ideals" would be of special interest for religious education, while not ignoring the role that other components would have in the lives of individuals.

Key issues / principles for religious education
1. Identity is a multifaceted property of individuals, which needs to be understood in its complexity.
2. There is a need for an educational perspective on identity, to give focus and direction to the role that religious education may have in fostering identity development.

Theory and Research on Identity

In this section I will briefly present the viewpoints of recent theories and research on identity and identity building, by referring to schools of thought and to openly discussed topics in this field of interest.

The Developmental Theorists: Contributions to Self-understanding

Theories and research on the nature and development of identity are concerned with interpreting the behaviour of individuals, trying to understand the underlying psychological processes that affect their development as human persons. Not all of the theories of human development focus specifically on identity; nevertheless, a number of them contribute helpful ideas for understanding the concept. Reference to these writings can help religious educators become better interpreters of what is happening in the lives of young people, more empathetic, and more capable of making their religious and moral education relevant to the human development of youth.

Because psychological theories help with self-understanding, especially with insight into the motivations that stem genetically from the organism at the different stages of biological development, and with perspective on the influence of the social/cultural environment, they can be used as resources for exploring identity. The theories of Piaget, Kohlberg, Erikson, Fowler, Kegan and Oser, which can be generically referred to as 'structural-developmental' theories, each has a distinctive viewpoint on personal development.

Identity formation is at the centre of Erikson's psychological theory[13]. Expanding and refining Freudian psychodynamic theory, Erikson saw the drive towards self understanding going through a series of

---

13. E.H. ERIKSON, *The Challenge of Youth*, Garden City NY, Doubleday, 1965; ID., *Identity. Youth and Crisis*, New York, Norton, 1968; ID., *Dimensions of a New Identity*, New York, Norton, 1974; ID., *Identity and the Life Cycle*, New York, Norton, 1980.

'developmental tasks' that predominate at particular stages of the individual's life cycle; human development proceeds as individuals gradually resolve the distinctive conflicts characteristic of each developmental stage. For the adolescent, Erikson proposed that the major task be in exploring relationships – seeking personal intimacy and moving away from a sense of isolation.

Piaget's initial ideas on the emergence of moral reasoning in the child were expanded by Kohlberg[14] (1984) who focused on the different levels at which moral reasoning relates to behaviour. However, it needs to be recognised that moral reasoning is only one of the factors that influence the development of a 'moral identity'. Other cultural factors like social conditioning and genetic factors like personality type have an influence on behaviour; the level of moral reasoning is not always the prime determinant.

Fowler's theory of human faith development focused on the changing patterns in the believing process[15]. It reflects the evolution of the ways the individual's beliefs shape personal meaning – from more dependent, derivative meaning from family and social groups, through conformity to authority and dominant groups, towards a more autonomous and eventually an expansive faith. By contrast with Fowler's theory, Oser's theory of spiritual development focused more exclusively on the level of cognitive activity linked with different stages of belief[16].

The structural developmental theories of Piaget, Kohlberg, Fowler and Oser all imply that the universe of personal meaning within which individuals understand their own behaviour can be very authority dependent at earlier stages and more autonomous and interpersonal later on. In the later stages, individuals are better able to cope with conflicting views without collapsing the tensions between them. The universalist stage in the Fowler scheme suggests that the sense of personal identity has developed such intrinsic security that it no longer needs the sharp boundaries between belief systems / religions.

14. L. KOHLBERG, *Essays on Moral Development. The Psychology of Moral Development*, San Francisco, Harper and Row, 1984.

15. J.W. FOWLER, *Stages of Faith. The Psychology of Human Development and the Quest for Meaning*, San Francisco, Harper and Row, 1981; ID., *Becoming Adult, Becoming Christian*, New York, Harper and Row, 1986; ID., *Faith Development and Pastoral Care*, Philadelphia, Fortress Press, 1987.

16. F.K. OSER, *Toward a Logic of Religious Development. A Reply to My Critics*, in J.E. FOWLER, K.E. NIPKOW, F.K. OSER, F. SCHWEITZER, *Stages of Faith and Religious Development. Implications for Church Education and Society*, London, SCM Press, 1993, 48-88.

Key issues / principles for religious education
1. Self-understanding is an important process in the development of identity.
2. Reference to theories of human development can contribute to educators' understanding of young people's spiritual and identity development; and can inform their teaching about identity.

Reflections on Writings about Identity

Only a limited comment will be offered here on other writings about identity, which I have found helpful for education; the discussion begins with reflection on two review articles by Wilna Meijer[17].

Meijer considered that the more traditional understandings of personal identity were too biological and inflexible; they tended to define identity as a relatively fixed entity that is influenced by particular group self-understandings into which individuals are socialised. She saw this emphasis as educationally problematic because in Western countries the cultural milieu is characterised by rapid social change and international, interethnic, intercultural and interreligious communication. She claimed that it was inappropriate to propose the development of identity as an educational aim because its narrowness was incompatible with the democratic and pluralistic ideals of these communities.

While not agreeing with all aspects of Meijer's argument, I think that the points she raised need to be addressed because there is much evidence that a narrow, exclusivist view of personal and group identities is at the centre of much human conflict – conflict that ranges from arguments between students about sporting teams through to the centuries old ingrained hatreds that continue to fuel killing and displacement in the name of ethnic cleansing.

Meijer examined two views of identity at opposite ends of a spectrum. The first understood personal identity as a fixed inner core or kernel to the individual, which remains constant throughout the life cycle. Another extreme is the view typified by Nietzsche that personal identity is an illusion or an artificial construct; the individual is an aggregation of changing emotions, desires and ideas. In rejecting both the inherent

---

17. W. MEIJER, *Religious Education and Personal Identity. A Problem for the Humanities*, in *British Journal of Religious Education* 13 (1991) 89-94; ID., *The Plural Self. The Hermeneutical View on Identity and Plurality*, in *British Journal of Religious Education* 17 (1995) 92-99.

identity and the option of no identity at all, Meijer turned to the philosophy of Paul Ricoeur, which understood identity as a process of *interpretation* of personal history. This psychological understanding regarded identity as the end product of reflection on personal experience, allowing for continual adjustment.

Meijer attempted to sidestep the problems within a socialised personal identity with its relatively permanent, unchanging, and externally defined characteristics by stressing personal interpretation as the primary identity forging process. "This human potential for reflection is more fundamental than identity, for identity-as-interpretation is the outcome of reflection. Personal identity, therefore, is necessarily tentative, to be reflected upon, reconsidered and revised again and again. Education should therefore not aim at identity-development or identity-formation, but at rational autonomy, independence and responsibility, the capacity to make informed choices or at personhood"[18].

Meijer's approach, which stresses the need for continual change and development in identity, is useful for identifying problems that result from defining identity as fixed or as an illusion; also she shows how personal interpretation of experience can be a valuable component of identity which allows for change and development in self understanding. However, she seems to overstate the importance of psychological reflection and to underrate the place for the less reflective, unconscious elements. This does not give an adequate account of the important role that the externals of culture and social interaction play in identity processes. Also, a legitimate concern in education for identity development need not necessarily be thought of as opposed to efforts to promote rational autonomy, independence, responsibility and informed decision making; all of these elements seem to be desirable, natural qualities in a person with a healthy, mature identity. Meijer's ideas on identity seem more relevant for mature educated adults who are in better position to choose components in their identity; young people are only taking initial steps in this direction. Intercultural, interethnic and interfaith communication are desirable processes but they are not so much a given in pluralistic communities (an impression one gets from Meijer's writing). Such levels of dialogue and communication are difficult goals to work towards even with adults – tolerance, respect and desire to communicate across social/cultural/religious boundaries do not come easily. Education (religious education) can aim at fostering first

18. W. MEIJER, *The Plural Self* (n. 17), p. 95.

steps in such communication; this is not incompatible with a sense of particular religious identity. Meijer's conclusions do not give an adequate account of the role of given or cultural elements in the formation of identity, and consequently, her ideas about the links between education and identity development are too limited.

Contrasting with Meijer's view, but also complementing it, is that of psychoanalytic theorist Brennan who argued that the identity of the individual depended on perceived relatively fixed points because it depended on its identifications with others and ideas to maintain its sense of individual distinctness or identity[19]. The sense of identity depended on images of the self received from others – images that remained relatively constant in relation to the movement of life. Individuals needed these psychic fixed points. But these fixed points could hold the individual back from further change and development. Brennan argued that these relatively fixed points for the definition of identity were reinforced by the construction of commodities in the social world. She claimed that while psychic fixed points "blocked the mobility of psychic energy", technological commodities, unless they were constructed with care, could block the regeneration of nature and natural energy.

In response to the question "Who are you?", individuals could answer immediately and directly "I know who I am" from their sense of personal continuity; given basic mental and physical health this remains a constant. But at a deeper level, the answer to that question will always be changing, even if slowly as the individual grows older, responding to new experiences and new challenges; and these change factors are often external to the individual; they may catalyse (or in strong/traumatic cases, *force*) a personal revision of identity to a greater or lesser extent. Having both a sense of permanence and flexibility in identity is not contradictory; Meijer's view gives the impression that we need to opt more exclusively for the latter. While some may change their self-understanding and behaviour in response to new circumstances and education in its various forms, others may not – consciously reinforcing an established self image against any invitation to change.

Personal identity is like a well established 'working hypothesis of the self' as to what sort of a person you think you are and would like to be.

19. T. BRENNAN, *History after Lacan*, Oxford, Oxford University Press, 1993, p. xii.

For most, this self-understanding is relatively stable and usually changes only gradually, especially if individuals like this picture of self (positive self-esteem). For others, the self-hypothesis may be insecure and fragile – often, or from time to time.

This understanding of identity acknowledges that externals and social interaction are crucial reference points and raw material for identity. For some, the problem with identity is precisely a lack of the sort of reflection that Meijer sees as constitutive to identity; they may give little or no thought to identity but may live with the stereotypes and values they have absorbed unconsciously; they display an identity by default. The implied identity that is embedded in behaviour can be linked with the thought of the French sociologist Pierre Bourdieu[20] on what he calls 'life structure'. He defined this as the presumed values, ideas and beliefs that are implied in the way individuals spend their time and engage in activity. It is like an identity portrait of individuals painted through the way they spend time and invest energy. No matter what individuals might say about identity and preferred values, their life structure is the litmus test of their authenticity. Bourdieu's ideas as relevant to identity are explained in Warren[21].

Some individuals could be considered to have identity conflict or identity ill health. This means a hiatus between self understood identity and the implied identity that others perceive and interpret in their behaviour. This hiatus would indicate a lack of realistic reflection on self; or the self-reflection being deluded.

A major point of relevance for education is the hope that the educational process may in some way inform self understanding – fostering an identity that is open to enhancement through education – so that individuals' identity might include the resource of being 'reflective' and 'evaluative', helping them be open to considered change. This would imply that one role for education (religious education) is to help people understand something of the complex processes in the formation of identity – hence the relevance of research and developmental theories.

20. P. BOURDIEU, *Outline of a Theory of Practice*, New York, Cambridge University Press, 1977.
21. M. WARREN, *Life Structure and the Material Conditions of Living. An Ecclesial Task*. Paper presented at the Conference of the Association of Professors and Researchers in Religious Education in the United States and Canada, Chicago, 1994.

Key issues / principles for religious education

In the light of these considerations, it is proposed that an understanding of personal identity needs to include three elements:

1. some sense of 'fixed-ness' and permanence at one psychological level;
2. relationships with the world outside the individual, which serve as identity reference points and identity resources;
3. The capacity for revision or change in parts of the individual's identity, in response to physical and mental development, to experience, education and to reflection on the self.

Education and religious education could make some contribution with respect to the second and third aspects.

4. Identity can be understood as a working hypothesis of the self, which is influenced by external and internal factors; and which, hopefully, is open to enhancement through education.
5. Identity development needs some basic socialisation into values and stereotypes and into some sense of group identities – hopefully positive, non-exclusivist and altruistic. But these components should not be fixed and immutable but open to confirmation, reinforcement, evaluation and modification.
6. Education (religious education) should try to help inform individuals' self-understanding as well as their understanding of the complexities of identity formation.

Social Psychological View of Identity (the Symbolic Interactionist Theory)

Another avenue in social psychological theory which underlines the importance of external reference points for identity development is the Symbolic Interactionist school of sociology. The writings of the early sociologist C. H. Cooley (1864-1928) proposed the idea of the *Looking Glass Self* – that the image of self is in part derived from reflections of the self that an individual encounters through interaction with others[22]. This followed through into the thinking of the symbolic interactionist school of sociology – for example, Herbert Blumer's views that social interaction had a major influence on self-understanding[23]. How individuals are viewed and treated by others have a significant bearing on their acquisition of values, beliefs, self-image and self-esteem. This thought is

22. C.H. COOLEY, *On Self and Social Organisation. Charles Horton Cooley (1864-1929)*, Chicago, University of Chicago Press, 1998.
23. H. BLUMER, *Symbolic Interactionism. Perspective and Method*, Englewood Cliffs NY, Prentice Hall, 1969.

also prominent in theories for the social construction of reality – as evident in the sociological theory Berger and Luckmann[24]. It is also pertinent in writings / research concerned with education for self-esteem – more will be said about this area later.

Key issues / principles for education
1. A view of identity that sees its ongoing development linked interactively with cultural elements, personal and social discourse, as well as private reflection seems less prone to identity problems that might arise from an excessive emphasis on self analysis.
2. In addition, this view of identity leaves more room for an educational contribution. Education for identity (including religious identity) requires both intentional components for communicating to young people some sense of continuity with their heritage, as well as attempts to foster reflection on, and evaluation of, the processes of identity development.

Other Psychological Insights into Identity: Exaggerated Individualism

How individuals think about and relate to others is influenced by their own self-definition. Getting the basic personal, gender and cultural identity boundaries clearer is one of the developmental tasks for children and adolescents. The earlier, brief discussion of developmental theories looked at changes in thinking about self at different phases of the life cycle.

What we will be considering here are theories about the way people may be seduced into a sense of identity that is subtly constructed for them as a marketable package by power/economic/advertising/media groups in society. One of the crucial tasks for religious education would seem to be alerting young people to these dangers to their own humanness and authentic identity.

Max Weber in his book *The Protestant Ethic and the Spirit of Capitalism,* suggested that the religious revolution of the Reformation and its influence on the rise of individualism set the stage for the development of capitalist societies in the West[25]. He did not claim that this was the only factor which promoted the rise of capitalism; but he saw it as an important influence which contrasted with a more spiritual interpretation of culture and history.

24. P.L. BERGER & T. LUCKMANN, *The Social Construction of Reality. A Treatise in the Sociology of Knowledge,* London, Penguin, 1967.
25. M. WEBER, *The Protestant Ethic and the Spirit of Capitalism,* London, Unwin University Books, 1974 [1930].

The French psychoanalytic theorist Jacques Lacan proposed that in turn, capitalist society has accelerated the emphasis on individualism to the point that many people suffer from a social psychosis of individualism – trying to live out a massive ego fantasy. He considered that much of their anxiety comes from the frustration of unrealistic personal desires; the drive for higher production rates and profits has an ever increasing negative effect on the psychic environment in which people live, and it tends to strongly colour the social reference points they draw on for self understanding and identity[26].

These identity reference points are reinforced by the manufacture and marketing of commodities which strengthen the hold of the psychosis; and the reference points become entrenched, trapping people into an identity and search for meaning in what are ultimately unrealistic, naturally frustrating and basically antisocial fantasies. The result is a psychotic idea of identity in the service of free enterprise. Brennan, an interpreter of Lacan, suggested further that this post-enlightenment psychosis of individualism blocks flexibility to human identity development involving relationships with other people and nature, and in turn this causes degradation of the social and physical environments[27].

Lacan's theory suggests that individualism tends to "make the world over in its own image by reducing the lively heterogeneity of living nature and diverse cultural orders to a grey mirror of sameness. And it can only do this by consuming living nature in producing a proliferation of goods and services whose possession becomes the *sine qua non of the good life*. Of course, if nature is endlessly consumed in the pursuit of a totalising course, then that course is dangerous for living; it constitutes a danger to one's own survival, as well as that of others"[28].

Brennan then went on to assign a new meaning to the familiar acronym PMT – Pre Millennial Tension – to describe the condition in a society ambivalent about its various descriptions as postindustrial, post-modern, poststructural, post cold-war etc. while being anxious that it has no analysis that will readily give a hopeful sense of future direction.

26. J.A. MILLER, *Index: J. Lacan, Ecrits: A Selection* (translated by A. Sheridan), London, Tavistock, 1977.

27. T. BRENNAN, *History after Lacan* (n. 19), pp. 1-25.

28. *Ibid.*, p. 4.

Key issues / principles for religious education
Exaggerated individualism is a contemporary problem for identity, which
warrants attention within education for identity development.

The Relationships between Self-esteem and Identity

Care is needed with the idea of self-esteem as it relates to identity. Self
esteem may not always be unconditionally positive; for example, some
individuals may have a sense of identity that is arrogant, intolerant,
aggressive and hurtful to others – and they may feel comfortable and
happy with this picture (high self esteem?) The moral value of the 'content' of identity cannot be dismissed under the democratic guise of
being equally respectful and tolerant of all identities. The limits to tolerance are set by the rights, freedoms and responsibilities of citizens pro-
tected by law. This would also become an important consideration in
any examination of the relationships between identity and violence.

In responding to this issue, I find that a useful working definition of
self esteem is: the dynamic link between *what* individuals think about
their personal identity and *how* they feel about this; it has both a
descriptive content (their self perceived qualities as a person) and a powerful *affective dimension* (how comfortable or satisfied they feel with that
image of self). For example, people may feel more or less comfortable
with their self understanding and about how this is reflected to others;
or there may be a fundamental, almost unconscious, unarticulated,
doubt about their value – they may feel that if others only knew what
they were really like, they would find them unattractive and undesir-
able.

While it may be transparently evident to an adult that a particular
young person feels he/she is unloved and perhaps unlovable, this may
be something that the young person is not able to comprehend or
admit. Sensitive adults and teachers often make an accurate diagnosis
of this condition in young people; but it is not easy to change. It is not
just a matter of identifying the problem for the young person; neither
is it resolved by a small dose of what has been called 'unconditional
affirmation.' It can be a psychological difficulty that individuals carry
throughout their lives, often a cause of distress to themselves and to
those close to them.

One of the issues for educators (and for the community generally) is
how to address problems of low self-esteem in youth. What people usually describe as poor self-esteem has two aspects:

- Firstly, the image of self that individuals with low self esteem have is often harsh and unfavourable; it may not be an accurate picture, but for them it represents reality.
- Secondly, despite any outward show of self-confidence, they feel unhappy and uncomfortable with their self-image.

Any therapeutic efforts to redress the problem, as well as any generally supportive educational process, need to focus on the dual aspects of self-esteem. They should look at the question of the *degree of satisfaction* individuals have with their perceived identity, and at some *evaluation* of its 'human-ness' or personal qualities. By stressing the evaluative element, I seek to address the limitations in the so called 'self esteem movement' in education that seems to operate out of a too simplified understanding of self-esteem, and also out of questionable empirical measures of self-esteem.

While few people would oppose the idea that education should help improve students' perceptions of their own worth, the related theory, research and practice are, in my opinion, somewhat vague and unconvincing. I refer specifically to the analysis of Kohn, which I have found insightful[29]. Part of the problem has been the way self-esteem is conceptualised and operationally defined for purposes of empirical research.

Coopersmith, one of the earliest self-esteem researchers in the United States, understood self-esteem with an evaluative emphasis: "a personal judgment of worthiness that is expressed in the attitudes the individual holds toward himself"[30]. However, when it came to developing self-report questionnaires for measuring self-esteem, the evaluation of personal characteristics (a complex task) was not prominent. As a result, the many instruments for measuring self-esteem were concerned primarily with subjects' responses to questions about how favourably they felt about themselves. Immediately there was a problem in that the findings might say more about how individuals *wished* to appear than about what they really felt about their 'true' self, presuming that this could be known accurately. The findings reported on confidence and self-satisfaction – but not about what sort of person individuals perceived themselves to be. Hitler may well have scored well on self-esteem scales! Some researchers suggested that those who

29. A. KOHN, *The Truth About Self-Esteem*, in *Phi Delta Kappan* (1994) 272-283.
30. S. COOPERSMITH, *The Antecedents of Self-Esteem*, San Francisco, W.H. Freeman, 1967, p. 5.

scored highly tended to be the ones who demonstrated "a willingness to endorse favourable statements about the self as a result of an ambitious, aggressive, self-aggrandising style of presenting themselves"[31]. With difficulties like this, it is not surprising that many research studies linking educational programs with gains in self-esteem (or research linking behavioural problems with low self-esteem) have, in the main, shown no significant correlation – and therefore questionable evidence of causation.

The ambivalence and inconclusiveness of this psychological research does not seem to have inhibited the educational interest in fostering self-esteem. The focus of curriculum materials concerned with self-esteem which have appeared since the 1970s has been on simple, unconditional student affirmation – telling students 'how special they are'[32]. While no doubt such student materials may have been helpful to the limited role that classroom teaching might have in fostering self-esteem, they did not try to present a picture of the complex personal processes through which self-understanding, self image and self valuing develop. There are two dangers in the 'I am special' approach. Firstly, it can trivialise the importance and complexity of the concept as far as student personal growth is concerned. Secondly, its focus on the individual is yet another aspect of education that could tend to encourage self-centredness and self-preoccupation. An approach to self-esteem education that focuses primarily and directly on psychological self enhancement might end up being narcissistic (this will be referred to again later in the essay); it might distract attention from social and community aspects; it could overlook the importance of analysing economic, political and social factors that have an influence on how people are valued and devalued. These structural aspects might be having more influence on self-esteem than any simple self-analysis procedures.

---

31. A. KOHN, *The Truth About Self-Esteem* (n. 29), p. 273.

32. See for example the titles in J. CLARK, *Self Esteem. A Family Affair*, Minneapolis, Winston Press, 1978 and C. BORBA & M. BORBA, *Self Esteem. A Classroom Affair. 101 Ways to Help Children Like Themselves*, Minneapolis, Winston Press, 1978.

Key issues / principles for religious education
1. Attempts to link education with the fostering of self-esteem need to
   acknowledge firstly that self-esteem it a very complex, obscure, but vital
   factor in identity and psychological health.
2. Hence, the role of education, and of religious education in particular,
   will not be in the realm of clinical psychological analysis, but more likely
   in providing background studies that contribute in a limited way to an
   understanding of self-esteem as a component of identity.
3. Perhaps even more important an influence on sense of self-worth than
   the formal curriculum will be the quality of the personal relationships
   between teachers and pupils.
4. Of great importance in educational programs would be attempts to
   study how structural factors can value or devalue human persons.
5. Care is also needed to help avoid the self-development focus reinforcing
   self-centredness and narcissism.
6. Care is needed in interpreting the empirical research on self-esteem.
7. The possibilities and limitations in the use of self-esteem curriculum
   materials in the classroom need to be considered carefully.

Film, Television and Advertising: the Most Prominent Identity-building Resources in the Culture

Perhaps more than any element of culture and socialisation, film and
television provide young people with access to a vast range of identity
building resources. A detailed discussion of this issue has been presented
in Rossiter[33].

Film, television and commercial advertising are well attuned to a
number of the critical tensions/polarities in the psychological identity-
building processes for young people. For example: between the group
and the individual; between internationalism and nationalism; between
group required behaviour patterns and autonomy; between freedom and
responsibility.

Film and television have contributed to an increasingly internation-
alised perspective for young people; however, while this tends to soften
boundaries and distinctions that seem to be more important for older

33. G.M. ROSSITER, *Science, Film and Television* (n. 12); ID., *The Shaping Influence of Film and Television* (n. 12); ID., *The Shaping Influence of Film and Television* (n. 10).

generations, and while it promotes a greater sense of global 'brother-hood/sisterhood' and 'neighbourhood', it does not extinguish a sense of nationalism in identity. Certainly the commercial world is pragmatically alert to the tension between universalism and individual distinctiveness; it targets young people for purchases that will reinforce both aspects. While we may tend to think of identity mainly as a psychological sense of self, something that is primarily internal, it is a mistake to underesti-mate the importance of externals which can contribute much to self expression.

Items like clothing, hairstyle, preferred music, and fashion have something to say about identity, especially for teenagers. The quest for identity is easily exploited by commercial interests and the media. What may appear to another generation as unthinking conformity is of importance to the younger generation as a way of finding security and belonging within a group. Many commercial industries have developed more or less to cater for the identity experimentation of youth; they manufacture not only the clothes, food, CDs etc. for individual self-expression, but, through advertising, promote the images and moods that will be most likely fuel young people's desire to purchase their products. Music and fashion, especially that generated initially in the United States and the United Kingdom, serve as an international fund of resources for the self-expression and self-understanding of youth.

The problems with universal marketing are that advertising focuses on how to sell values increasingly geared to processes, not things. Sales appeals directed toward the values of individualism, experimen-talism, person-centredness, direct experience, and some forms of plea-sure and escape will need to tap intangibles – human relationships, feeling, dreams, and hopes – rather than tangible things or explicit actions.

While consumerism and advertising laud and reinforce both the ideas and images of 'freedom' and 'individuality', at the same time they may subtly seduce people into thinking that the acquisition of marketable commodities will satisfy identity needs. The meshing of market strate-gies with perceived identity needs may be successfully promoting what might be called a 'retail identity' or a 'commodity identity'. Any educa-tional investigation of identity forming processes needs to address these issues.

Key issues / principles for education

1. An education in the process of identity formation needs to include a study of how film, television and advertising can contribute significant identity-building resources[34].

2. Key topics in 1 should include:
   – the importance of externals for self expression and self understanding;
   – how advertising can promote a 'retail identity' – where self understanding and self expression are tied to marketable commodities;
   – the psychology of advertising;
   – the capacity of media advertising to seduce people away from their personal individuality towards a 'pre-packaged public individuality' proposed in consumerist terms.

The Crisis of Identity for Young Males

About twenty years ago, Australian education authorities were funding programs for girls which aimed at increasing access and equity in educational opportunity for young women. Programs such as these tried to address some of the effects of the long standing and ingrained cultural bias against opportunities and status for women in the community. However, as far as school is concerned (for example in New South Wales), girls now significantly outperform boys in more than 75% of study subjects in the final year of schooling. But the issue is not just a difference in academic performance.

There is increasing evidence in Australia especially, and in other post industrialised countries, that boys have disturbingly high rates of personal and social problems. A peak indicator is the high suicide rate. This is also a problem for young women, but for young men the rate is significantly higher. Other measures of disturbance show in the high risk of dropping out of school, alcohol abuse, taking drugs, being involved in criminal activity, being unemployed and being homeless. Beneath these indicators there is probably a level of depression, unhappiness, dissatisfaction and purposelessness amongst boys that warrant serious attention.

As noted in the earlier discussion, a part cause of the youth problems for both boys and girls is the lack of sufficient meaning to give direction

---

34. This is considered in more detail on the site: wwwdev.acu.edu.au/mre/spirituality_identity/.

and motivation for life. However, there seems to be some other factor for boys, and it could well be related to their sense of male identity.

Almost 30 years ago, an interesting reader was published about the experience of growing up male. In the introduction[35], editors Pleck and Sawyer summarised the male identity crisis as follows. I have included an extended quotation because of its significance. "Boys are treated, and are expected to behave in certain ways defined as masculine. ... The masculine role says that we males are supposed to seek achievement and suppress emotion. We are to work at 'getting ahead' and 'staying cool'. As boys we learn that getting ahead is important in both work and play. Grades are handed out in school, teams are chosen on the playground and both of these events tell us how well we are doing and how much better we could be doing. Here our masculinity is tested in immediate physical competition with others. Moment by moment, our performance is measured in relation to others. Both in winning and in losing, the masculine role exerts strong influence. It is not enough to win once; we have to keep winning. The continuing evaluation in relation to others encourages us to keep trying, but also insures that we can't ever really make it, once and for all. Our learned need to keep proving ourselves helps explain why many of us – no matter how hard we work or how much we achieve – remain vaguely dissatisfied with our lives. As males grow older, the bases for evaluation change, but the importance of establishing a ranking of work among individuals remains. As adults, the physical skills that were reflected in sports become less important than the mental and social skills that are reflected in prestige and income. What we learn growing up prepares us for these adult skills and rewards. As adolescents, one important area we were rated on was our social facility with females. Trying to get on well with females created anxiety for many of us, but mainly we accepted the situation as just another place where we should try to ignore our fears and go ahead. Staying cool, no matter what, was part of what we learned growing up male. We knew that big boys didn't cry, and that real men didn't get too excited except in places like football games. Spontaneous emotion – positive or negative – was suppressed or restricted to certain settings. We learned to mute our joy, repress our tenderness, control our anger, hide our fear. The eventual result of our not expressing emotion is not to experience it. Our restriction of emotionality compounds the stress put upon us by our striving to

---

35. J. PLECK & J. SAWYER, *Men and Masculinity,* Englewood Cliffs, Prentice Hall, 1974, pp. 3-4.

get ahead: we are often unable to acknowledge fully how the striving makes us feel. We suffer in many ways that may relate to the strain our emotional denial places upon our physical body. Compared with women, we die younger, have more heart attacks, and contract more stress related diseases. The drive towards getting ahead and staying cool has functioned, more or less well for men as individuals and for society as a whole for a long time. Much work has been accomplished, and many troubling feelings have been avoided. The masculine role has provided answers about who we are and what to do. But for ... some men what the masculine role offers is insufficient. Some of us no longer find our fulfilment in external rewards that come from meeting masculine standards; instead we seek internal satisfaction that comes form fuller emotional involvement in our activities and relationships".

It is disconcerting to think that these issues raised so long ago still seem to be very pertinent to the stressed situation of many young men – even though issues like poor employment options and a greater sense of public anomie are now more prominent. One might ask why have these issues not been addressed more successfully in the community in ways that might make significant inroads into changing the patterns through which young men seek a sense of masculinity. This remains the case, even though there have been many recent books and articles on masculinity[36]. There is an urgent need for more carry-through from the researchers on masculinity to young people, families and educators.

By contrast with the apparently slow progress of a 'men's movement', in the same thirty year period since this reader was published, the objectives of the 'women's movement' have had extensive coverage and many of them have been achieved. Boys have acknowledged that girls seem to have more social support and sense of direction from the women's movement in its various forms[37]. Traditional concepts of masculinity

36. R.W. CONNELL, *Masculinities*, St Leonards NSW, Allen and Unwin, 1995; N. EDLEY & M. WETHERELL, *Men in Perspective. Practice, Power and Identity*, London, Prentice Hall, 1995; S. BIDDULPH, *Manhood. An Action Plan for Changing Men's Lives*, Sydney, Finch Publishing, 1995; ID., *Raising Boys. Why Boys are Different and How to Help Them Become Happy and Well Balanced Men*, Sydney, Finch Publishing, 1997; D. TACEY, *Remaking Men. The Revolution in Masculinity*, Ringwood Vic, Viking, 1977; ID., *Reenchantment. The New Australian Spirituality*, Pymble NSW, Harper Collins, 2000.

37. This term is used with considerable generalisation here, without the opportunity to look at the many issues and meanings attached to the phrase 'women's movement'. The point being made is that young males do not seem to have similar useful cultural identity resources compared with those available to young women.

have been challenged by the women's movement, adding to the uncertainty, confusion and questioning of the male role. Greater freedom of expression and acceptance for homosexuality within the community might also add to young men's identity problem. For some young men, perhaps even a significant proportion, the way to express their masculinity in a satisfying way remains a considerable problem.

Key issues / principles for religious education
1. Educational strategies which intend to help young people study and reflect on the processes and resources in identity formation need to include consideration of an identity crisis that seems to affect many young men.
2. Research and other writings on masculinity and gender identity can inform this educational process.

Other Identity Related Issues

While it is beyond the scope of this essay to extend the analysis of identity related issues further, I think it is important to signpost some other areas that warrant investigation. These are areas where educators need to have background information and critical reflection that will inform their educational interactions with young people whenever issues for identity surface[38]:

– The extent to which individuals define themselves in terms of their work can contribute much energy to work, but it can be a source of psychological and social problems – especially for men, and for families. New flexibilities in work and employment in technological societies call for different understandings of the human meaning of work and leisure.

– Economic policies, and the often unarticulated values that underpin them and resultant effects on industry, trade and employment, are having a significant influence on the physical, social and cultural environment in which people live. Consideration needs to be given to the ways in which individuals can live creatively and happily in such an environment, and to how they might call into question the values and economic processes in society that are ultimately dehumanising.

38. See: wwwdev.acau.edu.au/mre/spirituality_identity/.

- Individual and community identities need to be referenced not only to human interactions but also to the non-human world – in its physical and biological aspects. The separation of human identity from the non-human world (earth, plants and animals) has been an influential component of the thinking that underpins the continued degradation of the environment; it sustains a mentality of dominance and exploitation. A more holistic (and ecologically sustainable) understanding of human identity is needed.
- How education might relate to questions about ethnicity and multi-culturalism in a pluralistic community need to be worked out in more detail.
- Human conflict often has a strong identity component to it. There is a need to explore the issue educationally in the hope that the boundaries set by different cultural, ethnic or national identities will not be used as a justification for conflict and violence – either psychological or physical.

3. A Conceptualisation of Identity that Is Useful for Religious Education

Taking into account the components to identity and the ideas in the literature considered earlier, the following conceptualisation is proposed as one that is helpful for thinking about the role of religious education in fostering identity development. It presumes that *interpretation of meaning* is central to religious education and that helping individuals to become *wise interpreters of life* is one of its foremost aims. For educational purposes, identity can be regarded as a process in which individuals draw on both internal and cultural resources for their self-understanding and self-expression.

Identity, from this perspective, is a complex of internal and external elements; the externals are relevant to identity when they are important reference points for self-understanding and self-expression. 'Identity health' can be thought of as a harmonious balance between internal and external identity resources. It can be proposed that identity should be based mainly on internal elements like beliefs, values and commitments – these are tied up with attitudes and motivations; too great an identification with externals weakens individuals' autonomy and makes them slaves to expectations from outside, rather than inner directed. However, it would be problematic to expect individuals to be so spiritually strong and independent to be totally dependent on their own internal resources for identity and meaning. It seems to be a fundamental part of the human condition to need the help of others and access to external cultural resources for making sense of life, for the experience of happiness and a sense of fulfilment. Identity development and maintenance have an important interpersonal component.

What individuals think of themselves and what they do to express themselves, particularly their individuality, display their identity. This view of identity is useful for education because it emphasises the importance of education generally, and religious education in particular, in helping give young people access to cultural resources – including religion – to assist with their self understanding and self expression. Also, this view lends itself to the interpretation of behaviour in the light of motivation, beliefs and values. It has a strong psychological focus and is related to self-knowledge and self-esteem, and to purpose and meaning in life. This view of identity is like spirituality viewed from the perspective of self-expression and self-understanding.

This view sees identity as the consistent moral picture of the individual that emerges from their behaviour; it is an expression of what sort of a person they are; what they think of themselves and what sense they make of life and of their behaviour. Identity has a momentum about it; it is relatively fixed, but it can change. It can be influenced by things like new experience that requires interpretation, personal reflection on life, relationship with God, a need for action, social change and comparisons with others; it can be affected by perceptions of the view that others have of the individual; also it can change in the light of perceptions of the identity of others – especially if they are favoured role models. Just as sense of self can be very dependent on social interaction so identity can be influenced and sustained by it.

This view provides a useful *interpretative framework* for the educator which helps give focus to teaching related to identity development. What is taught relates to this in two ways. Firstly, giving students educational access to the content (traditions, wisdom, experience, theology etc.) provides them with initial contact with potential identity building resources that they might not otherwise encounter. Formal education can open them to larger cultural horizons, and to a broader imagination of the sort of person they could be, than they might otherwise encounter in their ordinary lives. How such content is taught, how it is presented and studied in relationship with people's quest for meaning and identity, can help students sense that the educational process and its content are relevant for their personal development. Secondly, this approach models for youth useful ways of interpreting their own identity development (indeed their whole spiritual development) in the light of a critical interpretation of culture. It suggests to them that they need to learn to understand how cultural elements and their own internal needs/drives can contribute to the way they understand and express themselves.

This approach can foster young people's understanding of their own spiritual/moral development from an identity perspective. For example, it might foster the following understandings:

- A strong sense of identity can be the driving force behind idealistic and humane action; it can reinforce links with others from various groups; and it can serve as a source of courage in adversity.
- But at times, for various reasons, individuals' identity can be fragile.
- A diffuse identity can lead to erratic and immoral behaviour.
- A natural interest in maintaining and enhancing identity is healthy; however, a concern to project a particular identity may be a facade protecting inner uncertainty and weakness.
- Individuals may appeal to a particular identity to justify their actions – both moral and immoral ones.
- Various things can cause anxiety about identity, for example, ranging from the poor form of one's favourite sporting team, to fear that immigrants may threaten one's lifestyle, jobs and cultural dominance, or to moods that are biologically based.
- How individuals and groups define themselves, and what cultural elements they draw on to do this, will reveal something about their values and their understanding of what it means to be human and to be spiritual.
- There may be conflict between the identity individuals would like to propose for themselves and the identity that is actually implied in the way they live and express themselves. "As individuals express their life, so they are"[39].

This view of identity stresses the importance of inner identity resources – this shows identity intimately linked with spirituality. The advice that Polonius gave to Laertes in Shakespeare's *Hamlet* is relevant: "To thine own self be true; then if follows as surely as the day follows the night that thou shalt not be false to any man". Inner truth is

---

39. K. MARX, *The German Ideology,* London, Lawrence and Wishart, 1970.

achieved firstly by knowing what one's moral identity and values are; then there is *fidelity* to those commitments.

This 'languaging' of identity is essentially spiritual. It is the same language that is appropriate in the exploration of Christian spirituality where love, inner truth, fidelity to commitments, social justice and identification with the marginalised are core gospel values. This sort of language has been described elsewhere as a *psychological spirituality*[40] – I consider this to be one of the most important developments in Catholicism since the Second Vatican Council. Psychological spirituality evolved out of a blending of theology and psychology where the language focused the religious tradition on contemporary issues to help it become relevant to the lives of Christians. This quest for relevance (and hence the focus of psychological spirituality) is even more crucial now if the faith tradition is to be of any perceived relevance to young people. This language is useful because it helps translate gospel values and theology into contemporary psychological principles; it helps relate the Christian gospel to people's lives. As will be considered later in the essay, one of the apparent reasons for the current decline in mainline Christianity is that the words the churches have traditionally used to encapsulate Christian teachings have lost much of their force. The language of psychological spirituality could help make Christian spirituality and ministry more relevant and accessible for people today.

While this approach has much to offer, a caution is needed. It is basically concerned with 'self development' and it is essentially 'self focused'. It needs correctives to ensure that it does not deteriorate into narcissism – that is, into self-centredness and self-preoccupation. Stressing the importance of internal identity resources does not have to imply self-centredness; individuality does not have to exclude altruism; autonomy does not have to exclude interdependence. Christian spirituality has much to offer in its emphasis on fidelity to others – a distinguishing feature of Jesus. It states parabolically that individuals may find themselves best in the very process of giving themselves away for others; social justice is central to Christian spirituality, and service is central to Christian ministry. This view calls into question modern society's preoccupation with individuality and also its materialism. The study of spirituality and identity in religious education needs to give voice to these values.

---

40. G.M. ROSSITER, *Historical Perspective on the Development of Catholic Religious Education in Australia. Some Implications for the Future*, in *Journal of Religious Education* 47 (1999) 5-18, esp. p. 8.

As noted above, the languaging of Christian spirituality in psychological terms has been one of the great advances in the Church since the
1950s. However, this has been more or less limited to those who have
studied the Social Sciences and Theology / Scripture (and related spirituality) from this perspective. It has not yet made its presence felt widely
in the regular homilies in parishes, although the situation is still changing slowly. It is interesting to note that the movement called *Spirituality
in the pub* in Australia in recent years is an example of this development,
along with the programs in adult religious education and counselling
institutes.

Spirituality is a core expression of identity. The tendency towards secular spirituality in many youth is consistent with their inclination not to
see religion, including their own particular tradition, as likely to have a
prominent place in the way they work out their identity, values and purpose in life[41]. It can be said that this is not a new phenomenon because
the description fits many nominally religious adults. However, today's
youth, as well as inheriting a tradition of secularisation, are subject from
birth to an electronically conditioned, global village culture that colours
their view of religion itself and offers many alternative sources of meaning and values that can be used for developing a sense of identity.

Young people do not start life with a relatively static cultural baseline;
for them, the constant as regards education, lifestyle, employment and
entertainment is *change* itself. Change may have become more of a natural ingredient in the formation of their personal identity. They can
tend to seek self understanding and self expression through keeping in
tune with the latest trends in music, film, fashion, leisure, sport and
technology with little reference to traditional beliefs and values; even
family traditions may have a minimal place in their self definition.

Also relevant to this discussion are questions about the maintenance
of ethnic and national identities. In the sort of world that today's young
people live in, many conventional distinctions between groups of people
have tended to lose their meaning and force. They can go beyond common boundaries and draw elements of spirituality, identity and lifestyle
in a trans-religious, trans-ethnic and trans-national way. This could be
regarded as valuable for developing a sense of global human community; but there remains an ambivalence about identity that is evident in
a tension between wanting to be universal yet distinctive, and in out-
bursts of racial prejudice and violence.

---

41. M.L. CRAWFORD & G.M. ROSSITER, *The Secular Spirituality of Youth* (n. 11).

Key issues / principles for religious education

1. For educational purposes, identity can be thought of as a process in which individuals draw on both internal and cultural resources for their self-understanding and self-expression.
2. This understanding of identity can guide the ways that religious education fosters identity development both through content and process.
3. Religious education can foster in young people greater understanding of the identity development process, helping them become better 'interpreters' of both their experience of life and of their own spiritual development.
4. A language of 'psychological spirituality' can facilitate 2 and 3 above as well as providing a way of making the theological traditions of the Church more accessible to people today and more focused on what they perceive as 'real' spiritual/moral issues.

The identity forming process needs to be supported by communities' efforts to communicate some basic sense of identity to children by giving them access to elements of familial, cultural and religious heritage that can be resources in helping them understand themselves and make sense of their life in society. Otherwise their education could be presuming wrongly that they should be brought up in a type of identity vacuum until they are mature enough to determine their own identity, choosing rationally in the light of an appraisal of the many values and identity components available in a pluralist, multicultural society.

Educational efforts to communicate a particular religious identity do not have to be exclusivist, trying to impose a 'package deal' identity that precludes individuals' growing involvement in a more autonomous, reflective process of identity development. Also, the values and identity components that a group wants to hand on to its young people should be kept open to evaluation; the identity that a group desires to communicate should never be a hidden agenda. It could serve as a basic starting point or baseline in identity development. There can be the hope that young people might later affirm, embrace and enhance their religious identity; but what eventuates is theirs to determine.

As well as an obvious interest in *religious identity*, Religious Education is concerned with fostering *moral identity* in young people. Either consciously and/or as illustrated in their behaviour, they will have a moral profile of values, beliefs and commitments that gives direction to their lives and colours their interaction with others. The *conscious* moral identity may not always coincide with the *lived, operative* or *implied* moral identity.

4. General Implications for School Religious Education

The focus here will be specifically on school religious education. However, as suggested in the introduction, the issues also have relevance for theology and ministry.

Interpretative Background for Religious Educators

The first, and probably the most important, proposed implication for religious education flowing from this discussion of youth spirituality and identity has to do with the role of religious educators as interpreters of meaning. Religious educators, both those who teach and those responsible for curriculum development (and indeed all school educators) need to have an understanding of the life world of young people in all its complexity.

Religious educators need an understanding of spirituality and identity issues for youth that will serve as an interpretive background to their educational work and their personal interactions with youth. It is needed as a source of wise insight into what is happening in the lives of individuals and groups; such insight can inform the comments they make in class – where they should be modelling the committed, adult 'searcher for meaning'; and it can inform a range of personal interactions with youth ranging from silent, knowing empathy to personal advice given to individuals. It is also needed as a source of perceptive interpretation of the ways in which various components of culture can have a bearing on youth spirituality and identity. Here, religious educators are modelling the critical interpreter and evaluator of culture.

Such an understanding of spirituality and identity issues becomes recognisable in educators as a language of meaning, which explores and expresses reasons for living. They need to show young people through their language, both in the classroom and in personal interactions outside the classroom, that they are sensitively conscious of the questions and issues that the young are having to deal with. This is another way of talking about the language of psychological spirituality noted earlier.

With a language of meaning evident in their professional and personal contact with youth, religious educators will better be able to identify with their life questions and to assist them in becoming wise searchers for meaning. This role in supporting young people's search for meaning needs to fit comfortably and naturally within teachers' larger educational role. It must not be exaggerated – otherwise educators could be perceived by youth as goodwilled, obsessive, amateur psychiatrists, bent on giving advice at every opportunity. Sensitivity to the needs of youth spirituality has to be a balanced part of the educator's human interface with young people and should be perceived as a naturally important, but not an overbearing part of their professional commitment.

An Understanding of Youth Spirituality and Identity Evident in the Religious Education Curriculum

What was said above about educators as interpreters of meaning also needs to be translated into the school religious education curriculum in tangible ways.

In other words, the religion curriculum needs to have the search for meaning and identity as one of its central themes, which influence the selection of content, and the way in which content is presented and researched by the students.

In the eyes of students, the religion curriculum (in church related schools) should clearly have a dual responsibility:
– to ensure that students get adequate access to the religious tradition;
– to help students learn how to become informed and think critically about spiritual and moral issues.

Whether or not they take up active membership in the Church, young people's experience of school religious education should leave them with a sense that the curriculum has tried to help them study and think through issues related to the search for meaning and identity. Hopefully this will become a part of their life long learning. From this perspective, they should be able to see how the Church and its theology have tried to respond to the perennial search for ultimate meaning in life. Hopefully too, this impression will be more vivid than that of the school trying desperately to give them a lasting 'injection of Catholicism' before they leave.

In addition, they should have experienced a 'critical' religious education. This will have alerted them to the ways in which elements of culture may have a shaping influence on people's beliefs and expectations of life.

If this has happened, young people will not have difficulty seeing the religious education process as essentially one of 'interpretation'. The students' use of research and formal study will have helped them to become critical interpreters of meaning and of the culture.

Problems with Current Religion Curricula in Catholic Schools in Australia

Elsewhere I have argued that formal religion curricula in Catholic schools in Australia are much less relevant and effective than they could be because the content is too 'tame'[42]. In other words, the curricula are generally perceived by the majority of students as of little relevance to their own quest for spirituality and meaning. I believe that this sense of irrelevance is masked by students' overall satisfaction with their experience in Catholic schools which often reflects appreciation of the community spirit, friendships, quality of education and the commitment of staff to their education and personal development – as well as a relatively patient and uncomplaining acceptance of the good will behind religious education. This is clearly an area that warrants systematic research.

There are two types of religion curriculum in Catholic secondary schools in Australia. The first type responds to the official *diocesan religious education* guidelines that apply. This type covers the full range of schooling from Kindergarten to the final year (Year 12).

The second type is the state education authorities' *religion studies* courses, which are usually taken up in the final two years of schooling. These courses are academically accredited and examined in the same way as all other matriculation subjects. Catholic school students in Australia make up more than 95% of the candidature for state religion studies courses, even though Catholic schools teach just over 20% of the country's school children. The reason for this disproportion is that, in the main, the Catholic schools (and some others like the Lutheran schools) are the only schools, which have consistently committed substantial resources to the teaching of religion. In New South Wales, more than 75% of Catholic secondary schools offer the state Studies of Religion course at year 12 level as the principal classroom religion curriculum.

---

42. G.M. ROSSITER, *Historical Perspective on the Development of Catholic Religious Education* (n. 40), p. 15.

I believe that the first type, the Catholic religion curricula are too preoccupied with what I would call "institutional maintenance" – at least this is the dominant perception that I think the students have. The Catholic curricula emphasise traditional areas of content: sacraments; Scripture; Jesus; morality; Church; liturgy etc. My concern is not that such topics should be removed, because they have an important central place. However, what I consider lacking is enough content on questions related to the search for meaning and identity – that is: content on spiritual, moral and cultural issues that make it evident to students that a major concern of the curriculum is to foster their search for meaning and identity. In addition, I believe that the teaching of the traditional areas of Catholic content can often be better related to the theme of the search for meaning than is currently the case. As noted elsewhere, I am also concerned that religious education is lagging behind other subject areas such as English language and history (and other secular subjects) which, in the final years of schooling in Australia are increasingly becoming more values and issues focused, with the students being challenged to become critical interpreters of culture[43]. I am pleased to see such a development in general education; but I am disappointed that this focus is not more strongly evident in religious education, the subject area which *par excellence* should be about the search for meaning and values.

I consider that the content of the state religion studies courses are also too 'tame' and are not as relevant to young people's search for meaning and identity as they could be; but for different reasons from the Catholic religion curricula. In Australia, the state courses in religion are, in my opinion, still too tied to the content selection principles and teaching methods of phenomenology that developed in British school religious education after 1970. They are too descriptive and focus too much on what students tend to perceive as "useless religious paraphernalia"[44]. This phrase echoes the research findings of Nipkow[45] who found that this was the judgment German youth made of religious education content which did not focus in some way on what they perceived to be the main spiritual and

---

43. G.M. Rossiter, *Historical Perspective on the Development of Catholic Religious Education* (n. 40), p. 11.

44. *Ibid.*, p. 15.

45. K.E. Nipkow, *Pre-conditions for Ecumenical and Interreligious Learning. Observations and Reflections from a German Perspective* (Moral and Religious Education Project), Sydney, Australian Catholic University, 1991.

moral issues of the day; they showed little interest in content which seemed more or less exclusively concerned with institutional maintenance and not enough with people's search for meaning and values. Similar findings appeared in the extensive Italian survey of Malizia and Trenti[46]. I have heard similar interpretations from religion teachers and scholars in Britain and I suspect that research would come up with similar findings in Australia. It would be important to test the extent to which students today are not antagonised by a lack of relevance in the content of religious education – they may be tolerant, regarding it with a type of detached, clinical, anthropological interest. My concern is that too many youth have little expectation for religious education to be relevant to their search for meaning and identity.

Elsewhere I have described the evolution of state religion studies courses in Australia, which have drawn heavily on the British county school traditions[47]. In the quest for educational respectability, such courses have steered away from both Christian theology and contemporary issues and towards less controversial content in descriptions of world religions. In addition, where there is scope for addressing issues[48], there still seems to me to be too much dependence on description; the evaluation of particular issues needs to be written more strongly and unambiguously into state religion studies courses.

In British schools and in religious education theory, there have been significant moves in the 1980s and 1990s towards more issue-oriented teaching in religion studies courses[49], but there is not much evidence for this yet in Australian state religion studies courses. One state education official recently acknowledged this about the Australian courses; he considered that they were constrained to stay with

---

46. G. MALIZIA & Z. TRENTI, *Una disciplina in cammino. Rapporto sull'insegnamento della religione cattolica nell'Italia degli anni 1990*, Torino, Società Editrice Internazionale, 1991 (English translation: *An Evolving Enterprise. Report on the Teaching of Religion in Catholic Schools in Italy in 1990*).

47. M.L. CRAWFORD & G.M. ROSSITER, *The Nature of Religious Education in Public Schools. The Quest for an Educational Identity*, in *Panorama. International Journal of Comparative Religious Education and Values* 5 (1994) no. 1, 77-94.

48. See for instance the role of women in religion, ecology and religion etc.

49. M.H. GRIMMITT, *Religious Education and Human Development. The Relationship Between Studying Religions and Personal Social and Moral Education*, Great Wakering, McCrimmons, 1987; R. BEST (ed.), *Education, Spirituality and the Whole Child* (n. 2).

what he called "traditional religious content", while social science, English language, history and other subjects, were more free to address contemporary spiritual issues. This restriction on religion studies, in my opinion, takes too narrow an epistemological view of religion itself. And it is a view, which tends to domesticate religion and reinforce for many students their feeling that much of religion is irrelevant to their lives. The religion studies courses in Australia need to venture further from the structural confines of Smart's dimensions of religion[50].

The Need for More 'Issue-oriented' Content in Religious Education Curricula

My conclusion in 3 above is that the two sorts of religion curricula, both Catholic diocesan and state religion studies, for different reasons, fail to engage students sufficiently at the level of contemporary spiritual and moral issues. In other words, they do not adequately touch the spirituality of young people – the areas of life where they are confronted by its spiritual and moral dimension. The syllabuses are in effect too domesticated. It is not that every line of the syllabuses needs to be issue-oriented. But the present pattern needs to shift more in this direction. This is the direction that would make religious education more relevant to the majority of young people. I also believe that it is the best option for the classroom in representing the Church and fostering Church participation. Because there is difference of professional opinion about where the balance should be, I would see the urgent need for more in-depth research on students' perception of the role of religion in giving people meaning in life and on their perceptions of the content of religious education. My fear is that a significant number of young people are indifferent, but not antagonistic, to religious education because they felt that it was not really concerned with their lives.

A good way of illustrating the formula I am proposing here is to look at particular topics that might be studied. These could be of variable length and could be integrated with the study of more traditional religious content. This is not a whole curriculum, but the sort of topics that I think should appear in the secondary school religion curriculum.

50. N. SMART, *Secular Education and the Logic of Religion*, London, Faber, 1968.

Examples of issue-oriented topics in religious education

Critiques from a religious perspective:
The values – or lack of values that underpin economic rationalist thinking.
Globalisation policies and free markets: whose interests are being served?
   What values are involved?
How do film and television influence the spirituality and identity of people?
What are the links between contemporary music and youth spirituality?

Theological issues:
The contemporary research on the historical Jesus: implications for the
   beliefs of Christians.
Current debates about the role of women in religion: the problem of patri-
   archy and gender bias in the Christian church – even in the New Testament.

Psychological spirituality:
The development of identity – secular, ethnic, and religious – and its influence on human behaviour.
The possible links between identity (including religious identity) and problems like racism, violence and ethnic cleansing.
How do religions search for answers to fundamental questions about meaning, purpose and transcendence in life?

Science and religion:
The new Physics: Its impact on religion, and on people's ideas of God and
   creation.

World religions:
Judaism: Understanding the meaning of the holocaust for contemporary
   Judaism; Jewish controversy over the religious and secular significance of
   the state of Israel; Controversy in Jewish views of out marriage and
   homosexuality.
Islam: The interpretation of Jihad or holy war. Islamic fundamentalism.
Sect and cults: Why do people join them? Are cult members attracted
   because of their psychological needs or because of their personality type?
   How harmful is membership for their psychological and spiritual health?

These recommendations are controversial and they need further consideration and debate. There needs to be a balance. However, the overall credibility of our representation of the Catholic tradition in religious
education may be jeopardised if religious education is perceived more by
students as concerned with maintenance of the institution than with
addressing the critical spiritual and moral issues of the day.

Method in Classroom Religious Education: Should It Be More Personally Oriented?

In the earlier-mentioned review of the history of Catholic religious education in Australia[51], I proposed that the need for relevance and a personal focus in school religious education was more important now than at any previous time; however, I argued that the general failure of the personalist movement in religious education in the 1970s was because it was perceived as a 'low key', discussion-oriented activity which did not involve serious study and research by the students. Personalism and relevance in contemporary classroom religious education will never be achieved in an authentic fashion without academic credibility. The notes of student research, critical reading, interpretation and evaluation are central to the activity; on this basis, class discussions tend to be more focused, more relevant and often more personal.

For many years in Australian Catholic religious education (and I suspect the same in other countries) it was mistakenly thought that an *academic* approach could not be *relevant* and *personal*. Getting into some perspective the place for personalism and the development of faith have long been, and still remain, central problems with the practice of Catholic school religious education[52].

I will refer to this question again in a later section which reflects on relationships with the religious education theory of Herman Lombaerts.

Language of Meaning and Reasons for Living within Theology and Religious Education

The following are words from a Catholic hymn, which was prominent in Australian Catholic piety in the 1950s:

---

51. G.M. ROSSITER, *Historical Perspective on the Development of Catholic Religious Education* (n. 40).

52. M.L. CRAWFORD & G.M. ROSSITER, *Teaching Religion in the Secondary School. Theory and Practice*, Sydney, Christian Brothers Province Resource Group, 1985; ID., *Missionaries to a Teenage Culture. Religious Education in a Time of Rapid Change*, Sydney, Christian Brothers Province Resource Group, 1988; G.M. ROSSITER, *The Centrality of the Concept Faith Development in Catholic School Religious Education*, in *Word in Life* 46 (1998) no. 1, 20-27; ID., *Historical Perspective on the Development of Catholic Religious Education* (n. 40).

Soul of my Saviour sanctify my breast
Body of Christ be Thou my saving guest.
Blood of my Saviour bathe me in Thy tide.
Wash me with water, flowing from Thy side.
Deep in Thy wounds Lord, Hide and shelter me.
So shall I never, never part from Thee.

Religious educators have no difficulty seeing the lack of congruence between this sort of religious language and contemporary experience/ spirituality – and hence its inappropriateness. Many would tend to think: "Fortunately we do not have that problem now." But they are wrong. While the language of present day Catholic theology and religious education is nowhere near as sentimental as was the case in the hymn *Soul of my Saviour*, its lack of *relevance* to the experience of many young people still remains a fundamental problem. Theorists and practitioners in theology/religious education do not seem to be sufficiently aware of the radical extent to which a lack of relevance in their language and content remains a problem for youth and many adults as well. They do not seem to understand that a lack of antagonism on the part of youth for religious education should not be interpreted as an indication that it is relevant for them. Hence my concern for more finely focused research on this question. In curriculum content, student resources and teachers' language, there is still insufficient overt connection with the ways people experience the contemporary moral and spiritual realities of life. My concern is that many youth – even those who are not antagonistic to religious education – feel that it has little consequence for their search for meaning and values: the spirituality of the organised church seems to have little or no relevance to their lives.

While this problem has no easy, quick answer, it is vital for both theology and religious education to pursue relevance. This has always been a central issue for theology and religious education, but now more than ever, because of rapid social and cultural change.

However, the problem is not just with the relevance of the theological language, but with the fundamental framework out of which the language flows. The question: "How can we more effectively communicate the Catholic tradition?" is not, in my opinion, an adequate framework within which to work, because it is too exclusively institutional. Rather, the question, which illustrates a more useful spiritual, starting point for many youth is: "How can we better help young people explore the spiritual and moral dimensions of life?" Within this framework, the case for Catholicism can be best presented. It is very encouraging for religious educators to find that this is precisely the emphasis emerging in the recent Vatican document *The Catholic School on the Threshold of the Third Millennium*[53].

While not a complete solution, I believe that Catholic theology and religious education need to take on more seriously a *language of meaning*, as suggested above. They need to show plausible *reasons for living* in response to people's search for meaning. For a long period of history Catholic theology was expressed mainly in Thomistic and Aristotelian language (I do not want to debate here its relevance for any of that period.) But what is needed now is expression in language and concepts which 'bite' into all of the issues and problems of the contemporary search for meaning, values and identity. The identity issues explored earlier in this essay are examples of the thinking and language that need to be incorporated into theology and religious education; the faith tradition needs to be explored and expressed anew in these terms, very much focused on the issues people experience today. This means not trying to be 'trendy' but seriously engaged with the content and processes through which people draw on cultural elements in their search for a meaningful human life.

5. Relationship with the Hermeneutic-Communicative Theory of Religious Education

The implications I have proposed for school religious education harmonise with the hermeneutic-communicative model described by Herman Lombaerts and his colleagues[54]. This is particularly the case with respect to their diagnosis of the cultural and spiritual context of youth in Western countries.

Lombaerts' idea of young people's "self-thematisation" is another way of describing how they make use of cultural elements to construct a sense of identity; this they do in a comparatively secular way: "Young

---

53. CONGREGATION FOR CATHOLIC EDUCATION, *The Catholic School on the Threshold of the Third Millennium*, Homebush NSW, St Paul Publications, 1998.
54. H. LOMBAERTS, B. ROEBBEN, G. GINNEBERGE, *Godinet: Religious Education on the Internet – A Flexible Working Tool for a Subject on the Move*, Discussion paper, Leuven, K.U. Leuven, 1999.

people are not so much interested in the understanding of religious or Christian 'realia' than in the world that surrounds them and the concrete experience of their lived relationship to that environment"[55]. The authors refer to the research of Roebben which highlights the individualism and questioning that characterise this process: "Young people understand themselves particularly as authors of their own moral and religious biography and they want to question religious traditions as regards their plausibility and legitimacy"[56]. This is the mood and orientation of young people that make it so difficult for educators to find ways in which the study of religious traditions might be perceived as relevant and personal.

Given this cultural situation, a hermeneutic learning process for religious education is of fundamental importance. In such a process, the students are engaged as interpreters of meaning; they are encouraged to be critical interpreters of culture; they learn how to interrogate their cultural conditioning[57] – to become more critically aware of the shaping influence that culture can have on beliefs, attitudes, values and behaviour.

In these aspects, the hermeneutic-communicative model is strongly endorsed. However, I consider that the methodology that Lombaerts and his colleagues propose, as I interpret it, needs further refinement according to the context – especially formal classroom religious education. My view is based on limited contact with their writings; perhaps the different estimate I make of school religious education may not turn out to be so different from their view in the light of further dialogue; the comments here contribute to that dialogue. The methods the group proposes I find suitable for adult religious education and youth ministry. But I suggest modifications for use in the school classroom where young people participate in compulsory religious education.

The Lombaerts' model is based on the view that "young people, as a group, design a collective 'discourse' regarding questions on meaning, values and lifestyles, and that the task of the teacher especially consists of investigating, evaluating, broadening and deepening this 'discourse' in a critical way with the students"[58]. This approach was articulated as an alternative to a 'didactic' approach to religious education which was

55. H. LOMBAERTS, B. ROEBBEN, G. GINNEBERGE, *Godinet* (n. 54), p. 3.
56. *Ibid.*
57. B.V. HILL, *Is Value(s) Added Education in the National Interest?* (Harold Wyndham Memorial Lecture), Sydney, NSW Institute of Educational Research, 1993.
58. H. LOMBAERTS, *A Hermeneutical-Communicative Concept of Teaching Religion*, Unpublished research proposal, Leuven, K.U. Leuven, 1999, p. 1.

found wanting. The model proposed that the first step in classroom religious education is a diagnosis of the group discourse, which taps into the expressed thinking, and beliefs of youth. It is only after such a diagnosis that relevant content can be devised: "Acknowledgement of the dialectic character of the so-called 'group discourse' guarantees that relevant learning content can be identified in order to realise a meaningful hermeneutic learning process for the students"[59]. The teaching/learning process presumes, and becomes structurally dependent on, the active participation of the students in a hermeneutic dialogue.

My concern about this method is that, even though it proposes an attractive ideal, the presumptions built into the process do not always hold true. While young people are vitally concerned about a search for meaning and identity, this does not mean that they will automatically see obligatory religious education as the place and time when they will seriously engage in personal dialogue about this search. An approach is needed which does not presume that openness to personal dialogue is a prerequisite and starting point for the process. This may well develop, and it is desirable that it does; but it depends on a number of factors and it is, therefore, counterproductive to make it a starting point for religion lessons. This is of course very different from the voluntary group context where such an openness to dialogue is usually one of the main reasons that individuals participate.

The Lombaerts model, in its appraisal of so called 'didactic' methods, rightfully questions the relevance of excessive dependence on descriptive and institutional content and authority-based teaching. I have an impression, and this may not be correct, that it also seems to eschew the ideas of content and intellectual focus as somehow inappropriate and antithetical to the interactive group process. In so doing, it seems to have overemphasised personal group dialogue as the only alternative to didactic teaching.

I believe that a more appropriate approach to classroom religious education presumes that engagement in a student-centred 'study' process is the starting point. Study and student research are justified and accepted as legitimate educational processes in the compulsory context – as they are for other learning areas like science, language and mathematics. This is not the case for a personal dialogue, which needs an implied acceptance of special circumstances by the group. However, what I would

---

59. H. LOMBAERTS, B. ROEBBEN, G. GINNEBERGE, *Godinet* (n. 54), p. 5.

describe as 'academic dialogue', which does not commit students to tes-
tify to their own beliefs and commitments, is perceived as a natural, core
part of the learning process. The differences between these two dialogues
are subtle, but very important for the students' perception of religious
education as educational and not indoctrinatory[60]. The students can presume the academic dialogue as appropriate and required for the educational process; this is not necessarily the case for the personal dialogue,
which needs a voluntary component. The latter may flow from the former if the conditions are right – and this is educationally desirable; the
two may overlap and merge naturally. But to require or presume a personal dialogue at the very beginning of the process exerts a subtle psychological pressure which inclines students not to take the process seriously as it compromises their sense of freedom. I believe that this
problem has been one of the principal factors that have militated against
the success of efforts to make Catholic religious education personal and
relevant since the second Vatican Council[61].

It is not that personalism and relevance are unimportant; in fact they
are more much important now than they were perceived to be in the
1970s – because of the urgency of the contemporary search for meaning.
What is in question is the most appropriate formula for fostering relevance and personalism in the obligatory classroom context.

Certainly much can be done to choose content that links with the
search for meaning, values and identity. Engagement in academic dialogue can have an important role in informing young people's personal
search for meaning; this role is probably underestimated, because the
language of Catholic religious education has tended to give too much
attention to achieving personal dialogue. However, to emphasise what
was said above, adding the additional level of personal dialogue, where
participants reveal their own feelings and beliefs, should not be felt by
them as a requirement of the public hermeneutic process. Whether or
not such a level of personal interaction eventuates is not fundamental to
the success of the lesson – what is crucial is that students be well
informed and learn how to think critically about the issues. The important personal learnings will in most cases be private. If an authentic personal dialogue is to develop in the lesson, it must be free. Anecdotal evidence suggests that the approach proposed here, where academic

---

60. M.L. CRAWFORD & G.M. ROSSITER, *Missionaries to a Teenage Culture* (n. 52).
61. G.M. ROSSITER, *Historical Perspective on the Development of Catholic Religious
Education* (n. 40), p. 8.

dialogue and study maintain a sensitive respect for, and protection of personal dialogue, actually provides the most appropriate classroom environment for allowing such a personal dialogue to occur. It is ironic that an approach which takes care not to presume or force personal dialogue is the one most likely to promote it; the question of perceived freedom is so important for the students. The conditions for an academic study have built in respect for this freedom.

What I am proposing is that the approach to obligatory religious education is better situated within a context that emphasises critical study more than personal dialogue. In the classroom (but not necessarily in other contexts), the former is the best precursor to the latter, and it actually makes the dialogue more relevant and less likely to remain at a level of superficial opinions. Hermeneutics is central to this critical study process in which students are encouraged to become well informed, critical interpreters of culture. No matter how negative their view of what they refer to as 'organised religion', this approach to religious education can encourage them to consider that their religious tradition is a very old repository of wisdom, a study of which can give them basic access to its cultural resources for spirituality and identity building. They need to develop an awareness of the complex ways in which components of culture can become incorporated into views of life's meaning and into people's self understanding and self expression[62].

As with all good education, it is *hoped* that the study process in classroom religious education will flow into personal implications. However, to be authentic and enduring, this flow cannot be forced. Since the 1970s, one of the problems with Catholic religious education has been its excessive preoccupation with personal/spiritual outcomes; too much emphasis on making religious education personal and relevant, and on fostering faith development have in fact been counterproductive[63]; so much so that students have become alienated from religious education by a felt pressure to be personal.

The best formula, I believe, is in a student-centred study process, which suffers nothing in comparison with the academic and intellectual challenges students experience in other subject areas. Increasingly,

---

62. A recent book by R. PENASKOVIC, *Critical Thinking and the Academic Study of Religion*, Atlanta, Scholars Press, 1997, provides a useful analysis of some aspects of what teaching for a critical study of religion means – in terms of critical thinking and problem-solving, decision-making and metacognitive skills.

63. G.M. ROSSITER, *The Centrality of the Concept Faith Development* (n. 52); ID., *Historical Perspective on the Development of Catholic Religious Education* (n. 40).

school studies, especially in history, language and social science are hermeneneutical, and sensitive to values and justice issues[64]. Given the content of religious education, it should be leading the way in this regard.

Often the personal reflections of students and their interaction with the content / issues during religion lessons are not always expressed verbally; probably their important personal learnings are rarely articulated in dialogue with others in the public forum of the classroom. However, academic dialogue – where they can explore the meaning and implications of different views, where they can identify and appraise social issues, and test arguments, without having to identify the views to which they are really committed – can be a valuable process that develops them as critical thinkers and which in turn can catalyse personal change. Precisely because the academic process does not emphasise overt personal dialogue, it provides the most sensitive classroom environment for promoting personal change in students (also more appropriate for allowing personal interactions to take place).

Conclusion

This essay has touched on a number of spirituality and identity related issues for young people. These may be useful starting points for more systematic research on the ways they perceive a spiritual and moral dimension to life, and on the ways in which school religious education might make a more relevant contribution to their search for meaning, values and identity. Hopefully too, the discussion will enhance the background from which teachers can address these issues within religious education, modelling the role of wise spiritual interpreters guiding young people's efforts to become themselves critical interpreters of culture in their personal quest for meaning, and for values to which they can commit themselves.

In considering implications for religious education and theology, the main proposal is the need for a focus and language which show that they are in tune with the ways young people ask questions about meaning, purpose and identity. In other words a focus on *search for meaning* and *an exploration of reasons for living*.

---

64. G.M. ROSSITER, *The Characteristics of an Excellent Student Text in Religious Education*, in *Journal of Religious Education* 48 (2000) no. 2, 14-18, esp. p. 15.

The perceived relevance of Catholic theology and religious education in these times remains in a crisis as far as a significant number of youth and adults are concerned. They will quietly ignore the Catholic faith tradition unless it is saying something serious to them in response to contemporary personal, social, and political life. This even applies to practising members of local faith communities; increasingly, Catholics will be less inclined to remain practising members of a parish out of cultural inertia. If the way the Church's theology and spirituality are presented do not engage sufficiently in the real spiritual and moral issues that people experience, then they will get used to an expectation that their faith tradition remains marginally relevant to their lives.

Empirical Orientation of Research in Religious Education

Hans-Georg Ziebertz

In the following text I have used the concept of practical theology as a header for practical theological sub-disciplines, such as catechetics, religious education, homiletics, church development, poimenics and diaconics. I do not see the adjective "practical" as simply the opposite of "theoretical". Rather, "practical" refers to the material object of practical theology – the practice of religion. Unlike systematic theological disciplines, practical theology focuses on the real-life human acting ("Handeln")[1] within religious practice rather than logic. The sub-disciplines mentioned above reflect religious practice within different fields of human acting ("Handeln"). As a form of *theology*, practical theology is not just looking to describe religious practice, but also to understand it, explain it, and lay out possible alternatives for future decisions. The goal of orienting decisions is particularly relevant to normative theology. Some would see the formal objective of practical theology as analyzing the tension between what is, what could be, and what ought to be. This does not mean that theology analyses normative aspects in order to compare these with real-life practice. This would relegate the discipline back to being an applied science. Rather, the goal is to find the theories that define the practice. Practical theology must focus on the practice itself, methodically explaining *how* it focuses, and *how* it arrives at conclusions. This definitely requires an empirical emphasis, which may take on several forms; either by taking in empirical data or independently doing empirical research within the scope of practical theology. Nowadays, we know that an empirical orientation does not automatically mean a *positivistic* science; it can indeed have very *critical* characteristics.

This article has been written with an empirical orientation in mind, with empirical research within itself. The following issues will be discussed; firstly, the subject matter of the research, secondly, the

---

1. Due to the several unsatisfying possibilities for translating the German "Handeln", the term "human acting" will be used in this document to mean the process of decision-making and taking action within the real-life practice. The term will be highlighted to mean "Handeln" each time it is used.

methodological basis, thirdly, the methods used, and finally, the role played by empirical research within the field of practical theology.

1. The Material Object of Empirically Oriented Practical Theology

There are many aspects to religious practice, the material object of practical theology. Several options are available for gaining data about a particular practice that is to be supported or encouraged. One could analyse the efficiency of a religious curriculum, the religious[2] and moral attitudes of young people[3], the teacher-student interaction in religious classes, religious biographies, etc. In western Europe, one particular topic of research in the empirically oriented practical theology has gained in popularity recently. This topic is the changes within religion on the macro-, meso- and micro level. The church, and theology in general, is becoming ever more estranged in response to the presence of pluralistic religion in our society. At the same time, more and more people are becoming estranged towards religious content, as presented by church and theology, as well as towards the church's social structures[4].

The lines were fairly clear as long as the process could be explained by the secularization theory, which holds religious degeneration to be inherent to the modern age. Those phenomena which fell outside Christianity as represented by the church were abandoned. As far as the Christian church was concerned, having a monopoly on society's religious needs meant being able to accept the loss of a few believers without considering the need to make any radical self-changes. New modernization theories, however, challenge the notion of a negative correlation between modernity and religion. Their ever-changing relationship is considered, at the very least, *ambivalent*. On the one hand, there is the secularization effect which does impact religion as repre-

2. H.-G. ZIEBERTZ, *Religious Pluralism and Religious Education*, in *Journal of Empirical Theology* 6 (1993) no. 2, 82-98.

3. H.-G. ZIEBERTZ, *Heteronomy and Autonomy. Moral Pedagogical Goal Conflicts of Professionals in Ecclesiastical Youth Work*, in *Journal of Empirical Theology* 4 (1991) no. 1, 39-58; ID., *Sex, Love and Marriage: The View of RE Teachers in Germany*, in *British Journal of Religious Education* 14 (1992) 151-156.

4. H.-G. ZIEBERTZ, *Continuity and Discontinuity*, in *International Journal of Practical Theology* 2 (1998) 1-22. See also the website www.uni-wuerzburg.de/religionspaedagogik/forschung.

sented by the church. On the other hand, the modern age has proved to be a pool of religious creativity and vitality[5]. These two phenomena combined do not necessarily lead to the conclusion that religion is in a crisis, or that it is incompatible with the modern age. Rather, it appears to be particular forms of religion that are in trouble. In any case, the situation is more complex than the secularization theory makes it out to be[6].

According to new modernization theories, religion as such can no longer be exclusively identified with the Christian church. Theologians now admit, more or less openly, that the Christian church has lost its religious monopoly, that the very definition of religion must be stretched (outside of what the church represents), and, finally, that we are in a market force situation where the future of competing religious traditions and institutions is unknown. Moreover, religion is no longer controlled 'from the top down'; rather, the people themselves make the decision as to what and how much religion they want[7].

These phenomena are characteristic for a deep structural change. The roots are to be found within the very process of modernization. With the continuing differentiation processes in modern society our experience increasingly shows that church and culture, theology and religion, theory and practice are coming further and further apart:
- the societal structure is no longer identical to the world view held by the Christian church,
- contemporary religious styles deviate from the frames of Christian theology, and
- academic dogmatic theology and religious practice are neither identical nor deductive from one another.

These changes had already been noticed in the 18th century, and were considered to be a deep crisis[8]. One response was the establishment of

---

5. K. GABRIEL, *Christentum zwischen Tradition und Postmoderne*, Freiburg – Basel – Wien, Herder, 1994[3].

6. H.-G. ZIEBERTZ, *Religion, Christentum und Moderne. Veränderte Religionspräsenz als Herausforderung*, Stuttgart – Berlin – Köln, Kohlhammer, 1999.

7. V. DREHSEN, *Wie religionsfähig ist die Volkskirche? Sozialisationstheoretische Erkundungen neuzeitlicher Christentumspraxis*, Gütersloh, Kaiser – Gütersloher Verlagshaus, 1994, pp. 250-285; N. METTE, *Individualisierung und Enttraditionalisierung als (religions-) pädagogische Herausforderung*, in U. BECKER & C. Th. SCHEILKE (ed.), *Aneignung und Vermittlung. Beiträge zu Theorie und Praxis einer religionspädagogischen Hermeneutik*, Gütersloh, Gütersloher Verlagshaus, 1995, 69-84.

8. V. DREHSEN, *Neuzeitliche Konstitutionsbedingungen der Praktischen Theologie*, Gütersloh, Gütersloher Verlagshaus, 1988.

practical theology as a further department within the theological canon. This new scientific discipline was created to analyze the relationship between theory and practice, explaining why religious plans failed in practice. It would help priests and catechists, who only had knowledge of theological structures and felt unprepared, come to grips with the real world[9]. Historically, practical theology has oriented its studies of practice to applicable results; one has to understand the actual practice in order to have an influence on it. However, understanding religious practice in order to implement religious programs that, in essence, remain static cannot work in the long run. This perspective neglects those subjects who are not necessarily 'out of tune' religiously (M. Weber), but for whom certain religious traditions are simply strange. These traditions are, in fact, becoming increasingly strange today, because they were never introduced in a social or family environment. This also means that this group is not just made up out of 'previously lost', but also those who are 'religiously neutral and open'. Quite apart from the instrumental interest in influencing the situation, it has become absolutely necessary to understand the changes and the subjects acting within them. This essentially hermeneutical interest is combined with an empirical orientation. Empirical procedures are coupled with hermeneutical thinking, and can only be processed though the latter[10]. For Schweitzer, empirical methods are a continuation of hermeneutical methods[11], without concretely abandoning the original concept.

The theories construed are often not enough to understand the religious estrangement. In the field of religious education, for instance, the limits of correlating didactics are becoming clear. These assume that there is a fitting Christian interpretation for every event, like a key for every lock. Religious practice, however, is now leaving its church cradle to develop outside of institutional limits. Religious traditions, used to a historical monopoly on the truth, now sees itself confronted by conflict. People who derived their norms more or less naturally from tradi-

9. N. METTE, *Theorie der Praxis. Wissenschaftsgeschichtliche und methodologische Untersuchungen zur Theorie-Praxis-Problematik innerhalb der praktischen Theologie*, Düsseldorf, Patmos, 1978.

10. Cfr. H.-G. ZIEBERTZ, *Representations of Church Among Young Theologians*, in *Journal of Empirical Theology* 9 (1996) no. 2, 5-29; ID., *Types of Church Leadership in the Context of Catholic Ecclesiology*, in P. HANSSON (ed.), *Church Leadership*, Stockholm, 1998, 218-236; ID., *Religion, Christentum und Moderne* (n. 6).

11. F. SCHWEITZER, *Praktische Theologie und Hermeneutik. Paradigma – Wissenschaftstheorie – Methodologie*, in J.A. VAN DER VEN & H.-G. ZIEBERTZ (eds.), *Paradigmenentwicklung in der Praktischen Theologie*, Kampen – Weinheim, Kok – DSV, 19-47, p. 39.

tion and authority now do so based on their own subjective experiences. Religion and religiousness are now a claim for autonomy, preventing judgement by tradition and authority, subjecting it to the light of subjectivity. What people believe and how they express themselves religiously is unconnected to the Christian religious monopoly. Individual and institutional religion may be identical or simply cross over in some areas, they may co-exist peacefully or they may compete with each other – in the modern era, there are no rules. When people are forced to learn about and practice Christianity (e.g. religious courses in school), there are considerable normative problems and a great need for interactive discussion. Consequently, modern religious classes have conformed to stressing a 'didactics of communication'[12]. Discussion then ensues, even over 'truisms'. One example thereof is 'superstition'. For school children in the 8th grade (approximately 13 years old), it is up for discussion as to what 'true faith' and 'superstition' is. The authors of their school book, however, have no such problems. The only doubters are the children, who miss a certain sense of freedom when exploring different value systems. These are, however, truisms that theologians use everyday as a matter of course. If we do not encourage discussion from the very start, then we just add to the estrangement in progress.

One consequence we must deal with is the dominance of dogmatic thought in practical theological discourse. This, in turn, means that imparting the subject and context of religion becomes the principal task. But the subjects want to play a role in the very definition of religion. This situation is new to most theologians, who have never had to deal with such a myriad of faiths and conflicts. These are now so complex, that they cannot be categorized according to church or non-church, Christian or non-Christian, believer or atheist etc. The (changing) strangeness itself has become the structure. For the objective sub-disciplines of practical theology this means:

– Practical theology goes beyond churchly theological content and turns towards the socio-cultural presence of religion, which will eventually always be confronted through education. Seen objectively, 'religious practice' becomes very loosely defined, going far beyond what religious education presumes, be it in the school, church, or in another directed form of learning.

---

12. E. FEIFEL, *Didaktische Ansätze in der Religionspädagogik*, in H.-G. ZIEBERTZ & W. SIMON (eds.), *Bilanz der Religionspädagogik*, Düsseldorf, Patmos, 1995, 86-110.

- Practical theology picks up the task of analysing modern religious styles, trying to understand them on the personal and biographical level as well as on the cultural level. Another goal is to understand both their estrangement from classical religious institutions, and the search for existential functionality which lead to their adoption.
- For practical theologians, it is not just about a new religious landscape becoming estranged from tradition and which *estranges tradition itself*. 'Estrangement' has at least two sides to it. The responsibility carried by e.g. the very social structures propagated by (practical) theology must also be considered.
- Understanding the practice is not just interesting instrumentally for connecting the unchanged programs with the contemporary. It is also important for evaluating the cultural worth of the Gospel today. The practice has a theological dignity all its own.
- As a theological discipline, practical theology has its base within Christian tradition. However, it can always take in other points of view as long as neither the contemporary Christian church and religion, nor a particular socio-cultural context is taken as a 'truism'. This also means that a purely theological interpretation of the contemporary situation is insufficient, other points of view must be integrated and theologically developed.
- These other views must be classified empirically. Practical theology as a whole must have an 'empirical orientation'. It is clear from the above that a technical knowledge alone is insufficient, processes for understanding should be the key element.

2. Methodology: Hermeneutics, Empirical Orientation and Ideological Criticism

In his discussion of theoretical sciences, the German philosopher Jürgen Habermas pointed out the connection between "knowledge and interest"[13]. He showed that there is no naïve use of method since methods imply a particular view of reality, and because methods of knowledge, and interest of knowledge are in a dependent relationship to one another. Within the context of a critical scientific theory, he mentions three relational systems, used to scientifically define the connection between logical methodical rules and the interests that guide knowledge

---

13. J. HABERMAS, *Erkenntnis und Interesse*, Frankfurt am Main, Suhrkamp, 1968.

in the research practice. He differentiates between empirically analytical, hermeneutical, and critically oriented sciences, and arranges these types into their technical, practical and emancipating knowledge interest.

Empirically analytical research is interested in the scientific statements related to experience. The goal is to find rules for the construction and description of theories as well as for their final test. Empirically testable prognoses are gathered from deductive hypothetical connections, which should lead to basic conclusions. Habermas points out that these basic conclusions are not something objectively evident, but rather something drawn out of their preceding perspective (guiding interest) in order to assure and expand successful human acting ("Handeln"). This is different from the *hermeneutical* method, where formalized language and objective experience remain one and the same. The development of theories is neither done deductively, nor with a view to the operational success of systematic experience. Rather than systematically observe and describe facts, the hermeneutical method concentrates on form and meaning. What could be construed as 'pure theory', is in reality a developed relationship between the initial comprehension gained from the very start by an interpreter, and the hermeneutically produced knowledge, applied within the framework of the original comprehension. Habermas finally turns to an *ideologically critical* type of science. Using ideologically critical means, the goal is to turn unanalysed consciousness into a critical consciousness through self reflection, and thus free the subjects from their dependence on hypostatic forces. "Self reflection is defined by an emancipating knowledge interest"[14].

This analytical differentiation shows three different knowledge-guiding interests to be connected to the process of research. First of all, the production of experienced knowledge, secondly, adding to our understanding of the purpose and meaning, and thirdly, furthering an emancipation. Should these three issues be understood as 'pure types', and, if not, should they be ordered next to, above or below each other? This article takes the position, suggested by J.A. van der Ven[15], that, in a practically ordered discipline, the systematic examination of experienced knowledge is of the utmost importance. Without this, theories run the risk of becoming pure speculation. The concept of adequacy would become random, e.g. when developing learning goals or estimating the point of origin for learning processes. A modern science analyzing a

14. J. HABERMAS, *Erkenntnis und Interesse* (n. 13), p. 159.
15. J.A. VAN DER VEN, *Practical Theology: From Applied to Empirical Theology*, in *Journal of Empirical Theology* 1 (1988) no. 1, 7-27.

complex practice cannot afford to be that inexact. Empirical methods can serve to illuminate the *material* object of practical theology: the present religious practice.

Hermeneutics is also very important, and for three very good reasons. Firstly, religious education contain certain concepts which lay down the educational goals. Clarity is required to understand which general perspectives, concrete goals, specific interventions are meaningful. Secondly, hermeneutically understanding meaning and purpose is necessary within the scope of the experienced knowledge, for this is neither completely without theory, nor does experienced data contain its own program that explains what it is good for. According to Habermas, there is a "previous organisation within our experience". Its contours must be highlighted to make the inter-subjective reflection accessible. Thirdly, the hermeneutical thought is constantly in line with the dialectics of normativity and factivity, theory and practice. Understanding the meaning and purpose of the *formal* object means using theological hermeneutical thought to reflect on the tension within a practice; what it is and what it ought to be.

Finally, a critical perspective is necessary to set up a forum of ideal meta-communication with both hermeneutical thought and the highlighting of experienced knowledge. It should question new ideas and concepts, search out their implicit presumptions which would hinder the person's own independence and freedom. It should similarly question the methods used[16] and whether they further the goal of independence or not. These three perspectives are not exclusive, but rather, should be seen as complementary to each other. That is what the following theses show:

- Hermeneutics without ideological criticism runs the risk of producing ideology.
- Hermeneutics without empirical orientation runs the risk of losing sight of reality.
- Empirical orientation without hermeneutics runs the risk of being understood in a positivistic manner.
- Empirical orientation without ideological criticism could mean taking factual knowledge at face value and use it as a truism.
- Ideological criticism, as shown, is inextricably related to empirical orientation and hermeneutics.

16. H.-G. ZIEBERTZ, *Religionspädagogik als empirische Wissenschaft. Beiträge zur Theorie und Forschungspraxis*, Weinheim, Deutscher Studien Verlag, 1994.

Practical theology with an empirical orientation will therefore look for a complementary use of the three systems. According to Nipkow, empirical knowledge cannot allow religious educational theories to be based on the personal experience of the researcher. What he means is that personal experience should not be drawn out into generalizations, e.g. that all children in the local neighbourhood go to church every Sunday. Experienced knowledge must be gathered systematically using empirical methods. Empirical analysis makes correct and result-oriented human acting ("Handeln") possible, but it is still not enough. These methods are limited by the fact that the actual norm for taking action is indefinable. Empirical research must therefore be brought into line using a hermeneutical dimension. It should be mentioned that Nipkow argues for the use of a dialectic ideological criticism to gain a meta-theoretical corrective value, thereby keeping the actual social values and connections within reach[17]. This leads to the following conclusion: Empirical research is absolutely necessary for a factual study of religious education, but is not enough in itself. It must be supplemented by hermeneutical and ideologically critical methods in order to gain useful theological theories in regards to Christian socialization, contemporary Christian educational and political history.

3. Quantitative and Qualitative Orientation in a Constructivist Perspective

The 'understand-or-explain controversy' (inspired by Dilthey's quote "we *explain* nature, we *understand* the life of our souls") loses a lot of its significance when one considers the close link between hermeneutical and empirical methods. To 'explain' something was seen as a principle of empirically oriented (natural science) research, related to issues of exactitude and objectivity. The humanities, on the other hand, were reconstructive and interpretative sciences, based on 'understanding'. Dilthey criticized the way methods from natural science were incorporated into the humanities. His reasoning was that it was insufficient (or just plain wrong) to look for firm laws and cause-and-effect scenarios in human acting ("Handeln"). The humanities were more about the purpose and goals achieved through decisions[18]. To come up with those sorts of

---

17. K.E. Nɪᴘᴋᴏᴡ, *Religionspädagogik*, vol. 1, Gütersloh, Gütersloher Verlagshaus, 1984, p. 185.
18. R. Uʜʟᴇ, *Qualitative Sozialforschung und Hermeneutik*, in E. Köɴɪɢ & P. Zᴇᴅʟᴇʀ (eds.), *Bilanz qualitativer Forschung*, vol. 1, Weinheim, Deutscher Studien Verlag, 1995, 33-73.

results, hermeneutical work was needed. With the subsequent adoption of empirical methods (empirical quantitative procedures, to be exact) in the humanities, the argument arose as to whether this natural science (i.e. foreign) way of thinking and working wouldn't overshadow or simply forget to take into account issues of purpose and goals within human acting ("Handeln").

With the increasing use of qualitative methods over the last two decades, the understand-or-explain conflict is no longer one of 'empirical orientation vs. hermeneutics', but rather a discussion *within* the empirical field on the use of qualitative and quantitative procedures. One important argument brought up is that if understanding is defined as "laying something out in terms of something else", then the process of explaining and understanding is nothing more than particular explanations of the world[19]. What the world is, and what it is made up of, would then be a question of how it is laid out. Whether one uses quantitative or qualitative methods is then of secondary importance, because, whatever it is, the method is just an instrument of precision used to sharpen the image the same way a telescope does. Whether that image actually means anything is by no means guaranteed through the use of the telescope. What is the relationship between object and analysis?

There are several views on how empirically oriented practical theology arrives at its object. Three main positions spring to mind, each with a different take on methodology:

- The first one assumes, quite simply, that empirical orientation is the tool for establishing reality. In other words, that empirical methods guarantee a perfect reproduction of the object, the way it really is.
- The second position deals with the method for establishing an object. Certain methods are suitable or correct, others are unsuitable or wrong. This position has sparked a controversy dealing with the use of quantitative and qualitative procedures, first in the empirical social sciences, and then, to a greater extent, in practical theology.
- The third position is based on conclusion theory, and highlights the constructive character of all theories – including empirically oriented ones. On the one hand, it rejects the possibility of directly relating to an object. On the other hand, the choice of method is seen as secondary, since 'construction' precedes and accompanies methodology. The focus is on the changing relationship between empirical practice and scientific practice.

19. R. UHLE, *Qualitative Sozialforschung und Hermeneutik* (n. 18).

The first position, where empirical procedures focus immediately on the practice, is characteristic, not just for a high degree of consciousness for the every-day, but also for empirical studies. It is also common (although often hidden) in those cases where one method is seen as superior to another. One example is the discussion in regards to induction and deduction. In this case, induction is seen as letting the data speak for itself, whereas deduction is felt to push the practice into a system into which it doesn't fit. Accordingly, the practice is more closely defined by induction than by deduction. The third position adds to this argument, since it realizes that both procedures have 'self-referral' elements to them. This would mean that the original question in regards to the practice must be supplemented by what preceded it, and how the use of this method influenced the question.

This assumption is based on the fact that all empirical references are drawn from observations. Observation hones two particular skills; firstly, the ability to see differences, secondly, the capacity to make sense of those differences[20]. The existence of differences in the real world is not enough for an observation, one also has to be able to recognize them. In other words, conclusions are not drawn from the data itself, nor from the method with which the data was processed. What is important are the *references* that *were* relevant *before* and *during* the observation, and that *are* relevant during later analysis. To recognize something in and through an observation is a very human ability. Because of this, it is also dependent on the human historicity and contingency. Observation and self-reference cannot be separated from each other. Self-reference is both a *presumption* and a *consequence* of observation. It is a presumption, because there has to be something identical to use as a key, and it is a consequence, because observation constantly produces processes of self-reference. This means that the learning subject is itself a large part of the learning process. Every conclusion is tied to the own methods of observing and understanding. There is no method that fully guarantees reporting the object the way it 'really' is. The method defines the possibilities for observing, and establishes 'how' something is to be observed. Whatever the choice made, it is contingent. The thing being studied can never be seized in its ontological being[21].

It would, however, be exaggerating if all methodical observations were suddenly to be labelled 'subjective constructivism', with the actual

---

20. H. WILLKE, *Systemtheorie II: Interventionstheorie*, Stuttgart, Fischer, 1994.
21. *Ibid.*

object fading into the background. Obviously all processes of discovery based on methodical observation attempt to find a fitting explanation for the phenomenon at hand. At the same time, no explanation can claim to be the *real* explanation. The search for truth is open for a long time into the future. In this context, objectivity is not an adjective for a particular researcher or research procedure, but is, rather, the overreaching goal of the research[22].

This does not change the fact that every observation reveals at least as much about the logic of the researcher as it does about the object at hand[23]. This is the same for all processes of discovery, whether they use qualitative or quantitative methods. For this reason, the constructivist position questions if and how 'scientific practice' should become the second priority after the 'practice' itself.

In view of this latter question, a research tradition like Popper's concept of critical rationalism finds itself facing some very serious issues. This paradigm has made some very noticcable marks within empirical methodology, particularly the so-called quantitative research uses many of Popper's ideas. Within the three-prong approach to a research project, i.e. the context of discovery, the context of justification, and the context of application, critical rationalism focuses intensely on the context of justification. This is where scientific reflection and scientific practice come into play. Theories are then tested against standards of validity and dependability. The context of discovery, where the concrete research problem and question come up, is relegated to the pre-scientific field. The is where the ingeniousness of the researcher, and his or her creative spirit and inspiration play their greatest roles. The presumption is that these sorts of variables take away from the scientific core value. The same goes for the eventual use of the results, the context of application, which, in reality, has nothing to do with the actual scientific proofing that preceded it. This is the way, then, to turn off the greatest amount of subjectivity on the part of the researcher. This concentration on the context of justification brought about a picture of an 'exact' research, worthy of (or at least similar to) the precise ideals of the natural sciences. The fact that certain limitations were essential was shown, not just within the context of justification, but also in the relationship between the contexts of justification and discovery.

---

22. W. MEINEFELD, *Realität und Konstruktion*, Opladen, Leske und Budrich, 1995, p. 271.

23. H. WILLKE, *Systemtheorie. Eine Einführung in die Grundprobleme einer Theorie sozialer Systeme*, Stuttgart, Fischer, 1993, pp. 178-213.

In regards to the context of justification, there is another point to consider. When analysing the steps that make up the empirical analytical procedure we see several areas where a decision or interpretation on the part of the researcher becomes necessary. One example thereof is factor analysis. Factor analysis serves to filter out hidden dimensions (a plan, a structure) within a large number of items, thereby reducing the amount of data. This analysis is not just about randomly pushing a key on the computer. Mathematical statistics have produced and keep producing more and better methods for this form of analysis, and only a study of the factor clusters, commonality and variance can tell us which is the right method. One could opt for a high level of factor discrimination, but that could lead to a weaker variance among other things; one could go with a higher variance, but would then have to accept clustering a single item on two or more factors. The decision as to which result ought to be used for future analysis is not possible without an estimate on the part of the researcher. The result must be meaningful and relevant as well as interpretable. This also means that both theoretical knowledge gained by deduction and experience gained by induction are essential in order to make a well-founded decision.

If you relate the context of justification to the context of discovery, the subject and individual that is the researcher becomes a constitutional element of the observation process and its results become an even looser variable[24]. This influence is not taken into account within the context of justification, nor is it even empirically controllable. It would be doing too little to classify this problem as "theory steering" in empirical quantitative research. Already at the stage of limiting the research field and problem, there is a relevant, albeit not conscious, influence by the researcher. There are the contours of expectation which structure the perception of the problem, producing a certain perspective (the interconnected selectivity) which, in turn, influences the research[25]. This influence escapes methodological control.

When considering the choice of methods, one realizes that quantitative and qualitative research procedures do not have an impact on the two perspectives above. In both cases, there are several areas in the critical methodology that depend on decisions, value judgements and interpretations. These may be methodologically controllable to a certain extent. However,

24. W. MEINEFELD, *Realität und Konstruktion* (n. 22), pp. 264-270.
25. H.-G. SOEFFNER & R. HITZLER, *Hermeneutik als Haltung und Handlung. Über methodisch kontrolliertes Verstehen*, in N. SCHRÖER (ed.), *Interpretative Sozialforschung*, Opladen, Westdeutscher Verlag, 1994, 28-54.

they do rely on previous experience gained by inductive and deductive reasoning which cannot be 'neutralized' by any one method. In the case of qualitative procedures, this scenario arises when people are called to an interview, and one has to explain what is expected of them, what the purpose of the study is, and what knowledge or results are expected to be gained. The actions of the researcher ought to be kept out of the analytical process (context of justification) since it isn't methodologically controllable there, and because it definitely influences the research and its results. If one then ignores the three-prong approach to the research process, and starts to look at the problem from a time-line perspective, it becomes clear that this plays an important role, too. The influence exhibited by this context show that proofing and justification, the very core of the analytical process, has itself been dependent on the development of methodological knowledge throughout the course of history[26].

On that note, the constructive portion of empirical procedures clearly steps into the spotlight. Between radical constructivism, which holds objectivity to be impossible, and the theory of objectivism, which holds the object to be immediately definable, there is the mixture of the knowledge focus and the knowledge system, of object (practice in the field) and scientific practice. None of these must be allowed to become an absolute value. The question of quantitative or qualitative procedures becomes secondary. The method, from this point of view, is merely one means chosen out of several because it promises to produce a maximum of information and knowledge. It also answers the question as to what the (quantitative or qualitative) research is meant to achieve. In other words, methodological precision must not be allowed to overshadow what the result is based on and what it represents. Knowledge through practical (human acting) sciences ("Handlungstheorien") is not gained without purpose (nor for its own inherent value). It is gained in order to orient what is going on in the world. On this platform, methods lose their aura of exclusivity, which grants them a special place. This aura is based on the assumption that certain methods allow true knowledge and a direct link to the object whereas others do not. Rather, they ought to be seen as complementary, even though this complementing ("Triangulation") will not undo the limitations that come with certain particular methods[27].

26. W. MEINEFELD, *Realität und Konstruktion* (n. 22), pp. 287-293.

27. M. FROMM, *Zur Verbindung quantitativer und qualitativer Methoden*, in *Pädagogische Rundschau* 44 (1990) 469-481; D.T. CAMPBELL & D.W. FISKE, *Convergent and Discriminant Validation by Multitrait-Multimethod Matrix*, in *Psychological Bulletin* 56 (1959) 81-105.

4. General Functions of Empirical Research in Practical Theology

The goal of empirical research in practical theology is to measure effect and control success. It means to orient practical human acting and take on a critical function in theology, setting it apart from deductive normative theology[28]. These general functions will here be dealt with briefly.

Firstly, empirical research within practical theology will continue to play an important role in *controlling human acting in religious education*, i.e. research used for a practical purpose. One example is religious didactic material used for education. For all grade levels and forms of curriculum there are particular learning goals, content, and mediums available. From a certain point of view, these educational materials do what they promise; didactically and effectively guide learning processes. They implicitly answer the question what the best content for such and such a goal is, where to begin learning, what knowledge is assumed on the part of the student, where the problems lie, how the content should be structured, what the learning phases are, what means should be used and how a learning process can be evaluated. One also has to consider what inter-personal learning processes are taking place between the students, what 'constitution' makes up the point of origin, and how educational content relates to the students' self-image. Using this example, then, it could be asserted that such educational models are never tested for their actual effect – particularly not tested in such a way that not just a personal experience forms the base of the results. The result is often a mish-mash of the hopes and assumptions of teachers and students within their respective learning circumstances. It is clear that, among other things, the concept of education (faith, problem or experience oriented), the educational style (frontal, multi-media etc.), the religious attitudes and social background of the students, the quality of the material (additive use of different content, study plan based on increasing difficulty, systematics, etc.) make up a complex network, the 'effect' of which is almost impossible to estimate. Other examples are central theoretical concepts such as "learning through models", "learning through ideals", or "the religion teacher as a witness of the faith", all of which need to be re-examined. What are they capable of, what are the conditions they need to meet the expectations (assuming they do at all) of religious educators? With such central concepts, educators need experience data in order to know if they achieve what they promise.

---

28. J.A. VAN DER VEN, *Practical Theology* (n. 15).

A *second* function of empirical research in practical theology is the production of knowledge needed to *orient human acting*. To put it in the words of Max Weber, the goal is to develop empirically based scenarios that give people in those scenarios the knowledge they need to responsibly make decisions. According to Weber, researchers should use their data to make grounded value judgements possible[29]. Understanding reality in a social setting does not happen in a neutral way, nor without interest. Gadamer reached the conclusion that the lay-out of a scenario (*subtilitas explicandi*) is a part of understanding (*subtilitas intelligendi*), and that both are connected to a sense of application (*subtilitas applicandi*)[30]. What he is clarifying is that the lay-out of observations, images, texts etc. are more than the sum of their implicit meaning. Processes of understanding (and explaining) also target a certain judgement, as will be discussed later. Especially for the human acting sciences ("Handlungstheorien"), it is true that they are difficult disconnect from the context of their inherent task. Gadamer has defined this context of the task even more precisely. Processes of knowledge (understanding and explaining) serve to rebuild the interrupted accord. As Habermas points out, this is the understanding of what is strange and what has become estranged. The above introduction pointed out what has become strange for practical theology. In this sense, understanding does not mean the Wittgenstein-type sense of understanding as 'knowing a rule' and 'participation in a common sense'. Understanding means uncovering every cultural truism in a research process which was close at hand, yet hidden. Understanding is the final point of an investigation. Another definition for understanding is finding a meaning which can only be established through interpretational processes. In other words, an investigation that means to understand does not mirror the 'true reality', but simply adds a scheme for interpreting it. It is, then, the insimultaneousness, the non-identity etc. which challenges understanding[31].

In-depth interviews with youth have shown that a lot of them see themselves as removed from the church. At the same time, many of them go to church and claim to be touched by the atmosphere in there, pray, light candles etc. These young people, who must be classified as on

29. H.-G. ZIEBERTZ, *Objektivität und Handlungsnormativität. Ein Dilemma der empirisch orientierten Praktischen Theologie?*, in *Theologisch-Praktische Quartalschrift* 144 (1996) 412-428.

30. See more in detail R. UHLE, *Qualitative Sozialforschung und Hermeneutik* (n. 18), p. 39.

31. *Ibid.*, pp. 40-42.

the 'church fringe', use religious symbols, take part in religious rituals, and incorporate Christian images into their world view. Even among those who classify themselves as "non-religious", the majority want to baptize their future children, get married with a church ceremony, and, of course, be buried by a priest. For religious educational purposes (in particular the church catechism), deeper knowledge of the religious views of these young people is essential. It is quite possible that a treasure trove of 'theologization of the real world' is waiting to be discovered[32].

Obviously the purpose of such investigations is not the detailed restatement of fact, but overcoming an ever-changing estrangement. Understanding social situations is all about forming a will or judgement – it is not 'neutral'. Because of this, the method for gaining knowledge must not be more important than the knowledge itself. A reference to the future application makes it clear that such measures for understanding and explaining have a practical function. Texts, statements, actions etc. must be understood and explained, because they serve to create judgements, because they make those scenarios possible that are based on "if" and "then", because they give the basic information necessary for overcoming difficult life situations and orient human acting. Practical theology is, after all, partly about religious education, preaching and announcing, establishing the deaconry and the community.

Thirdly, empirical research in practical theology has a *critical function within theology itself*. Practical theological fields may be seen as 'application areas for theological normativity'. This is not just true for systematic theology, but also for the practice itself, which has certain expectations. At the same time, it is certainly clear the practical theological fields must not simply be reduced to deducing theologically developed normativity. In other words, the object field of 'religious practice' is not just a field to be sowed, the field has expectations of the seed. Not everything will grow on this soil, and certain mixtures won't grow at all. The object field 'practice' is more than just an 'application field', the practice makes demands on the theological reflection.

In the roman catholic church, there is an increasing tendency to deduce theology 'from top to bottom'. The era of new scholastics have clearly shown how dangerous it is when theologians lose their grass-root attachment, creating schemes and concepts that must fit into the actual

32. H.-G. ZIEBERTZ, *God in Modern Individualized Religiousness?*, in H.-G. ZIEBERTZ, F. SCHWEITZER, H. HÄRING, D. BROWNING (eds.), *The Human Image of God*, Leiden – Boston – Köln, Brill, 2001, 329-346.

practice. Today we ask the question what theologians are to do with an ever more abstract picture of God. Is this an effect of secularization, or is it a rejection of a personal model which had always been misunderstood as an "anthropomorphic" picture of God? Have there really not been any other theologically justified abstract pictures of God in the 2000 years of Christian history? Should we not see such finds as a call to renewal for modern theology rather than as a danger?

Practical theology makes such new issues comprehensible, and introduces them to the theological discourse. As traditional as it may be to want to shape the practice, the practice now makes demands on the theology that wants to form it. The practice now has a critical function, confronting the theological normative thoughts and its assumptions with new data. On a theoretical level, this is how ideologies are formed.

Beyond this issue, 'sensus fidei/fidelium'[33] is a concept with a lot of theological dignity. It is of great theological importance how the people whose practice is being studied shape their faiths. For this reason, practical theology can not stay outside the discourse that forcibly arises when tradition and situation conflict in the educational process. Theology as a whole would lose out on critical knowledge if practical theology abandons the task of critically judging the terminological and conceptual traditions of religious socialization. It is not enough to study the practice on a speculative level. Practical theology must make use of the procedures of other sciences which focus on human practice ("Handlungstheorien"). It thereby fills a regulating function necessary for all of theology[34]. Particularly in the case of religious socialization, with all its new and compelling problems, the call for a normative basis for the practical theological fields is getting louder. This tendency should be viewed with a critical eye. This is not just a question of principle, based on a practical theology that has developed its own identity. Rather, it is about a problem of socialization where practical theology, used to extending dogmatism in a 'downward direction', is losing its grip. An empirically oriented practical theology adds to all theological fields when it uses its studies on the practice to develop normative concepts for the conflict between tradition and experience.

---

33. S. WIEDERKEHR, *Sensus vor Consensus: auf dem Weg zu einem partizipativen Glauben – Reflexionen einer Wahrheitspolitik*, in ID. (ed.), *Der Glaubenssinn des Gottesvolkes – Konkurrent oder Partner des Lehramts?*, Freiburg, Herder, 1994, 182-206.
34. J.A. VAN DER VEN, *Practical Theology* (n. 15).

Working empirically within practical theology means having both a theological education and knowledge of empirical methods. Empirical thought as a paradigm must be established even further in education and research. The problems faced by religious educators in the schools and church communities cannot be resolved without empirical research forming theories and stimulating practice. The basic methodology of practical theology, however, must face up to new questions. The methodological debate cannot be given over to the humanities, leaving practical theology to eclectically choose particular procedures. Methodology is the scientific grain of a discipline, and questions of methods and methodology must be decided by those who use it. This means, among other things, incorporating methodology into the canon of theological education. In the systematic fields, particularly the historical and exegetic ones, this has been the common practice for quite some time. Students participate in seminars teaching 'historically critical', 'linguistic', 'psycho-analytical' and 'materialistic' methods, giving them the skills they need to critically analyse texts. Are the practical theologians of tomorrow learning the hermeneutical, ideologically critical and (in regards to the practice) empirical skills they will need?

Catechesis and (or) Religious Education
Another Look

Michael Warren

One might think the distinctions and correlations between catechesis and religious education have been clarified in writing done in the late 20th century. Having done some of this writing myself[1], I ordinarily would be reluctant to revisit this topic, except that the recent essays of Herman Lombaerts shed important light on the question, still a puzzle in some countries[2]. Gifted with an ability to write well in several languages, Lombaerts exhibits a broad social and cultural perspective that gives his work an enduring quality. He explores the conditions under which institutions arise and flourish or falter. I begin my examination of catechesis and/or religious education with events that were going on fewer than 500 miles from my home, but of which I was unaware until Lombaerts brought them to my attention: the seemingly sudden collapse of Roman Catholic religious affiliation in Québec Province, Canada[3].

1. Cfr. M. WARREN, *Catechesis: An Enriching Category for Religious Education*, in *Religious Education* 76 (1981) 115-127; *Youth Ministry in Transition*, in ID., *Youth and the Future of the Church*, New York, Seabury, 1982, 8-16; *The Future of Youth Ministry in Canada*, in *The Canadian Catholic Review* 3 (1985) 249-255; *Ministry, Catechesis and Religious Education*, in *Catholic School Studies (Australia)* 59 (1986) no. 2, 45-48; *A Dilemma for Youth Catechesis: Finding the Right Context*, in *Doctrine and Life* 38 (1988) 458-465; *Don't Expect the School to Be the Church*, in *Catholic New Times (Toronto)*, 17 April 1994, p. 8; *Schools, Education, and Catechesis*, in ID., *Faith, Culture and The Worshiping Community*, Portland OR, Pastoral Press, 1997, 1-17; *The Catechumen in the Kitchen*, in *ibid.*, 89-105.

2. See especially H. LOMBAERTS, *Van generatie tot generatie*, in L. LEIJSSEN, H. LOMBAERTS, B. ROEBBEN (eds.), *Geloven als toekomst. Godsdienstpedagogische visies en bijdragen aangeboden aan Professor Jozef Bulckens bij zijn emeritaat*, Leuven – Amersfoort, Acco, 1995, 213-230; *Godsdienstonderricht als communicatieve gebeurtenis*, in H. LOMBAERTS & B. ROEBBEN (eds.), *Godsdienst op school in de branding. Een tussentijdse balans* (Cahiers voor Didactiek, 7), Deurne, Wolters/Plantyn, 2000, pp. 81-107; *Religion, Society, and the Teaching of Religion in Schools*, in M. WARREN (ed.), *The Sourcebook for Modern Catechetics*. Vol. II, Winona, St. Mary's Press, 1997, 306-329; *Catechetics and the Formation of Catechists*, in *ibid.*, 178-191; together with B. ROEBBEN & G. GINNEBERGE, *Godinet: een flexibel werkinstrument voor een vak in beweging*, in *Verbum* 66 (1999) no. 1, 11-20. Finally, see his essays in H. LOMBAERTS *et al.*, *The Management and Leadership of Christian Schools*, Groot Bijgaarden, Vlaams Lasalliaans Perspectief, 1998. This book is the most comprehensive analytical work on various issues affecting Christian [church] schools I have seen.

3. But from hindsight, not so suddenly and not without signs that a shift was coming, as one finds in the following account: G. BAUM, *The Dumont Report*, in J. PROVOST

In a seven year period, between 1960 and 1967, this predominantly Roman Catholic province with a high rate of sacramental practice saw an "abrupt severance of ties with the church and of religious initiation among a high percentage of the young generation and adults"[4]. The "severance" led to a shift in religious affiliation so dramatic that its significance and scope is still being researched and assessed[5]. Many were astonished at the sudden cessation of centuries-old patterns of life. A similar shift is underway in the Republic of Ireland, where 91% attended weekly Mass in the early 1970s, whereas today that percentage has fallen below 50%[6]. Either case, Québec or Ireland, raises questions about the effective means of communicating faith to the young generation. The purpose of this essay is not so much to probe what happened in Québec to religious practice or what is happening to it now in Ireland as to deal with the larger issue of effective means of fostering Christian faith. Communicating faith is difficult in a time when vivid and compelling narratives are electronically communicated in an endless stream designed to be entertaining. An ethos of entertainment is unable to tolerate the kinds of troubling questions about the purposes of life posed by Jesus of Nazareth.

How was the sudden collapse in Québec of religious orientation and religious practice possible? If a seemingly solid and historically important building collapsed suddenly, investigation would quickly show its causes, say, termites silently eating away the wooden frame from within or a hidden structural flaw's strains finally causing disaster. Cultural causes of a collapse of religious meaning and religious practice are less

& K. WALF (eds.), *The Tabu of Democracy within the Church*, London, SCM, 1992, 106-113.

4. Cfr. H. LOMBAERTS, *Van generatie tot generatie* (n. 2).

5. For some examples, see H. LOMBAERTS, *Godsdienstonderricht in Franstalig Canada*, in *Korrel* 7 (1985) 304-312. In *Van generatie tot generatie*, Lombaerts lists the following studies: J. GRAND'MAISON (ed.), *Le drame spirituel des adolescents. Profils sociaux et religieux* (Cahiers d'études pastorales, 10), Montréal, Fides, 1992; ID., *Vers un nouveau conflict de générations. Profils sociaux et religieux des 20-35 ans* (Cahiers d'études pastorales, 11), Montréal, Fides, 1992; ID. & S. LEFEBVRE (eds.), *Une génération bouc émissaire. Enquête sur les baby-boomers* (Cahiers d'études pastorales, 12), Montréal, Fides, 1993; ID. (eds.), *La part des aînés* (Cahiers d'études pastorales, 13), Montréal, Fides, 1994; J.M. CHARRON & J.-M. GAUTHIER (eds.), *Entre l'arbre et l'écorce. Un monde pastoral en tension* (Cahiers d'études pastorales, 14), Montréal, Fides, 1993; J. GRAND'MAISON, L. BARONI, J.-M. GAUTHIER (eds.), *Le défi des generations. Enjeux sociaux et religieux du Québec d'aujourd'hui* (Cahiers d'études pastorales, 15), Montréal, Fides, 1995.

6. M. KENNEDY, *Tracks into a New Civilization. A View from the Irish Roman Catholic Church*, in M. WARREN (ed.), *Changing Churches. The Local Church and the Structures of Change*, Portland OR, Pastoral Press, 2000.

easily charted[7]. My assumption in this essay is that erosions of religious affiliation are also failures of pastoral ministry, particularly of the "ministry of the word". They are catechetical failures, not schooling failures. I assume that further study of the Québec phenomenon will show catechesis had become non-existent or improperly located in schools or perfunctory and routine. In many places today, schools are expected to bear a burden of communicating the Word of God in a full and final way that schools of their very nature are unsuited for and unable to bear.

This essay proceeds in two steps. In the first step I wish to make two proposals helpful for thinking about the connections between catechesis and religious education, while maintaining the distinctiveness of each[8]. One proposal is about the proper use of categories and the avoidance of categorical errors. The second proposal is about the proper use of procedures and avoiding procedural errors. I will give examples of each kind of error. In the second step, I will examine the origins of education and the origins of catechesis to see how the distinctive character of each is disclosed in those origins.

1. Finding the Proper Categories and Procedures

Religious Education and Catechesis are often used interchangeably, as synonyms, but they should not be. Both terms describe "learning activities around religion" but their goals are so distinct that they are not two species of a common genre of education, but two species of separate genres. Catechesis is a species of the genre, pastoral ministry; but religious education a species of the genre, education. Their origins are different; their goals are different; their outcomes are different; the identities of their participants are different.

Sometimes people use a religious education language when they actually wish to speak about the activities and processes of catechesis. This is a categorical error. But sometimes people use a catechetical language when they mean to speak about religious education. This is also a categorical error. Categorical errors are conceptual errors with practical

---

7. For an attempt to explain what happened in Québec, see G. BAUM, *The Dumont Report* (n. 3), pp. 109-112 and M. KENNEDY, *Tracks into a New Civilization* (n. 6), pp. 92-101.

8. In dealing with these terms, I deliberately use the term "catechesis" for what some Protestants prefer to call Christian education. I do so because I find so much insight in the catechetical tradition but also because more and more Protestants are adopting catechetical language for its obvious connections with pastoral ministry and worship.

consequences, that is, leading to erroneous practices. Categorical errors are analogous to absentmindedly starting to button your coat with the wrong button. The error cannot be corrected without an attentive undoing the wrongly placed buttons and attentively putting them right. In my view the distinctiveness of the two categories is valuable for appreciating their distinctive values.

The second kind of error I wish to get at here is a procedural error. Procedural errors result in conceptual confusions. There are two forms of this error related to catechesis and religious education. Using religious education means to achieve catechetical ends is the first procedural error whose consequences are not easily corrected. Using catechetical means to achieve religious education ends is the second procedural error not easily corrected, though it is not so common as the first procedural error. Catechesis is aimed basically at the transformation of sensibility and practice, while religious education is basically aimed at clarification and enlargement of understanding. I will use two examples of these errors, one a procedural and categorical error currently being corrected in the Republic of Ireland, the second a categorical error in the mistranslating of a French text that had (and has) implications for procedures.

Example 1 – Ireland's New RE Curriculum

At the time of my writing, national education policy makers in Ireland are attempting to sort out the correct categories for the teaching of religion in secondary schools. From my position in North America, at least, it appears the attempt is encountering difficulties[9]. The nation has adopted a religious education curriculum aimed at teaching persons of any or no faith stance about the societal phenomenon called religion[10]. Ireland wants those in its secondary schools to understand religion in its varied historical complexity, its contributions to the world, its destructive tendencies as well as its positive transformative power. The nation also recognizes that religion's phenomena are mainly particular, and that

---

9. In Ireland the term "religious education" has been used to mean catechesis for years, at the same time its users deny they are proselytizing. Change in language is slow, even in the face of new curriculum seeking "education in religion". See F. HURL, *Religious Education: Catechetics or Academics?* and A. HOLTON, *Religious Education. An Examination Subject*, in *The Furrow* 51 (2000) resp. 279-286 and 287-295.

10. The new Irish program is crafted to speak to various levels. Its program for children allows children to rejoice in celebrations of the world, of their own feelings of joy and freedom, as a route to grasping "the religious".

learners need to examine the history, tenets and practices of particular faiths: Judaism, Islam, Christianity, etc. The new curriculum does not *propose* any particular religion; it rather *exposes* the features of religion in general and of particular religions.

Just as you don't have to be a poet, playwright, or novelist to appreciate literature, neither do you have to be a religious adherent or practitioner to appreciate religion's place in the human quest. However, it may not be possible to be an educated person in the modern world without grasping the character and power of literature and religion. The appreciation of both literature and religion can give perspective on the world we live in. And so the new Irish curriculum does not propose religious belief; it exposes it to examination. In holding these views, the curriculum developers would not deny that attempts to create original literary works or to live out a religious commitment can give one a heightened appreciation of literature or religion in one's own life. These distinctions and clarifications are essential for grasping the logic behind the new Irish curriculum.

The Republic of Ireland is a nation where what is called "RE" in schools has till now actually been the teaching of Roman Catholic doctrines meant to foster Roman Catholic religious affiliation. From the earliest grades, children have had mandatory classes in RE that taught and proposed Roman Catholic "faith", sometimes called "the faith". As a result little of what is called catechesis has been located in the local churches. This system has had some narrow results in the way religion itself is understood, something the new curriculum is trying to change. Catholic adults have been known to stand in public and speak about Christians of other denominations as if they were adherents of other religions. The success of these classes, the competence of those teaching them, and the quality of the study materials being used has long been questioned, partly due to the complaints of students about the lack of focus or vagueness of what is being taught. What has been called RE is not religious education at all but a dangerously denatured form of catechesis. What we have here is a double error: a categorical error misnaming what is intended to be catechesis as RE, compounded by the procedural error of trying to do catechesis in a school context suited for religious education.

So when RE is the preferred term to describe an activity that is seeking to achieve ends achievable, not by RE but by catechesis, or when the idea in the heads of most people speaking of RE is more properly catechesis (though badly distorted), how is the scramble of categories ever to be sorted out? The Republic of Ireland in its new curriculum has, it would seem, moved in the proper direction of letting education in religion be *education in religion*, understood as broader than Roman Catholicism or even Christianity. As a result of this shift, the Christian churches in Ireland must begin to relocate catechesis in the local churches as a distinctively ecclesial pastoral activity. At the parish level, catechesis hardly exists in Ireland, a fact that explains the burden put on the school and on the family as the carriers of faith but not on the local church, which according to recent Catholic thinking is the key carrier.

Example 2 – The Mis-Translations of Options and Methods

In the 1960s, Pierre Babin, the great French catechetical leader who sought to do catechetical work in different languages and cultures, wrote two little books about adolescent catechesis, called *Options and Methods*. In these books he deliberately moved away from schooling language toward a more neutral, and I would say a more catechetical language, of people influencing one another by their questions and counter questions about the meaning of their Christian faith; by probing their human situation with one another; by seeking norms for interpreting reality and making decisions about faith; by engaging one another on level ground as fellow human persons equal in dignity before God. Babin's books were not about classes but groups, not about teachers and students but about facilitators/animators and group members/participants, not about curriculum but about follow-up sessions, and so forth. (Most often he named the young participants as "les jeunes" or young people.) He never once used the French word for student.

At the time, Babin's careful use of non-schooling language was an imaginative way of getting at the distinctive language needed for distinctive activities involving ministry with youth. He sought new categories for describing a new way of interacting with young people on matters of faith. To describe the process by which young people willingly engaged faith questions on their own time and in the spaces they themselves opted for, Babin employed a school-neutral language. He wanted to avoid the then all-pervasive language of education and its focus on planned curriculum. What he seemed to be doing was laying the groundwork for a ministry with youth done outside the structures of schooling. At the time he wrote, Catholic schools in France and in the U.S. were the main location for pastoral interventions with Roman Catholic youth.

When, however, *Options and Methods* were translated into English in the late 1960s for use in North America, the translators recast Babin's neutral categories back into fixed educational categories. Groups became classes; leaders and facilitators became teachers; young people became students, and so forth[11]. As a result, the books became practically useless for implementing in North American the kind of transformation of activities with the young that Babin had in mind, activities of pastoral ministry rather than of schooling. The revolutionary character of Babin's work was decisively undercut by the mis-translation, and Babin's inventive categorical breakthrough was effectively cancelled by his translator's categorical error. Now long been out of print, these potentially wonderful books of Babin, deserve to be properly translated and thus have their pastoral power restored[12].

Readers here should note that the mistranslation was appropriate if one accepted that catechesis is the key form of religious teaching in Catholic schools, something I deny. A procedural error was the basis for shifting the categories in these books from those of pastoral ministry outside schools to those of schooling. As stated above, this error was a setback for non-school pastoral ministry with youth. Knowing the distinctive histories of schooling and of catechesis could help both educators and catechists rethink their particular tasks and the means by which they are fulfilled. In the next section I will examine the originating history of education and of catechesis to show the distinct interests behind these activities. If successful, this examination will disclose the distinctive character of particular context and why they must not be confused or conflated.

2. Education and Catechesis in Antiquity

Education in Antiquity: The Origins of Western Education

On the first page of the Introduction to his famous *The History of Education in Antiquity*, Henri Marrou claims this history reveals the founda-

---

11. The reason for such a translation, I have been told, was that the publishers thought the schooling language was the language teachers in religious schools would understand.

12. For details on these translations, see M. WARREN, *The Approach of Pierre Babin to Adolescent Catechesis and Its Influence on American Catholic Catechetical Literature. 1963-1972*, Washington DC, Catholic University of America Dissertation, 1974, pp. 267-277.

tion of our own modern educational tradition. For Marrou everything important in our own civilization derives from the civilization of the ancients, especially "our system of education". His capsule statement on education in antiquity is put in terms not of education but of culture:"the progressive transition from the 'noble warrior' culture to a 'scribe' culture"[13]. Long after the schools of antiquity had vanished, continual attempts were made to imitate them by organizing according to their principles, and even today much can be learned by studying these principles.

Marrou, the descriptive historian, offers scant critique of the cultural and social structures of those times and institutions. Today many will see the culture served by Greek education as elitist and class-based, offering education to the aristocracy and civil servants but excluding the under classes of peasants and manual laborers (and slaves). Such education clearly served social and political power. Even further, education in antiquity served males, and so his book has very little to say at all about the place in education of women of any age[14]. In our own 21st century, however, the evident use of education to enforce social privilege and its lack seems to surface in almost every nation, presenting a problem of equality most societies recognize but are unwilling to change – but quick to deny the lack of will[15]. Not all educators are willing to face this dark side of education's social structure; with magical slight of hand, they prefer to abstract education from social structure and then sacralize it. That said, it is more and more difficult today to ignore education's connections to social structures.

Those connections are the subject of today's "critical education" literature. Those who advocate or practice critical education know the difficulty of inviting people to become aware of how they are aware, and of how their minds are shaped socially and culturally. Schooling is a social institution designed to hand on and reinforce a society's values and

13. H.I. MARROU, *A History of Education in Antiquity*, Madison, University of Wisconsin Press, 1982, pp. xi-xv (translation: George Lamb). Though Marrou does not advert to the sexist and classist structures of these societies, he generally offers more detailed and nuanced accounts of ancient life than do my summaries of his positions. Readers should consult his important text themselves for their important details.

14. An exception comes in two pages where the place of Spartan girls in sports competition and in singing and dancing performances is mentioned, see H.I. MARROU, *A History of Education in Antiquity*, pp. 17-18 and p. 23.

15. As a bald example of such elitism, see *Social Principles Determining Secondary Education*, chapter 9 of A. INGLIS, *Principles of Secondary Education*, New York, Houghton Mifflin, 1918. This chapter is filled with principles that could be challenged as anti-democratic and elitist. For a recent critique of the same elitism, see *School Colors. The Racial Politics of Public Education: A Forum*, in *The Nation*, 5 June 2000, pp. 13-18.

ways. To say this is not to damn schooling, but to open educational structures to scrutiny.

Writing descriptively not critically, Marrou offers a compelling account of Hellenic education, as being much more about a way of inhabiting the world than about the acquiring of literacy (though literacy was essential). Marrou names this aspect of education with the word the Greeks themselves used: *paideia*, a word with positive connotations. "What is ... [*paideia*] but the principle behind all education, pushed to its farthest limits and made absolute. Paideia here is no longer the technique by which the child is equipped and made ready early in life for the job of becoming a man ... [but it] denotes the results of this educational effort pursued beyond the years of schooling and lasting throughout the whole of life, to realize ever more perfectly the human ideal. Paideia comes to signify "culture" – not in the sense of something active and preparational like education, but in the sense that the word has for us today – of something perfected: a mind fully developed, the mind of a man who has become truly man; it is a striking fact that when, later, Verro and Cicero had to translate paideia into Latin, they used the word *Humanitas*"[16]. Marrou goes on to say this: "Classical education was essentially an initiation into the Greek way of life, moulding the child and the adolescent in accordance with the national customs and submitting him to a particular style of living – the style that distinguished man from the brutes, Greeks from barbarians"[17].

Marrou is obviously impressed with the idea of *paideia* as an outcome of education at its best, possibly because from his position in 1950, he saw it as an educational ideal far beyond the technicalized and product-oriented education he found in mid-twentieth century France[18]. And while there is much about Greek paideia that deserves attention, at the same time the term needs critique of its snobbish elitism and its claims to intellectual superiority that might just as well describe the self-appraisal of a Nazi in 1939, as that of a self-congratulating Greek of the post-Alexander empire[19]. Still, as we will see, shorn of its elitist conno-

16. H.I. MARROU, *A History of Education in Antiquity* (n. 13), pp. 98-99.
17. *Ibid.*, p. 99.
18. J.F. DUNNE wrote *Back to the Rough Ground. Phronesis and Technè in Modern Philosophy and Aristotle*, Notre Dame, University of Notre Dame, 1996, as a way of countering a tendency to technologize education and lose its character as creating the "humanum". See esp. his introduction, pp. 1-27.
19. In all his writings Raymond Williams rejects the elitist definition of culture in favor of a more Marxist and critical analysis of culture. See, for example, *The Long Revolution* (1961), *The Year 2000* (1983), and *The Sociology of Culture* (1982).

tations, paideia becomes a concept useful for distinguishing catechesis and religious education. Let us have a closer look at the tension between paideia and the school.

The Greeks were confident the Greek Way was humanizing. Convinced their culture itself was educative they did not have a high regard for school teaching, at least not during the Hellenistic period of the third century BCE. Schools did not play the key role in education they came to play in the Middle Ages and beyond. For grasping the limited role of schooling in Greek Hellenistic society and the limited role of the schoolteacher, Marrou's own words are best: "The schoolmaster was only responsible for one small section of children's education – the mental side. He did not really educate his pupils. Education means, essentially, moral training, character training, a whole way of life. The "master" was only expected to teach them to read – which is a much less important matter. The connection between elementary education and moral training, which seems so natural to us today, is a heritage from the Middle Ages – to be more precise, from monastic schools, in which the same person found himself obliged to unite two quite distinct roles – that of the school teacher and that of the spiritual father. In antiquity the school master was far too insignificant a person for any family to think of giving him the responsibility of educating its children, as it so often does today. If anyone other than the parents was ever given the job, it was the pedagogue, who was only a slave, no doubt, but who was at least one of the family. Through his daily contact with the child, and his own example – whenever possible – and at any rate by his precepts and the careful watch he kept over him, he made a far greater contribution to his education, especially his moral education, than the purely technical lessons provided by the school master"[20].

---

20. H.I. MARROU, *A History of Education in Antiquity* (n. 13), pp. 147-148. – Readers who read Marrou's sections on *paideia*, will see that he is fascinated by the proposal of *paideia* and convinced of its power, but at the same time somewhat uncertain of exactly how the culture's most important convictions are passed on. See how he returns to the issue in his chapter "Classical Humanism" (pp. 217-226): "When the Greeks spoke about the 'training of the child' – what they really meant was essentially moral training. ...From the Hellenistic period onwards the word 'pedagogue' gradually changed it meaning until it came to have its modern sense of 'educator'. The fact is that the humble slave who was known as the 'pedagogue' was a more important person with regards to the training of the child than the schoolmaster. The schoolmaster was simply a technician, and he only affected a limited area of the child's intelligence; but the pedagogue was with the child all day, he taught him how to behave, how to be a good boy, how to get on in life, in society – all more important things than knowing now to read. We have made the school the decisive factor in education; for the Greeks the decisive factor

These facts help us face the difference between our current understanding of the school and that of ancient times. Today "education" is often used as a synonym for schooling, signaling how the popular imagination tends to identify the two. "Educational reform" usually means the reform of schools. But in the numberless writings on the education of children done in the Greco-Roman age, little attention is given to school problems, with the greatest space given to the moral atmosphere needed for education. Education was not so much a matter of instruction as of the formation of character, a task far beyond anything the school was expected to do. "The teaching profession remained a humble, somewhat despised occupation, ... requiring no special qualifications"[21]. For the moment my concern here is to focus on our different assumptions about the nature of education and the place of schooling within it. Eventually these values became reversed with the school and the role of teachers highly prized, even dominating the educational process.

Most instructive in the origins of Western education is that the school was the place for learning skills of literacy but not expected to form character. The formation of character was the task for the household and the overall society. The household was to find a person who could initiate the child into what it meant to be a good person and a good citizen, but Greek culture itself and its proposal of humanization in the Greek mode was carried out by living in Greek society. Society was the carrier of the Greek imagination of the meaning of "a good life". The religious life was part of the culture and handed on by absorbing that culture. These aspects of Greek education are, as I hope to show, helpful for understanding the distinctive character of catechesis as well as its function as a kind of "paideia". They may also clarify the choices religious people face today in handing their faith on to the rising generation.

Marrou's description of the difference between schooling and paideia offers wisdom for today as we sort out the possibilities of the school and those of the church in fostering faith. Ireland's new religious education curriculum is meant for the school, not for the believing community. To say this is not to deny that the community of worship is enriched when

---

was the surroundings in which the child grew up – the family, with its servants and friends ... At this stage, Greek culture [was] not so much concerned with the inmost nature of the universe and society as with the practical inculcation of an ethical ideal – a system of moral values and a way of life in conformity with it" (p. 221).

21. *Ibid.*, pp. 145-146 *passim*.

its adherents understand the functions of religion, its positive and negative outcomes, and its varieties of forms. These understandings offer to
committed faith greater perspective on its own uniqueness.

The course in religion is completed when its goals and objectives are
completed, with efforts graded along a statistical line of more accuracy or
less, of better grasp or lesser grasp. The efforts of the community of worship, however, do not bend to such evaluation or even to such completion. These efforts, unending and less open to quantitative evaluation,
are about living faithfully its religious vision. While the religion course is
mandated by the state, the commitments of the believing community are
of a different sort altogether. They are not state-mandated with successes
or failures recorded in State documents but are understood to come from
God's own Self, as a loving invitation, with some successes and some failures as part of the unfathomable effort to be true to one's summons from
God. Religious convictions might oppose state-endorsed teaching and
policies, like slavery and war. In the end faith is not a study but a practice, and practice is of its nature open to endless enhancement. To con-
fuse the study of religion and the living of faith helps no one, while
understanding the uniqueness of each area enriches both.

The Greek insight that paideia was about the formation of the whole
person deserves much consideration today[22]. Education is broader than
schooling and, according to some, lifelong. Paideia is useful for helping
us understand the role of the churches as different from the role of
schools. The church, as I hope to make clear below, is meant to be a
place where the life of the whole community is the chief educative element, inviting the young to live what it lives. The life of the whole
invites the young to a whole way of life, pursued through the whole
course of life. That such is the character of catechesis is clear from its
origins and from its most current literature.

Catechesis in Antiquity: The Origins of Initiation

The ways by which persons initially move toward Christian faith are
varied, as can be seen in various first-person accounts. Paul was knocked

---

22. 'Required' reading for background on these matters in the U.S. include:
J.S. COLEMAN et al., Youth: Transition to Adulthood, Chicago, University of Chicago, 1974
(Part 2: Background, pp. 9-125); NATIONAL PANEL ON HIGH SCHOOL AND ADOLESCENT
EDUCATION, The Education of Adolescents, Washington DC, Government Printing Office,
(HEW Publication # (OE) 76-00004), 1976; and J. TAYLER GATTO, The Underground
History of American Education, NY, Oxford Village Press, 2000. This last is actually a
social history of U.S. education which examines its exploitation by social engineers.

off his feet by a blinding light. Augustine's final jolt toward conversion was his hearing outside his walled garden a snatch phrase from child's song. A woman tells a priest friend how she grew up in a completely non-religious home, but came to be enrolled in a Catholic elementary school, where instructions about Catholic faith led her to search deeper into it, and finally to baptism. Emilie Griffin's powerful account of the vague and gradual stages of her own conversion, makes one think of the slow, even tedious positioning of a massive ocean liner by a bevy of tug boats, gradually moving the ship into a safe berth[23]. The initial step-by-step process by which any person begins to move, like Moses, ever deeper into the Mountain of God is highly varied. This variety is to be respected in any general account of the process of coming to faith. Still, the deeper and extended process by which one eventually comes to stand with those who embrace the perils of Jesus-faith is not one of happenstance but of deliberation and choice by an individual and a community.

The original procedures for helping people become followers of Jesus are historically vague. Whatever they were, they were dangerous and probably cautious. After Jesus's execution as a revolutionary, his followers most likely were suspect. "Danger is clearly a fundamental category for understanding his [Jesus's] life and message and for defining Christian identity. ... Danger and being in danger permeate every NT statement"[24]. Still, in *Acts* the procedures of incorporation into the Christian Way are not well-delineated. For example, Cornelius the Roman centurion, is suddenly recognized as filled with the Spirit of Jesus and quickly baptized (Acts 10,1-48). Within a century and a half, however, there had evolved a sophisticated process for ensuring those seeking baptism had changed their way of life before being able to proceed to baptism. That process was the catechumenate, and from it comes the contemporary understanding of catechesis. The very design of the catechumenate in the early church exposes the features of contemporary catechesis.

Made possible only by initial conversion and the pursuit of a lifelong conversion, catechesis was seen as an activity done in the context of worship and the search for deeper faith. This means that catechesis is a view of the Christian "thing", not from outside but from inside. Being outside a circle is very different from being inside the same circle. From

---

23. E. GRIFFIN. *Turning. Reflections on the Experience of Conversion*, Garden City, Doubleday, 1980.
24. J.B. METZ, *A Passion for God*, Mahwah, Paulist Press, 1998, p. 48.

outside you can see the entire circle, take it in, comprehend it visually. However, once you step inside, you no longer comprehend the circle, especially not visually; the circle comprehends you, and you see it only one part at a time. The circle of faith is similar, though it is not a circle of concepts only but one of commitments grounded in insight. If by means of conversion you pass the bounding circumference and enter into that circle, you find it now envelops you. There is more to the reality of it than you can ever express. Catechesis expands conversion via movement deeper into the core of the circle. That move is a lifelong process. This means that all catechesis is partial, incomplete, and ongoing. The astute catechist knows she doesn't have to do everything at once, but only the partial thing possible right now. God's spirit functions beyond the catechist's well planned intervention. While an educator may need educational goals and objectives and measurable outcomes, the catechetical process is more open-ended, less "tight".

The following are features of catechesis that show its distinctiveness from schooling but without diminishing the value of schooling as a vehicle of education.

Catechesis was meant to be an option but not a casual option.
In today's post-industrial societies, schooling is not an option. The State enforces it. Choice, however, is the heart of catechesis. The move to catechesis was an optional move initiated by persons presenting themselves as wishing to become Christians. They were accepted into the process of initiation only after an examination or scrutiny of their understanding of what they were doing and of their motives. From the first, initiation is a step to implicate oneself in the way of Jesus-faith. In *The First Catechetical Instruction*[25], his famous essay on dealing with seekers after baptism, Augustine explains that some, say a Carthage shopkeeper, might want to become Christians because it could be good for business – and for that reason should be discouraged. Thus the community's very first step was to examine motives. This was a discreet note of hesitation on the community's part, asking in effect, Are you sure you know what you are asking for or getting yourself into?

Technically then catechesis begins only when a person reaches out to the Spirit of Jesus. Persons are not shoved into catechesis; any shoving

---

25. AUGUSTINE, *The First Catechetical Instruction*, Chicago, Henry Regnery Co., 1966 (trans. Joseph P. Christopher). The Latin name for this treatise is *De Catechizandis Rudibus*, loosely: "About Catechizing Those with Little Knowledge".

negates catechesis. Catechesis is an exercise of freedom and choice. The community says to the chooser, We will be there with you and for you on your path to become a seasoned disciple, to help you decide if discipleship is even possible for you. Some readers will be aware that the "catechesis" they encountered as yesteryear's shoves lacked this character of choice and option. What was called catechesis was done to them whether they wished it or not. Lacking this character of option, it was inappropriately named as catechesis. While Christian living is not an option for those wishing to be disciples, the process of catechesis itself never loses its character as a willing and self-involving process. Wherever it loses that character, it has ceased to be catechesis.

This feature of catechesis raises questions about catechetical procedures in church-related schools. Vatican documents, like the *General Directory for Catechesis* (1997) and *The Religious Dimension of Education in a Catholic School* (1988) clearly distinguish the school as the zone of education in religion rather than catechesis[26]. In these schools one can find examples of all the following: those who have *not opted* for the schooling itself (which when mandated by the state is compulsory under penalty of law); or, for the particular church-related school (having been sent there by parents but against one's will); or, for the classes in religion (being desirous of the secular classes but resentful of the religious classes); or for the distinctively Christian atmosphere (finding it distasteful on any number of grounds)[27]. In such circumstances, competent teachers realize they cannot teach well without being aware of varied agendas in a group. A class about religion may for one person be perceived as deeply satisfying catechesis but for another be a painful indoctrination or a hateful religious exploitation for a third. Persons alive to the character of catechesis as option would seek, in non-optional circumstances, to expand the options of those involved in the circumstances[28]. Explaining in detail how this might be done would involve a

26. See CONGREGATION FOR CATHOLIC EDUCATION, *The Religious Dimension of Education in a Catholic School*, in *Origins* 18 (1988) 213 and 215-228.

27. Important research on the influence of church schools on students has been done by Leslie J. Francis and Josephine Egan. Their research shows the greatest predictor of the growth of religious consciousness and faith from such schooling to be the faith filled practice of the parents. See L.J. FRANCIS & J. EGAN, *The Catholic School as 'Faith Community'*, in M. WARREN (ed.), *The Sourcebook for Modern Catechetics*, Vol. 2 (n. 2), 291-305.

28. Of course it is true that no learning is possible without the cooperation of the person being educated. Teaching is in part a work of creating among learners the conditions for the achievement of the educational goals, which include the willing, self-involving participation of the learner in the process. An insightful and entertaining book

separate essay. The general principle I would recommend is to respect all hesitations about religiousness, especially when honoring a mandate to teach about religion.

As someone who teaches theology in a church-related university that requires students to complete a sequence of courses in theology-and-religion, I find there are ways of respecting students' hesitations about religious proposals while inviting them to reflect seriously on what it means to be a self in today's world and its multiple kinds of relationships. After all the Christian community's original hesitations about who might become members via the catechumenate were an authentic way of facing both the complexities of the human self and the community's own distinctive requirements. This concern over the possible abuse of educative power is not just an important educational matter but an essential aspect of all pastoral work. The real problems occur when teachers assume their activity is beneficent or even beneficial for all in the group. For teachers, conscious doubt is the way to wise action in such a situation. In Ireland, the *educational* aspect of teaching about religion has been finally aided by approaching education in religion, not as a means to confessional affiliation but to intellectual appreciation and critique.

Catechesis is an initiation into a new sensibility, a new way of perceiving the world and of being in that world – in Greek terms, a distinctive paideia. Catechesis holds to the Greek idea of paideia, with its inability to be communicated by schooling only. From the start, catechesis knew one learned the ways of Jesus-faith by becoming members of a group that embodied that faith. Life in the *ekklesia* was the means of communicating the secrets of Jesus-faith. In the fourth century North Africa catechumenate, moving into this alternate culture was not an overnight affair, but took about three years of difficult transition. It took time to come to see other persons as proxies of Jesus and even more time to master the skills of the Jesus Way. Tied to the new sensibility were habitual ways of responding to situations involving the ill, the imprisoned, the physically and mentally impaired, the hungry, those lacking shelter – and also, those named enemies. It was useless for the catechumen to claim these habitual ways of thinking and acting were in place; only

about the various problems encountered in teaching about religion is, C. ARTHUR, *Biting the Bullet. Some Personal Reflections on Religious Education*, Edinburgh, The Saint Andrew Press, 1990. See, his wise observations about teaching about ritual, "The Mimicry of Faith" (pp. 10-15).

actions could effectively exhibit the new ways[29]. Those admitted to the period of formation in the Jesus-Way did not proceed to baptism because they claimed to be followers but because they demonstrated the behaviors of discipleship after being coached in these behaviors by virtuosos who exhibited them. Those tempted to shove people into the new Jesus sensibility may well have lost their confidence in the community's ability to display that sensibility in credible ways.

Catechesis is a lifelong process and the community is its agent.
The initiation process and baptism were the start of a lifelong process whose chief agent was not any single person serving as catechist, but the vitality of the believing community itself. As Berger and Luckmann say in the final third of their important book on the sociology of knowledge: Conversion is no big deal; the big deal is the maintenance of the conversion, that is, of the new sensibility with its new perceptions and new ways of acting[30]. The agent of conversion-maintenance is the community itself.

I have already noted how a variety of events and circumstances might prompt a person to move in a search for God, but that the process by which that same person could become a faithful follower of the Jesus Christians name as the Christ, is not happenstance but a carefully marked out process – an achievement of intentionality on the part of both the seeking person and the welcoming community. I am dealing with a double intention here: one on the part of the seeker to become a disciple of Jesus, plus a complementary intention on the part of the community to assist the seeker to become in fact a disciple. Of course it could happen that the seeker might come to see that the discipline of discipleship is too difficult and unsustainable – and abandon it. The maintenance of conversion is not so much the task of any one individual but of the community of followers. This point is made over and over

---

29. The early Christian teacher, Origen, wrote: "When it becomes evident that the disciples are purified by the word and have begun, as far as possible, to live better, only then are they invited to know our mysteries" (*Contra Celsum* 3,59). This quote is found in B. Capelle, *L'introduction du catéchuménat à Rome*, in *Recherches de théologie ancienne et médiévale* 5 (1933) 129-154, p. 151, note 38.

30. P. Berger & Th. Luckmann, *The Social Construction of Reality. A Treatise in the Sociology of Knowledge*, New York, Doubleday Anchor Books, 1966 (Chapter 3: "Society as Subjective Reality", pp. 129-183). The actual quote is: "To have a conversion experience is nothing much. The real thing is to be able to keep on taking it seriously; to retain a sense of its plausibility. This is where the religious community comes in. It provides the indispensible plausibility structure for the new reality" (p. 158).

again in the 1997 *General Directory of Catechesis*, the most authoritative current statement about catechesis.

Here are a few of its passages about the sacramentality of the community of believers.

> #77 The agent of catechesis [is] the church animated by the Holy Spirit.

> #78 Catechesis is essentially an ecclesial act. The true subject of catechesis is the Church which, continuing the mission of Jesus the Master and, therefore animated by the Holy Spirit, is sent to be the teacher of faith. ... This transmission of the Gospel is a living act of ecclesial tradition.

> #87 To fulfill its tasks, catechesis avails of two principal means: transmission of the Gospel message and experience of the Christian life.

> #105 The ecclesial nature of catechesis confers on the transmitted Gospel message an inherent ecclesial character. Catechesis originates in the Church's confession of faith and leads to the profession of faith of the catechumen and those to be catechized. ... Catechesis is nothing other than the process of transmitting the Gospel as the Christian community has received it, understands it, celebrates it, lives it and communicates it in many ways.

> #106 This faith, *transmitted by the ecclesial community*, is one.

> #141 From her very beginnings the Church, which "in Christ, is in the nature of a sacrament," has lived her mission as a visible and actual continuation of the pedagogy of the Father and of the Son. She "as our Mother is also the educator of our faith". These are the profound reasons for which the Christian community is in herself *living catechesis*.

The church is not perfect.

Another feature of catechesis, little addressed in any literature of catechesis I know but logically important, is this: the community of followers can tolerate the presence of those who have become uncertain of their way, who have slipped back into habits they themselves supposed they had left behind, or who find the new way far more a burden than a joy. These long for the old ways unobstructed by reminders of Jesus' teachings or the community's exhorted way. The community holds these persons lovingly in its circle because it is to be a healing space for those at its perimeter, who may even long to be free of it. In other words the community is not a circle of "pure ones" but rather of those who are called to be more than their worst impulses. The community holds repentance as sacred and the possibilities of new efforts as a sign of God's presence.

Conclusion

The power of today's communications media to shape our worldview and values according to the interests of consumerism is alarming to many of us. We conclude that any strengthening of family, folk, and religious cultures are an important antidote providing an alternative sensibility to the ever-rushed sensibility of more profit, more comfort, more privacy. In my view all social institutions should foster humanization: the ability to recognize our fellow beings as fellow creatures of God. This *ability*, when successfully instilled in children and maintained, represents a *sensibility*, that is deeply attuned to the human, to what fosters the *humanum* and what diminishes it. The stakes of consumerization or humanization are what confront all of us for the future. For the church (or any worshiping assembly) humanization is the issue. The same is true for all educational institutions, including schools and families. When each agency does well what it is equipped to do, the world is oriented toward healing and away from destruction.

To Teach Religion or Not to Teach Religion: Is That the Dilemma?

Kieran Scott

There is hesitation, confusion and perplexity in the United States as to what to do with religion. Reactions vary. There is empathy for learning religion but not for teaching it. In some settings, there is fear of evangelizing. While in others, it is explicitly assumed and advocated. In some circles, the *meaning* of "to teach religion" is understood as a confessional act. In other circles, the meaning is nearly the reverse, or simply a blur. In the US, we are in a dilemma as to whether to teach religion or not. And, I suspect the situation is not unique to the US.

Three brief examples will illustrate the muddled confusion:

1. In the Spring semester 1994, I was assigned to teach a course titled, Toward a Theology of Christian Marriage, on the undergraduate level. Some thirty-five students enrolled. My operating assumptions were: The setting is a classroom in a school; the content for engagement is marriage from a Christian perspective; the process is academic discussion and critique. Shortly before mid-term, I discovered not everyone shared my assumptions. We had just completed a unit on sexuality. James B. Nelson's book, *Embodiment: An Approach to Sexuality and Christian Theology*[1], was a key resource. The text is standard in the progressive and liberal theological tradition. A student approached me a few days before mid-term examinations. He expressed his opposition to the text, its ideological framework and viewpoints. Confessionally, he was a devout practicing Evangelical. The text was a source of temptation, he claimed. It was antagonistic to his fundamentalist hermeneutic. After consultation with his local minister, he requested exemption from the mid-term examination and exemption from studying the text. I refused. Was I correct? What is at stake in teaching religion? What is involved in learning religion? From the teacher's perspective, is it a work of advocacy? From the student's side, is it confessional confirmation? Or, is it something else?

---

1. J.B. NELSON, *Embodiment. An Approach to Sexuality and Christian Theology*, Minneapolis MN, Augsburg, 1978.

2. On June 19, 2000, Edward M. Egan was installed as New York's ninth archbishop at St. Patrick's Cathedral. The ceremony reflected many of the elements that will inevitably shape his tenure as archbishop. In his homily, Egan expressed his hope to be a teacher[2]. He emphasized his role as a teacher of faith and values. Being a teacher, he proclaimed, means working directly to shape the spiritual understanding of the faithful by clearly expounding church doctrine. He cited a national opinion poll (taken several years earlier in April 1994) that showed that more than 60 percent of American Catholics were uncertain of basic a doctrine, that the bread and wine at the Mass are changed into the body and blood of Christ. On this belief, Egan said, there can be "no compromise". What do we mean when we say: "The bishop is the chief teacher in the diocese"? Does he teach by being the primary guardian of doctrinal orthodoxy ("correct believing")? Are his teaching competencies, purposes and assumptions different than the classroom teacher of religion in an archdiocesan high school or Catholic college/university? Are these teaching forms compatible or conflictual? Are they simply variations within a common and assumed confessional stance? Or, are they not? Does the teaching act change according to settings? Does the teaching of religion depend on the mission of the school?

3. During my graduate studies, I enrolled in an intensive inter-session course. It was a deep and rapid immersion into the subject-at-hand. It was also a good way to quickly add three credits to one's transcript! The course topic was titled, Sexuality and the Social Order. The course would change my life and world view. First, I had the experience of being a minority. I was one of four men in a class of thirty-one. Second, the course was my introduction to feminism and feminists. It was an experience in transformational learning. One element in the course, however, unsettled me. As the classes progressed, assigned texts tended to be left aside. A personalistic group pedagogy took over. It represented a turn to the subject. The importance of personal experience as a source of knowledge was recognized. Permission and encouragement was given to self-expression, self-revealing, emotional unloading and confessional declarations. Psychic turmoil, sexual violence, emotional hurts, incest and sexual ambiguity were shared with all. In retrospect, it seemed like a forerunner of an Oprah Winfrey or Sally Jesse Raphael afternoon TV talk show. At one stage, the professor asked the four men to excuse themselves from the class because the women had "female stuff to work

---

2. *New York Times*, June 20, 2000, pp. A1 & B10.

on". As the course turned more into a form of therapeutic encounter, I felt more ill–at-ease. The dynamics seemed more appropriate in a counseling setting or in a church confessional[3]. Is the classroom of the school the place to work on psychic turmoil? Is it an area for acts of confession? Can we replace the school desk with the psychologist couch? We may be living human documents, but is classroom teaching a therapy session? What kind of space is the classroom? Is it a place where personal grief is traded for consolation? Or, is it something else?

This essay will attempt to unclutter, distinguish and clarify the issues at stake in the three examples noted. The focus of my attention is to uncover the meaning(s) of "to teach religion". The technology of teaching does not claim my primary interest here; nor does the disposition of the learner/student to learn; nor does the impact of social and cultural forces on the learning situation. These are, of course, vital components to consider in every educational context. Contemporary literature on schooling and (practical) theology is attending extensively to these poles[4]. But I wish to look at the issues from the other side, that is, from the perspective of the teacher, or to be more precise, from the side of the act of teaching. I will explore the meaning of the verb "to teach" and its object "religion" as they intermingle, interplay and intersect in contemporary United States. This particular US embodiment, however, may have universal implications.

Specifically, I will explore the meaning(s) of to teach religion in two settings: first, in Public or government sponsored schools and, secondly in Parochial or church sponsored schools. I will attempt to untangle the meaning(s) in each of these educational arenas and their respective interrelationship. Our exploration, however, begins with the unveiling of the meanings of the verb "to teach", a naming of its multiple forms, languages and settings. Prior to linking the verb to teach with its object religion, a comprehensive interpretative framework and consistent linguistic pattern is needed. I will propose an emerging meaning of religious education as a heuristic framework. Whether one conceptualizes this project, as a form of practical theology is a question I keep in abeyance until the conclusion of the essay.

---

3. On the risks of personalistic teaching methodologies, see K. HOMAN, *Hazards of the Therapeutic. On the Use of Personalistic and Feminist Methodologies*, in *Horizons* 24 (1997) 248-264.

4. For an excellent new resource see the journal *Teaching Theology and Religion*, published by Blackwell Publishers in cooperation with the Wabash Center for Teaching and Learning in Theology and Religion.

1. Liberating the Verb "To Teach"

Reclaiming the richest meaning of the verb "to teach" will involve a four step process. First, the moral dilemma at the heart of teaching is raised. Second, in an attempt to solve the dilemma of teaching, a variety of teaching acts or forms are named and recognized. The third step is to distinguish among the many forms of speech in teaching. And, fourth, the task is to match one of these languages or a pattern of languages with the appropriate institutional setting. When the latter is accomplished the dilemma is solved and teaching can become a moral act[5].

The Moral Dilemma of Teaching

Teaching is an important test case of whether we understand what education is. Yet, it is the learning aspect of education that gets attention today. We have prolific discussion on the student's readiness to learn, dispositions to learn, and social-cultural influences on the learning process. Little or no ambivalence is expressed about learning. In contrast, the nature of teaching goes nearly unexplored. Teaching and learning are taken to be separable processes. Learning is treasured. Teaching seems to be an optional extra or an oppressive interference. Why is this so?

Gabriel Moran proposes a thesis: people are uneasy with the very idea of teaching. At some level of consciousness and conscience, they sense a moral dilemma in the idea of teaching[6]. They have an ethical problem with the activity and have a deep suspicion that it is an immoral activity. Teaching is equated with the exercise of power by an adult over a vulnerable child. It is identified with a powerful adult trying to control the thinking of a powerless neophyte. It is telling the young the truth. Moran traces this reductionist meaning of teaching to its seventeenth century roots. John Locke and Jean-Jacques Rousseau did not eliminate the term, but they narrowed its meaning to a rationalistic core devoid of religious meaning. Its chief embodiment in the modern world is a classroom. In educational literature, it is assumed that teaching is an explanation from the front of a classroom. It becomes confused with a certain

---

5. The recent work of Gabriel Moran is a major inspiration for this section of the essay. I note in particular my indebtedness to his *Showing How. The Act of Teaching*, Valley Forge PA, Trinity Press International, 1997.

6. *Ibid.*, pp. 15-33.

arrangement of power – one of great inequity. In addition, the coercive influence is exercised mainly or exclusively through words. It seems only reasonable, then, with this domesticated meaning, to shift the attention to learning.

There are two places in particular in modern educational literature where teaching has an explicitly negative history: It is either attacked or avoided. This is most obvious in the literature on "moral education" and "adult education". In the literature on "moral education", teaching is suspect. At one end of the pendulum, it comes under direct attack (for example, "value clarification"). The teacher should never say something is right or wrong. At the other end, teaching becomes moot as "moral development" is subtly affirmed. In Piaget's framework, to teach morality to the child is almost a contradiction. The task of the parent or the schoolteacher is to foster discussion and get out of the way. Teaching receives its poorest press in contemporary "adult education" literature. "Adult education" literature intentionally abandoned the term pedagogy. If pedagogy or teaching is the exercise of power over a child, then, adults want no part of it. A new vocabulary was invented. "Androgogy" was and is the centerpiece of the literature. "Adult education" proceeds to define and demarcate itself over against the child, the teacher and religion. The assumption was and is: children need teachers, but adults need "mentors", "facilitators", "guides" or "counselors". The moral dilemma associated with teaching is palpable on nearly every page.

The Variety of Teaching Acts

We need a rich meaning of teaching to discuss religious education. At the same time, the contemporary practice(s) of religious education can unveil a more adequate meaning of teaching. Most writers on teaching are aware that they should not equate teaching with classroom instruction. However, after this initial acknowledgement, they proceed to discuss the activities of a schoolteacher in a classroom. The result is that most kinds of teaching disappear, and with it, much of the language, imagery, and techniques for improving classroom instruction. Classroom teaching needs a wider context of teaching. When it lacks that, it can indeed become coercive and negative. The initial turn toward solving the moral dilemma of teaching is the recognition of the variety of teaching acts. It is helpful to focus on the act or event of teaching and to ask: what exactly does a teacher do when engaging in the act of teaching? A sense of history and geography is helpful to arrive at a clearer answer. Etymologically, to teach, means to "show how". It means to show someone how to do something. It is captured in the American pragmatic sense of "know-how". A teacher not only knows something but also knows how to show the knowledge or skills to someone else. Most comprehensively, to teach is to show someone how to live and that includes how to die. Here we can sense, most teaching has a religious dimension. This comprehensive meaning lives on in people's ordinary speech. They know they are taught everyday in numerous ways. Teaching is a central characteristic of the human animal.

Teaching and learning, then, should be viewed as poles within a single process. Learning always implies teaching. People learn things because they have been taught. The proof that teaching exists is the existence of learning. Learning, however, may not always follow from teaching. But, teaching is showing how and learning is responding to this showing. The relation of teaching -learning is a cooperation in power that leads toward mutuality. Gabriel Moran seeks to re-appropriate the meaning of teaching by grounding it in foundational forms of teaching that occur with little or no conscious intent and with few if any human words[7]. In other words, most of the teaching in the world is nonverbal and unintentional. It is communal, symbolic, physical showing how. Every religious tradition reminds us that the community teaches. It teaches by being an example – by demonstrating (showing how) a way of life: this is the way to live and to die. Teaching goes on everyday in the way the community and its traditions functions. Virtue is learned when adults and children grow up in a virtuous community. Teaching here includes a wide range of people doing a variety of things in diverse settings with various groups. Intentionality and the verbal are for the most part in the background.

The moral problem of teaching begins to surface, however, when an individual is designated as "teacher" and the teaching is consciously intended. When the teaching is of a physical act (swimming, dancing, bicycle riding), the learner can receive precise directions. If the learner shows a willingness to try again and again, the signs are that the teaching is not oppressive. Speech here functions as choreography of the body, and the moral problem is quickly resolved. However, there can be teaching in which speech takes center stage. Speech becomes the focal point of the teaching. Human language can be viewed as human activity or movement and, consequently, the object of teaching. In other

---

7. G. MORAN, *Showing How* (n. 5), pp. 34-58.

words, we have the human capacity to distance ourselves from our own speech. This is both the glory and the danger of the human. As speech moves to the center, the great danger is that it can loose its rootedness in bodily life. Some academic teaching (and writing) stumbles into this pitfall. Speech can never loose its connection to the body. It draws power by being situated at the center of bodily life. Speech, in this case, can still be viewed as choreography – precisely indicating movement to someone who can accept or reject the direction. This may lead to reshaping or redesigning the person's relation to the community. The redesign or reshaping however, may be of the speech itself. What best goes on in classrooms is this redesigning of linguistic patterns. The reshaping of the movement of speech holds center stage. But human language can be used for many purposes. To resolve the moral dilemma of teaching, we need to distinguish between forms of speech in teaching, and to match the appropriate form with the appropriate institutional setting.

The Languages of Teaching

Before a teacher begins to teach, he or she needs to ask why are these people in front of me? The question is critical for each: teacher, parent, coach, preacher, counselor, kindergarten teacher, teacher of religion, university professor. Under what assumptions are these people present? What kind of license to speak have they given me? What can I say that will relate to their bodily lives? What is appropriate (moral)? What is inappropriate (immoral)? The basis on which an individual or group appears before a teacher signifies a moral consent to a particular form of discourse. Much of the misunderstanding surrounding the term "to teach religion" arises when people are confused about the nature of the institution they are in. Why are they assembled? What have they consented to? What language form is operating? Toward what is it directed? When the answer to these questions is unclear, the consent of the people gathered in front of the teacher is sometimes blurred.

Gabriel Moran's most original contribution, in this regard, is his delineation of three groups or families of languages for discussing teaching. He names them the homiletic, the therapeutic, and the academic[8]. The homiletic and the therapeutic forms of speech are opposite in many

---

8. G. MORAN, *Showing How* (n. 5), pp. 83-145; see also ID., *Religious Education as a Second Language*, Birmingham AL, Religious Education Press, 1989, pp. 69-80.

ways. The contrast is based upon a difference in relation to *end*, that is, a good it wishes to reach. The homiletic has an end in view. The therapeutic does not. Both languages can be effective and moral in acts of teaching when used in the appropriate setting. They need, however, to be held in a healthy tension. The setting for academic speech is distinctive and circumscribed. The academic is, as it were, one step removed from ordinary life. It overlaps the homiletic and therapeutic. Communal / bodily life is mediated to the academic through the latter two languages. Academic speech can be powerful in transforming the world and redesigning people's lives. It simply needs the right setting. I will now layout in more detail the nature of each linguistic form.

Homiletic Speech

The best example of homiletic speech is the church sermon. However, the homiletic, as a way of speaking, includes more then preaching. Representative of this first family of languages is storytelling, lecturing and preaching. Homiletic speech presupposes a community and arises from a community. The community has convictions, an agreed-upon text. The end, or good to be attained, is known to the group. This family of languages is "rhetorical", that is, the intention is to persuade people to act on the basis of their (already-accepted) beliefs. The teacher in this situation steps into the center of the community, enable people to tap into their past, retrieve what underlies their beliefs, so as to energize them in the present... toward an end in the future. Moran writes, "The homilist's or preacher's job is both to remind the community of what it has agreed upon and to bring out implications of that agreement. Thus, the homilist is not mainly concerned with providing new information to a community. The point of homiletic speech is to arouse people to action beyond the assembly, to inspire people to get up from the seat and change the world for the better"[9].

Storytelling is one form of homiletic speech. Communities develop stories (fairy tales, myths, literary fiction) that embody who they are, what their agreements are, what are good and bad. The homilist teaches by telling the story. He or she adds a layer of commentary on the (communal) text. When the story is told well, it can spark the imagination and inspire the reshaping of the communal life. Lecturing is a second form of homiletic speech. Academics may be surprised to find it here. To lecture means "to read". It is a particular kind if reading for an

9. G. MORAN, *Showing How* (n. 5), p. 70.

instructive or didactic purpose. It usually requires a ritual setting, personal involvement in the message, carefully crafted words, and appeal to reason. The lecture aims to convince and change the audience. The lecture can be an effective form of teaching, but contrary to university custom, it has little or no place in the classroom of a school. Preaching, for the most part, is preaching to the converted. It is an act of rhetoric persuasion. The community has an inner language and a text that expresses the community's beliefs. The preacher steps into the pulpit to stir the hearts of the people, to exhort them to keep their commitments and to go out and resist the injustice in the world. Preaching is to be affirmed and valued as a form of teaching. When the conditions are right, it is a powerful form of pedagogy. In other circumstances, it is completely inappropriate.

Homiletic speech is indispensable in some educational settings. However, where it flourishes, there is little space for critical thinking. Homiletic teaching can become vulnerable to manipulation. Stories can be romanticized, lectures dogmatic, and sermons indoctrinative. How does one protect the community from these impositions and violations? The only sure prevention is the introduction and rich presence of the other two families of languages.

Therapeutic Speech

The best example of therapeutic speech is the work of the professional psychotherapist. However, the therapeutic, as a way of speaking, includes more than what transpires in the therapist's office. Acts of praising and condemning, welcoming and thanking, confessing and forgiving, mourning and comforting come under the canopy of therapeutic speech[10]. The therapeutic is rooted in communal and bodily life. That is, it emerges out of the nonverbal realm of life. Unlike the homiletic, that accepts and celebrates the communal text, the therapeutic attempt to subvert it. It assumes the community is fragmented and the individual within it needs healing. Therapeutic speech seeks to undermine the individual's text. There are obstacles to wholeness in his or her way. The function of therapeutic speech is to remove these obstacles for the purpose of healing the individual within the community. It aims at quieting the interior. The language is restorative: it soothes, calms, heals. It is indispensable to human life, and central to teaching. The teacher in this situation is healer.

---

10. G. MORAN, *Showing How* (n. 5), pp. 103-123.

Therapeutic languages tend to be indirect and even illogical. It is a form of speech that operates in ordinary everyday life. It does not go directly at its object – like homiletic speech. Rather, its language is more silence than sound. It tries to get us to come to terms with our personal and collective conflicts. In therapy, the client does most of the talking. The process of talking unearths hidden texts, enables the individual to come to terms with them and bring them into a healing experience. The therapy is in the talking. On the part of the therapist, however, the speech tends to be minimalist. He or she refrains from pronouncements on how the world ought to be. In fact, therapeutic speech distrusts proclamations and is suspicious of speech. It calls attention to the roots of speech and how we can con ourselves with our own language games. It seeks to free us from our egocentric predicament. Moran writes, "In those situations where people need healing words, the therapeutic is appropriate. One uses speech to soothe, to relieve feelings of anger, guilt, or sorrow … In therapeutic speech we temporarily suspend some of the intellectual, aesthetic, and moral standards for the sake of recon-ciliation. In therapeutic speech the aim is not achieving an object of choice but reestablishing the ability to choose"[11]. The assumption is: there has been a rupture in the life of the community. The therapeutic family of languages seeks to recreate that world.

Sometimes in life, in particular situations, therapeutic speech is urgently necessary. It can be a valuable and vital form of speech in teaching people how to live (and how to die). However, there is a dan-ger. The danger is twofold: (1) therapeutic speech in the wrong context can be counterproductive; and (2) the hegemony of therapeutic speech in society can cloud our visibility to vital areas of life. We can avoid these dangers by (1) using the therapeutic in its appropriate setting, and (2) by introducing as complementary the other two families of lan-guages.

Academic Speech
The best example of academic speech is classroom instruction. How-ever, the academic, as a way of speaking, includes discourse beyond the walls of the school. Discussions with colleagues, friends and parishioners could get into raising questions and examining one's presuppositions. Academic speech, on the other hand, requires a specific set of conditions that may be difficult to establish outside the classroom of a school. This

---

11. G. MORAN, *Showing How* (n. 5), pp. 74-75.

family of languages includes dialectic discussion and academic criticism[12]. Academic speech is the use of speech for critical understanding. Here speech moves to center stage and is examined in relation to it. The act of teaching, in this case, is speech about speech. The teacher employs academic discourse to turn speech back on itself and to investigate its assumptions, biases and meanings. In order to achieve this, a certain distancing from ordinary life is needed. Academic speech is disinterested speech. To engage in it, we temporarily put on hold our involvement and convictions, as far as we are capable, to examine assumptions, contexts, blind spots. On the other hand, the academic teacher is an advocate. The advocacy is linguistic. He or she advocates how to speak so that greater understanding is possible.

Academic discourse presumes the homiletic and therapeutic. The latter two mediate communal / bodily life to the academic. Whereas the homiletic affirms the text of the community and the therapeutic subverts it, the academic aims to talk about the nature and meaning of particular texts. The main question it raises is what do the texts mean. It has no end beyond that. Moran writes, "the homilist says: 'We must believe and act upon the agreed text'; the therapist says: 'We must be free from a text that dominates us without our choice'. The academic teacher says, 'Accept no text uncritically; it might be false. Reject no text uncritically, it might be true'"[13]. Teaching academically is not directed to get students to believe the text or to reject (or dissent from) the text. The teacher's task is to playfully and imaginatively direct students to bring their own metaphors under suspicion and passionately propose richer metaphors for understanding. If the teacher succeeds, students may reshape the pattern of their discourse, and, in effect, redesign their world. The schoolteacher, then, does not tell people what to think. Nor is it an exercise in truth telling. It is an invitation to examine their way of speaking. The words of the teacher, students and assigned texts are placed between them. The ground rules are civility and tolerance. Everything else is open to critique. No opinion is uncritically accepted as the truth. The assumption is every statement of belief, every linguistic expression of truth and every viewpoint can be improved upon. This saves the process from being authoritarian.

The classroom is a place for a particular kind of discourse, nothing more and nothing less. Within this family of languages, we can recognize

---

12. G. MORAN, *Showing How* (n. 5), pp. 124-125.
13. ID., *Religious Education as a Second Language* (n. 8), p. 78.

two forms: dialectical discussion and academic criticism. Dialectical discussion often takes the form of debate. There is a sense of back and forth, a dialogue, with a reflective use of language. Particular attention, however, is directed to the meaning of the words in the dialogue. The dialogue, as an oral exchange, can only bear fruit if the participants are willing to listen to the words of the other, and the voice and otherness of the assigned text. Texts that tend to preach or be dogmatic defeat the purpose of the academic. Good texts need to leave open the possibility of imagining different viewpoints and alternative worlds. Dialectical discussion is oral debate where the movement of speech is the (inter)play of ideas. This prepares the participants for academic criticism.

Classrooms are designed to teach people to be skeptical. They are places to cultivate an attitude of questioning everything. Academic criticism can be a powerful form of teaching language in the service of this cause. What is called into question is language itself. The classroom is an arena of criticism. The established world or assumed truth is called into question. It is the student's written and spoken words that are the direct object of concern – not the person. The academic dialogue is between the teacher and the students. Both are participants. Assuming the teacher is competent, a further prerequisite for a valuable exchange is that students are in touch with a variety of sources for the topic at hand. In other words, students are required to bring some formed knowledge to the arena of criticism. If they don't, there will be no genuine dialogue. Students are invited to place their (informed) words on the table. Their words become the focus of attention and criticism. The academic search is to understand the words on the table between teacher and students. The task is to distinguish meanings in a way that leads to greater understanding. The teacher does not describe or prescribe. He or she does not try to change the student or the student's thinking, only the student's words. The teacher is advocate, but the advocacy is for a certain way of speaking. The schoolteacher's job is to propose a reshaping of the student's words. That is what is appropriate and academically permissible (moral).

Academic speech, then, is concerned with meaning, with intellectual understanding. It questions the adequacy of every form of expression. This critique if it has communal support does not end in negativity. Rather, it can facilitate the emergence and flowering of new meaning. That is the purpose of classroom teaching. When academic criticism is absent, the classroom is simply not functioning as a genuine classroom. This form of teaching can never substitute for the other two, but when it complements the homiletic and the therapeutic, it can be powerful and transformative in people's lives. However, the central issue remains: when and where is each form of speech appropriate.

Matching Languages with Educational Settings

The final step in resolving the dilemma of teaching is fitting the appropriate family of languages to the appropriate institutional setting. Each educational setting has one or several forms of language appropriate to it. Each setting has specific limits that protect the learner. A moral problem arises when an inappropriate pattern is used. Each institution signals to the learner the family of languages suitable to it. The learner (parishioner, client, student) by entering the institution (parish, therapist's office, school) signifies what language he or she is ready for. In a word, he or she consents to a particular form or a few forms of speech.

When parishioners congregate in a church they consent to homiletic speech. Preaching and storytelling is what they have come to expect. Imaginative and creative storytelling and preaching is what the congregation deserves. These are important languages to every religion. The teacher is obliged to make them accessible. The teacher here may be the preacher, parent, catechist, or lecturer. Those assembled believe in the text. The teacher's task is to enable its members to reflect on its readings and to live up to their commitments. Homiletic speech can function in and outside of church. When all the conditions are right, it can be one the most powerful forms of teaching. It can be morally appropriate and educationally effective. However, when the right conditions are absent, homiletic language can be morally offensive and educationally counterproductive. It is no accident that sermonizing and preaching have, at times, negative connotations. One does not enter a therapist's office to be lectured. On entering the classroom of a school, one does not consent to being preached at. Therapy is not lecturing. Classroom instruction is not preaching. The homiletic has almost no part to play when the classroom teacher is engaged in instruction. Teachers of religion can easily ignore this principle when they slip into moralizing and semi-indoctrinative attitudes.

When a client enters a therapist's office he or she consents to therapeutic language. But the therapeutic, as noted above, is not confined to the professional therapist. The therapeutic can operate in congregational life, in family settings and in the arena of the school. Congregations can experience fracture, families may be ripped apart, and students in school may be wounded. This is the right time for the therapeutic. The teacher's task is to provide comfort, praise, hospitality and rituals for mourning. The aim is to heal, to restore the individual /community to wholeness, so that the ability to choose may be re-established. The teacher here may be the pastor, parent, counselor, spiritual director, chaplain, or schoolteacher. These therapeutic languages are important to all religions. At the right time and place, they are morally appropriate and educationally effective. However, when these conditions are absent, therapeutic speech can be morally offensive and educationally futile. One does not assemble in church on Sunday for therapy. A student does not enter a classroom of a school for therapy treatment. A worship service is not predominantly designed for comforting and consoling. And, therapy should not predominate in the classroom. Teachers of religion who ignore this principle cloud students' view of large areas of life, sacrifice intellectual excellence and pander to students' needs.

When a student enters a classroom in a school he or she consents to a particular kind of discourse, namely, academic speech. Dialectical discussion and academic criticism are what they have come to expect. The schoolteacher is obliged to make them accessible. They are important languages to every religion. While academic discourse can emerge outside the school, the classroom in the school is particularly designed for it. The teaching act here is designed for discussion of ideas and their assumptions. The teacher and students are partners (but not peers) in searching or researching the truth. If the right conditions prevail, the dialogue goes back and forth. The purpose is to move closer to the truth but without fixity, finality or absolutizing. It is academic criticism that keeps open the meaning of words. Its form is interrogative. The students' words, the words of the text and the teacher's words are all subject to public scrutiny. The first question of concern is: What do the words mean? There will be a difference between the intended meaning of the speaker and multiple meanings of what is voiced. This is the space for academic criticism. The teacher asks: What do you mean? Who says so? Why? What are the assumptions? Is there a better way of saying that? The teacher, as advocate, shows and proposes a better way of how to do it. Here, the teacher, par excellence, is the classroom instructor. In the right place and time, academic speech can be the powerful form of teaching, both morally appropriate and educationally effective. However, when these conditions are absent, academic discourse can be educationally counterproductive and morally offensive. A liturgical assembly is not the place for dialectical discussions. A therapist's office, for the most part, is not suitable for academic criticism. Preaching is not dialectical and therapy is not critique. Academic discourse, like every other language, presumes a community. One can not begin or end with criticism. But, when teachers of religion ignore academic discourse beliefs become dogmatic, interpretations closed and traditions idolatrous.

2. Religion: An Academic Construct

In the title of this essay, religion is the direct object of the verb to teach. In twentieth century English, religion has two distinct and very different meanings: (1) It is a word for a set of practices that particular communities engage in. These (religious) communities, with their beliefs, rituals and moral practices, show a way of life. Religion here is what one lives. (2) Religion is also a word to designate a field of academic inquiry[14]. It is an object of scholarly and academic investigation. It is the name of a curriculum subject. Both meanings are well established today, and, both meanings arose together out of the Western Enlightenment. The second meaning is the focus of my attention here and the one I wish to connect to the verb to teach.

Religion is an idea and a concept that was invented in scholarly circles. It appeared as a general idea applicable to a set of things called religions. Religion was adapted as a neutral term by scholars who sought to study particular (religious) communities and compare them to other particular (religious) communities. The focus is on understanding. But one can understand only if one compares. The single act of understanding is directed at multiple objects: the phenomenon of religion. In a world of religious multiplicity, with each group espousing to be the way, religion represents an understanding that the conflicting claims of traditional groups can be examined, critiqued and compared. The concept implies understanding one (or one's own) religious position in relation to the other possibilities. This is a quite recent idea. The claim is: religion can be a subject in the school curriculum. It can stand next to psychology, politics or pharmacology. As an idea (of comparison) and a method (of inquiry) posited by scholars, it represents a commitment to use the mind in a search for truth. This willingness to use the mind to understand one community (e.g. Christians) in light of other people (e.g. Jews) deserves to be called "the study and teaching of religion".

---

14. G. MORAN, *Religious Education as a Second Language* (n. 8), pp. 123-124.

Where is the appropriate setting for this form of inquiry? The modern classroom in the school is surely one place where it belongs. "It was practically invented for the classroom," notes Moran, "there is no place where religion more comfortably fits than in the academic curriculum"[15]. One preaches the Christian message, but one academically teaches religion. The school teacher steps back from the practice of the Christian, Jewish or Buddhists ways of life so as to examine Christian, Jewish or Buddhist discourse. The teaching tools for this activity are dialectical discussion and academic criticism. When used properly these languages open up richer meaning(s). They can be transformative.

3. An Interpretative Framework: Religious Education

Before exploring the state of teaching religion in various settings in the US, I will briefly set a comprehensive context for the discussion. In some of his most recent writings, Moran calls attention to the ambiguity in the term religious education in different parts of the world. He points out the term operates with two different and contrasting meanings on both sides of the Atlantic Ocean. There are very good reasons, he claims, why these two distinct realities need to have the same name. His project is to unveil the richest meaning of religious education. This emerging meaning can embrace both sides, honor the distinctiveness of each, and, yet affirm their relatedness[16].

In this comprehensive framework, religious education has two faces. A complete contrast between the two faces would include describing the who, what, how, where, and why of each. This would take us beyond the scope of this essay. However, I will briefly sketch a number of these components. The two faces of religious education can be described as 1) teaching people to be religious in a particular way and, 2) teaching people religion. The two forms have sharply contrasting aims, processes, recipients and settings. The two aspects of religious education are not simply parallel; nor do they locate people in separate compartments. They are necessarily bound together. People need access to both, although at some moments in life one of them is likely to dominate. The first face of religious education is to teach people to live religion i.e.

---

15. G. MORAN, *Religious Education as a Second Language* (n. 8), p. 124.

16. *Ibid.,* pp. 216-242; see also M. HARRIS & G. MORAN, *Reshaping Religious Education*, Louisville KY, Westminster – John Knox, 1998, pp. 30-43.

a particular religious way of life. This is the educational work of formation, initiation or induction into the practices and mission of the group.
In this process, the aim is to teach the recipient to be a devout Catholic,
observant Jew or practicing Muslim. One is trying to form new members "in the faith". This is an ancient process familiar to the great religious traditions. Catholics have named it catechesis and Protestants
Christian nurture/education[17]. This meaning of religious education
flourishes in the US. With respect to age, the recipients tend to be children, although there is an emerging recognition that formation can continue throughout life[18]. The teacher here is the catechist, preacher, parent and, in fact, the whole community. People accept the community
text – or are inquirers or initiands. The teaching languages are mostly
homiletic and therapeutic. However, most of the teaching is non-verbal.
This is especially true for the moral and /or religious life. The two major
teaching forms are liturgy and the works of service. And, the appropriate educational settings are the family, religious community, and the
school – but not the classroom of the school. This face of religious education shows peoples how to live. It is the teaching of activities, a set of
practices, and a code of conduct and rituals, for immersion into a concrete and particular communal way of life. This form of religious education is indispensable in the (post) modern world. The second face of
religious education is to teach religion. Religion here is an academic
construct. This is the educational work of stepping back from the practices of a religious way and trying to understand them. This form of
education is mostly a matter of the mind. We use the muscles of the
mind to explore, question and critique. In this process, the aim is to
teach the recipient to understand religion. In order to understand, however, one must compare. Teaching religion aims at understanding one's
own tradition in relation to the religious life of others. The aim is not
change of behavior but change in understanding. This meaning of religious education flourishes in Great Britain and other parts of the world.
In terms of age, this process could begin with older children, increase
during the teenage years, and reach its full fruition during the adult
years. The teacher here is the schoolteacher. The teaching languages are
dialectical discussion and academic criticism. And, the appropriate educational setting is the classroom in the school. In (post) modern times,

17. I trace the history of these terms in my *Communicative Competence and Religious
Education*, in *Lumen Vitae* 35 (1980) 75-96.
18. See the US Catholic Bishops Pastoral plan for adult faith formation in their document, *Our Hearts Were Burning Within Us*, Washington DC, USCC, 1999.

this form of religious education is indispensable to peace and harmony in the world.

Religious education, then, stands Janus-faced. One side faces practice. The other faces understanding. Each are inextricably related to the other. Practice without understanding can become blind, narrow and prejudicial. Understanding without practice can become abstract, detached, and lacking in appreciation. Of course, not every religious educator can do both kinds of education. Most teachers may devote themselves to accomplishing one of these aims. However, they should know another aim exists. It is in the interplay and integration of the two aims, however, where religious education is most developmentally mature. This is the comprehensive context in which I wish to explore the academic teaching of religion in public schools and religiously affiliated schools in the United States.

4. To Teach Religion in US Public and Church Related Schools

Public School

If my explorations to this stage have been logical, intelligible and credible, the parameters I have set for discussion of the teaching religion in the US are restricted and narrowly circumscribed. There is real strength in this restriction. It can clarify the meaning of the terms under discussion, and, thereby, shed light on the particular form of teaching, its object, and its appropriate setting. This, I hope, has been achieved. There is something quite ironic about the state of religious education in the United States. Even though the contemporary movement and Association, as we know it, was born on these shores[19], religious education tends to fly on one wing here. Religious education can mean many things in the US. It can even function under different labels, but one thing it does not mean is "to teach religion" in a public or state school. In the US, religious education never means a subject in the curriculum of the state school. Yet, the teaching of religion in the context of the school is a crucial part of the field of religious education. The teaching of religion in US public schools is constitutionally permissible and educationally desirable, yet, it hardly yet exists. Why the anomaly?

19. Historical sketches of the movement and Association can be found in K. BARKER, *Religious Education, Catechesis and Freedom*, Birmingham AL, Religious Education Press, 1981, pp. 25-72, and in S. SCHMIDT, *A History of the Religious Education Association*, Birmingham AL, Religious Education Press, 1983.

The role of religion in US public schools has always been a topic to stir fiery emotions, controversy and resistance. One might presume that thoughtful discussion on the subject would flourish in educational contexts. However, the opposite is the case. The "taboo" against the schooling in religion has largely been imposed by educators themselves. While a persistent effort has been made by a small group of people over the past four decades to get religion into the curriculum of the public school, progress has been slow[20]. Minimal signs are discernible on the elementary level. In the high school, some initial promising efforts are emerging. While community colleges currently show the most hope. In some states, children do have the opportunity to study religion as a subject, or to study units on religion within literature, social studies, and other subjects. The state of California, for example, has introduce a curricular model for adding the study of four great religions – Judaism, Buddhism, Confucianism, and Christianity to its elementary schools[21]. However, for the most part, the discussion is mired down in fears of law suits and suspicions of indoctrination. The continuing debate on prayer in public school, the posting of the Ten Commandments, and the current focus on character education[22] is also distracting from the central issues. The fundamental problem is the framework in which the discussion takes place. The debate is caught in fixed formulas that seriously limit discussion. The result: there is no readily available language in which to situate the question. Before attending to the linguistic framework, however, the ambivalence toward religion in the US needs to be acknowledged.

The United States is one of the most religious places on earth. Religion (as a lived way of life) is omnipresent in the culture. Since World War II about 93% of US people have expressed allegiance to a religious group. Most people actually engage in religious practice. By almost any scale of measurement, this is a very religious nation. This generally comes as a surprise to most first time visitors. But it was not a surprise

20. I note in particular the journal *Religious & Public Education*, published by the National Council on Religion and Public Education.

21. Two noteworthy publications have appeared recently that describe some curricular developments nationwide, namely J.T. SEARS & J.C. CARPER (eds.), *Curriculum, Religion, and Public Education. Conversations for an Enlarging Public Square*, New York NY, Teachers College Press, 1998; W.A. NORD & C.C. HAYNES, *Taking Religion Seriously Across the Curriculum*, Alexandria VA, Association for Supervision and Curriculum Development, 1998.

22. On character education see T. LICKONA, *Educating for Character*, New York NY, Bantam, 1991. For a survey of the movement, see R. ROSENBLATT, *Teaching Johnny to Be Good*, in *New York Times Magazine*, April 30, 1995, 36-74.

to Alexis de Tocqueville. He cautioned us not to forget that "it was religion that give birth to the English colonies in America" [23]. These religious roots are deep and pervasive today. On the other hand, as Stephen Carter claims in *The Culture of Disbelief* [24], religion has been marginalized and trivialized in public life and culture. It has been distorted as idiosyncratic, exotic, and toxic. Carter chronicles the current US obsession of either brushing off religious convictions as the ravings of the fanatic fringe or domesticating them as private pastimes. In academic circles, religious beliefs are treated as exotic. They are ignored because they emanate from a "foreign epistemology". Scientific rationality remains the dominant way of knowing. And, in a therapeutic obsessed culture [25], religion is an obstacle to mental health. Non-belief is the public sponsored orthodoxy. One of the ironies, then, in US public life, is that for all our religiosity, a profound ambivalence remain. This is also the case in US public schools.

Religion has always been intertwined with the schools in the United States of America. Since the mid-nineteenth century, a "common faith" [26] flowed through the public schooling system. Elements that were presumed to be part of a common religion in the country held a prominent place in the school [27]. Bible readings became prominent rituals and prayers became common practices. This pattern would prevail until the Supreme Court declared the unconstitutionality of devotional exercises in state school [28]. But to this day religion blows through the hallways of the public school. What the school will not do with it, however, is teach it. It simply will not take it seriously as a subject in the curriculum. The assumption is the public schools do not teach religion; That task belongs to religious organizations. Logically it follows: the public schools want no part of teaching religion. This is a great educational scandal in the United States. To shed light on this current predicament, it is necessary to draw attention to the artificial and convoluted language that sets the terms for the debate.

The public school shies away from the language of teaching religion. One has to look far and wide for any discussion by school people of the

---

23. Quoted in ASSOCIATION FOR SUPERVISION AND CURRICULUM DEVELOPMENT, *Religion in the Curriculum*, Washington DC, ASCD, 1987, p. 1.

24. S.L. CARTER, *The Culture of Disbelief*, New York NY, Doubleday, 1993.

25. See R. BELLAH *et al.*, *Habits of the Heart*, Berkeley CA, University of California, 1985, esp. pp. 113-141.

26. J. DEWEY, *A Common Faith*, New Haven CT, Yale University, 1934.

27. See J. WESTERHOFF, *McGuffey and His Readers*, Nashville TN, Abingdon, 1978.

28. *Abington versus Schempp*, 1963.

school doing with religion what schools are supposed to do, namely, teach it and study it. The biggest problem is the absence of a language to discuss religion as a normal part of public education. The discourse gets caught up in a particularly artificial jargon. The two phrases which run throughout the literature are: "Teach about religion" and the "objective study of religion". These two phrases structure the current linguistic framework. And, neither phrase is very helpful. The first phrase is taken from a Superior Court ruling of 1963, although the history of the phrase goes back to the 1940's. Justice Arthur Goldberg in *Abington versus Schempp*[29] offered the distinction between the "teaching of religion" and "teaching about religion" in the public schools. At the time, this comparison was a useful tool of thought in clearing the way for further discussion of religion in state schools. Unfortunately that discussion was not forthcoming except in scattered instances. The court gave a clear directive with the legally orthodox phrase "teaching about religion". The problem emerged when educators take this legal speech and incorporate it into educational language. This is precisely what transpires in the literature. The authors adopt the prevailing and standard legal distinction. The question and the issue becomes: Is it possible to teach religion in public school? The educational literature declares: No, one may only "teach about religion". The phrase is uncritically repeated adnauseum. At its best, it failed to clarify the issue with an artificial language. At its worst, it hides the issue by failing to hone out meaningful educational distinctions.

The two phrases "to teach religion" and "to teach about religion" are now set in logical opposition. On the one side, "to teach religion (or the "teaching of religion") is given over to parents and religious bodies. It is identified with religious nurturing, inculcating and proselytizing. On the other side, "teaching about religion" is given over to the public school. It is identified with being objective, intellectual and critical. Here there is a deliberate distancing of the teaching from a properly academic subject called "religion". The phrase "to teach about religion" creates an artificial notion of objectivity. The same could be said of the phrase "the objective teaching of religion". Schooling emphasizes distancing. It seeks to bring a wide perspective to our premises and personal data. The attempt is to get a question or situation in front of us for careful examination. In this sense school "objectifies". To a degree, in schooling, we bracket our biases, interests and viewpoints in order to

29. *Abington versus Schempp*, 1963.

explore other worldviews. This objectivity is required in all teaching and study. However, the words to a degree are critical. Total or complete objectivity is impossible and indeed unadvisable. Some subjective involvement in the subject matter is vital. It is critical for existential relevance and meaningfulness.

This is important particularly when the subject matter is religion. Objective and subjective, however, when applied to religion can do violence to the material. A subjective approach gets eliminated from schools because it is not objective enough. While a purely objective approach reduces religion to a set of cold data. The key is an interplay between the subjective and objective. This kind of teaching and study is appropriately called inter-subjective[30]. Little progress will be made as long as the discussion on religion in public schools remains captive to clumsy legal phrases and false notions of objectivity. We need to reshape a language of education. In a renewed linguistic framework, an obvious place to examine the meaning of "to teach religion" is the public school.

School is where religion belongs. It can enable the pubic schools to become more public. It can foster religious literacy, cultivate religious understanding and lessen religious prejudice. Religion, however, has been discriminated against in the public sector of education in the United States. Until schoolteachers embrace religious traditions as meaningful and deeply significant educational content, schools will encourage Balkanization rather than genuine pluralism. Ernest Boyer, a leading national commentator on public education, writes, "While no school should impose religious beliefs or practice, I believe, it is simply unimaginable to have quality education in the nations schools without including in the course of study a consideration of how religion has been a central thread in the very fabric of the human story, both here and all around the world … And yet the harsh reality is that in many schools a blanket of silence has smothered this essential study"[31].

Church Related Schools

School is precisely where religion dwells most comfortably. It is an academic category. As an idea and a method, it represents a commitment to use the mind in search for truth, a truth that transcends all

30. See P. PHENIX, *Religion in Public Education: Principles and Issues*, in D. ENGEL (ed.), *Religion in Public Education*, New York NY, Paulist, 1974, p. 67.
31. E. BOYER, *Teaching Religion in the Public Schools*, in *Journal of the American Academy of Religion* 60 (1992) 515-524, p. 517.

institutions. While schools cannot carry all the burden for the formation and the development of a religious way of life, never-the-less, its
limited contribution is vital to intelligent religiousness. Are Christian
(Jewish, Muslim) communities in the US committed to religion? Are
their church affiliated schools hospitable to the idea and method? Or,
are they suspicious and defensive of teaching it? The irony is religiously
sponsored schools in the US are as leery of teaching religion as are public schools. They are not yet doing the teaching job in religion that
needs to be done. Why is this? The problem is not only in what (content) is taught but in the root metaphor (language) of teaching that
undergird their total educational mission. Both, of course, are related.
And, the same problems are shared by Catholic and Protestant schools.

Catholic and Protestant communities give a prominent place to
teaching. What is to be taught, however, is usually very restricted. One
is expected to teach the Word of God (Bible), Christian Doctrine, the
catechism, and the (moral) way. The teacher is also expected to teach by
example. Jesus, the teacher, is the paradigmatic reference point[32]. The
New Testament directs the disciples how to pass on a way of life after
Jesus has departed. The dilemma was: the founder is gone; so how does
the new community engage in traditioning (the process of passing on) a
way of life that can be grasped largely through texts? The early church
initiated a two step (educational) process: preaching and instruction.
First, the word is preached. On the occasion of this announcing, one is
called to conversion. Second, when one becomes a member of the
assembly, he or she is ready for instruction (teaching) in the details of
the faith. The first step is proclamation. The second step is catechetical.
In this model, teaching (as instruction) is a follow up to preaching. And,
in the terms I have employed above, both are part of the homiletic family of languages. The Christian Churches have largely inherited this educational model. Education is initiation, incorporation, induction into
the faith. It is a process of religious socialization, enculturation and maturation in the faith. On the Protestant side, the root metaphor is *nurture*. On the Catholic side, the directing metaphor is *formation*. The
New Testament did not advocate the teaching of religion. (It is after-all
a modern concept). And, in the Christian Churches today, one is not
expected to teach religion. US Catholic and Protestant communities
have a consensus: church education is teaching with an end in view. The

---

32. NATIONAL CONFERENCE OF CATHOLIC BISHOPS, *To Teach as Jesus Did*, Washington DC, USCC, 1973.

end is to produce practicing church members. However, teaching religion does not aim to produce church members, but indirectly it may be necessary for intelligent religious affiliation in a (post) modern world.

Protestant church education in the US operates under the term Christian education. No one has had greater influence on the nature of the enterprise than Horace Bushnell. Bushnell, the honored Father of Protestant education, published his classic work Christian Nurture in the 1840's[33]. It remains influential to this day. Bushnell wrote mainly about the family. His agenda was to offer an alternative to revivalism with its focus on conversion. He stressed the goodness and positive capacities of the child in contrast to the fallenness and depravity emphasized by the revivalists. Bushnell's work had and has a constructive and liberating effect on the church and especially the family. However, his metaphor of nurture became too much of a good thing. The Protestant Sunday school became the "nursery of the church"[34]. Other educational agencies also came under its captivating spell. By lumping all educational activity under the word nurture, Bushnell obscures the distinctive role of the schoolteacher. To this day teachers in Protestant church schools are described as people who nurture children in the faith. When teaching is absorbed by nurture, the teaching of religion (as an academic activity) is excluded. Academic speech is mute and critical inquiry suppressed. This, in large part, is descriptive of Protestant elementary and secondary school classroom instruction. Christian education needs a healthy tension with a complimentary form and family of languages, namely, the academic. This can only come about if it resists the imposition of the nurturing metaphor on all form of teaching.

Catholic church education in the US operates under the term catechesis. Its educational activity revolves around the word and its cognates (catechetics, catechize, catechism). Catechetical language has its roots in the New Testament and the early Church. However, as an internal pattern of language, it is largely a post Vatican II phenomenon in Roman Catholicism. Catechesis is understood as formation in the faith. Its constitutive interest is to awaken, nourish, and develop one's religious identity, to build up the ecclesial body, to hand on the tradition. Its process is one of induction, socialization and maturation in the faith. In any survey of official church documents in the US and beyond, the catechetical

---

33. H. BUSHNELL, *Christian Nurture*, New Haven CT, Yale University, 1967.
34. See J.L. SEYMOUR, *From Sunday School to Church School*, Washington DC, University Press of America, 1982.

enterprise is defined as the total process of formation in the Catholic communal body[35]. It is unabashedly confessional. The communal text is accepted. The educational act is to proclaim and instruct. This is education with an end in view: "to form the faith". The family of teaching languages is predominately homiletic. There assumptions are carried over into Catholic schooling in the US in all its work and mission. Catechesis is the Catholic equivalent of Christian nurture / education.

The scope of catechetical activity also has been significantly expanded in contemporary church literature. The US *National Catechetical Directory* says that the tasks of the catechist are "to proclaim Christ's message, to participate in efforts to develop community, to lead people to worship and prayer, and to motivate them to serve others"[36]. Message, community, worship and service are the four aspects of the work. This, I believe, is over extending the catechetical aspect of the Catholic Church. Etymologically and historically, such a meaning is not well supported. All four aspects are part of the Catholic Church's internal language of religious education. Only the first of the four tasks – proclaiming Christ's message – is clearly the work of the catechist. While the four aspects are clearly related, catechesis is rooted in "echoing the word". Announcing the Gospel, to be followed by an exploration of Christian doctrine, historically has been the core of its activity. It is understood to be one of the Church's educational ministries. Expansion of the term places an excessive burden on catechists, obstructs cooperation between ministries and collapses distinctions critical to the educational work of the church. This can be clearly seen when catechesis enters the Catholic school system, particularly the classroom of the parochial school.

In current catechetical literature, religious instruction in the classroom is understood as a form of catechesis. It is conceptualized as church ministry, has an evangelizing and conversionary intent, and is directed toward formation in the Catholic community of faith[37]. The confessional character of catechism in Catholic school is not disguised. Nor does it need to be. However, classroom instructors in religion have to examine what motivates their teaching. What have the students consented to?

35. Some representative examples include *To Teach as Jesus Did* (n. 32); *Sharing the Light of Faith. National Catechetical Directory for Catholics of the United States*, Washington DC, USCC, 1980; *General Directory for Catechesis*, Washington DC, USCC, 1998.
36. *Sharing the Light of Faith*, # 213.
37. See for example *To Teach as Jesus Did*, # 101-111; *General Directory for Catechesis*, # 73-75 and *The Religious Dimension of Education in a Catholic School*, Washington DC, USCC, 1988, # 66-96.

What languages are appropriate? What assumptions are operating? What processes prevail? Teachers of religion in a Catholic school have to maintain the integrity of their own work. If religion is a part of the school curriculum, there is an academic standard to be met. Academic instruction should not be burdened with the role of catechizing. The child who walks into the classroom of a church related school has the right to expect not catechizing but intellectually demanding accounts of religion. School teachers work in the context of classrooms and an academic curriculum. Catechists work in the context of sacramental life. School teachers teach religion; catechists teach the Gospel and Christian doctrine. Schools, whether public or religiously affiliated, attend to symbols, practices and documents. The catechetical venture is firmly within the framework of forming people to lead a Christian life. Catechetical language is important to preserve. It is an intimate, caressing language that nurtures Catholic life and identity. However, we need an educational language to complement the catechetical. That language transcends the Catholic Church. This academic family of languages is what should hold center stage in Catholic school classrooms.

Graham Rossitier insightfully observes, "there often remains some uncertainty about what teachers in schools are trying to achieve in their religion classes. Too strong a focus on the potential influence of Catholic schooling can obscure the focus on what should happen in a religion class"[38]. The vast scope of its (catechetical) aims, he notes, can cover over and neglect the (academic) teaching of religion. This comes into clear relief when we scrutinize the assumptions in official Catholic documents. The standard phrase in Vatican and US diocesan guidelines is "to present clearly what the church teaches", or "what the magisterium teaches". Clearly that is the what the catechist (or preacher) is supposed to do. But is it the school teacher's task to present that to students? The answer is yes, if the material is relevant to the class topic of the day. But if one wants to teach religion that is a preliminary step in school teaching. As Moran noted, "The schoolteacher's questions are: What does the teaching mean? Where did it come from? What are its limitations? How is it changing? And dozens of similar questions … A schoolteacher's vocation is not to tell people what the truth is or tell them how to act". "The schoolteacher's modest task", he writes, "is to explore the meaning of what is written from the past and to help students articulate their own

38. G. ROSSITER, *The Gap Between Aims and Practice in Religious Education in Catholic Schools*, in *The Living Light* 18 (1981) 158-166, p. 158.

convictions"[39]. The truth or falsity of the church's teaching is not a direct concern of the teacher or student. This tends to upset Catholic Church officials. Their concerns are "orthodoxy" and "heresy". These concerns, however, are on a different wave-length. Both words are irrelevant in the classroom. The teacher of religion teaches the subject matter. He or she teaches the student to think. He or she aids in the understanding of texts. What the student does with this understanding (affirm or dissent) is up to the individual student.

The first aim, then, in teaching religion is to make the material intelligible – or at least to show how it is not unintelligible. The object to be understood is religion, including one's own religion. Some degree of otherness, some basis of comparison is necessary to understand. The other, as Emmanuel Levinas, informs us reveals us to ourselves[40]. The second task in teaching religion is to make the religious text accessible to the students with "disciplined inter-subjectivity"[41]. The text is a mediator between the community of the past and a community of the present. The school teacher's job is to see that the text has a chance to fulfill that role. The discipline of the teacher is key. It must be done with fairness and fullness. Thirdly, the teacher of religion must attend to classroom design. The atmosphere and shape of the setting teaches[42]. While the attitudes of today's students cannot be the curriculum content, neither can these sensibilities and dispositions be ignored. As soon as students step into the classroom space, they enter a zone of freedom. The space ought to be an "ideal speech"[43] situation conducive to a hermeneutic-communicative competence. This teaching-learning design is indispensable if students are to discover the link between (religious) understanding and external (religious) practice[44].

39. G. MORAN, *Of a Kind and to a Degree. A Roman Catholic Respective*, in M. MAYR (ed.), *Does the Church Really Want Religious Education?*, Birmingham AL, Religious Education Press, 1988, p. 30.

40. See T.A. VELING, *Emmanuel Levinas and the Revelation of the Other*, in *Eremos* 61 (1997) Nov., 23-25.

41. P. PHENIX, *Religion in Public Education* (n. 30), p. 67.

42. G. MORAN, *Showing How* (n. 5), pp. 59-79.

43. See J. HABERMAS, *Theory of Communicative Action*. Vol. 1: *Reason and Rationalization in Society*, Boston MA, Beacon, 1984. See also H. LOMBAERTS, *Religion, Society, and the Teaching of Religion in Schools*, in M. WARREN (ed.), *Sourcebook for Modern Catechetics*, Vol. 2., Winona MN, St. Mary's Press, 1997, 306-329, esp. pp. 321-326 for some characteristics of the teaching of religion in the school environment in light of changes in the European continent.

44. G. MORAN, *Showing How* (n. 5), pp. 59-79.

The question may be asked: Would there be a difference in a course on religion in a public school and in a church affiliated school? The question can be answered on two levels: the level of principle and the level of practice. On the level of principle, the teaching act remains constant irrespective of the mission of the school. In the church related school, there will probably be more contextual meaning available because students, it might be assumed, are already practicing a way that embodies some religious meaning. This leaves room for a difference in emphasis but there should be no contradiction between what is taught in the two schools.

On the level of practice, however, the question of context can get very complex. Some Catholic schools in the US today have a student body that is less than 50% Catholic. Many have faculties that are predominately non-Catholic. Some Catholic students also may be in a state of rebellion against their religious formation and resistant to religion. In various geographical regions in the US, some public schools have a large Hindu, Buddhist, Jewish or Catholic student body. In each case, the material can differ but what is done with the curriculum should not essentially differ whether the school is related to the church or not. A course on the sacraments could be taught in a public school. While sacred Jewish texts might be taught in a Catholic school. Indeed, Gabriel Moran writes, "A good test of whether religion is being taught to Catholic students is whether the class is appropriate for non-Catholic students. If the school has to exempt the non-Catholic student from religion class, that would be an admission that what is going on in those classes is something other than the instruction proper to a classroom"[45]. There may be political and institutional difficulties, but the direction is clear: to teach religion in public or church related schools is an academic vocation. Its teaching languages are dialectical discussion and academic criticism.

Throughout this essay, I have held in abeyance the proposal to reconceptualize religious education as practical theology. As you might guess, I am resistant to the proposal. The face of religious education explored here is part of a larger and wider *educational* venture. Practical theology may find a place *within* the other aspect of religious education, namely, to teach people to be religious. Christian theology, of course, can be a rich source of study. However, when theological content is taken into the classroom of the school it becomes the teaching of religion. The

---

45. G. MORAN, *Religious Education as a Second Language* (n. 8), p. 158.

texts are not assumed to be believed. The process is not "faith seeking understanding" (Anselm). Rather the theological content becomes subject to the same investigation, critique, interpretation, comparison, rejection or acceptance as any curriculum content. The teacher of religion is not an evangelized for the church. He or she is an advocate for richer words and meaning. The aim is to understand one's own religious tradition in relation to other people. Religious pluralism has been the condition that has led to teaching religion, but teaching religion in the US public and church related schools is the condition for sustaining religious pluralism in the Third Millennium.

Catechesis and Religious Instruction in Catholic Schools Perspectives of the *General Directory for Catechesis* (1997)

Catherine Dooley

The attempt to address the issue of the nature of religious instruction in Catholic schools and its relationship to catechesis is one of the innovations of the 1997 *General Directory for Catechesis* (GDC)[1]. The first *General Catechetical Directory* in 1971 made almost no mention of the schools except in the framework of the developmental level of the child and the importance of the home environment. The focus of the GDC is catechesis, both initiatory and life long; therefore the GDC makes a clear distinction between religious instruction and catechesis. It does assert, however, that there is a complementarity between these two forms of the ministry of the word (73). Admittedly, the discussion of religious instruction in the schools in the 1997 Directory extends to only a few paragraphs (73-76; 259-260) but offers some important clarifications and directives. In this article, I will focus on three aspects. The first is the fundamental themes of the GDC that provide the context for religious instruction in the schools. The second aspect is the purpose delineated by the GDC for religious instruction in the schools, and thirdly, some of the implications of these directives.

Introduction

The 1997 GDC is a revision of *General Catechetical Directory* promulgated in 1971[2]. Although it retains the basic structure of the 1971 Directory, the GDC addresses new needs and new developments in catechesis. The GDC aims to balance two aspects: to contextualize catechesis in evangelization as proposed by Pope Paul VI in *Evangelii Nuntiandi*

---

1. The paragraphs of the GDC that are discussed in this essay, will be placed between brackets in the corpus of the text.

2. For notes and commentary on the 1971 Directory, see B. MARTHALER, *Catechetics in Context*, Huntington IN, Our Sunday Visitor Press, 1973.

(Evangelization in the Modern World) and to appropriate the content of the faith as presented in the *Catechism of the Catholic Church* (7). The purpose of the Directory is to offer "reflections and principles, rather than immediate applications or practical directives" (9) and is addressed primarily to the Bishops, Episcopal conferences and in a general way to those who have responsibility for catechesis. It aims to provide fundamental theological and pastoral principles drawn from the church's magisterium and particularly those inspired by the Second Vatican Council that can better orientate and coordinate the pastoral activity of the ministry of the word, concretely catechesis (9). Its immediate purpose is to assist in the adaptation of the guidelines and principles of the GDC to local circumstances.

Along with evangelization, the appropriation of the *Catechism of the Catholic Church* (CCC) is foundational in the GDC. The CCC is an official text of the Church's magisterium and is offered to the entire Church[3]. The CCC and the GDC are two distinct but interdependent means of handing on the faith. The 1971 *General Catechetical Directory* contained a chapter on doctrine under the title, "The Most Outstanding Elements of the Christian Message". The new Directory does not include a specific section on doctrinal concepts but acknowledges the CCC as a reference and "methodological norm" for the concrete application of the Christian message (20). The CCC with its four integrated pillars of profession of faith, the sacraments of faith, the life of faith, and the prayer of the believer, seeks to deepen the understanding of faith so that it might be lived in the service of others. Its structure arises from the unity of the Christian life. It is a call to integral Christian education in the four interrelated tasks of catechesis and for the compilation of local catechisms (122). These local catechisms will take into account the various situations and cultures of particular peoples of the world, while maintaining unity of faith and fidelity to the teachings of the Gospel. In comparison to the GCD of 1971 but in continuity with it, the GDC offers a broader perspective of the nature and purpose of catechesis/religious education.

The GDC draws its vision from the Scriptures, the teachings of the early Fathers of the Church, the writings of Vatican II and the *Rite of Christian Initiation of Adults* (1988). The apostolic exhortation of Pope Paul VI in 1975 *Evangelii Nuntiandi* and the exhortations and encyclicals

---

3. See J. KOMONCHAK, *The Authority of the Catechism*, in B. MARTHALER (ed.), *Introducing the Catechism of the Catholic Church*, Mahwah NJ, Paulist Press, 1994, 18-31.

of Pope John Paul II, are of particular importance in the formation of the GDC. Catechesis has been a major theme in the writings of John Paul II beginning with *Catechesi Tradendae* (Catechesis in Our Times, 1979) and continuing through all of his works, especially *Redemptoris Missio* (Mission of the Redeemer, 1990)[4]. There is both continuity and development in the thought expressed in these documents.

In the GDC, evangelization is the umbrella or organizing principle. It permeates all the aspects of the document. Pope Paul VI writes that evangelization means "bringing the Good News into all strata of humanity, and through its influence transforming humanity from within and making it new" (*Evangelii Nuntiandi*, 18)[5]. In the activity of evangelizing, there are certain interrelated elements. These are a personal commitment and witness of a Christian life, proclamation of the word and preaching that elicits a response of conversion, initial and ongoing catechesis, participation in sacramental celebrations, and actions of charity and justice. No one element alone identifies evangelization. Paul VI wrote that evangelization always begins with the person and comes back to "the relationships of people among themselves and with God" (*Evangelii Nuntiandi*, 20). In beginning with the person, evangelization is intrinsically bound to inculturation, popular devotions, ecumenical and interreligious dialogue. Evangelization is the work of the entire church. It is directed toward non-believers; the religiously indifferent; those entering the church or the baptized who are uncatechized, and also for those who are committed Christians (*Evangelii Nuntiandi*, 49).

In the GDC, catechesis is described as "a moment, an essential moment in the process of evangelization". It is a fundamental ecclesial service for the realization of the church's missionary mandate of Jesus (59). In the context of evangelization, catechesis is an integral part of the primary proclamation, which is addressed to non-believers and those who are indifferent to religion. Its purpose is to call the hearers to conversion by the proclamation of the word of God. Although catechesis is distinct ("complementary distinction") from primary proclamation, its function is to promote and deepen the initial conversion,

---

4. For a review of the development of the church's official teaching on evangelization and catechesis from the *General Catechetical Directory* (1971) to the *Catechism of the Catholic Church* (1992), see P.C. PHAN, *Catechesis and the Catechism as an Instrument of Evangelization: Reflections from the Perspective of Asia*, in *Studia Missionalia* 48 (1999) 289-312.

5. The quotations from *On Evangelization in the Modern World* and *Catechesis in Our Time* are taken from *The Catechetical Documents: A Parish Resource*, Chicago, Liturgy Training Publications, 1996.

educate in faith and initiate the individual into the Christian community (61). The GDC, however, admits that in pastoral practice, it is not always easy to separate these two activities. The *"missio ad gentes"* is usually achieved in the pre-catechumenate (62). This first proclamation prepares for catechesis. The task of catechesis is to provide a period of formation, an apprenticeship in the Christian life that encourages a living, explicit and fruitful profession of faith within the experience of Christian living. This initiatory catechesis is the bridge between the first call to faith and the ongoing catechesis that is addressed to the Christian community. This initiatory catechesis must be comprehensive and systematic, include not only instruction but also formation in the Christian life, and initiation into the Christian community.

Continuing or lifelong formation follows this initial catechesis. The life long catechesis depends upon a Christian community that welcomes the newly initiated, supports them and forms them in the faith. This ongoing formation is not only directed to the individual Christian but to the Christian community in itself. Ongoing catechesis can take many different forms, for example: study of the bible, the social teaching of the church, liturgical catechesis, spiritual formation, theological education, and theological reflection. Consideration is also given to the nature of religious instruction in the schools. This instruction is also evangelization in so far as "it is called to penetrate a particular area of culture and to relate with other areas of culture ... it sows the dynamic seed of the Gospel and seeks to keep in touch with other elements of the student's knowledge and education" (73).

In all of these forms of catechesis, there are the same basic elements: knowledge of scripture and tradition, moral formation, worship and prayer. Two other tasks are education for community life, which includes an ecumenical dimension and a missionary initiation that comprises interreligious dialogue. The GDC is clear that all these tasks are necessary: "When catechesis omits one of these elements, the Christian faith does not attain full development" (87).

1. Basic Themes of the GDC

Evangelization is the heart of the document. All of the themes on which the GDC is based are interrelated with evangelization. The main themes are the responsibility of the whole community in the process of catechesis, the baptismal catechumenate as the model and inculturation. These aspects provide the framework for religious instruction in the schools.

Catechesis is the Responsibility of the Entire Christian Community

Many of the catechetical documents focus on the formation of community as one of the tasks of an evangelizing catechesis. The GDC states that not only is the community the locus for catechesis but adds that the community is also the content of catechesis. Catechesis not only takes place in the community but it takes place through the community. Moreover, the GDC declares that the primary agent of catechesis is the community as community (168). "Catechesis will be effective to the extent that the Christian community becomes a point of concrete reference for the faith journey of individuals" (158). The role of the community is to be a place of visible faith witness that provides for the formation of its members. It constitutes itself as the living context for growth in the faith. The GDC is realistic when it asserts that "Christian community life is not realized spontaneously. It is necessary to educate it carefully" (86).

The school is to be an educational community. The Declaration on Education of Vatican II, *Gravissimum Educationis* (28 October 1965), made "a decisive change in the history of Catholic schools: the move from school as institution to school as community"[6]. This change can sometimes create a tension. The aim, methods and characteristics are the same as any other school, yet the school is a Christian community whose entire philosophy is rooted in Christ and his gospel. The context of this educational task is the community, all who are directly involved in the life of the school. Enlivened by a spirit of liberty and charity, this community is to orient the whole of human culture in the light of the gospel (259). This will be accomplished by the relationships within the school community. It is not just what teachers and other authority figures say but what they are and what they do and how they relate to the young person.

---

6. See *The Religious Dimension of Education in the Catholic School* (document of the Congregation of Catholic Education, April 1988), quoted in *The Catechetical Documents: A Parish Resource*, pp. 493-529, here paragraph 31.

The Baptismal Catechumenate is the Model of All Catechesis[7]

The emphasis of the GDC on the baptismal catechumenate as model for all catechesis is based on the premise that catechesis is by nature ecclesial. The document notes that initial catechesis takes place in the context of the catechumenate. Characteristics of this initial formation are that it incorporates the individual into the community through the community's life, prayer and worship. It is educational in that it is a critical reflection on experience in the light of the Gospel and faith tradition. It is instructional in that it enables the catechumen to acquire knowledge and skills to live a responsible, personal and communal Christian life. A systematic presentation of Christian belief enables the catechumen to articulate faith. Post-baptismal catechesis is to draw its inspiration and its dynamism from the baptismal catechumenate. This does not mean that structure of the catechumenate is to be "slavishly followed" but rather, on-going or post-baptismal catechesis is to have a catechumenal style, an integral formation rather than mere information. It includes the same elements of gradual formation, word and ritual. It must act "as a means of arousing true conversion" (29).

The GDC offers some principles that are to be the source of inspiration for post-baptismal catechesis (69-72). These are:
– The need for a Christian community to support ongoing conversion.
– The importance of the sacraments of initiation for the whole of the Christian life. All other sacraments are in relationship to them.
– The paschal mystery is the heart of catechesis and the paradigm of the Christian life. The Easter vigil and its spirituality of baptism is the motivating source of all catechesis.
– Catechumenate is the initial locus of inculturation. Inculturation is the work of the whole community. God became human in a concrete,

---

7. The baptismal catechumenate as the model of all catechesis is not an innovation of the GDC but is found in the "Message to the People of God" (8) following the synod on "Catechesis in Our Time" in October of 1977. The document of the 1990 International Council for Catechesis, "Adult Catechesis in the Christian Community" (66) states that the baptismal catechumenate is the most appropriate mode. The Congregation for the Clergy sent questionnaires to the presidents of the catechetical commissions of the Episcopal conferences, to the major catechetical centers, to the members of the International Council for Catechesis (Coincat) and to other catechetical experts. The final drafts were written by Bishop Estepa Llaurens, Military Ordinary for the Spanish Armed Forces, and Don Cesare Bissoli, SDB of the Salesian University in Rome. Both are recognized leaders in the catechetical field.

historical moment; the church receives catechumens together with their cultural ties.

- The Eucharistic celebration, the table of the word of God and of the body of Christ, is essential for the journey of faith. The homily has importance in the liturgy of the word because it fosters the journey of faith promoted by catechesis.
- Catechesis has many forms. Some of these are study of the sacred scripture, of the social teaching of the church, liturgical catechesis, and reflection on daily life in terms of the gospel, spiritual formation, and theological instruction.

Inculturation

The purpose of the directory is to adapt to new situations and needs. Churches in almost every country now have a multi-cultural face. Many peoples with the hope of a better life, free from poverty and oppression, are fleeing their native countries. Vatican II was a significant turning point, where a large number of Roman-Catholic Bishops came from Africa, Asia, Latin America and Oceania. The church took on a world-view, characterized by pluralism and new theological and pastoral issues. As A. Shorter notes: "The theology of this multicultural Church is Inculturation Theology, the recognition that faith must become culture, if it is to be received and lived"[8]. Inculturation is not simply an external adaptation designed to make the Christian message more attractive. On the contrary it means the penetration of the strata of persons and peoples by the gospel which touches them deeply, going to the very center and roots of their cultures. The criteria for inculturation are compatibility with the gospel and communion with the universal church. Inculturation needs to take place gradually in such a way that it really is an expression of the experience of the Christian community (109). The GDC describes inculturation as a profound and global process and as a slow journey (109). Many theologians describe stages of inculturation: enculturation as the process of socialization into one's own culture; acculturation is the dynamic encounter between one culture and another; and inculturation which is a theological concept[9]. Shorter gives

8. A. SHORTER, *Toward A Theology of Inculturation*, Maryknoll NY, Orbis Books, 1988, p. xi.
9. *Ibid.*, pp. 1-16, gives a good understanding of the terms. Some authors are dissatisfied with the term inculturation because it seems to imply a one-way process. Some, for example J. Blomjousk, uses intercultural to emphasize the reciprocal character of

a brief description of inculturation as the ongoing dialogue between faith and culture or cultures. Inculturation is not only the first insertion of the Christian message into a culture in which the Gospel has not been proclaimed and preached, but it is an on-going mutual process of dialogue.

Catechesis has several tasks in this process of inculturation; namely, to recognize the ecclesial community as a primary agent of incultura-tion; to produce local catechisms that respond to the needs of particu-lar cultures; to make the catechumenate and catechetical institutes into centers of inculturation. Its task is also "prepare those who are to pro-claim the gospel to be capable of giving reasons for their hope in cul-tures often pagan or post-Christian" (110). It is this last aspect that is a particular responsibility of Catholic schools.

2. Religious Instruction in Schools

The GDC provides some basic principles for religious instruction in Catholic schools. The first is that every student has "the right to learn with truth and certainty the religion to which they belong. This right to know Christ, and the salvific message proclaimed by Him cannot be neglected" (74). The GDC recognizes that there are different contexts in which religious instruction takes place and instruction must be adapted to that particular situation. In the Catholic school the confes-sional character of religious instruction must be guaranteed and be completed by other forms of the ministry of the word (catechesis, homilies, liturgical celebrations, etc). In state schools or non-confes-sional schools the teaching of religion will take on a more ecumenical form and include a greater interreligious awareness. In other circum-stances, religious instruction will focus on all the great world religions, including the Catholic tradition. The local church and the Episcopal conference have the responsibility to establish guidelines for these par-ticular situations.

mission [*Development in Mission Thinking and Practice, 1959-1980. Inculturation and Interculturation*, in *African Ecclesial Review* 22 (1980) 393]. Shorter supports the use of the term intercultural. Other terms are contextualization (role of context) indigenization (theology is done by and for a given geographical area), and localization (dynamic inter-action among gospel, church and culture). Although there are different nuances in meaning all point to the need to bring the Gospel into the very heart of culture and cul-tures. A discussion of this terminology can be found in R. J. SCHREITER, *Constructing Local Theologies*, Maryknoll NY, Orbis Books, 1985, pp. 5-21.

Secondly, the GDC states that there is an absolute necessity to distinguish clearly between religious instruction and catechesis (73)[10]. For many people these two terms are synonymous. In fact, many of the religion programs used in schools are billed as catechetical materials but are in fact textbooks for religious instruction. Moreover, there is often very little clarity about the nature and purpose of the religion program in some schools. The GDC offers a clear position: religious instruction is a "scholastic discipline with the same systematic demands and the same rigor as other disciplines" (73). This instruction is to be complemented by catechesis within the context of an educational community. This position provides a starting point for discussion and evaluation of an individual school.

In distinguishing the two endeavors, the GDC refers to the publication of the Congregation for Catholic Education, "The Religious Dimension of Education in the Catholic School"[11], which states that the aim of catechesis is maturity: spiritual, liturgical, sacramental and apostolic. Catechesis is life long and occurs within the local Church community. Catechesis is the responsibility of the entire community. The Congregation for Catholic Education delineates the distinct characteristic of catechesis: "Unlike religious instruction, catechesis presupposes that the hearer is receiving the Christian message as a salvific reality"[12]. The assumption here is that catechesis fosters conversion and Christian faith is a lifelong process of conversion to Jesus Christ. It is a complete and sincere following of Jesus Christ, making oneself his disciple. This transformation of mind and heart causes the believer to live that commitment within the context of the community of believers and in the faith of the church (53-55).

The purpose of the school, according to the GDC is to impart a systematic knowledge of Christian faith. Religious instruction in the schools is to have the same depth and systematic presentation as other subjects in the school (73). The distinctiveness of the Catholic School is its religious dimension that is manifested in the educational community, the personal development of each student, the relationship established between culture and the Gospel, and the perspective of life in the light of faith. In

---

10. See M. WARREN, *Catechesis: An Enriching Category for Religious Education*, in ID. (ed.), *Sourcebook for Modern Catechetics*, Vol. 1, Winona MN, St. Mary's Press, 1983, 379-394. This remains the best discussion to date in English on the complementarity and distinction between religious education and catechesis.

11. *The Religious Dimension of Education in the Catholic School* (n. 6).

12. *Ibid.*, par. 68.

other words, the school aims to foster an integrated formation that prepares the students to contribute to the welfare of others and to "work for
the extension of the Kingdom of God so that by living an exemplary and
apostolic life they may be, as it were, a saving leaven in the community"[13]. The education community includes the parents since education
in the Christian home, together with religious instruction and catechesis
are basic to the formation of children and young people (60).

The distinction between religious instruction and catechesis does not
obscure the fact that the school plays a significant role in the process of
catechesis[14]. All authentic formation includes information but that
information needs to be within the context of a community, celebrated
in liturgical ritual and relevant to the life of a Christian. Religious
instruction is part of and completed by liturgical formation (74). Religious instruction, as an original form of the ministry of the word[15],
makes present the gospel in a personal process of cultural, systematic
and ritual assimilation (73). It challenges the students to think through
the religious questions that relate to their own particular field of learning. Religious instruction aims to enable students to see their faith not
just in terms of religious practices but rather in all aspects of their life.

A third directive of the GDC is that religious instruction needs to be
interdisciplinary so that that there is a link between human learning and
religious awareness (73). "In this way the presentation of Christian doctrine influences the way in which the origin of the world, the sense of
history, the basis of ethical values, the function of religion in nature, the
destiny of humankind and its relation to nature is understood" (73). An
interdisciplinary approach presumes a different mind-set on the part of
teachers and curriculum planners. As Professor Herman Lombaerts

---

13. *Gravissimum Educationis*, par. 8.

14. At the May 2000 meeting, the Bishops' conference of England and Wales published a statement on Religious Education in the schools, describes the school as a catechetical community and states that the purpose of religious education is primarily educational because its "primary purpose is to draw pupils into a systematic study of the
teaching of the church, the saving mystery of Christ which the church proclaims". This
educational mission includes daily prayer, celebration of the sacraments, works of charity, a striving for justice and a sharing of the life of faith (see www.catholic-ew.org.uk).

15. B. MARTHALER, *Sowing Seeds: Notes and Comments on the General Directory for
Catechesis*, Washington DC, United States Catholic Conference, 2000, p. 22, clarifies
the meaning of "an original form of the ministry of the word": "It refers, as the context
and reference to *Catechesi Tradendae* suggest, to a characteristic that distinguishes such
ministry from other forms. Religious instruction in schools is distinctive not because it
engages in dialogue with culture in a generalized way, but rather because it promotes
'dialogue in a personal process of systematic and critical initiation and by encounter
with the cultural patrimony promoted by that [particular] school'".

notes, the linear way of thinking about the catechetical task is that the content (theology) is taught by an appropriate method (pedagogy) to the student. Lombaerts asserts that this mode of thinking must give way to a process that focuses on the "interaction between the church as institution and the sociological, economic, and political environment"[16]. In an interdisciplinary approach that incorporates various other disciplines, the catechetical question would change from an emphasis only on the learning of content to the meaning for one's life and to action out of Christian values. Religious instruction, integrated into the overall education of the students, is the special character of a Catholic school and the underlying reason for its existence[17].

An interdisciplinary approach presupposes the concept of culture. Culture has several aspects. First, it is a system of beliefs, values, attitudes and norms for behavior. It provides a particular way of looking at the world that shapes one's actions and deepens one's identity. Secondly, rituals, particularly communal celebrations, constitute culture. Celebrations affirm one's identity as belonging to the group and offer a worldview that shapes one's actions. Thirdly, there are the symbols and the objects, such as language, food, clothing, music art, and creation of space. All three aspects need to be kept in mind in understanding a particular culture. Because of the large amount of time that students spend in school or in school related activities, the school has an opportunity in an interdisciplinary way to explore aspects of culture and to acculturate students. Time is an important factor in addressing these issues and the years of schooling provide that time.

The GDC points out that teachers of religion need to be aware of the fact that the life and faith of students are in continuous change (75). Some students are believers, some are searching and some are non-believers. The teacher needs to be sensitive to the different levels of involvement. The student's faith and life is in continuous change and so the questions for each group will be different. In situations like this there is a tendency to explain (and sometimes moralize) rather than to explore the issue. The teacher's input is necessary but only after the student has been challenged to think about the question. It has to be an honest exchange.

---

16. H. LOMBAERTS, *Catechetics and the Formation of Catechists*, in M. WARREN (ed.), *Sourcebook for Modern Catechetics*, Vol. 2, Winona MN, St. Mary's Press, 1997, pp. 185-186.

17. *The Religious Dimension of Education in the Catholic School*, par. 66.

The distinctiveness of the Catholic school, an interdisciplinary scholastic approach, relation with culture, and complementarity of catechesis and religious education are then some of the aspects that the GDC sees as foundational to religious instruction in the schools.

3. Implications for Catechists and Teachers

What then are some of the implications of these directives? First, it is essential to see the unity of the catechetical tasks. One of the ways in which catechesis can complement religious education in the schools is to bring to the fore the organic whole of the process. Sometimes it seems as though placing the emphasis on doctrine will cure all the catechetical woes that are so often bandied about. Knowledge of the basic teaching of the church is essential to the Christian life. Students need to be able to reflect upon, appropriate and articulate their faith. Faith a relationship with God; this relationship is expressed in various ways. Unless the faith that students profess is celebrated and lived, it often becomes intellectualized and compartmentalized without real effect upon daily lives. This unity of faith professed, celebrated, lived and prayed is the structure of the CCC, which time and again speaks of organic unity and the presentation of the Catholic faith in its entirety. This unity is also given attention in many sections of the GDC, which states emphatically that all the tasks of catechesis: knowledge of the faith, liturgical life, moral formation, prayer, belonging to community, missionary spirit, are essential. "When catechesis omits one of these elements, the Christian faith does not attain full development" (87). This is the reason that the GDC insists that religious instruction should be complemented by catechesis. The homilies, the liturgical celebrations, family life, the life of the community and its apostolic mission are powerful means of catechesis. The effectiveness of catechesis depends upon all of these factors and not on religious instruction alone.

The GDC affirms the need for interdisciplinary education. The questions involving religion and science, the bible and literature, environment and ethics, life issues, oppression of peoples, racism, poverty are just some examples. Certainly concern for social justice and the social teachings of the church should permeate the entire curriculum. The Bible is a rich source for the discussion of an ethical response to the obligations inherent in the pursuit of justice, mercy and peace. Another source is the CCC in its treatment of the commandments. The section on the moral life incorporates the social teachings of the church and offers a contemporary way of understanding the covenant. Themes presented in the Bible and in the CCC need to be related to the discussion of the papal encyclicals and episcopal writings on Catholic social teachings. The Synod of Bishops in 1971 made a very emphatic statement on the social ministry of the church: "Action on behalf of justice and participation in the transformation of the world fully appear to us as a constitutive dimension of the preaching of the Gospel, or in other words, of the Church's mission of the redemption of the human race and its liberation from every oppressive situation"[18]. An interdisciplinary approach will increase awareness of the responsibility to a global community. It exposes the social and economic inequalities and dictates the need to actively promote the dignity of all human persons.

Interdisciplinary education includes an ecumenical and interreligious content. Most teachers recognize that the homogenous Catholic culture is a thing of the past and are becoming more and more aware through their classroom and neighborhood experience that we live in a multicultural, world community. It is essential that students know, respect and esteem one another's beliefs and traditions. This is a way to overcome the prejudices of the past and raise a barrier against the forms of anti-Semitism, racism and xenophobia, which continues to crop up in different places and at different times. Such an education leads to a transformation of the individual and to preparation for engagement in secular society.

Religious instruction needs to be completed by liturgical catechesis. The examples of liturgical catechesis indicated by the GDC are catechesis, homilies, liturgical celebrations, etc. The CCC describes liturgical catechesis as initiating people into the mystery of Christ by proceeding from the visible to the invisible, from the sign to the thing signified, from the "sacraments" to the "mysteries"[19]. Liturgical catechesis is an integrated process, rooted in rites, symbols and biblical and liturgical signs in the context of the community within the framework of the liturgical year. The ultimate aim is to enable the Christian community to have full and active participation in the liturgy so that they might express that faith and live it in their daily lives. Very often teachers and catechists see ritual and prayer as a kind of an add-on, another activity

---

18. SYNOD OF BISHOPS (1971), *Justice in the World*, in *Acta Apostolicae Sedis* 63 (1971) 923-942.
19. CCC, par. 1075.

that can be included if there is time. We live in a world in which the
rational is the measure of school entrance, of intelligence quotient and
test scores. Catechesis not only involves rational thought, content and
memory but also imagination, action and transformation. Teachers need
to recognize the role that ritual, symbols and images play in the formation of an individual's faith and identity. The power of ritual and symbol to "teach" in its own way, that is non-discursive, intuitive and open-
ended, needs to be affirmed. The ritual signs used in the liturgy: the
gathering of the assembly: signing with the cross, proclaiming the word;
laying on of hands; anointing, illuminating, being immersed into water
and sharing the eucharistic bread and wine are not something outside
the experience of young people. Rather these rituals build on the human
experiences of children, such as the activity of the community, exchange
of greetings, capacity to listen and to seek and grant pardon, expression
of gratitude, experience of symbolic actions, a meal of friendship and
festive celebrations[20]. Teachers and catechists have the responsibility to
help students to see the connection and the meaning of these actions.
Above all, teachers and catechists need to learn to trust the non-verbal
and the experiential nature of ritual, which has the power to form and
transform those who participate.

It is almost a truism to say that parents are the first and primary educators of their children. Parents are not always aware of this and it is the
school's responsibility to help them to recognize their role as educators.
The school often holds parents' meetings to explain procedures and
policies but the meetings should also provide an ongoing formation in
faith (71). We often speak of parents as partners but need to evaluate the
extent to which they are involved in the educational aims of the school
or are incorporated into the school community.

The greatest challenge underlying these qualities of religious instruction
in the schools is the training of teachers and catechists. The formation of
catechists requires that they have a sufficient knowledge of the message
that they transmit, of those to whom they hand on the message and
of the social context in which they live (238). Teachers/catechists need
to interact with the broad social situation in which catechesis
and religious instruction takes place[21]. Such interaction comprises four

20. *Directory for Masses with Children*, Washington DC, United States Catholic
Conference, 1965, par. 9.
21. See par. 193-214 of the GDC on socio-religious and socio-cultural context of catechesis.

interpretive analyses[22]. The first of these steps is to discern the impact that the culture or social context has on the church; secondly, to listen to what is happening in the midst of ecclesial life; and next, to discern what skills and competencies are needed to enable Christians to live as disciples of Jesus. The final step is to evaluate in light of these three analyses. Some catechists only focus on the content or the activities and are unaccustomed to looking at the context in which young people learn. We cannot, however continue to be blind about the current situation in which we live. The multi-cultural and multi-religious groups, which fill our classrooms, will of necessity impel teachers to look at the social situation and to be attentive to the questions and concerns that the learners have. In this way, the teacher will also become a learner. The next step is to discern what are the skills and competencies that are needed. More than likely, they will be different than the ones the teacher may have proposed before following this process. There are several questions to be asked in this process of discernment. What is it that prevents people from developing a life that is lived in God? What attitudes, language, rituals, way of thinking and acting are needed to enable individuals and community to come to an awareness of the Good News as integral to their lives? Finally, evaluation means to look at the total situation and not just test results. In what concrete ways, have we been attentive to the particular needs of particular cultures? Have we fostered learning and respect for various cultures? How have we enabled students to see their responsibility in the social-political realm? Have we taught them to analyze television, radio, video games and other media to see the impact on their lives? These questions of context are as important as the questions of content.

The GDC (133) echoes these same concerns. In the section on local catechisms, quoting the CCC, the GDC states that any synthesis of faith must exhibit the adaptations which are required by the difference of culture, age, spiritual maturity and social and ecclesial conditions among al those to whom it is addressed. The aspects of adaptation in a local catechism apply also to the whole process of religious education or catechesis. The particular culture of those being catechized must be taken into account as well as the way in which religion is lived in a particular society. Is the context one of religious indifference or of strong religious belief? This determines the approach. Local catechisms must also take into account social and political conditions and also the

22. This schema of analysis is found in H. LOMBAERTS, *Religion, Society, and the Teaching of Religion in Schools*, in M. WARREN (ed.), *Sourcebook for Modern Catechetics*, Vol. 2, Winona MN, St. Mary's Press, 1997, p. 307.

concrete ecclesial situation. In this way the context becomes an integral aspect of the content. The vision of the GDC in its brief paragraphs on the Catholic schools is very challenging. Students today live in a global society. Schools must prepare them to live in this world of cultural pluralism, by inculcating the ability to be open-minded, to listen and to dialogue, to analyze critically, to search for truth and to take action to promote the dignity of all human persons. The religious dimension of the Catholic School must be such that it leads its students to build up the Kingdom of God.

Multifaith Education in the Europe of Tomorrow
A Civic Responsibility for Universities and Schools

Flavio Pajer

Citizens now of what the political analyst Michael Emerson calls the *multinational Euro-village*[1], we live within the confines of three superimposed and correlated institutional horizons: the national horizon, the community horizon of the Economic and Monetary Union (EMU), and the continental horizon, foreshadowed by the Helsinki agreements on security and cooperation (OSCE) and by that cauldron of ideas and cultural initiatives, the Council of Europe, which at present includes 30 or so countries, many of which are eastern. Of the three, it is the intermediate horizon which clearly occupies the imagination of our contemporaries, if only because it is the one which is being constructed with the greatest outlay of economic resources and a more clearly defined political will. But both inside and outside the process of the economic and political construction of the continent, a great deal of uncertainty surrounds its cultural recomposition: in addition to creating a Europe that is united economically and institutionally, there remains the problem of constructing a common cultural identity.

Given that one of the determining factors of cultural identity is the religious factor, it is not surprising that – uniting until now regional populations, whose identity had been historically identified with one or other of the three major Christian denominations, and integrating, in the meantime, a massive influx of extra-European immigrants belonging to non-Christian cultures – Europe must rethink a certain number of criteria, to make it possible to live together harmoniously in a society that is now also multicultural, and create the necessary conditions for education in *European citizenship* in the new socio-religious context that is being created.

While the candidature for admission to the EU of eastern countries with Orthodox majorities creates some problems, the problem posed by the candidature of Turkey is very much greater. An Ankara daily newspaper, the *Hurriyet*, proudly announced the candidature last November

---

1. M. EMERSON, *Redrawing the Map of Europe*, London, Macmillan, 1998, p. 251 in the Italian edition, Bologna, Il Mulino, 1999.

as "the first muslim candidature". The problem lies in the fact that Turkey wishes to be integrated in a continent characterised not only by its *Christian* culture, but by a *secularised* Christian culture, endowed with political, juridical and educational institutions, which, as a result of the separation of Church and State, *are independent of religions*. It is known from the outset, that of the three institutions mentioned above, the last two in particular are not easily reconciled with certain tenets of Islam and of its social ethos.

More generally, however, and according to the often repeated warnings of socio-religious observers, made even more alarming by the media, it would seem there are some spectres haunting Europe. There is the spectre of religious wars which has been recently revived in the Balkans; there is that of religious intolerance, reflected in isolated, but not at all unexpected, incidents reported in the press; there is the spectre of the sects or of the "new religions" which exploit the disenchantment of many Europeans with the traditional faith, and seduce them with the fascination of the exotic and the occult. What do these symptoms represent, ask contemporary historians and analysts of social phenomena? Are these "the last flames of a past that cannot return? the flames of the vanguard of our future? or signs of a malaise we can still cure"[2]? Must we "believe the idea according to which our societies, which were once directed by religion, have now freed themselves of its guardianship"? or believe that "even in the most secularised societies, religious belief, from a statistical point of view, is professed by a majority, and that this is by far the most widespread social phenomenon of a voluntary nature"[3]?

1. Europe in Search of a New Identity

It is clear, of course, that between Europe and religion, or more precisely, between European society and Christianity, the links that used to exist must now be much weakened, if the synod of European Bishops, at the close of the last millennium (October 1999), felt it could speak of the "apostasy of Europe" (*Instrumentum laboris*, n. 14), and had to recall that it was not possible "to identify Europe with Christianity, an identification

2. S. FERRARI & I.C. IBÁN, *Diritto e religione in Europa occidentale*, Bologna, Il Mulino, 1997, p. 7.
3. R. RÉMOND, *Religion et société en Europe*, Paris, Seuil, 1998, pp. 16 and 283 of the Italian edition, Bari, Laterza, 1999.

that had never existed and one that now is less than ever possible to suggest" (n. 51); and if the unity of the continent was desirable and, in some aspects, inevitable, it "cannot be seen in terms of "Christianity alone", but in terms of "pluralism with dialogue and collaboration", so as to bring about that "*living together of cultures*", which can transform the temptation to present itself as forms of opposition between mutual service and acceptance, into a synthesis scaled down to the needs of individuals and citizens, and into a great reality in which so many small nations and cultures can find a home" (n. 10)[4].

But already ten years previously, just after the Wall fell – and with its ideologies – a prophetic voice such as Ernesto Balducci's urged people to abandon for good any thought of a new Christian era, and instead, realise that "in the post-ideological Europe the meeting of minds must be founded on an entirely fresh basis, given an ecumenism which goes beyond the boundaries of Christian denominations and religions, to include also human convictions justified by the principle of fidelity of reason to its own independent resources. The pre-modern age was the age of the wars of religion; the modern age was that of ideological war; and the post-modern age is the age of the free meeting of minds, prepared to contribute to a common historical project, on the basis of a cosmopolitan ethos"[5].

A Europe in which Christianity has become again a *diaspora* – in which the statistical majority of the citizens, although baptised, are, in fact, baptised persons who "believe without belonging" and others who continue "to belong without believing"(Grace Davie); to which individuals and groups come seeking for shelter, and bringing with them styles of life and religiosity unknown to western man; where the very reasons for society no longer find a unifying ethical inspiration either in denominational beliefs or in secular ideologies – is without doubt a Europe destined to suffer from a lack of identity for a long time.

This Europe must be able, in the medium to long term, to preside over the transition from a mosaic of ethnic, national and mono-religious identities to a state of *plural citizenship*[6], or of *society citizenship*[7], under-

4. *Instrumentum laboris* of the Synod of Bishops of Europe, Italian translation in *Osservatore Romano/Documenti*, supplement to issue no. 179, August 6, 1999, p. 20.

5. E. BALDUCCI, *La paideia europea nei prossimi anni*, in *Testimonianze* 33 (1990) no. 12, 26; the thesis is amply developed in *L'Uomo planetario*, Fiesole, ECP, 1990.

6. K. FOUAD ALLAM, *Religione, identità e cittadinanza in Europa*, in *Laicità e religioni nella scuola del 2000*, Bari, Progedit, 1999, 59-71.

7. P. DONATI, *Modelli culturali e processi di integrazione: quale progetto per l'Europa di domani?*, in *L'Europa, sfida e problema per i cattolici*, Bologna, EDB, 1999, 19-55.

stood already not as an unlikely, shapeless and levelling melting pot, but as a form of associative living together, capable of accepting and making accepted, that cultural and religious differences are legitimate and productive; and one which avoids the opposing creeping tendencies of syncretistic indifference or fundamentalistic intolerance, as well as the outbreak of indiscriminate proselytism. Regarding the latter, only recently, various countries have passed a number of laws intended to make missionary activity by new and old religions self-regulatory[8].

It is not surprising, therefore, that in this connection, for more than ten years, it has become increasingly evident in all European educational systems, that there is an urgent need for *multicultural education* in schools and in universities[9]. Such an education would not evade the "religious" dimension by leaving it exclusively, on one pretext or another, to the competent pastoral structures of religious institutions; or worse still, ignore it, considering it irrelevant to the critical maturing process of the individual and of the citizen. Rather, it would recognise the religious factor, and would treat it as one of the historically ineradicable dimensions of cultures or, more precisely, as one of the keys to the understanding of people's lives all over the world. Today, it is not only religious organisations or groups of believers who defend the right of inclusion of some critically presented religious courses in State education, but it is also the national and international organisations responsible for the management of the cultural heritage and for educational policy. For example, in its last report to Unesco, the international Commission on education for the 21st century, proposed, with good reasons, that one of the four supporting pillars of education should be learning to live together with others who are different: "by teaching young people to adopt the point of view of other ethnic or religious groups, it is possible to avoid the lack of comprehension which leads to hatred and violence among adults. The teaching of the history of religions and customs can

8. Cf. S. FERRARI, *Proselitismo nell'età della globalizzazione: autodisciplina delle religioni*, in *Il Regno-attualità*, Feb. 15th, 2000, 132-140. A new European Watchdog of racist and xenophobic phenomena was officially inaugurated in Vienna on April 7, 2000. Its brief was "to organise research on the development of xenophobia in Europe, create networks and information campaigns in every member State, combat racism with every means, such as, for example, education and the media". According to the directors of the Watchdog, "the future of Europe will be determined by its cultural, ethnic and religious diversity. Mutual understanding and non-discrimination are the fundamental pillars of the EU. Racism, xenophobia and antisemitism are radically incompatible with these principles and are a threat to them" (from the monthly *Europe Infos*, April 2000, p. 4).

9. F. GOBBO, *L'educazione interculturale in Europa: elementi per un dibattito*, in *Studium Educationis* (1999) no. 4, 691-704.

serve as a useful point of reference for future behaviour"[10]. Another example comes from the recent international convention on "Building a common European identity", organised by the Agnelli Foundation at Turin, February 28th-29th 2000, which set itself the task to study "a common model of society for the 21st century, based on a shared European identity, rooted in the cultural, ethical and spiritual heritage of Europe, but which is necessarily reformulated in the light of the new challenges posed by modernity and by a critical examination of recent history".

It is more than obvious that the responsibility for a cultural and formative challenge of this importance cannot be entrusted solely to present-day religious teaching curricula (more or less denominational in the whole of Europe, with rare exceptions) to be found, for one reason or another, in the complex mosaic of national educational systems. Despite their constant praiseworthy modifications to content and didactic approach, their point of view still seems to be based on the assumption that European society is Christian, legally at least, if not in reality. Today, however, in a Europe that has become post-Christian and multireligious, schools and universities inevitably give more importance now to examining and interpreting the phenomenon of religion – and secularisation, its necessary reflection – with a view to research and multicultural and multi-faith formation.

2. Lack of Structures to Communicate Knowledge

In this connection, the mechanism for the promotion of religious education in State schools – governed only by the norms of the concordat – is becoming increasingly inadequate. It has to be remembered that, in western Europe, many countries, whether catholic or protestant, still regulate religious education in school on the basis of one or other form of concordat, para-concordat or special agreement with the "national Church" (Anglican, Lutheran). On the other hand, the authority to establish concordats is certainly not one that the EU has at present, and it is not even imaginable that in the future the EU could negotiate concordats with this or that Church. On the institutional

10. J. DELORS et al., Learning: The Treasure within. Report to Unesco of the International Commission on Education for the Twenty-first Century, Paris, Unesco, 1996, p. 86 of the Italian edition, Roma, Armando, 1997.

level, the construction of Europe does not include plans to homogenise relations between States and religions[11]. In fact, what is true is that the adoption of laws on religious freedom is making democratic and secular States recognise minority religions and new cults as legal entities and as having a social role. But this cannot include, obviously, the proliferation in State schools of religious courses promoting the various religious denominations, for the consequence of that would be to reduce State education to an ungovernable collection of particularistic options which would destroy the very meaning of an integrated public system.

The common tendency is rather the opposite: State schools in European countries, at least in the western ones, which are predominantly catholic or protestant, but now with an increasing Islamic presence, dealing with a population of young people belonging to different faiths or belonging to none, are increasingly less prepared – culturally and institutionally speaking – to retain in their curricula religious educational activities specific to a single religion, preferring to leave them, or return them, to the pastoral care of their respective religious communities. Faced with this difficult distinction of roles and areas of competence, it often happens that schools unlawfully abdicate a duty they cannot delegate, that is, to include in their teaching programme that huge sector of general culture represented by the religious heritage. This duty consists in equipping each one of its pupil-citizens, leaving aside their present or future religious options, with objective and critical information about religious facts, which will enable them to relate to the typical ethos of a multicultural society, and to interact with it constructively. This educational duty cannot be delegated in absolute terms to religious organisations (even if these, with initiation given at home and in a community that is open to the democratic values of personal dignity and of social solidarity, can contribute to a considerable extent to education in civic values), but remains the specific task of schools for everybody, and all the more so, at this particular point in history and in an area such as Europe, where the *raison d'être* of society runs the risk of being dissolved in the general "amnesia" of the religious roots of the continent and of the powers which function according to a just separation of Church and State.

A pluralistic society is also democratic if, ensuring freedom of belief, it ensures also the freedom to know. The enjoyment of both of these in equal degree must be guaranteed to all citizens. But we still see today a

11. H. MENDRAS, *L'Europa degli europei*, Bologna, Il Mulino, 1999, p. 74.

blatant discrepancy between the juridical dispositions guaranteeing religious freedom and the scarcity of means made available to civil society to satisfy its right to a secular knowledge of the phenomenon of religion. And so today in Italy, to give a concrete example, more than a million students, having chosen not to avail themselves of denominational courses, and not being offered as an alternative some appropriate subject, can spend years in the primary and secondary school and leave them "religiously illiterate", without ever having received the minimum critical equipment to be able to examine and understand the meaning of the phenomenon of religion inherent in the culture and experience of people past and present. The other students, those who voluntarily sign up for courses in the catholic religion (these form a clear majority, numbering about 8 million), in principle, should be able "to confront the problem of religion from an historical and anthropological angle; be able to tackle at some depth some of the great pages of the biblical text; be able to deal with a culturally based idea from history or Christian theology". These are some of the basic aims indicated in the national programme for the catholic religion. In reality, the results which have been trickling out in the last few years, in verifiable terms regarding cultural information and religious competence, show that this ambitious programme is grossly unrealistic, and that the overall picture of the teaching given is one of disorganisation and problems (however, there are some aspects which are emotionally gratifying for the students), producing results which are very unflattering, if we are to believe the regular empirical checks that are made, and the opinion of the young people themselves once they have left school[12].

The simple fact of treating religious facts, met by chance in some school subject or other, and treated in the light of, and according to the methods of that subject, is not enough, even if it is appreciable and

---

12. "Non-existent curriculum", "a complicated lesson", "a weak lesson", "a discipline in crisis", "incomplete religion", "nanny religion", "a course in all -ologies": are some of the names, not too disguised by irony, given to the catholic religion lessons prescribed by the concordat, in investigations conducted in recent years on a national or regional scale. The courses are judged *a posteriori* as being somewhat irrelevant especially by young university students or workers, of whom, looking back on their school experience, a third said they were relatively satisfied, a third were disappointed by the insignificance and inconclusivity of a subject left completely to personal opinion, and a third had a totally negative opinion. Only 1.8% had a totally positive opinion. This type of RE, even apart from unofficial generalisations, "was and is for some children and adolescents perhaps the most confusing and disconcerting experience they encountered in school" (M. POLLO, *L'esperienza religiosa dei giovani. 2-1: Adolescenti*, Turin, Elledici, 1996, pp. 348ff).

necessary. The reasons for this are as follows: (1) by its critical potential and epistemological basis, religious knowledge, whether deduced from theological or non-theological sciences, is not of itself inferior by nature or quality to other subjects on the curriculum, and so, only ideological and anti-religious prejudice could accuse it of being irrelevant or undeserving to be included in the curriculum of a school open to all; (2) if other school subjects (history, philosophy, art, etc.) were to expel a priori the religious element from their courses, they would be the first to fall short of their own scientific standards, degrading themselves by partisan considerations; and so, when different disciplines include the teaching of the religious element in their programme, they are not doing anything exceptional or ambiguous, but are simply being consistent with their own epistemological statute. After all, it is not a question of trying to introduce surreptitiously a religious viewpoint, understood as an ideological interpretation of reality into school programmes, but to make pupils understand in an elementary way, what the significance is, for example, of religious experience in the history of peoples and the lives of individuals; what symbolic codes encode it; what are its distinctive characteristics by comparison with other human experiences; what theories have interpreted them; what influence have they had on the society of their own country and continent, etc.

It is obvious that each school subject can make its own useful contribution to ensuring that pupils acquire "religious competence", but none can take on the onus of studying the world of religious signs in an organised and systematic manner. And so it seems singularly inconsistent in the culturally democratic system the West has – or purports to have – that the intellectual, critical and ethical contribution of the sciences which explore the world of religion, continues to be exploited negatively, minimised or excluded from State school education.

On the other hand, it should be recalled here that religious knowledge which, in a "Christian" era now long gone, knew in practice no other model except that of theological rationality, is now refracted in a whole constellation of empirical and hermeneutic sciences of religion, which seem to have won acceptance in learned cultural circles, but which have still impinged too little on popular and school culture – a situation which, in neo-Latin countries, has been abetted by the centuries-old disregard of universities for religious questions. And yet, the more accepted discoveries of such sciences, if properly publicised and presented, could filter down quite naturally into the subjects on the school curriculum, beginning at least with the arts subjects. We know, however, how slow this osmosis is, and the fact that it is almost inexistent, slowed down above all by that inveterate error, diagnosed as anti-clerical and secularistic (a position more Latin than Anglo-Saxon, it has to be admitted), which confuses faith with superstition, religious history with myth, belief with credulity, theology with dogmatism. Often, the official religious teacher is not put into a position, as might be expected, to take advantage of the contribution of religious sciences, locked in as he is, from the days of his professional training, in mainly theological curricula, on which non-theological religious sciences manage to impinge only in a peripheral and subordinate role. And this happens, despite the fact that this theological research is in the process of freeing itself of its centuries-old institutional and self-referential isolation which had held it imprisoned in the role of being almost exclusively the body responsible for the training of priests.

3. Religion: From Belief to Memory, through *laïcité*

"Christian Europe", if it ever really existed in the pre-modern societies of past centuries, is certainly no longer recognisable in post-traditional Europe. What we have now are situations of diaspora (K. Rahner), of disenchantment (M. Gauchet, E. Pace), of cultural discontinuity/diffraction (M. Tomka), of crisis of the parochial lifestyle (L. Voyé); we have a Europe which endorses the society of instant gratification (G. Schulze) which, in a word, has become *post-Christian* (E. Poulat), in which people continue to "believe they believe" (G. Vattimo), "to believe without belonging" (G. Davie), all of which leads to the question: "What does a person who does not believe, actually believe in?" (C.M. Martini, U. Eco). The society of western Europe, recalls P. Berger, unlike other industrialised societies such as the United States, Japan or Australia, seems to be the only one in the world, in which the classic hypotheses of secularisation and de-Christianisation have been totally proved to be processes by which institutional religions become progressively irrelevant[13]. Christianity is no longer the social cement of national identity – a fact that innumerable analyses and counter-analyses recall ad nauseam. This means that if the national identity of yesterday was able to draw endlessly on values passed on from Hebrew-Christian tradition, with its

13. P. BERGER, *Una gloria remota. Avere fede nell'epoca del pluralismo*, Bologna, Il Mulino, 1994, pp. 31ff.

normative world of beliefs and religious rites, thanks to a solidarity that was at least implicit, if not always consciously practised; the national identity of today, under pressure all the time to see itself increasingly in international terms, is less and less nourished by those traditional roots, and it begins to lack those stable referents, which were socially plausible and binding, made possible once by the complicity of the political and cultural with the religious.

It is well known, in this connection, that almost all the constitutions of European countries have drawn, more or less extensively – but without stating it and sometimes perhaps without being aware of it – on the principles and values of the Hebrew-Christian tradition, combining them obviously, on the political and juridical level, with the modern values of freedom of conscience and the secular nature of institutions. But these cultural and ethical roots which inspired the basic texts of western society have almost completely disappeared from the collective memory of contemporaries. One hears frequently now expressions such as the "cultural amnesia" of the West (Ch. Duquoc), or "religion with no longer a memory". Secularisation is called "a crisis of religious memory" (D. Hervieu-Léger) or "religion without tradition any more" (R. Campiche)…

This is an amnesia which reveals not only a lack of appreciation for cultural, historical and phenomenological data, an amnesia which not only reveals ignorance of the biblical text as the "code of western culture" (N. Frye), but is rather a removal, an intentional dropping of something which is no longer interesting: "for many of our contemporaries, Christianity is nothing but an archaic monument on a par with Gregorian chant, Romanesque art or Greek tragedy. It can be beautiful, but it no longer holds any truth for us"[14]. As Johann Baptist Metz, the theologian of "Christianity as subversive memory" recalls, the European spirit gave birth to two kinds of rationality during the course of modern times: it developed a technical-scientific rationality, inspired at its origins by a

14. Ch. DUQUOC, *Fede cristiana e amnesia culturale*, in *Concilium* (1999) no. 1, 158. The author states that amnesia is not perverting only because it is ignorance, but because it leads to existential non-sense, to a scission between living and the reasons for living, to the "dia-bolic" in the etymological sense of the term. He gives the example of scholastic learning which, from secondary school to the university, can be marked by erudition in all tool subjects except in the one that offers a meaning to life. It runs the risk also of creating resentment against teachers and the whole of society, which accept the institutional duty of transmitting something which is not relevant to daily life. On the theme of the "value betrayal" of present-day school education there are also the reflections of the philosopher Guy COQ in *Démocratie, religion, éducation*, Paris, Mame, 1993, and in *Laïcité et République. Le lien nécessaire*, Paris, Félin, 1995.

desire for power over a nature still to be dominated, a decidedly exploita-
tive and inherent rationality, which seems in fact to have dealt a mortal
blow to the capacity of the symbolic religious memory of European
man. Fortunately, in the meantime, the European spirit was able to
develop dialectically, almost as an antivirus, another type of rationality,
that of the universality of human rights, "that rationality which founded
a new political culture, which aims at subjective freedom and the dignity
of all human beings"[15]. The first rationality was *euro-centred*: from its
ideas about power, colonialism was born, as were also the social utopias
of the 19th century, the movements born of scientism and bourgeois and
marxist secularism, culminating in the present-day imitators, economic
imperialism and computer globalisation. The other rationality, *anti-euro-
centred*, was essentially based on such values or ideals as States based on
law, freedom of conscience, social solidarity, recognising that others are
similar to me, but also different and independent of me, by their religious convictions and their ethical choices. It was this rationality that
was able to bring about that critical look and that typically European
habitus called secularity (*laïcité*).

After the golden age of the humanist secularity of Machiavelli, Erasmus and Thomas More, it is true that Europe experienced the effects of
the political secularism of the French Revolution and, above all, the great
flood of those ethical-philosophical secularist movements of every hue
which, based on the Voltairian Enlightenment and the positivism of
Comte, affected most of the continent until the first half of the 20th century. But it is true also that the "archeo-secularity" of the prejudiced
refusal of religion of the 1800's has evolved today into a "neo-secularity of
confrontation" (R. Rémond), into a "plural secularity" (J.-P. Willaime) or
"contractual" (J. Baubérot) or "dynamic" (P. Ricoeur), which is no longer
a neutrality hostile or indifferent to the religious factor, and which no

---

15. J.B. METZ, *Lo spirito europeo: crisi e compiti*, in *Concilium* (1992) no. 2, 138-147.
Metz gives an interesting definition of the biblical-Christian tradition, calling it "un-
amnesic rationality": "the rationality of biblical traditions had an un-amnesic structure,
which presupposed the indissoluble unity of *ratio* and *memoria*, exactly the memory
which, in my opinion was forgotten by the type of Enlightenment rationality which
sought freedom. The criticism which the Enlightenment levelled at dogmatism and tra-
ditionalism was based on its own good reasons. But, did it not forget, perhaps that a
particular image in the memory is always inherent in a critical reason which does not
intend to result in mere criticism? Did it not forget that this memory is needed not only
by faith, but also by every reason that wishes to be translated into freedom in practice?
And in the face of our techno-scientific system, this memory assumes the character of a
dangerous memory, deprived of which, the human being would no longer see itself as
subjective and interdependent freedom" (pp. 144-145).

longer writes it off as a peripheral factor or one without influence on the
formation of individual and national identity. Instead, it recognises positively its social and cultural function, to the point of requesting – as is
happening in France at the present time – that State schools and universities include as a matter of course in their curricula the objective religious
factor which was removed from them as one of the reciprocal preclusions
in the conflict among opposing forms of clericalism[16]. Today, "unlike certain commonplaces", recalls the catholic sociologist Émile Poulat, "secularity is not a kind of neutrality on the part of the State and of schools,
but consists of their commitment to ensure and guarantee the exercise of
all our freedom. And it is not true that secularity is the same as separation
from religion. It is rather a *solution* to the problems facing a society

16. Some recent educational policies in a secularistic and separatistic country such as
France are in fact moving in the direction of a cultural reconciliation of the so-called
profane and religious studies. In September 1989, the education Minister received the
Philippe Joutard Report, which rang the alarm bell to warn against the "lack of religious
knowledge" which characterised the pupils leaving State schools in France, and which,
among the recommendations it made, proposed the inclusion of the study of the history
of religions in the curricula of primary and secondary schools, giving some reasons,
almost unheard of until then in France, to justify its proposal: "The ignorance of the
religious dimension prevents many contemporaries, especially those who belong to no
religion, from having access to the major works of our artistic, literary and philosophical heritage. Secularity will seem all the more precious to our contemporaries if they are
able to recognise clearly the cultural and social importance of religions. The 'neutrality'
of schools does not imply at all the marginalisation of the religious factor from the field
of learning, but leads rather to openness to diversity and the refusal of all indoctrination" (Ph. JOUTARD, *Rapport de la mission de réflexion sur l'enseignement*, September 1989,
pp. 90-91). The École du Louvre, in collaboration with the Ministries of Culture,
National Education and Universities, organised in April 1996 a national colloquium on
the problem of "formation in the religious dimension of the cultural heritage", for the
purpose of "pointing out how extremely serious it would be for our culture, and consequently for our society, if its religious learning disappeared". And to demonstrate that
"the secularity which we need is not one which encourages denominational teaching in
our schools, but one which encourages openness to to the great religious movements
which, while it is true, have brought to our societies abominable confrontations and
conflicts, have also led to a prodigious cultural enrichment" (*Forme et Sens*, Paris, La
Documentation Française, 1997, pp. 20 and 260). In a dossier entirely devoted to *Laïcité, un idéal à réinventer*, the monthly *Le Monde de l'éducation*, May 1999, put forward
the idea that "the new secularity has become a necessary condition for reflecting on and
living in harmony with the religious pluralism which is increasing daily" (M. Gauchet),
and that it (the new secularity) "is the basis today for the exercise of freedom of conscience in a civil society ridden until recently by forms of clericalism of diverse extrac-
tion" (J. Baubérot). An impressive number of critical studies and popular publications
have appeared in the last ten years, that are devoted to the subject of secularity, viewed
from an historical, juridical, institutional, philosophical, theological and pedagogical
point of view. For a commented survey of thirty or so titles published in the 1990's, see
my essay *Laicità, educazione morale, cultura religiosa in Francia*, in *Pedagogia e Vita* (a
bimonthly of the Catholic University of Milan) (1999) no. 2, 79-115.

divided by beliefs and convictions which, being so, bases that society on basic human rights, which have to be guaranteed to all the members that compose it, without discrimination"[17].

Seen as a strategy for the transmission of culture, the new secularity, then, is a method which makes it possible, on the one hand, to value the religious factor as a cultural capital fund, the memory of which must be preserved as the interpretative key of all human culture (*cognitive secularity*), which must not be hidden. On the other hand, it seeks to guarantee to all citizens of multicultural societies the exercise of the right to personal freedom of conscience and of ethical choices (*axiological secularity*). This idea has recently been developed by the sociologist from Strasbourg, Jean-Paul Willaime who, pleading the case for *open secularity*, identifies its basic characteristic as "the defence of a public pluralist space, where uninterrupted questioning can take place, not only of the age-long religions and visions of man and of the world, but also of the beliefs which are the very basis of modern ideals and practices. This open secularity can integrate the understanding of the religious dimensions of cultures and societies to a much greater extent, if it is itself secularised, by having learned to develop a critical approach to non-religious concepts of man and the world. It corresponds to what Edgar Morin calls *open reason*, that is to say, a reason which recognises 'that there are realities at the same time rational, irrational, a-rational, super-rational, such as myths; whereas a closed reason can see only errors, stupidity and superstitions'"[18].

Secular reason, therefore, to the extent that it can free itself from *exploitive reason* (that is, from the imperialism of techno-scientific knowledge and expertise) and from the *sectarian* or *identity* temptation (that is, from denominational or atheistic self-referentiality), is the postulate if the religious factor is to be valued as one of the cultural components to be included in the partial and sectarian memories of the continent that is being constructed. To give the beginnings of an answer to those who have been asking in these past years: Why is it, in this Europe of ours, we can make a common market, but we cannot also make a common memory[19]?

---

17. É. POULAT, *La solution laïque et ses problèmes*, Paris, Berg International, 1997, pp. 7-11.

18. F. BOESPFLUG, F. DUNAND, J.-P. WILLAIME, *Pour une mémoire des religions*, Paris, La Découverte/Essais, 1996, p. 189. The quotation from E. Morin is in *Pour sortir du XX siècle*, Paris, Nathan, 1984, p. 281.

19. Some attempts to harmonise, for example, school history textbooks commonly used in European schools have already been completed, and others are being considered [cf. *Le Monde de l'éducation* 7 (1997) 88]. *A Manual for a Europe without frontiers*, in French and German, and from the 1999-2000 school year, in the hands of 300 thousand

4. Going beyond the Identity/Otherness Dilemma

The fact that the Europe of the Enlightenment, on the basis of the Hellenistic-Christian concept of the human person, was able to create the concept of tolerance, and then that of freedom of conscience and of unalienable individual responsibility, and in doing so, also the social rules of democratic society, based on equality and justice and seen as regulatory ideals of society, this fact remains one of the greatest and most irreversible achievements of its spirit. But today, we realise, it was only a stage. It was a stage when the dignity of the individual was built up and when national identities were formed, but it was also a stage of linguistic barriers, patriotic rhetoric, religious enclaves and ethnocentric educational systems. Today, the new generations have to confront a new force, a multiform otherness which is not simply a superficial cosmopolitanism, and they have to go a step further than their predecessors, who recognised the legitimacy of the "other" who came from beyond national and denominational frontiers: they have to learn to live with the other in a social space which has no frontiers or hierarchies of any kind, and for this reason, they are tempted to build substitute defence "walls" on the pretext of preserving the "achievements of our civilisation that cannot be renounced", convinced perhaps that, in defending them, they are also ipso facto defending the orthodoxy of their own religious faith.

There is a need to create the educational rules and conditions necessary for a culture of plural citizenship. The first step along this road is to abandon the *identity ideology*, or better, the instinctive opposition in so many parts of European culture between identity and otherness. In fact, "for centuries, the word "identity" was seen as a synonym of such concepts as hegemony, dominion and monopoly. Worse still, in Christian circles, identity became synonymous with *truth,* leading even to intolerant and anti-liberal norms and behaviour. These are mental habits that

French, German and Swiss pupils, and pupils from the territory of Alsace, Baden-Württemberg, the canton of Basel, to be used in conjunction with courses in civic education, history, geography, language. The historian Jacques LE GOFF produced a very successful *L'Europa raccontata ai giovani* (Italian translation, Bari, Laterza, 1997; original edition in French, *L'Europe racontée aux jeunes*, Paris, Seuil, 1996, illustrated, p. 96). At the beginning of this year, in Malta, the University of Valletta organised a meeting for Jewish, Christian and Muslim teachers with a view to preparing the drafting of common texts for Mediterranean middle schools. But the "European view" is influencing also other subjects little by little and, as a tendency, the whole of school education, even because the normative texts of new educational legislation are prescribing, with increasing determination, greater openness by disciplines to the continental dimension.

are so deep-rooted that it is not easy to change them, especially if one is satisfied to accept otherness as a "joke played by history" or a "hypothesis" made necessary by circumstances, while waiting for the mono-cultural "thesis" to be restored to it. The quality of the approach needs to be improved if we wish to accept otherness as the new frontier of human plenitude: recourse to cheap syncretistic or wait-and-see attitudes would only lead to minimalistic and unsatisfying compromises"[20].

As the years go by, schools are filling up with pupils from other cultures, who have a right to complete respect for their otherness. The educational systems in place in the various countries, however, were created in order to integrate the children in their own territorial culture, a local culture, or European anyway, often mistaken for general knowledge. These systems now find themselves having to cater to a school population, increasingly not native, and above all bringing with it different cultures which are de facto a refutation of any kind of pretentious eurocentric universalism. Cultural proximity within the same educational space makes it necessary, first of all, to create a healthy dialectic between identity and diversity (this is the pedagogy of confrontation: overcoming stereotypes and prejudices, reciprocal knowledge, self-criticism), but also there has to be found a set of common values, which can be positively accepted to make it possible to live together by giving a new sense to this living (this is the pedagogy of consent: looking for agreement on important points, sharing common projects for a common cause)[21]. This cannot come about without the burden of all kinds of cultural mediation. Of these, *religious mediation* is one that is certainly at the basis of multiculturedness.

From cultural anthropology and from the history of religions it is known how relevant religious diversities are in relations between cultures.

---

20. G. ALBERIGO, *L'Europe et les autres Continents. Tensions, confrontations et relations*, in P. HÜNERMANN (ed.), *La nouvelle Europe. Défi à la théologie et à l'Église*, Paris, Cerf, 1994, 81-82. From a more philosophical-theological point of view, there are the reflections of Armido Rizzi (*L'Europa e l'altro. Abbozzo di una teologia europea della liberazione*, 1991), who dismisses the myth of "completed modernity", that is, of an "I" who makes himself consciously flexible to the point of embracing – paternalistically – the "Other", but proposes, with a provocative typically evangelical but also secular U turn, that one must take the "Other" as one's starting point in order to redefine the "I". Values like solidarity, peace, ecology, dialogue between cultures, quality of life, are the basic components of a type of a (religious) man, who is less eurocentric and more ecumenical.

21. Cf. G. DAL FERRO, *Libertà e culture. Nuove sfide per le religioni*, Padua, Messaggero, 1999, pp. 85-102; C. SIRNA TERRANOVA, *Pedagogia interculturale*, Milan, Guerini, 1999, pp. 119-130.

If religious identity creates in the individual certain symbolical representations, draws certain meanings from the universe and history, imposes
specific hierarchies of truth and ethical values, brings a particular sense to
living and dying, it is clear that it is the person in one's totality and continuity that is involved, and not only some isolated faculty. Even more
involved is the group to which the person belongs and the jealously
guarded link which identifies the individual with the community and its
traditions. For this reason, multicultural dialogue proves to be superficial
and illusory, especially if it takes place when teaching young and very
young children, if the religious component of the children's personal and
social identity is not taken objectively into account. Work in education is
all the more important – as the history of peoples, especially of European
peoples teaches us – as a great proportion of conflicts do not arise from
the nature or the objective contents of individual religions, but derive
rather from subjective defects in the religious teaching of religious (or
anti-religious) persons, and from the tendency to use religion as a tool for
improper purposes.

It is clear that in conditions of cultural and religious proximity, not
only would a *proselytising*, implicit or explicit, be anti-educational and
devastating, but the very *identity language* specific to a religion, to its
liturgical symbols, to its theology and catechesis, would be abusive or
discriminatory, "exclusive", in a State education which seeks to be multicultural and multi-religious. It is not surprising that, in Europe, in the
course of the last twenty years or so, all models of mono-denomina-
tional religious teaching have more or less reached a crisis point[22]. They
had been able to function in State schools so long as society was (or
could still appear to be) a "sociologically" Christian society. It was sufficient to use the self-referential language of the Churches, or better still,
that of one's own denominational tradition, with its spirituality, its exegesis, its liturgy, to be able to legitimise and impose a "religious knowledge" model in schools.

Already now, that educational model is proving to be widely unus-
able, not because of subjective shortcomings on the part of teachers,
pupils or of those in charge, but simply because of an objective change

---

22. For further information, see some of my essays: *Gli insegnamenti di religione nei
sistemi scolastici europei*, in *Aggiornamenti sociali* 43 (1992) 235-271; *L'enseignement scolaire
de la religion en Europe: vue panoramique d'une mutation*, in J. BULCKENS & H. LOM-
BAERTS (eds.), *L'enseignement de la religion catholique* (BETL, 109), Leuven, University
Press – Peeters, 1993, 31-57; *Quale religione insegnare a scuola nell'Europa di domani?*, in
Cultura, religione, scuola, Milan, F. Angeli, 2000.

of paradigm which is affecting seriously the whole social, and not only the educational, system:

- the socio-religious profile of the school population has changed and is very differentiated; religious experiences, involving fully the children and able to do so, are becoming very rare, especially if they are of a denominational character[23].

- the morphology of the present-day religious and spiritual phenomenon, in its social visibility as in its curves and psychological effects, is much more vast and variegated than that of the religious world codified in the west Christian tradition, and the Christian vocabulary is insufficient even simply to describe the phenomenon;

- at a time of ethical eclipse, or in a "ethically neutral society"[24], even the educational requirements many families have of religious schools have blatantly, and for self-serving reasons, changed: instead of wishing the child to study the classic "catechetical truths", they now want it to be taught the moral principles.

- in addition to the existing evaluative theological sciences, which legitimised traditional denominational religious teachings, the need was felt, but obviously not submitted for theological approval, for religious sciences which were autonomous and non-evaluative, to give cultural credibility and an academic profile to "religious knowledge" drawn up in the secular setting of a school or of a State university[25];

- in practice, the whole of school studies is dominated in western culture by the hyper-efficient primacy of formalised and scientific disciplines, to the detriment of the more informal humanistic disciplines, with their symbolical-religious codes. One result is that teaching in school succeeds now in playing down or saying absolutely nothing at all about the unsuppressable problem of meaning ("the real genetic code of society", as Niklas Luhmann says), which remains above all a secular problem, common to all types of pupils, before becoming a religious problem or, especially, a problem over which one single religious denomination can claim to have exclusive rights.

23. Cf. R. CAMPICHE (ed.), *Cultures jeunes et religions en Europe*, Paris, Cerf, 1997.
24. Cf. P. DONATI & I. COLOZZI (eds.), *Giovani e generazioni. Quando si cresce in una società eticamente neutra*, Bologna, Il Mulino, 1997.
25. Cf. J. GOMEZ CAFFARENA, *Por qué no una Facultad universitaria de "Ciencias de las Religiones"?*, in *Razón y Fe* 232 (1995) 73-85; J. JONCHERAY (ed.), *Approches scientifiques des faits religieux*, Paris, Beauchesne, 1997; P. GISEL, *La théologie face aux sciences religieuses*, Geneva, Labor et Fides, 1999.

These and other factors – which an endless socio-pedagogical literature never ceases to study (see the bibliographical selection included) –
have changed the social and cultural panorama of the school. They
oblige it to reconsider the "vocation" that was assigned to it in the modern period, and to check what role it can sustain in the post-modern
period (otherwise, one could not explain the recurring urgency for radical reform in schools and universities). This means that the traditional
insistence of the Churches to maintain in State or, for that matter, in
denominational schools, religious education that is *identifying* in nature,
conflicts with a cultural situation that, de facto largely post-Christian
and multicultural, is such as to make an exclusively denominational
approach to the religious problem, not only unpopular, but also sim-
plistic and unproductive.

For all these reasons, there is no easy solution to the problem posed
by the claims of religious groups (certain Islamic groups, certain "new
religions", but also, generally speaking, the Orthodox Churches of eastern Europe), which aspire to preserve or start up in State schools teaching and practices of a denominational character[26]. If a certain anxiety
about identity still exists or arises from time to time, it means that equal
recognition by the State for otherness is still a long way away. This is yet
another urgent reason for the competent State institutions to take steps
to set up a normative *State and secular* panel which, without abuse or
discrimination vis-a-vis any Church or religious organisation, can run *a
common "literacy" programme* on the phenomenon and problem of religion, supporting the *cultural difference* of all the pupils within the
framework of their *common citizenship*.

5. The Cognitive and Ethical Potential of Religious Culture

To say that *religion* can be seen (also) as a cultural product and therefore as an object of learning, is to say something that is very much taken
for granted and generally accepted now on a theoretical level. More
problematical is the affirmation that religion has a cognitive value, that
is, apart from constituting knowledge in its own right (the object of various religious sciences), it can serve as the *interpretative key* to so much

---

26. For a rapid survey of the positions taken by religions present in Europe regarding the question of RE in school, cf. J. BAUBÉROT (ed.), *Religions et laïcité dans l'Europe
des Douze*, Paris, Syros, 1994, pp. 141-271; F. PAJER, *Quale religione insegnare?* (n. 22).

knowledge that exists about man, society, the history of peoples, the universe. The first is a static knowledge, factual, descriptive and explicative, and an end in itself. The second is a dynamic knowledge, functional, that is, serving to discover the sense and values of facts, a medium and a source of an "understanding" vision of the world and of man's existence. To uphold the first knowledge, it is enough to invoke the principle of intelligibility of the religious cultural phenomenon as culture: it is accessible to the intelligence and can be taught to the extent that it can be documented, read, decodified, investigated, contextualised, analysed, compared. And seen from this point of view, it is not necessary to be a Jew to know the Mosaic decalogue, nor be a Catholic to understand the message of the Beatitudes, nor be a Muslim to read the Koran. If the postulate that the religious dimension is culturally intelligible were not accepted, it would mean that the whole of an enormous symbolic heritage of humanity, despite having been transmitted by traditions over the course of several thousand years, was no longer transmissible.

To uphold the legitimacy of the second "comprehensive" knowledge, a further step has to be taken without, however, abandoning the need for a critical sense:, we have to include as a part of human history the signs and effects of the activity of the "symbolic man" (Ernst Cassirer), called *religion*, whose sense transcends the limits of rational intelligibility. But since this sense has become a part of so many cultural expressions of man, in all ages, in all civilisations, these cultural expressions (models for life, philosophies, arts, literatures, etc.) cannot be thoroughly understood if the motive which inspired them, or the message they intended to convey, are not known.

"A knowledge of religions helps to know the world" – a thesis that has no need to be defended, if one accepts the historical indissociability of religions and cultures, the anthropological indissociability of culture and the meaning of life, the theological indissociability of life and faith in an afterlife salvation. The knowledge of religions can be justified, therefore, by a reason that is above all *functional*: they provide conceptual tools and symbolic material to make it possible to understand the world *in a significant way*, as well as oneself. Religion is not important only for the knowledge that it brings, but also and above all, for the second use of this knowledge in the process of school acculturation. Today, in school – whether it is a question of analysing the heritage of human culture, or wrestling with the major questions of the human condition, or learning to acquire a capacity for critical and self-critical judgement, or learning to live democratically in a pluralistic society – the knowledge of the religious factor is always of extreme relevance, if one admits that schools can and ought to contribute to the "construction of meaning" (R. Campiche).

"Religion is necessary because it provides the philosophical categories needed to understand the still very problematical experience we have of this world ... Religion offers interpretative categories, mythological figures, structures of meaning, without which we would not understand the problematical situation in which we are"[27]. In terms of historical progression, G. Gusdorf has traced out the trajectory of western consciousness in three stages: in the first, humanity, the spectator that it is of the unfathomable mystery of the universe, receives the *creative word*, which is imposed upon it from outside. It is both dominated and captivated by this word: this is the very long period of mythical consciousness. In the second, man works out for himself a word on the world, a word that vivisects reality into so many particulars of knowledge that eventually he loses contact with the primitive word, and in so doing, forgets the roots and the meaning of things: this is the recent period of the imperialism of science, of the rational consciousness. In the third, a more mature and conscientious conquest of rationality, capable of being open to mystery, brings about the recuperation of the forgotten primitive word, and the evolution into a new form of consciousness: this is the consciousness that G. Gusdorf called "existential", and that A. Rizzi, following H.G. Gadamer, describes by the more modern term "hermeneutic"[28].

---

27. S. GIVONE, in *Religioni e IRC nella cultura e nella scuola italiana*, Turin, Sei, 1998, pp. 10-11. L. PRENNA gives some clarifications along the same lines in *L'insegnamento scolastico della religione in una società plurietnica*, in *Pedagogia e Vita* 5 (1996) 94-107: "the aim of RE is not to seek ideological consensus or personal commitment, but to propose, as an study aim, what for believers is an object of their faith. Its aim is to form a habitual capacity to understand religion(s), that is, a intellectual virtue, a willingness of the intellect to identify the differences between the facts that mark the religious life of a person. Religious learning consists in this understanding of religion, seen as a 'forma mentis', capable of thinking, identifying, and evaluating religious facts" (p. 105).

28. A. RIZZI, *Il Sacro e il Senso. Lineamenti di filosofia della religione*, Torino-Leumann, Elledici, 1995, p. 116: "Hermeneutic reason is by definition 'secondary': it does not produce the Meaning of reality, nor does it really discover it, but it tracks it down in the signs in which the experience of meaning is pronounced. Like mythical-religious consciousness, every experience of meaning (esthetical, amorous, social, and others) is an element of that fundamental self-understanding, that for the human being is the source of self-becoming". On the role of the school in the "construction of meaning", cf. R. CAMPICHE, *École et construction du sens*, in *Revue Française de Pédagogie* (1998) no. 125, 28-41.

In this context, the cultural re-evaluation of religion appears related to *ethical-political re-evaluation*. We know how the growth of individualism limits the regulatory influence of institutional religion in the area of private life. In the meantime, however, institutional religions gain credit and relevance in the area of public life: faced with a society which is forming offshoots and fragmenting, which has lost the "focal points of polarisation" represented by ideologies, there is an urgent need for impartial mediators, institutions for dialogue, a reference to common cultural roots. For this reason also, religion is coming to be considered as a political authority of international importance. Although difficult to quantify, there exists "a generalised search for meaning which has grown over the last few years in western society, meaning by which, not only the capacity to respond to problems of meaning (confronted down the centuries by religious systems), but also to the general seeking for identification and social belonging, and to crises of welfare policy, which constitute areas of tension, whose solution is of fundamental importance for the equilibrium of the social system"[29].

Still in the same connection, in certain strata of society, there is social pressure on Churches and religions, and a demand they become once again – it is not known with how much historical probability of success – promoters of "world ethics" (Hans Küng), a force championing "a collective ethos, of historical memory, of a re-affirmation of universalistic values. It is a recognition that the foundations of a new "common dwelling" have to be sought in religious matrices, a view which contrasts with the particularistic and disintegrating tendencies that affect various social groups ... In this context, people look to the Churches and religions in universalistic terms, as 'dépositaires' of a *humanitas* which transcends the various cultures, capable of emphasising the common values that derive from specific and particularistic religious references"[30].

In these last years, there has been taking place a radical revision of ideas about the function of a school. In view of a reform, there has been much debate, among other things, about the identification of "essential knowledge" which must be guaranteed by the new basic school. Now, the fact that religious knowledge had been omitted, through "forgetfulness", from the knowledge that should be a normal part of a literate citizen's cultural baggage, caused many a strong reaction in authoritative

29. F. GARELLI, *Religione*, in L. GALLINO (ed.), *Manuale di sociologia*, Turin, Utet, 1997, p. 441.

30. ID., *Quando la ragione non basta. Ethos collettivo e religioni*, in *Il Mulino* (1997) no. 4, p. 606.

circles. The "planners" of the school education of the future were asked, and quite rightly too, by a variety of persons to give proof of greater consistency with the principle they themselves had enunciated, that is, that "the task of the school is to guarantee to those who frequent it the capacity to find their bearings in the world in which they live". But it is difficult to find one's bearings in the world, to understand its history and interpret critically its cultural heritage, if one does not have at one's disposal one of the interpretative tools represented by the knowledge of the role played by religion in the human experience, both in the past and in the present. If the school intends to open itself institutionally to "all culture" so that it can make "the whole pupil" open to it, it cannot allow itself to exclude from the list of human problems, the religious problem, even because, ignorant of it, one cannot objectively and exhaustively explain the other problems[31].

6. Training of Teachers: Religious Sciences in Advanced Studies

The fate of universities is a curious one: born as *denominational*, as one of the most prestigious "inventions" of the Christian Middle Ages, with theology, the queen of sciences at the time, as the most important discipline, they have subsequently become *secularised* to the point that

31. Among the many voices, leaving aside those of a denominational or militant political nature, that have been raised to insist that State schools, and therefore universities, must adopt a non-denominational approach when dealing with religion, we can quote Amos Luzzatto, president of the Union of Jewish italian communities: "It seems to me that schools must include in their curriculum, without any half measures, the history or philosophy of religions. They would be taught by a graduate in history or philosophy, without any endorsement by non-school authorities (...). There is the risk of having teachers of various kinds and tendencies, as is the case in other subjects. To avoid this, you would have to abolish schools. Since this is not possible, I would say it was worth taking the risk all the same" [from an interview by Sergio CICATELLI, *Religione e scuola* (1999-2000) no. 1, p. 8]. Luciano PAZZAGLIA, Catholic University of Milan, has written recently on this topic: "We believe that in the reformed school, time should be allocated to religious knowledge which, going beyond the Concordat provisions, leads every student without distinction to seek information even on religious phenomena. This seems all the more plausible as, in the context of the macro-transformation taking place, European countries will be increasingly asked to combine their cultures and traditions, in which the religious factor has played and continues to play a major role, with those coming from elsewhere. There is no need to emphasise that, when this teaching of religious knowledge becomes part of the State school programme, it will have to be on a par with other subjects, not only on the level of teaching approach, but obviously also on the level of the competence and juridical status of the teachers" [*Ispirazione e scelte del cristiano in Italia, in Europa*, in *Il Regno* (2000) no. 4, p. 50].

theology no longer has the right even to figure among the disciplines on the curriculum. This has been, and still is the case mostly in Latin countries with a catholic majority, and to a less drastic extent, in countries with a protestant tradition. The historical details are known. Responsibility lies not only with the State (Napoleonic centralisation, monopoly), but also with some of the choices made by the Church, not the last of these has been to restrict during the whole post-tridentine period the teaching of the sacred sciences exclusively to candidates to the priesthood, to certain institutions (seminaries, faculties staffed by members of the clergy or of male religious orders), kept segregated generally from the influence of the surrounding culture. The result has been two-fold: on the one hand, the impoverishment of the sacred sciences, cutting them off from the stimuli of parallel research in the human sciences (for example, it was not till the end of the 19th century that the first attempts were made to adopt the historico-critical method in biblical exegesis); and on the other, depriving the newly-born modern world of science and technology – and including the society born of the industrial revolution, popular education, urbanisation and democratisation – of the possibility of a systematic dialogue or at least of a healthy dialectic with theology.

Relations between Church and State have improved considerably with time. Even dialogue between State and ecclesiastical universities is no longer an exception. Conditions exist today to make possible the reestablishment of reciprocal agreements and collaboration. There are universities in Europe, dependent on churches, which can award diplomas officially recognised by the State. There are denominational faculties of theology, with full rights, in public universities. There are inter-university agreements whereby a diploma awarded by an ecclesiastical faculty of theology can be recognised in the public sector as being equivalent to an analogous diploma in religious sciences released by a Humanities' faculty in a State university[32]. These and other similar initiatives have been made possible because, in certain countries more than in others, the *non-involvement of the secular State* in matters concerning religious

32. "If in Italy, the culture of the Catholics and their values, starting with religious ones, have been excluded from the main stream of culture, and have found only a minimal space in the media and information channels, despite the fact that a catholic party held a large part of the political power, this is due also (perhaps, in fact, especially) to the tendency of Catholics – and started by Catholics – to consider themselves somehow different, apart, and to create their own ghettoes. As it happens, this fitted in admirably with their adversaries' intention to create ghettoes for them" (E. GALLI DELLA LOGGIA, *Corriere della sera*, March 4, 1995).

knowledge is now a thing of the past, especially as religious knowledge has left its mark on so much of the educational and cultural policy of the modern European State. A thing of the past also is the *jealous claim of the Churches*, in particular, of the catholic magisterium, to regulate the production of religious expression by making it comply with the norms of a self-referential orthodoxy.

One of the problems that was discovered – happily resolved in some countries, but far from a plausible solution in others – was that of the scientific and professional training of the teachers of religion who work in schools. In the measure that religious teaching moves on from the "school catechism" of the past, and, because of the new objective circumstances mentioned above, moves closer to becoming a common subject for all pupils, in line with the educational and critical aims of the school[33], so the type of academic and professional training given to the teacher must change. The State will have to create the necessary structures for this training. In Europe, some forms of initial training are already satisfactory, others are in the process of being restructured[34]. The same goes for continuing formation[35]. In the neo-Latin countries, all

---

33. T. GARCÍA REGIDOR, *De la "catequesis escolar" a la "enseñanza religiosa escolar"*, in *Sinite* 40 (1999) 417-438.

34. A bird's eye view of Europe shows that the basic training of teachers of RE (catholic or protestant) is normally provided in one or other of the following ways: either in a State or public university with a faculty of theology or pedagogical sciences (this is the case of Austria, Germany, United Kingdom, prevalently Lutheran northern countries, Greece and, by special statute from France, Alsace Lorraine): or in advanced institutes of religious, pedagogical and/or catechetical sciences, run by the Churches, and authorised to award diplomas qualifying the graduate to teach RE in State and/or denominational schools (this is the case in Belgium, Croatia, Ireland, Italy, Luxembourg, Malta, Holland, Portugal, Spain, Switzerland). In Germany, the candidate who chooses the career of a religion teacher, must have a degree also in an other subject. If he has his mandate revoked by his respective Church, or if posts for teachers of RE are scarce, he does not lose his post, but instead is employed as a teacher of his other subject: this is guaranteed by State law. In the United Kingdom and in northern countries, unlike other States, the religion teacher has no need of ecclesiastical approval (declaration of suitability, a catholic *missio canonica*, a protestant *vocatio*), he is not subject to revocations for pastoral reasons; he is recruited and admitted into the school system according to criteria which are exclusively academic and professional. In these countries, RE is usually cross-denominational or non-denominational, and as such, does not bring into play the denominational subjectivity of either the teacher or the pupil. Likewise free of the control of religious authorities, and dependent solely on State or regional regulations, are the teachers of secular morality, or natural ethics, or history of religions, or of other alternative subjects, as in Belgium, Germany, Luxemburg, Spain and in the 14 European schools functioning in various countries of the Union.

35. Where religion teachers have a clear juridical and professional status, they have to attend periodically one of the regional centres or institutes. In the United Kingdom, for example, there exist regional centres for teachers, polytechnic institutes, and the national

this seems at the moment unlikely, at least in the short term of course, the present prescriptions of the concordat governing catholic education, and the agreements signed in the last few years, and even in the last few months, with the various religious organisations, make it impossible even to think even of substantial or rapid changes. But political realism and educational responsibility suggest it would be better not to put off finding solutions, for this would only cause further degradation, in quality and quantity, of school religious knowledge, already very deficient.

Some challenges in particular appear urgent and not deferrable[36]. I shall mention them briefly, without saying whether the conditions exist to make it feasible to respond to them. In any case, conditions vary from country to country.

1. From now on, within the framework of the conditions of the concordat, there is a need to rethink the training of religion teachers, putting it within the framework of the principles and rules of the formation of the other teachers of State schools. The purpose of this is to remove the regrettable dichotomy which isolates artificially the programme of studies of the religion teacher from the common course followed by his colleagues, and to encourage more consistent collaboration between State and Church which, on the matter of formation, continue to ignore each other or almost[37].

2. Train teachers who can work with a "European" mentality and tools, in the sense that, they can educate through the specificity of the cultural-religious approach, as citizens capable of living with their own

---

Foundation for educational research: religion teachers benefit from these in the same way as teachers of other subjects. In Holland, there are catholic, protestant and secular pedagogical centres. In Belgium, active support is provided by the national Secretariat for catholic education and other mixed groups, which promote contacts among teachers and researchers, between schools and universities. In Denmark, as in England, even the religion teacher has a right to a sabbatical term every 7 years for his/her personal updating. In Bavaria, there is a regional institute for continuing formation (*Akademie für Lehrerfortbildung*), which has the task of dealing with subjective or objective needs, indicating the general areas for updating, drawing up a programme of activities each term, training or updating inspectors, heads and training staff, making materials and help available, even in cases of self-updating. All this is organised for all the teachers in general, and for the different categories, including religious teachers.

36. I have developed this more fully in *Stimoli e prospettive per la formazione dell'insegnante di religione dal contesto europeo*, in M. CIMOSA (ed.), *L'insegnante di religione nell'attuale rinnovamento dell'educazione scolastica*, Roma, Las, 1998, 11-24.

37. Cf. G. CAMPANINI, *La formazione degli insegnanti di religione: compiti della chiesa e responsabilità dello stato*, in A. GIANNI (ed.), *L'istruzione religiosa nelle scuole italiane*, Cinisello Balsamo, EP, 1991, 110-131.

identity and, at the same time, capable of living together with otherness in a pluralistic world. According to the philosophy of recent school reforms introduced more or less everywhere in Europe, and the specific guidelines which accompany the religious instruction programmes, it is expected, in general terms, that the teaching of religions will be a contribution to the development of the personal and cultural identity of the pupil being taught; will be a preparation for learning to live with others in a pluralistic society; will promote mutual tolerance and the possibility of dialogue between individuals and groups from different ethnic and religious backgrounds; will promote religious competence (or *key qualifications*, as they say in Germany) in terms of critical information, ability to judge and make personal decisions, of communicability; and will mature the ability of the pupil to deal with the historical, cultural and religious heritage of Europe, and especially, of his own nation.

3. Supposing, as was mentioned above, that religious courses in fact came under the direct responsibility of the State, the profile and the professional curriculum of the teachers of this subject would still have to be worked out. Experiments in other European countries, show that, with the specificity of the historical and cultural context saveguarded, this is something feasible. They also encourage other countries to try out new types of formation courses leading, for example, to the design of a new degree course in religious sciences.

4. But quite apart from the formation of the teacher of RE, in one or other of the typologies referred to, an urgent need is expressed to reform the general knowledge of all teachers, starting with the teachers of the humanities, who often continue to have, perhaps unconsciously, an incomplete idea of the cultural roots of their disciplines. They should be able to interpret correctly the religious factor when they encounter it in their discipline, treating it according to the epistemological logic of their own discipline, instead of expunging it or exploiting it unnaturally. This implies a newly-thought out academic curriculum, integrated, depending on the type of discipline, and with the specific contents and the specific methodologies provided by religious sciences[38].

38. Translated by Allen Geppert.

Identity Before or Identity Through Familiarization with Plurality? The Actual Discussion Concerning School Based Religious Education in Germany

Norbert Mette[1]

1. Two Opposing Viewpoints

The traditional form of religious education in public schools in Germany, based upon the principle of confessionalism, has recently been the focus of discussion. At stake here is not so much religion's role in the school curriculum, but whether the principle of confessionalism that directs religious education is still adequate in a context of cultural and religious pluralism in contemporary society. We can refer here to the exemplary position held by the famous educationalist Wolfgang Klafki[2] in an article in which he argues that it is necessary to assure the "introduction of problems of worldview, ethics and religions"[3] a proper and significant place in school curricula, beyond its being taken into account in other school subjects (such as history or art education). On the one hand, we see how "in our socio-political environment individual people and social groups of different denominations and ethical attitudes, developed under very different socialization conditions"[4], have more

---

1. In this contribution I will rely on and continue what I have debated on other occasions. See especially N. METTE, *Identität,* in V. DREHSEN *et al.* (eds.), *Wörterbuch des Christentums,* Gütersloh – Zürich, 1988, 503ff; *Identität ohne Religion? Eine religionspädagogische Herausforderung,* in E. ARENS (ed.), *Habermas und die Theologie,* Düsseldorf, 1989, 160-178; *Religionspädagogik,* Düsseldorf, 1994; *Begegnung mit dem Fremden: Aufgabe des Religionsunterrichts,* in R. GÖLLNER & B. TROCHOLEPCZY (eds.), *Religion in der Schule?,* Freiburg im Breisgau, 1995, 118-132; *Das umstrittene Konfessionalitätsprinzip,* in *Neue Sammlung* 37 (1997) 207-230; *Individualisierung und Enttraditionalisierung als (religions-)pädagogische Herausforderung,* in N. METTE, *Praktisch-theologische Erkundungen,* Münster, 1998, 117-131; *Der Beitrag des Religionsunterrichts zum Bildungsauftrag der Schule,* in *ibid.,* 143-156; *Identitätsbildung heute – im Modus christlichen Glaubens,* in *Katechetische Blätter* 124 (1999) 397-405. This paper was translated from German by Antoon Bekaert.
2. Cfr. W. KLAFKI, *Braucht eine "gute Schule" einen neuen Unterrichtsbereich LER?,* in K.E. GRÖZINGER *et al.* (eds.), *Religion in der schulischen Bildung und Erziehung,* Berlin, 1999, 197-209.
3. *Ibid.,* p. 202.
4. *Ibid.*

and more to work together and compete with each other. It is therefore necessary to establish rules for the common good and to be aware of the "possibilities of mutually enriching and widening each other's horizons"[5]. On the other hand, the problem of the personal life of the individual has sharpened. Klafki comments: "Under the conditions of modern secularization, of advanced worldwide net working, and so-called value pluralism, especially in societies where those tendencies have been unfolding for a long time – and that is certainly the case for our society – the problems of developing a personal identity, a responsible life concept, of developing one's capacities to deal with ethical and religious problems and of making responsible decisions are characteristic of our times"[6]. Other urgent matters include finding and promoting peaceful ways of living together, and finding adequate world food supplies, etc.[7]

Schools, therefore, have the task to let "experiences such as friendship, love, disillusions, guilt and forgiveness, trust and distrust, tolerance and intolerance, hope and despair, altruism and self-centeredness"[8] become themes of reflection. And, Klafki argues further, "religions and ideologies can be seen as historically evolved and unfolding 'powers', which in their capacity as cultural and political institutions influence life forms, social relations and the understanding of oneself and reality"[9]. Klafki endorses the position outlined in his dissertation, that every school should be given the opportunity "to further develop, in collaboration with religious communities, inter-religious cooperative forms and to open up classes of religious education for pupils who are not committed to a determined religious creed"[10].

However, Christian churches responsible for religious education at school – at least until now – are not in favor of such a proposal for cooperation. Although they recognize the far-reaching changes in social conditions, they seem convinced that they have to promote, in their view even in the interest of the pupils themselves, another idea. "We live", so we read in the memo of the *Evangelische Kirche* in Germany (EKD), "in a pluralistic world, characterized by contradictions. The dilemmas of national, ethnic, cultural and religious identity

---

5. W. KLAFKI, *Braucht eine "gute Schule" einen neuen Unterrichtsbereich LER?* (n. 2), p. 202.
6. *Ibid.,* p. 201.
7. *Ibid.,* p. 200.
8. *Ibid.,* p. 202.
9. *Ibid.*
10. *Ibid.,* p. 209.

globally increase. These dilemmas will be intensified by an oversimplified unification, that does away with individual, national and cultural traditions. On the other hand, it is necessary to refrain from a self-satisfied withdrawal into these forms and to aim intentionally at a greater communality. The person who does not fear for his/her identity, is able to open him/herself to others and take up social responsibility. Identity refers to one's own, immediate life horizon and ultimately to the final goals, the protection of the unity of the world, the preservation of creation"[11]. The German Roman Catholic bishops even more intensively stress the connection of "identity and familiarization" (*Identität und Verständigung*) in their letter on "The educative power of school religious education": "There is no multi-cultural identity. But there is a proper cultural identity that can familiarize itself with other cultural identities"[12].

It is clear that both positions point towards a problem that goes far beyond religious education. How do we come to a thoughtful identity at the level of individual development? Is it better when young people at first are deeply rooted in a determined culture[13] – and thus in a determined religion? Or do we have to say that there are no longer homogeneous life spaces and that children, therefore, in an early stage of their education, have to be familiarized with pluralistic life styles and with ways to deal with them? Is such a situation even favorable with respect to the development of one's own identity? Also, what is the role of religious education in the process of identity formation? Which role could or should religious education *optima forma* play in that process?

The following reflections aim at providing a useful contribution to these questions. A lack of empirical data tends to give rise to a theoretical or abstract treatment of such questions. A first step might involve a better grasp of "identity", as the concept is used in church texts, in order to critically confront that concept of identity with other concepts.

---

11. *Identität und Verständigung. Standort und Perspektiven des Religionsunterrichts in der Pluralität. Eine Denkschrift der Evangelischen Kirche in Deutschland*, Gütersloh, 1994, p. 82.

12. *Die bildende Kraft des Religionsunterrichts. Zur Konfessionalität des katholischen Religionsunterrichts* (Die deutschen Bischöfe, 56), Bonn, 1996, p. 28.

13. See F. SCHWEITZER, *Religion ist mehr als Ethik – auch aus evangelischer Sicht?*, in A. BIESINGER & J. HÄNLE (eds.), *Gott – mehr als Ethik. Der Streit um LER und Religionsunterricht* (Quaestiones disputatae, 167), Freiburg, 1997, 164-176, esp. pp. 174-176.

2. The Concept of Identity Determined by Christian Faith as Developed in the Letter of the German Bishops

In the two church texts cited above, we find what is constitutive for identity as fostered by religious education. The fundamental position of both churches is very similar and the differences do not seem insuperable[14]. The text of the EKD aims at giving equal weight to both principles: confessional determination and dialogical cooperation[15], in a strained but clear attempt at balance. Confessional orientation is given by the confessional commitments of the teachers and by teaching the doctrine of justification. From their confessional standpoint, it is only logical that evangelical education throws itself open for the whole community of pupils[16]. On the other hand, the position of the German bishops concerning the confessional principle seems to be more rigid, as becomes clear in the logical unfolding of its argumentation[17].

The text's global argument tries to establish that withholding the principle of confessionalism is not rooted in church motives, but is necessary for the sake of the matter itself. The kind of education the school has a duty to promote gives young people the possibility of finding a life horizon of their own[18]. It is accepted that self-education always has to take place within concrete contexts, in which the universal can manifest itself and can have its effects. It is only possible to recognize others in their particularity when one is aware of how culture has shaped one's own context. The theological sections of the pastoral letter display the same dialectics between the concrete and the general. In the center stands the Gospel in its educative potentiality. A quotation that can make this point clear reads as follows: "The Gospel as God's declaration

14. Cfr. F. SCHWEITZER, *"Identität und Verständigung" und "Bildende Kraft des Religionsunterrichts". Zum Vergleich von EKD-Denkschrift und Bischofswort aus evangelischer Sicht*, in R. FRIELING & F. SCHWEITZER (eds.), *Religionsunterricht und Konfessionen*, Göttingen, 1999, 71-86.

15. Cfr. *Identität und Verständigung* (n. 11), p. 59.

16. Cfr. the comments of R. SCHLÜTER, *Aufbau einer konfessionellen Identität?*, in *Religionspädagogische Beiträge* 36 (1995) 17-30; ID., *Die "Konfessionalität des Religionsunterrichts" in der Pluralität*, in *RHS* 40 (1987) 210-222.

17. This is not an easy task, because of internal inconsistencies in the document. It is therefore useful to go back to essays of one of the main authors of the document: H.P. SILLER, *Konfessionalität und Perspektivenübernahme. Der Beitrag des katholischen Religionsunterrichts zur Allgemeinbildung*, in *Religionspädagogische Beiträge* 36 (1995) 3-15; ID., *Der Beitrag des Religionsunterrichts zur Bildung der nachwachsenden Generation*, in R. GÖLLNER & B. TROCHOLEPCZY (eds.), *Religion in der Schule?* (n. 1), 57-73.

18. See *Die bildende Kraft des Religionsunterrichts* (n. 12), pp. 26ff.

of love makes it possible that the power that bears all reality, God's love, expressly turns into an educative power for all pupils. Putting our trust in that power, it is possible to cope with the pressures of daily life and the difficulties in one's personal life story, and to develop one's identity. The identity remains communicative and able to appreciate other identities. The other, the 'alien', is allowed to remain in his or her otherness. He/she has not to be as I am, because his/her very otherness displays the inexhaustible richness of reality borne by God's love"[19].

The bishops further argue that the Gospel would remain in a vacuum, if not represented and materialized in institutions. Here the pastoral letter criticizes a widespread attitude fostered by the individualization process in modern society, i.e., that institutions restrict individual freedom. On the contrary, according to the bishops, they strengthen identity by supporting the individual and his freedom[20], at least in the institutions not bent on opportunistic self-interest. They do so to the extent that they can be considered as institutions of the eschatological attitudes of Faith, Hope and Love – although marked by imperfection. This is also true for the Church. Together with the Church, these institutions are the holders of educative power, because in them it is possible to learn how to realize a life together with others on the basis of faith, hope and charity. To bring the matter more into focus: "If general education actually helps one to recognize not only other individuals, but life in general in its cultural particularity, then the preconditions are well established in Catholic religious education, since it reflects the manifold perspectives of the different local churches"[21].

Implicit in the bishops' statement is the argument that, as long as ecumenical unity has not been established, it will be necessary to maintain the concrete confessional 'Gestalt' of the Church with its different accents in practice and in doctrine, if its educative power is to be fruitful. "Confessional" should no longer be assimilated with "self-centered-

---

19. *Die bildende Kraft des Religionsunterrichts* (n. 12), p. 34: "Das Evangelium als Liebeserklärung Gottes macht es möglich, daß die alle Wirklichkeit tragende Kraft, die Liebe Gottes, ausdrücklich realisiert und zur bildenden Kraft des Schülers und der Schülerin werden kann. Im Vertrauen auf dieses Gehaltensein kann es gelingen, von dem täglichen Erwartungsdruck und zugleich vom Unheil in der eigenen Lebensgeschichte Abstand zu gewinnen, also Ich-Identität zu entwickeln ... Die Identität bleibt kommunikativ und verständigungswillig. Der andere, der Fremde, darf in seiner Andersheit verbleiben, er braucht nicht so zu sein, wie ich bin; denn gerade in seiner Andersheit verbürgt er den unerschöpflichen Reichtum der von Gottes Liebe umfaßten Wirklichkeit".

20. *Ibid.*, p. 39.

21. *Ibid.*, p. 44. Later in the letter the argumentation even goes as follows: "Die Kirche ist also schon in sich ein nahezu universales Medium der Allgemeinbildung" (p. 62 – sic!).

ness, self-satisfaction and isolation", but has to be understood and practised as "communicative identity"[22]. Against this background, the educative potentiality of Catholic confessional religious education for the
young is unfolded by means of six guiding principles[23]:
– Concrete existence – The students can see what it means to live in
  faith and in ecclesial community by looking at their teachers.
– Openness to different perspectives – Religious education is well
  adapted to the mutual integration of different perspectives, because
  many perspectives are represented in it.
– Autonomy – Religious education, on the one hand, gives young people many examples of becoming autonomous and of perceiving
  responsibility in a faith perspective. On the other hand, it also favors
  the self-distance necessary if one does not want to acquiesce to everything without distinction.
– The guarantee of a meaningful life – Instead of superficial ways of
  trying to make sense of the world in postmodern society, the Church
  manifests itself as an institution, represented by trustworthy persons,
  that guarantees the possibility of living a successful life.
– Being-for-others – As a counter to merciless competition, the Church
  responds to the cold stream of self-interest with the warm stream of
  "being-for-others"[24].
– Ego-identity – This implies continuity in the life history of a person,
  besides being recognized by the others as a social subject. Religious
  education is presented as "a counterpart to the functional expectations
  and the rigid role definitions that prevail and from which many suffer,
  on the basis of the remembrances, stories, traditions and richness of
  metaphors, of the analogous language it carries with it. Education has
  the potential to bring about a reinforcement of remembrance, of imagination and judgment, of the faculty of reading and interpretation, of
  resistance and therefore of identity of the ego. The overstrained world-
  liness that is so characteristic of all our conflicts is relieved in the educative perspective of the eschatological determination of all reality"[25].

---

22. *Die bildende Kraft des Religionsunterrichts* (n. 12), p. 49: "An die Stelle von Ver-
schmelzung und Vereinheitlichung tritt der in der eigenen Geschichte gewonnene Reichtum als Gewinn auch für die anderen. Die Geschichte der Ausbildung einer eigenen
kirchlichen Identität auf beiden Seiten rückgängig zu machen, ist nicht denkbar, aber
auch nicht einmal wünschbar. Das wäre abstrakt. Ökumenisch kann deshalb nur sein, wer
in diesem Sinne auch konfessionell ist".
   23. *Ibid.*, pp. 61-66.
   24. *Ibid.*, p. 65.
   25. *Ibid.*, p. 66.

Despite its logic, this line of argument becomes irritating, specifically when one tries to apply it to an actual group of students. A confessional claim on identity building and religious education, however, not only needs to be empirically tested, it also needs to be theoretically discussed.

3. The Significance of Religion or Faith in the Context of Actual Socialization

A very controversial point – not in the least with reference to daily life in schools – is the question whether the bishops' lofty ideal takes into account the real existing population of students or – sharply worded – if they have constructed an ideal student, who in principle can enter wholeheartedly into the educative potential of religious education, but who remains an exception in an actual student population. It is true that empirical surveys, even recent ones, have established that the school subject of religion, in comparison with other subjects, is better than it is reputed to be[26]. Such surveys also reveal, however, that the impulses to reinforce a conscious religious attitude and conduct are not very strong; all effort to bind them to a local church ecclesiastically is clearly a futureless enterprise, above all when the school career becomes longer and longer[27].

This finding need not imply that young people of today have an aversion to religion. The situation is more complex[28]. Very distinctive factors are of importance here. First, there are domains in which the Church still plays an outstanding role in the socialization process, whereas in others no influence at all is exerted by religion, at least not in its institutionalized form. This means that some children and young people cannot ignore the question of their confessional origin, whereas for others such a question is completely out of their reach. Only for an absolute minority is ecclesiastically institutionalized religion given significant place in their lives[29]. The organizers of the most recent Shell survey state in a laconic way: "Generally speaking we are at a stage where Christian

26. Cfr. A. BUCHER, *Religionsunterricht: Unersetzlich? Überflüssig?*, in *Katechetische Blätter* 123 (1998) 47-50.

27. Cfr. ID., *Religionsunterricht: Besser als sein Ruf? Empirische Einblicke in ein umstrittenes Fach*, Innsbruck – Wien, 1996, pp. 113ff.

28. Cfr. F. SCHWEITZER, *Die Suche nach eigenem Glauben. Einführung in die Religionspädagogik des Jugendalters*, Gütersloh, 1996, esp. pp. 19-49.

29. For up to date information and conclusions, see W. FUCHS-HEINRITZ, *Religion*, in DEUTSCHE SHELL (ed.), *Jugend 2000*, Band 1, Opladen, 2000, 157-180.

churches, under the actual conditions and in the way they have operated until now, have few chances to gain influence upon the young generation"[30]. We would certainly miss the point, however, if this would bring us to label young people as "post-religious", because it does not do justice to religion if we identify it with its ecclesiastical-institutional form. If and in what way such a (post-ecclesiastic) religiosity, without ties to a specific institution, will take shape, remain open questions[31].

The first lead that promises to be empirically productive results from the hypothesis that religious styles vary with respect to the youth cultures and scenes one belongs to[32]. Attention should also be paid to the manifold possibilities of "silent ecstasies" as are manifestly purchased and experienced by many young people[33]. Even where young people define themselves as "expressly religious", their opinions vary widely, from a vague attitude that puts aside the question of God's existence for the time being but simultaneously without excluding the possibility that in the future it might become relevant, to definite reflections about God, but generally without communicating them to others, and from undeniable sympathy for fundamentalist positions, to varying styles of church affiliation, to prophetically inspired political engagement, to occasional interest in non-Christian religions, and finally to different forms of a "modern-postmodern transformation of the faith in God"[34].

In order to give an adequate description of the general trends in the attitude of young people towards religion and religiosity, one might say:
– Young people do not constitute a religious no-man's land, but reflect the same plurality as can be found in society as a whole.
– The "heretical imperative" (P.L. Berger) as a result of prevailing pluralism most probably leads young people to compose in a syncretistic way a religiosity of their own by choosing what they like within the range of existing religions.

---

30. A. FISCHER et al., Hauptergebnisse, in Jugend 2000 (n. 29), 11-21, p. 21.

31. Cfr. F. SCHWEITZER, Die Suche nach eigenem Glauben (n. 28), passim; V. DREHSEN, Alles andere als Nullbock auf Religion. Religiöse Einstellungen Jugendlicher zwischen Wahlzwang und Fundamentalismusneigung, in Jahrbuch für Religionspädagogik 10 (1993) 47-69.

32. Cfr. K. GABRIEL, Jugend, Religion und Kirche im gesellschaftlichen Modernisierungsprozeß, in K. GABRIEL & H. HOBELSBERGER (eds.), Jugend, Religion und Modernisierung. Kirchliche Jugendarbeit als Suchbewegung, Opladen, 1994, 53-74.

33. Cfr. D. BAACKE, Die stillen Ekstasen der Jugend. Zur Wandlung des religiösen Bezugs, in Jahrbuch für Religionspädagogik 6 (1989) 3-25.

34. Cfr. K.E. NIPKOW, Jugendliche und junge Erwachsene vor der religiösen Frage, in G. KLOSINSKI (ed.), Religion als Chance oder Risiko, Bern, 1994, 111-136.

- The criterion for choosing is the one in direct connection with one's own life and the problems that arise there. The interaction with the existing religious interpretative schemes is guided by "occasional, situation-centered" reflections[35].
- What is offered by the churches stands out in an unfavorable light because young people experience it as coming from a distant planet. On the other hand, when they meet church representatives who stand open to their lifestyles and life patterns and adopt a positive attitude, such individuals are generally well received. Anyone who expects this to be a stable basis for recruitment, however, will soon be disappointed.
- In short: under the conditions of individualization and pluralization the very thing required by young people in general, also applies to the domain of religion: the right to self-determination[36]. Unconditional respect for that right is the only claim that can be demanded from a pedagogy of religion that wants to do justice to these young people.

If we examine the situation in a matter-of-fact way, we can see how, in the young generation, the attitude to life that is also to be found more and more in older people has become predominant: self-realization, having fun in life and enjoying one's life as one's ultimate goal. This does not at all mean – as is argued by M.N. Ebertz[37] – that commitment towards others and one's own convictions, partnership and harmony no longer matter. But also here no indications of (explicit) religious motives are present. That it is possible to conduct a meaningful life on the basis of traditional Christian faith seems no longer conceivable and is even no longer understood by the majority of young people. If a certain religiosity can be ascribed to young people or adolescents at all, then it is a very self-centered one which should be treated as a private affair – thus in any case a very "invisible religion" (Th. Luckmann).

4. Inappropriateness of a Religiously-Embedded Identity in (Post)Modern Society?

These empirical findings concerning the significance of religion and faith under actual conditions of socialization seem to correspond to theo-

35. Cfr. D. FISCHER & A. SCHÖLL, *Lebenspraxis und Religion. Fallanalysen zur subjektiven Religiosität von Jugendlichen*, Gütersloh, 1994.
36. Cfr. A. FEIGE, *Vom Schicksal zur Wahl. Postmoderne Individualisierungspraxis als Problem für eine institutionalisierte Religionspraxis*, in *Pastoraltheologie* 83 (1994) 93-109.
37. Cfr. M.N. EBERTZ, *Erosion der Gnadenanstalt? Zum Wandel der Sozialgestalt von Kirche*, Frankfurt am Main, 1998, pp. 122-129.

retical reflections about modernization and are all but coincidental. This implies that there are no indications that this situation is likely to change fundamentally in the future.

In support of that position, we can refer to an article of U. Schimank, where this author argues that the individual and systemic identity forms are linked with each other, and explains why this is the case[38]. Based on this premise, it must be concluded that an identity formation grounded in a (explicitly) religious, more specifically Christian basis – in its traditional form – is unfit in modern society and leads into unsolvable identity crises. By "traditional form", is meant that to a traditional social form there was a corresponding "substantial-teleological" identity form, i.e. an identity form that was intrinsically determined and oriented towards a predetermined life aim. It was completely dependent upon the unattainable Absolute (God), comprehending all domains of life and canon of all thoughts and actions. The differentiation characteristic of the development of modern society implied emancipation from the religious explanation of the world. Partial systems imposed themselves as functioning according to their proper rules. This process even took hold of the institutional agents of religion, the churches, which were "deprived of their society-encompassing claim on absoluteness and became one partial system among others"[39]. According to this theoretical concept, they will continue to be dysfunctional in modern society as long as they consider it necessary in these circumstances to cling to that traditional identity ideal. Because the identity form corresponding with modern society is "reflexive subjectivism", where individuals are no longer defined in terms of predetermined (theonomic) aims, but autonomously make their own subjectivity into the guideline of their life and actions.

C. Wippermann comes to a totally different conclusion in this respect[40]. When comparing religious, and especially Christian young people to some of their peers without a clear confession, he considers: "the stronger and earlier young people identify themselves with a particular

---

38. Cfr. U. SCHIMANK, *Funktionale Differenzierung und reflexiver Subjektivismus. Zum Entsprechungsverhältnis von Gesellschafts- und Identitätsform*, in *Soziale Welt* 36 (1985) 447-465; here quoted by C. WIPPERMANN, *Religiöse Weltanschauungen – Zwischen individuellem Design und traditionellem Schema*, in R.K. SILBEREISEN *et al.* (eds.), *Jungsein in Deutschland. Jugendliche und Junge Erwachsene 1991 und 1996*, Opladen, 1996, 113-126, pp. 113ff.

39. *Ibid.*, p. 114.

40. Cfr. C. WIPPERMANN, *Religion, Identität und Lebensführung*, Opladen, 1998, esp. pp. 207-209.

world view, transcend their every day life conceptions and think within the framework of their view, the better and earlier the stable formation of identity is likely to succeed, which in general enables them to integrate their further experiences"[41]. Wippermann found a specific "advantage" for Christian faith in the fact that it more strongly than other worldviews interconnects acting, thinking and communicating. In opposition to the thesis that an auto-referential identity formation is more functional for a differentiated society, he considers a hetero-referential world view to be more appropriate in finding a stable identity. Such a worldview at least frees the individual from turning around in circles[42].

The question is rather if it is advisable to build out a stable identity under the conditions of (post)modern society. This question is at the forefront in the actual discussions about identity[43]. G. Heinrichs has attracted attention by introducing and opposing two new conceptions into the discussion[44]. Influenced by the social interactionism of G.H. Mead, partially in addition to the stages model of psychosocial development worked out by E.H. Erikson, a conception of identity has been developed in the sixties corresponding to the ideal of achieving an appropriate balance between the proper claims and social expectations. "A successful identity is seen as the capacity of continuity and delimitation, as the capacity of unification under competitive role claims linked with the central philosophical-ethical concept of autonomy. Education should contribute to the acquisition of different roles, to reflection, to breaking away from conventionalism and making individuality possible"[45]. This normative conception of a successful identity, which at the same time is put forward as a precondition for the establishment of an egalitarian and just society, is radically criticized by theoretical conceptions labeled as postmodern, to which G. Heinrichs also adheres. The conception that a person has the capacity to be a 'self' in a consistent and ongoing way is refuted as untenable and even dangerous, because it might very well lead to overestimation and even to a situation where one might be tempted to impose it upon others as an obligatory attitude standard. On the contrary, the fact that such a state of affairs is no longer possible under the conditions of a plural and continually chang-

---

41. C. WIPPERMANN, *Religion, Identität und Lebensführung* (n. 40), p. 297.

42. *Ibid.* – Wippermann speaks of "tautologische Endlosschleife".

43. For a good overview of this discussion, cfr. H. KEUPP & R. HÖFER (eds.), *Identitätsarbeit heute*, Frankfurt am Main, 1998.

44. Cfr. G. HEINRICHS, *Identität oder nicht? Plädoyer für ein Denken der Differenz in der (Religions-)Pädagogik*, in *Feuervogel* 4 (1998) 31-37.

45. *Ibid.*, p. 32.

ing society, is seen as an opportunity: "The subject in a postmodern conception is the effect of discursive strategies, it comes into being, changes, disappears. The conception of autonomy is, on the contrary, criticized because it always objectifies, and thus tries to eliminate the others. The subject is put into perspective and is seen in its discursive dependence ... Experiences of fragmentation are considered in the postmodern theory as an opportunity not to want to do away with the impassable difference with the others, but to keep it upright, which is seen as a precondition of freedom. Identity in this context no longer functions as normative for education, the orientation towards plurality and multiplicity replaces the representation of a successful identity"[46].

The typological distinction that is operated between a modern and a postmodern concept of identity can be discussed. A certain doubt arises whether the alleged "modern" concept of "balancing identity" is not too rapidly disqualified. It tries to attract attention to the faculty of a subject capable of acting under ever-changing circumstances, but does not leave the continuity and consistency of the acting person himself unaffected. "A successful identity" means a progressing and lifelong search process and not a final and fixed point in a development[47]. It can be argued furthermore that especially in this conception, the relationship with the others on the basis of the unconditional recognition of their otherness is constitutive. It remains to be seen if the postmodern identity concept can answer the question whether the experience of difference, plurality and multiplicity does not presuppose the representation of a self-linked-with-others. Even the alleged patchwork-identity needs to have a foundation upon or at which the different and varied patches can be sewn together.

It is precisely this pointing back to something predetermined and constant that argues in favor of a completely different identity concept, neither modern nor postmodern[48]. It is assumed that persons only gain identity and thus sense for their individual life conception to the extent that they recognize they are embedded in a meaningful collectively-appreciated context wherein individual existence is integrated and which constitutes the only safeguard for security. The partisans of this concept warn for the widespread loss of sense and orientation in actual

---

46. G. HEINRICHS, *Identität oder nicht?* (n. 44), p. 33.

47. Cfr. L. KRAPPMANN, *Die Identitätsproblematik nach Erikson aus einer interaktionstheoretischen Sicht*, in H. KEUPP & R. HÖFER (eds.), *Identitätsarbeit heute* (n. 43), 66-92.

48. I rely for the following on the typology of G. NUNNER-WINKLER, *Veränderte Wertorientierungen, neue Identitätskonzepte*, in *Informationsdienst o.J.* (1990) no. 3, 3-8.

society, which they link to the fact that everything is put into question and nothing is recognized any longer as binding; therefore it would be better to return to the insights of the past and no longer neglect the tradition(s).

Even if this traditional identity concept is accepted and experienced by the individual as a relief from the incomprehensibility, that is felt as an overcharge, it is characterized by the fact that it remains a concept stamped by (post)modern society: to adopt it means it is a product of a consciously made choice. Because it cannot restrict the range of possible options, the choice that has been made has to be motivated – implying it can be reconsidered – on other grounds than in traditional societies where there was almost no range of options.

G. Nunner-Winkler draws attention to the fact that the postmodern and the traditional conceptions of identity have something in common, because both are oriented towards contents; in the first case towards completely changing and exchangeable contents, in the second towards contents predetermined by tradition(s), this point precisely constituting the aporia. A way out is only possible, it is argued, by adopting a concept which "links identity not to the nature of the contents, but to the way in which contents are assimilated. Identity is gained by the people who autonomously pose the question of their identity and resolve it"[49]. The highest level of autonomy – after the two preceding ones of freedom and self-determination – is characterized by the fact that the ego determines what it wants in accordance with criteria that it can decide upon. In this way, it goes beyond the level of conventional back-up of norms in the sense of considering something right because God or the church determined it that way or because it has always been so[50].

As a result of the reflections in the last two sections, we can state: there is not only a virtually universal absence of explicitly religious, especially ecclesiastic-confessional elements in the way the actual identity is construed, but beyond that, in the theoretical discussions, it is no longer considered advisable to fall back on them, whether it would mean to return to the traditional society form or because this would not be good for the constitution of a subject capable of autonomously judging and acting under the actual – plural – conditions.

---

49. G. NUNNER-WINKLER, *Jugend und Identität als pädagogisches Problem*, in *Zeitschrift für Pädagogik* 36 (1990) 671-686, here p. 675.
50. *Ibid.*, pp. 678ff.

Before starting up the discussion on the level of theology and religious pedagogy with the questions and requirements resulting from
empirical data and theory, we first want to treat, from different points
of view, the question of the significance of religion under (post)modern
conditions and the consequences these conditions bring along for individual and collective life conceptions, and reconsider the theorems that
possibly are taken for granted too easily or even have been oversimplified.

The social reality of every day life, in which a whole range of value
representations and norms, religious convictions and practices can be
experienced, not only results in an attitude that evaluates everything as
equally valid, but one that considers them indifferently[51]. In an alleged
magnanimous tolerance, one lets everything be without distinction. This
means that religions are no longer fought over, because this would presuppose a resolved atheistic position. The slogan "religion – why not?"
gives a perfect description of the prevailing attitude and we could add:
"on the condition that it does not require any commitment from me".

Another important question is whether the social climate is indeed as
plurality-minded as it would seem. Are there not some mechanisms at
work – probably under the surface – which require and indeed achieve
a collective consensus? If this were not the case, the normative foundation of modern and also postmodern society, the capitalist market,
could not function. Only when and insofar as the economic uni-
formization globally succeeds, will the luxury of a plurality on the cultural level be possible and economically determined and oriented.
Because capitalism does not function in such an unproblematic and
undisputed way as we might wish, it continually works at its protection
and propagation. It resorts to quasi-religious arguments and strategies –
every means is allowed to justify its program. Its endless praise of com-
petitiveness becomes a kind of sublime catechism to make sure that people cling to the real religion of our times[52].

Many assume that the fact of enduring religious sensibilities[53] proves
that the economic market is incapable of meeting all needs and desires,
or is at least incapable of addressing its own aporias. When religion
is invoked, it is important to ask if it only serves resignation and

---

51. Cfr. F.-X. KAUFMANN, *Religion und Modernität*, Tübingen, 1989, esp. pp. 146-171.
52. Cfr. J.M. HULL, *Christliche Erziehung in einem pluralistischen und multireligiösen
Europa* (EMW-Informationen, 109), Hamburg, 1995, pp. 15-20.
53. Cfr. K. GABRIEL, *Christentum zwischen Tradition und Postmoderne*, Freiburg im
Breisgau, 1992, pp. 157-165.

compensation and increases irrationality – or if it leads to reflection about the harmful consequences for individual and society when everything is subjected to market calculus.

5. Religion and Identity – Between Deformation and Construction

If these reflections and remarks are true, they point to the conclusion that even today there is a much closer connection between identity and religion than is generally accepted. This is especially true with a functional concept of religion, when speaking about the "services" traditional religion used to produce. But also, we see how the whole ambivalence of the religious reappears. Precisely because it is anchored in the depths of human existence, the religious can point to salvation or doom. It is not a coincidence that, in order to enforce certain market interests, a coalition with religion attempted to legitimize these interests, or to anoint them in advance as religious or quasi-religious. This strategy expects that people not only will allow themselves to be manipulated in the desired direction, but even accept the manipulation as the fulfillment of their desires. People do not want to be deceived in this. From the manipulators' perspective, (post)modern society appears all but unreligious or post-religious[54].

There is a further question about the relationship between religion, identity formation, and education. The key issue is not even whether in actual society religion still plays a role in the process of identity formation and thus in the educative work of the school. What is at stake is the nature of religion. Religion can still play a crucial role in society, even when it is not present anymore as religious consciousness. Could it be possible that the defective formation of religious competence and of critical judgment in the domain of religion not only gives way to an unlimited expansion of para-religious or pseudo-religious phenomena, but is simply used to propagandize a kind of progress overloaded with religious promises? As the traditional religious conscience wilts away, a technocratic conscience is unfolding and consolidating itself, argues J. Habermas. The market and the information industry aim at "forming" people the way they need them: fastened down on the model of a "computerized

---

54. Cfr. H. NOORMANN, *Religionsfreiheit, Religionskompetenz, Religionsdialog – drei Zeitansagen in religionspädagogischer Perspektive*, in ID. et al. (eds.), *Ökumenisches Arbeitsbuch Religionspädagogik*, Stuttgart, 2000, 31-56, esp. pp. 35-39.

intelligence" – without language and sense, without history and fantasy, without ethics and transcendence. According to Habermas, this means we have to deal with a situation of "regression behind the identity level that had been achieved by the great monotheistic religions, formed by communicating with the one God"[55]. J.B. Metz names this kind of identity "second infantilism": "European modernization makes people weaker rather than stronger in their subjectivity, in their inter-human relationships and in their sense of history, all under the banner of 'progress'. The ever-increasing acceleration in which we live, the on-going change of consumption and fashion, even cultural changes, do not guarantee any meaningful contemplation. Our perceptions tend to be more and more in-comprehensible, without sensibility, because we can only look up at people and objects, but only in retrospect, not when actually present to us. In this way individuals are more and more trained to adapt themselves to an abstract-incomprehensible, complex world. The fantasies of youth are only called upon to colonize them with neat machines, even before they can develop themselves. Where are the human beings we are familiar with from the past? It seems that the more they turn into adaptable animals, the more they are successful in surviving. This creeping, soft death of maturity will go on without meeting any resistance to the extent that this process is not experienced as a threat and repression, but rather as a pleasure and distraction. This is realized by our modern culture industry, the increasing superiority of mass media, above all television, which more and more quasi-transcendentally encompasses our every day life, and disconnects us from our own imaginations, our own dreams, our own stories and our own language and will one day turn us into 'experienced, happy illiterate' (H.M. Enzensberger). This second 'infantilism' is clearly more difficult to overcome than the first one, because the secondary 'infants' do not suffer from their 'infantilism', but consider it an advantage that contributes to their well-being"[56].

It would be a mistake to praise religion as a sovereign remedy for social ills. Therefore religion itself is in different ways too much entangled in this culture. At issue here is not so much religion itself but human beings, who have to realize their innermost ideal to become the responsible subjects of their lives and histories – together with others. The question is what capacities are needed therefore and how they can

---

55. J. HABERMAS, *Wozu noch Philosophie?*, in ID., *Philosophisch-politische Profile*, Frankfurt am Main, 1971, 11-36, p. 35.

56. J.B. METZ, *Wider die zweite Unmündigkeit*, in J. RÜSEN et al. (eds.), *Die Zukunft der Aufklärung*, Frankfurt am Main, 1988, 81-87, pp. 81ff.

be appropriated. We have already established that building up such an identity under the conditions of ever-ongoing modernization constitutes a very demanding and precarious enterprise and that traditional identity standards therefore no longer can be taken as an obligatory criterion. The kind of identity-building required can be characterized as self-reflexive. This identity of the ego is typified by the capacity to "build new identities and simultaneously integrate them with the ones already developed in order to organize oneself and one's interactions in a unique life history"[57]. To put it in another way, it means balancing personal and social identity as a lifelong process. Where this endlessly renewed integration does not succeed, identity crises break out. The capacity of an individual not to be fixed on given behavior patterns with their own requirements and interests, and the ability to decide autonomously about them, is constituted – under ideal circumstances – in education: in the widening of the scope of action and responsibility during childhood, and by taking up one's role identity during adolescence (and further). In this process of identity integration, a pedagogical interaction towards community-building which is directed by the fundamental principle of mutual recognition and creativity promotes the development of identity and generates identity safeguarding qualities, such as a special capacity for communication and empathy, for tolerating ambiguity and role distance.

Based on this model, it might be tempting to determine an identity based on religion – in its traditional form – as a standard of role identity. At the same time, some might say such a route makes identity development adequate to today's social structures impossible, because the kind of religion involved does not allow a reflexive identity formation. Instead, the individual becomes fixed in obligatory creeds and norms. Instead of leading individuals to autonomy, it keeps them prisoners of heteronomy. The different religious systems pretend to be universal, but are in fact particular and require membership of a group. The cognitive dissonances called up in present time by religious worldviews are immense. Furthermore, religious institutions, as for instance the churches with their authority-based hierarchical structure, do anything but assure a domination-free space needed for a reflexive identity formation. On the contrary, to the extent that people withdraw more and more from public life and try to establish a religious subculture as a

---

57. R. DÖBERT, J. HABERMAS, G. NUNNER-WINKLER, *Zur Einführung*, in ID. (eds.), *Entwicklung des Ichs*, Köln, 1977, 9-30, p. 11.

place to develop and assure identity, they promote regressive tendencies. In short: there is a kind of religiousness that is completely unable to take into consideration the central characteristics of identity of the ego, intersubjectivity, reciprocal reflexivity, universalist orientation, transparency and capacity to revise contents.

A different relationship of religion and identity occurs when the conditions of successful identity formation are approached from the angle of the identity of the ego. Then it appears that, although identity and its development are bound to social processes, they do not merge into them, but rather are confronted with their limits. This experience of limits and conditions generates a longing for a transcendence of these limits and conditions. "Without the trace of hope that confidence in the recognition of expectations will not be disappointed, without the occasion to take responsibility for one's actions, without the experience that shared singularities can be taken up in a just, satisfactory community, the attempt to keep up an identity would have been meaningless and even self-destructive"[58]. The attempt to form one's own identity and to develop it, makes those doing so very vulnerable. The process is very much dependent upon the cooperation of others. For Krappmann this finally means: "Only that which is not identity, can be represented. Identity-risks and perturbations can be interpreted by the fact that one's actions and those of others are acknowledged to be split, evasive and unreflectively adapted"[59]. What identity really is, cannot be measured with a successful example. The genuine religious affinity of the ego-identity is constituted precisely in and through this experience of not-relying-on-oneself. "Experiences of life and death, of limits and going beyond them, of being-given-to-oneself and of being-taken-away, of hopeless injustice and endless despair"[60] – discovering in oneself an immeasurable depth, this religious dimension appears and compels it to articulate itself. To that extent it does not appear as something added to or put on top of "normal" identity, but constitutes an ongoing moment.

Therefore, it is not accidental nor arbitrary that efforts to reformulate Christian faith in its basic content concerning identity[61] refer pre-

---

58. L. KRAPPMANN, *Identität,* in D. LENZEN (ed.), *Pädagogische Grundbegriffe,* Band 1, Reinbek, 1989, 715-719, pp. 718ff.

59. ID., *Identität – ein Bildungskonzept?,* in G. GROHS et al. (eds.), *Kulturelle Identität im Wandel,* Stuttgart, 1980, 99-118, pp. 111ff.

60. H. HÄRING, *Die Geschichte Jesu als Grund und Ursprung religiöser Identität,* in *Concilium* 36 (2000) 219-230, p. 228.

61. Cfr. more extensively N. METTE, *Identität ohne Religion?* (n. 1), esp. pp. 165-171; ID., *Religionspädagogik* (n. 1), pp. 102-155.

cisely to the above-mentioned elementary experiences. Faith in its Christian interpretation means to orient one's life toward the God who, according to biblical revelation, radically commits Godself to the otherness of the creatures God put into being and gave freedom. Precisely in this way God grants them their identity – as Jesus Christ experienced in an unsurpassed way in his own life and bore testimony to his surroundings. This unconditional confidence allows personal identity to be experienced as a gift and therefore makes us free from the burden to relentlessly have to realize ourselves; it rather compels us to share the experience of our own identity and the ground of it with others and in this way aims toward universal solidarity. In such an authentic religious context, the experience that everything is only fragmentarily possible and contingent does not lead to resignation or cynicism. The deeper question concerns the basis for unconditional solidarity in a situation of suffering and failing, which no longer can be humanly comprehended[62].

From such an identity the person can be in harmony with actuality through a determined (communicative) practice – a practice resulting from the experience of unconditional acceptance and confirmation[63]: to accept oneself as one is; to perceive others and recognize them in their otherness; to be able to have confidence in a reality full of contradictions; to take up responsibility for the given, historical situation; not to repress the fact of suffering and failing; to be sensitive to the violations of humanity and to actively oppose them. "The yes of God", Th. Pröpper writes, "relieves the final burden of existence, that is, the obligation of self-affirmation, the compulsory search for influence and power, being fixated to things, the drive to succeed. It changes the attitude towards property, re-evaluates work and productivity. It brings about a new receptivity to the gift of our existence and a changed interaction with the goods of creation. It does not weaken,

---

62. H.P. SILLER, *Religion an der Schule – Fortsetzung*, in *Impulse aus der Hauptabteilung Schule und Hochschule des Erzbistums Köln* No. 50, Köln, 1999, Beilage I-VI, here IV: "Wenn das Unverfügbare unsere humane Bestimmung ist, dann muß es uns radikal entzogen bleiben und als solches uns doch geschenkt sein. Unbegreifbares und unverfügbares Geheimnis kann uns nur begegnen und zugleich bleiben, was es ist, zu seinen eigenen, von ihm selber gesetzten Bedingungen. Tatsache, Ort, Zeit und Art der Begegnung bleibt seine Sache. Hier ist die Sprache des Glaubens und der Theologie unvermeidlich. Die Begriffe Gnade, Offenbarung, Befreiung, Erlösung, Nähe der Herrschaft Gottes suchen diesen Sachverhalt zu beschreiben".

63. Cfr. Th. PRÖPPER, *Erlösungsglaube und Freiheitsgeschichte*, München, 1988², pp. 220-224.

therefore, the impulse of wanting to shape the world, but detaches that impulse from ideology"[64].

It is a specific task, then, to look for an explicitly religious education, to promote the thus determined religious dimension of development of the ego. More particularly the above-mentioned limit experiences could be integrated and implemented in self-formation and in building capacities to act at a new level. A religion in the sense of promoting identity is, according to H. Küng, a religion,

- "which promotes the acceptance of oneself without regression;
- which is useful to individuation of the human being with its symbols, convictions and rites;
- which can offer our young generations spiritual orientation and unconditional ethical standards;
- which guarantees freedom to decide notwithstanding all insights in culpability and in the limits of freedom of will, and offers a guarantee of identity and dignity throughout all learning processes and attitudes;
- which is able to overcome fear and to found confidence, comprehension and respect, a ground for friendship and love;
- which leads to creativity, expansion of consciousness, engagement and true humanity by promoting sensibility and emotionality"[65].

6. Facilitation of Identity of the Ego – an Urgent Pedagogical Task

So far I have treated the fundamental question of how religion can contribute to the formation of identity on a post-conventional level and whether religion maintains the development of the individual at the level of role identity. This has been done on the ground of an identity-theoretical reconstruction of Christian faith. But this does not mean that Christian faith can pose an exclusive claim on this process. This position can be valid for other religions as well. In emphasizing that religions can offer a constitutive contribution to identity formation, we must not forget that they also can take effect, and often have done so, in identity deformation. Therefore it is necessary to maintain the connection between religion and identity.

---

64. Th. PRÖPPER, *Erlösungsglaube und Freiheitsgeschichte* (n. 63), p. 223.
65. H. KÜNG, *Vorwort*, in G. KLOSINSKI (ed.), *Religion als Chance und Risiko*, Bern, 1994, 9-12, pp. 11ff.

Two other issues should be addressed here. The first one is the connection between religious education and actual needs. My thesis is this: If, on the one hand, it is true that because of the changed and ever changing social situation it has become an even more precarious enterprise to arrive at one's own identity than ever before and, on the other hand, religion has a constitutive contribution to help people forge individual identity, then it is necessary to protect and promote, within the framework of education ("Bildung"), the conditions for gaining identity and to prevent the destruction of those conditions by thoughtless bureaucratic mechanisms[66]. If everything should be done to help people forge their identity and to offer them the necessary conditions to do so, all institutions participating in the education process, such as family, kindergarten, school, church and so on, should contribute to that goal. Therefore the identity of young people as well as of the adults involved should stand at the center of religious education processes. How to promote such an identity in its inalienability, under the incontrovertible conditions of cultural and religious plurality so typical of (post-)modern societies, has become a decisive question.

The second issue is: What have we learned in our research about the identity-involvement paradox? Plurality no longer consists of the juxtaposition of different groups in society; it has become a structural characteristic of every group in itself, even of churches and religious communities. There is no longer, in any religion or church, something like a uniform confessional identity. Even with consciously religion-oriented people, it cannot be denied that in the course of their lives changes occur in their "confessional identity"[67]. And so one can ask whether confessionalism is as productive as some church leaders claim. Would it not be better to promote differentiation and communication as fundamental rules for the pedagogics of religion – as is proposed by H.-G. Ziebertz[68] –, which means that one should engage in religious education as inter-religious and dialogical learning, where the common question of

66. What this means for early child education, can be read in U. PEUKERT, *Der demokratische Gesellschaftsvertrag und das Verhältnis zur nächsten Generation*, in *Neue Sammlung* 37 (1997) 277-293. The document *Identität und Verständigung* (n. 11), esp. pp. 31-36, is pointing in the same direction concerning the destiny, meaning and task of religious education in schools, in a changing society.

67. Cfr. the psychological theories of religious development by J. Fowler or F. Oser, following S. Freud, E.H. Erikson, J. Piaget and L. Kohlberg.

68. Cfr. H.-G. ZIEBERTZ, *Identitätsfindung durch interreligiöse Lernprozesse*, in *Religionspädagogische Beiträge* 36 (1995) 83-104; *Prinzipielle religionsdidaktische Grundregeln II*, in E. GROSS & K. KÖNIG (eds.), *Religionsdidaktik in Grundregeln*, Regensburg, 1996, 30-48.

the human being and his/her salvation is essential, in the presence of massive threats[69]? Developmental psychology seems to argue in favor of such an approach[70]. The different religious communities, moreover, remain free – and should be advised to do so – to make use, to the benefit of their believers, of their possibilities to transmit or make more appropriate an identity grounded on their creed.

7. The Contribution of Religious Education in Schools to General (Identity) Formation

I will finally try to develop some perspectives at this juncture that may be useful for rethinking religious education. Even when this sounds evident, I repeat my position: religious education in school is not for the sake of the church or any other religious institute, but for the sake of children and young peoples – with a view to promote their identity development and therefore to facilitate a common life in the future. I have also claimed that the subject, religion, constitutes a valuable contribution to the school, to the extent it compels the school to become a place "where the truth can be mastered in practice, where finding pleasure in truth and fighting for it, constitute the internal ground for learning"[71]. When a school does these things, it refuses to submit itself to social and above all economic interests. Of course, all school subjects have to contribute to the struggle for truth. Nothing is more desirable than that all school subjects become aware of the philosophical, ethical and religious dimensions they encompass and make them explicit, at least on some occasions.

This means that religious education must reflect and focus on its genuine concern. "The theme of religion deals with questions that cannot be answered either on an ethical nor a pedagogical, political, economical or aesthetical level. Religious education's questions are about the meaning and origin of the world as creation, including that of human suffering caused by human hands. Therefore the meaning of the commandment 'thou shalt not kill!' is not the same in an ethical as in a religious context. In the religious context it implies an anamnetic solidarity

---

69. Cfr. also Th. KNAUTH, *Religionsunterricht und Dialog*, Münster, 1996; W. WEISSE (ed.), *Vom Monolog zum Dialog. Ansätze einer dialogischen Religionspädagogik*, Münster, 1999².

70. Cfr. the very helpful insights of K. GOSSMANN, *Ökumenische Erziehung*, in W. BÖCKER et al. (eds.), *Handbuch Religiöser Erziehung*, Band 1, Düsseldorf, 1987, 267-278.

71. H.J. GAMM, *Allgemeine Bildung in einer Schule der Vielfalt in der Gemeinsamkeit*, in *Pädagogik* 47 (1995) 64-69, p. 68.

with the meaningless victims of history, meaninglessness which cannot be redressed by any progress", so argues the German educationalist, D. Benner[72].

Religious Education as Religious Obstetrics

It is a great temptation to perceive and judge people by their "shortcomings", rather than to recognize their possibilities as persons in their singularity and inalienability. In religious education, to deny religiously illiterate children all religiosity, would certainly mean a misjudgment of what possibly could be stimulated within them. As to religious education, this means that instead of a deficiency-oriented attitude (U. Baumann)[73], a resources-oriented attitude should prevail. The aim is not as much to remove the alleged religious deficiencies of pupils, but rather to discover the resources they bear within them, which could reveal an enormous religious potential, even when it usually is not interpreted as such.

For primary school children, R. Englert gives the following examples in this context: their need for true knowledge, their need for meaningful order, their need for ritual modeling, and their search for religious experience, religious clarification and religious distinction[74].

M. Veit has shown in a sensitive way how in everyday experiences of young people a religious search can be detected, which could be very salutary for them, if that search could be taken into account in an adequate way[75]. After all, they are relentlessly exposed to the rules of merciless "productivist society", oriented toward a consumer society which promises all they can imagine, but offers only artificial satisfactions. Good religious education has the potential to provide help in dealing with personal guilt, in giving perspective to young people's vision of the future, and to their own desire to be accepted.

---

72. D. BENNER, *Statement*, in Chr. GESTRICH (ed.), *Ethik ohne Religion?*, Berlin, 1996, 133-136, p. 134; Cfr. ID., *Thesen zur Bedeutung der Religion für die Bildung*, in ID., *Studien zur Theorie der Erziehung und Bildung*, Weinheim – München, 1995, 179-190; Chr. STORCK, *Zukunft oder Ende eines kirchlich verantworteten Religionsunterrichts?*, in *Katechetische Blätter* 123 (1998) 28-36.

73. Cfr. U. BAUMANN, *Gemeinsame Schritte in die Zukunft*, in *Katechetische Blätter* 121 (1996) 34-40; ID., *"Postchristliche" Religiosität als Herausforderung an den Religionsunterricht*, in *Schönberger Hefte* 27 (1997) no. 3, 2-11.

74. Cfr. R. ENGLERT, *Der Religionsunterricht an der Grundschule – gegenwärtige Probleme und zukünftige Möglichkeiten*, in *Im Zeichen einer veränderten Kindheit*, Bensberg, 1996, 9-21, esp. pp. 16-20.

75. Cfr. M. VEIT, *Alltagserfahrungen von Jugendlichen, theologisch interpretiert*, in ID., *Theologie muß von unten kommen*, Wuppertal, 1991, pp. 20-51.

R. Englert has defined what might, in this context, be the task for religious education in school in the following program: "Real pupil-oriented religious education therefore means not only dealing with the vital questions of children and young people – and demonstrating the potential present in Christian faith to give answers; it also means, beyond this and more particularly, looking for the answers that young people bear within them or are present in their environment, and consolidating them. It means looking for the problem solving strategies of pupils, for their interpretation standards, for their religiosity and their faith. The primary reference for religious learning is no longer the faith of the church, but the faith in life of the individual, no longer "objective religion" but "subjective religion", that toward which the pupils themselves are oriented and in accordance with which they organize their own lives. It is not advised to measure this subjective religion by the standard of ecclesiastic faith in order to be able to say: 'See how poor your religiosity, your religious consciousness is, and let yourself be helped now by accepting the greater fullness of ecclesiastic faith'. Subjective religion has to be appreciated in its autonomy. This means that the pupils should be guided in their search for their own truth"[76].

Therefore it is necessary for pedagogy of religion to make "a turn in the direction of living environment", which has the potential to enable people active in that field to assure a real process supervision to the benefit of young people. U. Baumann has concretely outlined a range of aims that might be pursued in religious education:
– "Religious education should enable pupils to discover and articulate their own religiosity.
– Religious education is the occasion for the pupils to gain religious information, to the extent that it helps them learn a religious idiom in which they can make themselves comprehensible in changing communities, by means of the religious tradition(s).
– Religious education helps pupils with the development of their own identity. This means that the pedagogical aim of religious education is not orthodox, but personal faith"[77].

The following points fit into the framework of such a fundamental conception of religious education as religious-pedagogical process supervision.

---

76. R. ENGLERT, *Der Religionsunterricht nach der Emigration des Glauben-Lernens*, in *Katechetische Blätter* 123 (1998) 4-12, p. 5.
77. U. BAUMANN, *"Postchristliche" Religiosität* (n. 73), p. 9.

Liberation from "the God Complex" (H.E. Richter)

Especially with respect to determined technological and economic developments, it is a central task for religious education to make pupils become aware of the way in which people have managed to acquire the attitudes that traditionally were ascribed to God, such as omnipotence, ubiquity and omniscience:

– Ultimately, to be able to do what until now only God could do, to create life, which is the promise of gene technology.
– To be in all places of the world at the same time, as the declared intention of communication technology.
– To submit everything to the market as globally pursued under the motto of economic globalization.

It cannot be the intention to demonize all possible technological acquisitions. The comfort they bring about should not be denied, but this technical and economic progress turns into disaster, if it has to serve a project of human infinity and incompleteness. With respect to such human delusions, the contribution of the religious conviction which maintains the strict distinction between God and humanity is truly liberating and salutary. This thinking oriented towards instrumental rationality and megalomania has even found a place in the school curriculum. H. Rumpf has called "Bescheidwissen" (assessment thinking) the 'knowledge ideal' that became dominant in school, fixated to learning general, preferably quantitative relations in order to use that knowledge to "construct" the world in as perfect a way as possible[78]. It is a 'knowledge ideal' that tends to submit everything to the logic of making and power and to do resolutely away with everything that resists, thus everything alien and different. Other reality experiences which are less accessible for the procedures of assessment thinking, such as experiences of human weakness and limitation, but also the whole domain of awareness of the senses and aesthetics, are said to be invalid. An education that means that one has the right to do away with other approaches, fails. It does not do justice to the humanity of men and women. H. Rumpf advises school programs to "say good-bye to assessment thinking" in favor of the practice of a knowledge oriented toward awareness of life. Maybe religious education can offer a contribution here by talking of God; talking of God also means keeping in mind one's own mortality as well as accepting that one need not have an answer for anything[79].

78. Cfr. H. RUMPF, *Abschied vom Bescheidwissen. Über Bildung und Sterblichkeit*, in *Katechetische Blätter* 119 (1994) 232-238.
79. Cfr. F. STEFFENSKY, *Wo der Glaube wohnen kann*, Stuttgart, 1989, pp. 79-90.

The Struggle to Understand God

What has been stressed in the preceding point, has to be extended unconditionally to its structural dimension. As explained, it is a serious mistake to think that modern society is a society without, or at best with a completely marginalized religion. On the contrary, if religion or faith are understood to be a system "which holds people spellbound, is accepted without question, which distributes and legitimizes power in the world"[80], then such a system does exist indeed in the market and its laws, money as supreme power, domination exerted by the economy over all other human activities. In the era of globalization it is no longer necessary to demonstrate where supreme, absolute and ubiquitous power in the world lies. Politics bows to it and has been reduced to export-promotion or ad hoc policy; social achievements have to yield to it; it determines cultural and spiritual life as well as living together. This power dominates all over the world in a way that has never been achieved by any world religion. Its symbols, values and rules have become deeply implanted in the heart of all people; it is worshiped with a devotion that traditional religions can only be envious about. What great sacrifices are not made in order to participate in its salvific promises! Happiness and unhappiness, riches and poverty, life and death are determined in function of market rules. It is not a coincidence that it envelops itself in typically religious vestments. We can already find cult markets and consumer temples and a sacred architecture around the money centers. They talk about the 'new gods of the market' ..., we undergo the ecstatic, intoxicating dance as in the Berlin love-parade, we celebrate the rites of the high feast of consumer religion, Christmas, but we also find what should not be lacking in any religion, the willingness to make sacrifices – road victims, animal sacrifices, whole regions, streams and seas are sacrificed to the power of the market. Because this happens with the greatest possible conviction and obviousness, we truly are dealing here with a religion. It is not yet self-conscious, has no dogmatics and no catechism at its disposal, and does not even know its own gods – but it does not require all this to be a religion. Indeed, most of the archaic religions did not either"[81]. It can hardly be denied that this religion operates a massive and sometimes sublime catechesis in order to try to conquer the hearts of men and women.

---

80. Th. RUSTER, *Wie kann die Kirche in der pluralistischen Gesellschaft dialogisch, solidarisch und missionarisch sein?*, Pro Manuscripto, 1977, p. 6.
81. *Ibid.*, pp. 6ff.

In a time when there is seemingly no alternative for the market, which therefore can globally expand its influence, a critical attitude toward its allegedly ineluctable rules urges itself upon us. Falling back on biblical tradition has the potential to introduce an alternative way of looking at and judging of things, whereby it can be seen how promises are kept in the Bible; that instead of so-called scarcity, as by miracle, there is enough for everyone. "With the God of the Bible and the gods of the market, fullness and scarcity stand opposed to one other. Both require faith. If we continue to believe the dogma of scarcity, we must submit to the merciless market. If we believe in fullness, in the fact that all people can have enough – of food products, living space, confirmation, love –, we make ourselves free of domination and can act in another way"[82].

Instigation to Hope and Solidarity

"Religious education is often the only occasion for children and young people to come in contact with a systematic representation of greater life ideals and dramatizations of hope"[83]. With this viewpoint, F. Steffensky has outlined a further task for religious education: with respect to over-all prevailing lack of perspectives, drill wells which give audacity to hope, a kind of hope that does not merely overcome reality, but makes it possible to keep reality upright and compels us to engagement[84]. To learn about hope goes hand in hand with learning about justice-and-solidarity. Where everything is placed on the dogma of scarcity, the hope for optimum conditions is fixed on one's own life. Where there is confidence that a ground exists for 'putting on' hope and love, one is urged to commitment to solidarity, to cooperate in building a common world, where self-responsibility and unconditional care for each other are no longer mutually exclusive[85].

Encounter with Religiosity that Takes Shape in Reality

Religious education has the essential task to refer to a practice of life built upon religion and faith, without giving the impression to its pupils

82. Th. RUSTER, *Wie kann die Kirche* (n. 80), pp. 9ff.
83. F. STEFFENSKY, *Konzeptionelle Perspektiven des Religionsunterrichts in der BRD*, in *Die Christenlehre* 39 (1986) 295-298, p. 297.
84. Cfr. especially the work of I. BALDERMANN, for instance his *Das Alphabet der Hoffnung buchstabieren*, in *LM* 29 (1990) 370-374.
85. Cfr. more extensively N. METTE, *Religionspädagogik*, Düsseldorf, 1994, chapter 3.

that the ideas and concepts proposed are too beautiful to become true in the real world. It is therefore necessary to find out – in an ecumenical and interreligious perspective – where such a practice of life is lived and to facilitate encounters with people who live in such a way. It is possible that religious education will ultimately catch on and be able to offer the opportunity to do things together with such groups[86].

86. See for this aspect also Chr. BIZER, *Kirchgänge im Unterricht und anderswo. Zur Gestaltwerdung von Religion*, Göttingen, 1995.

Religious Education Through Times of Crisis
Reflections on the Future of a Vulnerable School Subject

Bert Roebben[1]

This contribution is an attempt to understand the extent to which the changes undergone by institutionalised religious traditions have contributed to a process of transformation of Roman-Catholic religious education at school in the Netherlands and Belgium. In confrontation with late modernity, with the radical and difficult digestible shifts in theological thinking since Vatican II and with the not always appropriate responses of the church to this complex set of circumstances, the inner-church vision of the life of faith has lost much of its plausibility. This has brought about profound changes in the nature, function and content of religious education at school. In what follows, we will endeavour to outline, analyse and interpret these developments and to envisage a number of future perspectives in their regard. This crisis is both an unavoidable situation for which new religious-educational leadership is required, but also a chance for young people to deepen their commitments to their own learning. Education "through" crisis as mentioned in the title could therefore imply two things: learning in times of crisis and in conformity with a situation of crisis.

This study is rooted in practical theology, a scientific discipline which seeks to establish insight into the religious praxis of individuals and communities in relation to (in affinity with or in confrontation with) institutionalised forms of religious experience. The formal object of the study of practical theology is empirical and/or hermeneutical: the fundamental life options and religious convictions of individuals and groups are charted and interpreted against the background of social and cultural changes in space and time[2]. In its nature practical theology is not a sort of applied theology, coming 'down' from the

---

1. Translation by Brian Doyle. For more details about the theoretical framework of religious educational research at the Faculty of Theology of the K.U. Brabant in Tilburg (NL) see the research project SEEKING SENSE IN THE CITY that can be found on www.kub.nl/tft/ssinc.

2. See for example G. HEITINK, *Praktische theologie: geschiedenis, theorie, handelingsvelden*, Kampen, Kok, 1993; J.A. VAN DER VEN & H.-G. ZIEBERTZ, *Paradigmenent-*

more historical-systematic to the more church and society related areas
of theology. It is not a kind of post office that distributes fundamental
thoughts to the peripheries of theological and pastoral praxis. It is
rather a 'covenant' research, that is desperately searching for connections and relationships between religious practices and thoughts of
human beings. It is honouring the daily praxis of people in its own
value, to the extent that it is taking seriously the quests for meaning to
which people are committed in this praxis. It constantly reinforces the
reflective power of this praxis and critically evaluates it. Practical theology could therefore be described as "a critical theory of religious mediated praxis in church and society"[3]. The aim of practical theological
research is to clarify and improve the religious practices (aim 'ad extra')
and to re-imagine the possible role of particular traditions (i.c. the
Christian tradition) in responding to the needs and desires of the contemporary quest for faith (aim 'ad intra'). Contemporary religious education researchers are fully and explicitly engaged in this research tradition, focusing their attention on the moral and existential meaning
conveyed by religious formation and communication at home, at
school and in the faith community.

    In the context of the present volume we will endeavour to focus our
attention on the teaching of religion in secondary schools in the Netherlands and Flanders (which is the Northern, Dutch speaking part of Belgium). We will offer a survey of the central themes and perspectives at
work in this discourse, a survey which will no doubt have its parallels in
many other western European countries. In six distinct yet related steps
we will reflect on the manner in which "religious education as practical
theology" has endeavoured to envisage itself in a meaningful way in the
current situation: (1) the crisis of the faith tradition and of traditional
religious education, (2) the reaction in the schools thereto, (3) the situation of young people with respect to religiosity, (4) a renewed orientation for religious education rooted in the dynamics of teaching, (5)
points of departure for a hermeneutical-communicative religious-educational theory, and to conclude (6) some practical-theological implications.

---

wicklung in der praktischen Theologie (Theologie und Empirie, 13), Kampen – Weinheim,
Kok – DSV, 1993; N. METTE, Praktisch-theologische Erkundungen, Münster – Hamburg
– London, Lit-Verlag, 1999.
    3. G. OTTO, Grundlegung der praktischen Theologie, München, Kaiser, 1986,
p. 77.

1. The Religious Education Class and the Crisis of the Christian Faith Tradition

The fact that Christian faith can no longer be taken for granted is perhaps the only certainty which remains these days for those who profess some degree of ecclesial engagement. Indeed, faith is "under pressure" both literally and figuratively[4]. Young people are inclined to wonder what believers as such are all about. Why are they so bothered? The Church and its transmission of the faith is no longer plausible, no longer recognisable in the eyes of the coming generation. A study of this very phenomenon suggests that we are experiencing an "interruption" in the traditional continuum of faith transmission[5]. In the context of religious education theory, specialists speak of a "duplication crisis", the apparent lack of evidence or indeed total disappearance of "solid grounds" upon which one can engage in the transmission of faith, made concrete, for example, in the absence of religious socialisation in the family[6] or in the confusion of the group discourse among school pupils which tends to be indifferent to both the Church and the faith[7].

Two aspects of this complex situation deserve special attention. In the first place, Christian educators speak of a "correlation weakness" *(Korrelationsschwache)* in the Christian faith[8]. In the context of the modernisation of society – a phenomenon which has had a profoundly unsettling effect on every form of religious belief and not only on Christianity –, it would appear that the Church is unable to connect her story in any recognisable way with the sentiments of late modern men and women. Such individuals are no longer able to see the point of faith because the experience associated therewith has become alien to them and because the words they once used to "express" that

---

4. E. DE LANGE & B. ROEBBEN, *Geloven onder spanning. Sacramentencatechese anno 1999*, in L. BOEVE (ed.), *De kerk in Vlaanderen. Avond of dageraad?*, Leuven, Davidsfonds, 1999, 210-228.

5. L. BOEVE, *Onderbroken traditie. Heeft het christelijk verhaal nog toekomst?*, Kapellen, Pelckmans, 1999.

6. J. MAAS & H.-G. ZIEBERTZ, *Over breukvlakken en bruggehoofden: religieuze opvoeding in het gezin*, in *Tijdschrift voor Theologie* 37 (1997) 384-404; B. ROEBBEN, *Religieuze socialisatie vanuit en voorbij de kerk. Situatie, problemen en perspectief*, in *Praktische theologie* 23 (1996) 366-381.

7. H. LOMBAERTS, B. ROEBBEN, G. GINNEBERGE, *Godinet: A Flexible Working Tool for a Subject on the Move*, in *Journal of Religious Education* [Australia] 49 (2001) no. 1, 51-58.

8. R. BOSCHKI, *Dialogisch-kreative Religionsdidaktik. Eine Weiterentwicklung der korrelativen Hermeneutik und Praxis*, in *Katechetische Blätter* 123 (1998) 13-23.

experience have become meaningless. This is also related to the fact the religious awe and wonder have become objects of suspicion for our contemporaries.

A second aspect which complicates matters even further lies in the fact that the church would appear to be incapable of teaching late modern men and women to live an independent life of faith even when they do take initial steps in this direction. The Church is struggling with a "modernisation backlog"[9] and is finding it difficult to assist people to deal with the complexity surrounding their rationally justifiable, independent and at the same time profound faith convictions. When the Church calls people to faith today this implies simultaneously that those involved have the capacity to follow their own well-reasoned path. In modern society, meaning and authenticity are high on the agenda. People are no longer inclined to participate in a "meaning project" which they cannot make their own. As a consequence, many have turned their back on the Church only to follow their own path in matters of fundamental life option. A movement of religiosity has come into existence outside the Church which for many well-intentioned Church people has evolved into a tragic situation. The latter have become aware that many individuals no longer have a religious roof over their heads and that the Church leadership continues to maintain the notion that such homelessness can be remedied by re-assembling the collective under a single ecclesial-confessional roof. Thus the Church no longer appears to be capable of addressing the faith situation of men and women in a meaningful and integrated way without fostering instrumental ulterior motives[10]. The questions which emerge from such a situation are legion: What does the Church has to offer to critical and self-aware young people today[11]? How can the Church continue to defend and promote its interests, especially in the context of religious education? What ultimately is the "religious" potentiality of religious education[12]?

9. K. GABRIEL, *Christentum zwischen Tradition und Postmoderne*, Freiburg – Basel – Wien, Herder, 1994³.

10. V. DREHSEN, *Wie religionsfähig ist die Volkskirche? Sozialisationstheoretische Erkundungen neuzeitlicher Christentumspraxis*, Gütersloh, Kaiser – Gütersloher Verlagshaus, 1994, addresses the question whether or not the churches still are *"religiös integrationsfähig"* – this means whether or not they are still in a position to offer a valid and appropriate religious perspective on world and culture.

11. B. ROEBBEN, *Shaping a Playground for Transcendence. Postmodern Youth Ministry as a Radical Challenge*, in *Religious Education* 92 (1997) 332-347.

12. F. SCHWEITZER, *Die Suche nach eigenem Glauben. Einführung in die Religionspädagogik des Jugendalters*, Gütersloh, Kaiser-Verlag, 1996, p. 173.

2. The Reaction in Schools to the Tradition Crisis

Schools are frequently at a loss when confronted with the socio-cultural processes of change which also have an effect on the charter of Christian identity, educational aims and religious education they are endeavouring to maintain. Under societal pressure to modernise and reinforced by the deficient response of both Church and faith to this situation, many schools have sought to find a way out of the problems associated with their moral and religious formational task. In other words, schools are tending more and more nowadays to focus on self-preservation in face of the pressures presented both by society and the Church.

The Italian religious education researcher F. Pajer offers a summary analysis of the reactions of the educational establishment to the lamentable state of religious education in schools at the European level[13]. The interpretation of this data provided by H. Lombaerts points to three distinct clusters in this regard[14]. Some schools have trended to give in to modernity, effectively scrapping moral and religious formation from the school curriculum and either integrating them into other subjects or offering a sort of clinically detached presentation of religious movements without engagement or specific option. Other schools exhibit a different reaction to modernity: they realise that religious education as a subject constitutes a thorn in the flesh of our consumption based society and of the school as a technocratic institution and opt, therefore, to concretise the subject in a doctrinal manner by removing its critical perspective or to withdraw it completely into the ecclesial or pastoral arena. A third cluster of schools endeavour to confront the pressure of modernisation in stead of running away from it. Such schools consider religious education to be a critical-pedagogical instrument intended to assist in the interpretation of the context. As such, the subject represents an important perspective or form of rationality aimed at the provision of insight in matters of morality and fundamental life options between the fractures and challenges unique to the modern context[15]. This threefold division of the relationship between schools and religious education gives rise to three models of formation in

13. F. PAJER, *L'enseignement de la religion en Europe. Vue panoramique d'une mutation*, in J. BULCKENS & H. LOMBAERTS (eds.), *L'enseignement de la religion catholique à l'école secondaire. Enjeux pour la nouvelle Europe* (BETL, 109), Leuven, University Press – Peeters, 1993, 31-57.

14. H. LOMBAERTS, *Religion – société et enseignement religieux à l'école*, in *ibid.*, 3-30.

15. Th. GEURTS, *Leren van zin. Contouren voor de inhoud van de levensbeschouwelijke educatie in de katholieke basisschool*, Best, Damon, 1997.

regard to fundamental life options (transmission, clarification and communication)[16], in regard to religious openness (multi-religious, mono-religious, inter-religious learning)[17] and in regard to the teachability of religion in the context of religious education as a curriculum subject *(learning about religion, learning in religion, learning from religion)*[18]. The same threefold division is also in evidence with respect to moral pedagogy. Here too it is evident that the processes of modernisation are at work in the life and learning processes of young people, particularly in relation to individual acquisition of values and convictions in a plural society[19].

It is thus in the context of a mutual, critically-pedagogical appreciation, support and challenge on the part of the school, the curriculum in general and religious education in particular that the latter can achieve a degree of significance in the lives of young people today. Without such roots, religious education in schools will be seen as either an anachronism or an empty shell. In either case no one will benefit. Lombaerts concludes: "L'enseignement de la religion se voit confronté avec le conflit de l'option entre, d'une part, l'invitation à se mettre au service de l'attitude doctrinaire (qui ne supporte pas l'autre), et d'autre part, l'exigence éthique de permettre que l'épreuve de vérité se vive en toute honnêteté, de permettre à chacun d'aller à la plus forte affirmation possible, à la plus grande puissance possible de ce sur quoi il fond"[20]. Some kind of response to this conflict situation is unavoidable. It is associated with the idea that the primary option of faith communication is ethical by nature and essentially related to moral and religious freedom. Those who are concerned with the well-being of young people will support this critically-utopic fundamental option for informed freedom.

3. The Situation of Young People with Respect to Religiosity

What role do young people themselves play in the evaluation of the crisis of tradition and to what extent are they influenced in their position

16. G. SNIK, *Modellen van levensbeschouwelijke vorming*, in *Nederlands Tijdschrift voor Opvoeding, Vorming en Onderwijs* 7 (1991) 36-49.

17. H.-G. ZIEBERTZ, *Religious Pluralism and Religious Education*, in *Journal of Empirical Theology* 6 (1993) 82-97.

18. M. GRIMMITT, *Religious Education and Human Development*, Great Wakering, Mayhew-MacCrimmon, 1987.

19. B. ROEBBEN, *Moraalpedagogiek: een bewogen discipline*, in *Onze Alma Mater* 51 (1997) 436-462, esp. pp. 440-447.

20. H. LOMBAERTS, *Religion – société et enseignement religieux à l'école* (n. 14), p. 28.

by the school's formation programme in general and the function of religious education therein? These two questions will occupy us in the coming paragraphs. Taking the idea that young people exhibit an intense awareness of the crisis we have been discussing and play a highly significant role in the social and cultural event as our point of departure[21] it is clear that we focus our attention in some detail on their perception of religious reality. Those who would endeavour to provide young people with the capacity to clarify and prepare for their future in a free and responsible manner – and who likewise consider this to be among the ethical tasks of formation and education – will ultimately be obliged to allow them to have their own say, even in the analysis and interpretation of the tradition crisis. We will begin, therefore, with a brief survey of the religiosity of young people today after which we will attempt to formulate, in the broadest sense of the term, the various formational aims which tend to emerge from the confrontation between the tradition crisis and the attitudes to life exhibited by young people. In the fourth paragraph we will endeavour to focus this formational concept on religious education.

Young People and Religiosity

One of the most complex and yet challenging phenomena of our time is the way in which young people deal with religiosity. Researchers are at odds as to how they should approach their target groups, the questions they should ask and the research lens they should employ as they study this reality. Of course 'religiosity' as such is the focus of research, but this concept remains open to interpretation. Some employ the term as a collective for a colourful hotpotch of expressions related to morality and openness with respect to fundamental life options and conclude thereby that young people no longer make any connection between their own lives and the interpretation frameworks employed by Church and religion[22]. Others are more restrictive and appeal for a degree of reserve when engaging in research partly motivated by the idea that young people no longer recognise themselves in what sociologists consider to be youth religiosity. The latter group maintain, moreover, that young people continue to employ traditional schemas to describe

21. B. ROEBBEN, *Een tijd van opvoeden. Moraalpedagogiek in christelijk perspectief*, Leuven – Amersfoort, Acco, 1995, pp. 105-107.

22. H. BARZ, *The pursuit of happiness. Empirische Befunde zur Religion der ungläubigen Jugend in Deutschland*, in *Praktische Theologie* 29 (1994) 106-116.

their acceptance or rejection of religion[23]. Two interpretation frameworks tend to dominate: the modernisation thesis and the secularisation thesis. The former is convinced of the idea that religion is undergoing a process of modernisation in contemporary society and emancipation from the Church as an institution, the latter is aware of an ongoing decrease in Church practice yet can see no revival of religiosity outside of the Church. The first interpretation employs a functional understanding of religion ("What do people understand to be the purpose of religion?"), the second a more content related understanding ("What do the churches and their members say religion is about?").

Given the conviction that justice can only be done for young people if the traditional analytical schemas are somehow transcended, the present writer judges it advised to opt for a broad interpretation matrix. In line with Drehsen, Gabriel & Hobelsberger, Schweitzer and Ziebertz[24] we will follow the modernisation thesis to interpret the phenomenon of religiosity among young people. In a late modern context, young people (and not only young people) are in search of new ways to express what they describe as the ultimate meaning of their own lives and of society as a whole. In what follows we will endeavour to present a number of characteristics of this youth religiosity.

Religious syncretism
Taking the modernisation approach to the religious landscape of Western Europe as one's point of departure, one can discern an ongoing and steadily increasing process of "de-traditionalisation" at work with respect to religion and religiosity. Young people no longer experience religious sentiments in the conventional spaces of Church and faith community. They are engaged in their own search for spiritual foundations. Rooted in a concern for the way their lives are going, young people tend to spontaneously develop their own individualised pattern of values, norms and meaningful lifestyle. Religious elements which continue to survive from former patterns of religious socialisation (in the

---

23. A. BUCHER, *Stimmt die Entkoppelungsthese? Zum Verhältnis allgemeiner und kirchlicher Religiosität in einer Stichprobe von 2700 Schuljugendlichen in Österreich*, in C. FRIESL & R. POLAK (eds.), *Die Suche nach der religiösen Aura*, Graz, Zeitpunkt, 1999, 224-230.

24. V. DREHSEN, *Wie religionsfähig ist die Volkskirche?* (n. 10); K. GABRIEL & H. HOBELSBERGER (eds.), *Jugend, Religion und Modernisierung. Kirchliche Jugendarbeit als Suchbewegung*, Opladen, Leske & Budrich, 1994; H.-G. ZIEBERTZ, *Religion, Christentum und Moderne. Veränderte Religionspräsenz als Herausforderung*, Stuttgart – Berlin – Köln, Kohlhammer, 1999; F. SCHWEITZER, *Die Suche nach eigenem Glauben* (n. 12).

family, parish or school) tend to be redeployed and supplemented with elements from other religions, lifestyles and fundamental life options. Analysts speak of religious syncretism[25], of religious "mix and match"[26], and even of "off road"-religion[27] among young people.

Religion as control of contingency

Even from a modernised perspective, religion continues to be viewed as a point of support when one is confronted with experiences of contingency. Young people tend to contrive intermediary spaces which enable them to make a meaningful and integrated transition from one domain of life to another without being overwhelmed by contingencies[28]. While religion in this perspective can no longer be described as a co-ordinating master narrative, it does appear to be a source of assistance when people are confronted with contingencies and points of disjunction in their everyday lives. Religion helps people to endure the "surplus expectations" engendered by modernity (everything can be fixed but the facts themselves continually prove otherwise). This "therapeutic" aspect of religion tends to enjoy serious emphasis in our late modern world, particularly in the uncertain context of the day to day existence of young men and women ("What can I expect in my adult life as partner, professional, person, human being?")[29].

Religious pluralism

Assuming that authenticity and creativity enjoy a dominant position in the search for (religious) meaning and purpose it would seem obvious that individualisation must ultimately lead to pluralisation. "Tot capites, tot senses": there are as many interpretations as there are heads. The market in fundamental life options is skilfully working the situation. Local faith communities are constantly in search of ways to clean up their image, new religious movements present an attractive option, spirituality groups move from strength to strength via both traditional and contemporary media channels, lifestyle movements (with an ecological, economic or socio-ethical agenda), professional instances, clubs with

---

25. H.-G. ZIEBERTZ, *Religion, Christentum und Moderne* (n. 24), pp. 45-51.

26. J. DE HART, *Tussen hemel en aarde. Over jongeren en christelijke traditie*, in *Verbum* 59 (1992) 109-115.

27. H. STREIB, *Off-Road Religion? A Narrative Approach to Fundamentalist and Occult Orientations of Adolescents*, in *Journal of Adolescence* 22 (1998) 235-267.

28. K. GABRIEL, *Christentum zwischen Tradition und Postmoderne* (n. 9), pp. 81-85.

29. F. SCHWEITZER, *Die Suche nach eigenem Glauben* (n. 12), pp. 116-123.

sect-like attributes and even the official churches are all out to win the restless and inquiring hearts of their contemporaries. Pluralisation is also evident at the level of personal fundamental life options. A multitude of interpretation schemas can be discerned at work in the identity formation of men and women of all ages. Here too one might speak of a "patchwork" identity or even of intra-personal pluralism. Young people tend not to make much of this phenomenon, at least in so far as they remain on the surface thereof. Dallying in a multiplicity of different perspectives can be a pleasant experience. Young people like to be initiated in whatever is exotic or different, whatever offers an alternative to their experience so far. The current interest in world music and the revival of folk and roots music has its place here. People like to be inspired by whatever it is that makes others different. Music tends to have a unique role to play in this process. One might ask the question whether young people are not in the process of developing a new communicative praxis in this arena?

Religion and media

Religion has become a media phenomenon. In a world of information which has become accessible for many, religious instances, churches and communities present their message side by side. Important moral and doctrinal distinctions are in danger of collapse. Thresholds of communication are being crossed, boundaries are being broken, traditional certainties are being openly discussed. The Internet has clearly had a significant role to play in this democratisation of religion, religiosity and lifestyle. Dogmatic arrangements tend to be rejected while systematic (in which everything is connected to everything else) arrangements are widely accepted. Young people converse (in cyberspace they "chat") with one another on questions which preoccupy them, questions of life and death, intimacy and contingency, via the Internet. They challenge one another to take a stand, to "come out" of their anonymity, to reveal their mutual otherness. Media watchers consider this development to be a sign of a new "sensorium" which will characterise us as rational beings in the new millennium: we are being forced to be interactive on the world wide web of meanings which is in a state of constant flux. For some this development has become a new religion which has already replaced and transcended its predecessors[30].

---

30. B. ROEBBEN, *Spiritual and Moral Education in/and Cyberspace: Preliminary Reflections*, in *Journal of Education and Christian Belief* 3 (1999) 85-95.

Religious Modernisation, Tradition Crisis and Education

Young people have a well-determined role to play in the modernisation of society and the tradition crisis of faith. They adapt and re-adapt their potential in function of life and survival under the pressure of modernisation. This process also engenders religious meaning giving: syncretistic, contingency-related, pluralistic and mediatised. Indeed, traditional faith and church involvement only function in this context when they form a part of one's personal and unique patchwork quilt of fundamental life options.

Modernisation, however, also has its limits, and individualisation – including religious individualisation – has risks attached. Young people today are gasping for breath. They have become unconsciously dependent on external factors in the construction of their own identity. They "scan" their surroundings in search of potential contributions to their draft identity[31]. Many are left with the question: "What is my own contribution?" In addition, it is not unthinkable that skilful salespersons might exploit this therapeutic, individualised and mediatised hunger for religion. One might even suggest that a potential re-ideologisation of religion is at work, one no longer based on a content imposed by the religious institutions themselves but one which has become domesticated, as it were, by the market forces of supply and demand[32].

The central idea which the present contribution would hope to defend is that the responsive attitude of young people with respect to modernisation and the crisis of tradition must itself be transformed into an educational theme. As such it is not simply a question of religious education. In the first instance, the task of education in matters related to modernisation of society and the disappearance of traditional lines of interpretation has been entrusted to the school as a whole. The rationale behind such a vision might be described as follows: assuming that education, in its basic modern sense, intends to make a contribution to the development of a critical identity and a vision of life, and considering the fact that (young) people are in danger of becoming splintered, alienated and commercialised in their own life narrative by the pressures of modernisation, it would seem clear that the schools have an urgent task in front of them, one which is foundational to their very existence,

---

31. V. DREHSEN, *Wie religionsfähig ist die Volkskirche?* (n. 10), pp. 66-91.

32. B. ROEBBEN, *Do We Still Have Faith in Young People? A West-European Answer to the Evangelization of Young People in a Postmodern World*, in *Religious Education* 90 (1995) 327-345, esp. pp. 330-333.

namely to safeguard the education of young people. Under pressure from modernisation, the modern ideal of formation is in danger of allowing itself to be called off-side[33]!

A number of practical theologians have endeavoured to elaborate this anomaly. For Blasberg-Kuhnke[34] and Mette[35] the school must enable young people to develop an "I" identity with respect to the key problems of life and society. While modernisation and its pressures constitutes only one such key problem, it remains an important and indeed fundamental one. The goal of formation in the contemporary context needs to be reformulated: the nurture of subjects who have the capacity to sustain universal solidarity and intersubjectivity[36]. While young people today are forcing the educational establishment to re-examine the context, the educational establishment is also being challenged in the confrontation to assist young people to question the context, to seek clarification and change, or better still, to refuse to give in to the pressures of modernisation. In real terms this means that young people ought to asked to take time to reflect on their own identity in relation to the ruthlessness of market forces and the world of consumption, the experience of dissatisfaction and guilt, the lack of a sense of future, broken relationships etc. The identity of young people is "balancing", flexible and sophisticated, and herein lies its ultimate strength. At the same time, however, it is also vulnerable and brittle. By establishing educational expectations and refusing to avoid pedagogical responsibility the school can help young people to build a capable and resilient identity[37]. It is thus in the wider context of education's formational responsibilities that religious education is to be given its specific function: it must be able to exercise its moral authority and expertise at the level of supporting identity formation and the thematisation of fundamental life options in the lives of young people. It

---

33. H. PEUKERT, *Über die Zukunft von Bildung*, in *Frankfurter Hefte* 6 (1984) 129-137; ID., *Tradition und Transformation. Zu einer pädagogischen Theorie der Überlieferung*, in *Religionspädagogische Beiträge* 19 (1987) 16-34.

34. M. BLASBERG-KUHNKE, *Nachdenken über religiöse Erziehung*, in *Herder Korrespondenz* 58 (1994) 252-257.

35. N. METTE, *Religionsunterricht in nachchristlicher Gesellschaft*, in J. LOTT (ed.), *Religion – warum und wozu in der Schule?*, Weinheim, Deutscher Studien Verlag, 1992, 269-283; ID., *Der Beitrag des Religionsunterrichts zum Bildungsauftrag der Schule*, in ID., *Praktisch-theologische Erkundungen*, Münster – Hamburg – London, Lit-Verlag, 1999, pp. 143-156.

36. B. ROEBBEN, *Een tijd van opvoeden* (n. 21), pp. 111-121.

37. A. SCHRÖDER-KLEIN, *Jugend ohne Religion. Der Versuch einer Bestandsaufnahme angesichts von Sinnkrise und Traditionsabbruch*, in J. LOTT (ed.), *Religion – warum und wozu in der Schule?* (n. 35), 213-232.

must motivate not only children and young people but also adults (as teachers) to reflect on the modern individual's capacity to stand up under pressure. The literature which addresses this task in terms of the "diaconia" of Church and society with respect to young people is growing fastly[38]. In the words of the German religious education researcher G. Bitter: religious education has become a "socio-hygienic necessity"[39].

4. Religious Education and the Fostering of Religious Competence

In the context of determining the general aims of education in a modernised society it is now the appropriate point to outline the unique contribution and character of religious education. As a classroom course, religious education does not really exist on its own, it offers rather a set of materials, insights and teaching strategies to assist teachers and pupils to engage in that "other qualitative observation of reality and to engage in interaction with one another"[40]. It reinforces, explains and systematises this observation on the basis of a number of fundamental insights which function within religion and religiosity's moral and ideological discourse. Religious education thus intends to contribute to an attitude of active openness among pupils with respect to these insights. It gives shape to the *religious competence* of young people, with the words of the German religious education specialist R. Englert[41]. His Flemish colleague J. Bulckens speaks of "religious responsibility"[42], his Dutch

---

38. G. BITTER, *Religionsunterricht zugunsten der Schüler. Umrisse eines diakonischen Religionsunterrichts*, in *Pädagogische Rundschau* 43 (1989) 639-658; M. BÜKER & J. SAYER, *Zur gesellschaftlichen Relevanz diakonisch verstandenen Religionsunterrichts im Kontext struktureller Individualisierung und Pluralisierung*, in A. SCHIFFERLE (ed.), *Pfarrei in der Postmoderne? Gemeindebildung in nachchristlicher Zeit*, Freiburg – Basel – Wien, Herder, 1997, 275-296; W. FLECKENSTEIN, *Religionsunterricht für einen "heiligen Rest" oder "für alle"? Die diakonische Funktion des Religionsunterrichts als Zukunftsperspektive*, in *Religionspädagogische Beiträge* 24 (1989) 26-44; T. GOTTFRIED, *Religionsunterricht als Lebenskunde. Diakonische Orientierung des Religionsunterrichts in der postmodernen Gesellschaft* (Religionspädagogische Perspektiven, 24), Essen, Die blaue Eule, 1995.

39. G. BITTER, *Religionsunterricht als eine sozialhygienische Dringlichkeit*, in *Lebendige Seelsorge* 49 (1998) 135-138.

40. H. Peukert, quoted by N. METTE, *Religionspädagogik* (Leitfaden Theologie, 24), Düsseldorf, Patmos, 1994, p. 233.

41. R. ENGLERT, *Der Religionsunterricht nach der Emigration des Glauben-Lernens*, in *Katechetische Blätter* 123 (1998) 4-12.

42. J. BULCKENS, *Godsdienstonderricht op de secundaire school. Handboek voor godsdienstdidactiek. Deel 1: Doel, inhoud, leerkracht, (katholieke) school*, Leuven – Amersfoort, Acco, 1994, pp. 76-80.

colleague Th. Geurts of "autonomy with respect to one's religious rationale or perspective"[43]. The fundamental vision at work here is the following: religious education responds to the subjective (modernised) religion of young people by establishing a learning process in the context of which objective material can be introduced which can help to explain one's personal observation of the religious and enable individuals to develop a resilient and critical identity in a complex (and risk-laden) modernising reality. The competence we have in mind can be further subdivided into "identity formation" and "religious communication". In the context of religious this implies two significant tasks: biographical accompaniment and education in plurality[44]. Both aspects which, incidentally, have been incorporated in the new curriculum for the Roman Catholic religious education in Flanders and Holland, will constitute the main focus of the following paragraphs.

Identity Formation

The German researcher J. Lott[45] describes this competence as the process of re-arrangement and re-interpretation of the crucial moments in one's life with a view to the explication of one's own narrative identity. Elements related to religious beliefs have an important role to play in this process: for example the management of one's own religious growth, of the broken pieces of religious socialisation one has inherited from the past, of the diverse elements of other religions one has encountered or continues to encounter. The question: "Who am I thus far?" can only be coherently and authentically answered when one admits other meaning givers into the narrative. People grow into adults in the presence of other people. Fundamental questions are only given a chance because there are communities both past and present which challenge individuals to learn, think, interpret and take a stance. In so doing, every community is a discourse community that honours a particular fundamental life option, even though it may consciously try to avoid doing so. Children are raised in such environments in which they are urged (more or less) to differentiate themselves.

---

43. Th. GEURTS, *Leren van zin* (n. 15).

44. F. SCHWEITZER, *Die Suche nach eigenem Glauben* (n. 12), pp. 164-178.

45. J. LOTT, *Die Beschäftigung mit fremder Religiosität als Bestandteil eigener religiöser Sozialisation*, in ID. (ed.), *Religion – warum und wozu in der Schule?* (n. 35), 321-340; ID., *'Religion und Lebensgeschichte' in praktisch-theologische Handlungsfeldern zur Thematisierung von Erfahrungen mit Religion*, in A. GRÖZINGER & J. LOTT (eds.), *Gelebte Religion. Im Brennpunkt praktisch-theologische Denkens und Handelns* (Hermeneutica, 6), Rheinbach-Merzbach, CMZ, 1997, 157-174.

Religious education aims at making young people more aware of such individuality. We should not line up our defences against an over emphasis on individuality, according to Mette[46], but against a lack of self-awareness or a distorted, automatic individuality which is locked up in itself and exhibits neither resilience nor a critical stance when confronted by the processes of modernisation. At this juncture, the therapeutic aspect of youthful religiosity (see paragraph 3) understood as accompaniment in the process of socialisation, is exceeded and takes the form of life accompaniment: young people are challenged to reflect upon their own past and their own future with a view to the establishment of a conscious and mature personal identity. It is far from easy, however, to find good and well-differentiated material which can adequately and correctly accompany the process of identity formation in religious education. In the words of the Australian researcher G. Rossiter the *appropriate classroom* is often lacking[47]. Retreat days outside the classroom context often facilitate the process because they allow for emotional communication. The classroom situation itself, however, has a different character: one cannot force pupils in the religious studies class to reveal their identity either as a group or as individuals. For the most part, therefore, there is an evident need to procure cognitive structures and materials which are sufficiently dynamic to enable identity formation. In this context, of course, it is of vital importance that the religions which are being treated should be presented from within the perspective of their own internal coherence and potential logic.

Religious Communication

Identity formation is never free from conflict, friction and difference of opinion, certainly not within a multi-cultural and multi-religious context. In the seventies it was the task of the individual in religious education to explain him/herself within the framework of secularisation. Today, this occurs within the framework of radical plurality[48]. The moral and ideological market sets the tone: opinions alternate with one another and tend to get bogged down in meaningless and often elaborate argumentations which insist on mutual exclusivity. In this perspective, religious competence implies that one is obliged to sustain intra-personal

46. N. METTE, *Religionspädagogik* (n. 40), pp. 188-189.
47. G. ROSSITER, *Perspectives on Change in Catholic Religious Education since the Second Vatican Council*, in *Religious Education* 83 (1988) 264-276.
48. F. SCHWEITZER, *Die Suche nach eigenem Glauben* (n. 12), p. 174.

pluralism at liveable and controllable levels in the context of one's endeavour to construct a conscious and well-reflected narrative identity by ensuring that one maintains a critical yet tolerant openness towards the plural world outside of oneself. Such a process demands both humility and self-respect: it is a "process of informed critique (not just criticism) with *ethical regard* for the integrity of beliefs and commitments of students and teacher, and for the integrity of the subject matter"[49].

Well constructed dossiers, digestible knowledge which transcends the "opinion" character of immediate information and refined search procedures[50] can help young people make the transition *from opinion to knowledge* and become conscious participants in the ongoing conversation between human culture and society. In the context of inter-religious learning there is an evident necessity, therefore, for matter of fact information *(learning about religion)* as a basic condition for the success of inter-religious dialogue as a moment of enrichment *(learning from religion)*[51]. Only then, when the critically-utopian fundamental option of informed freedom is present, will the conversation speak for itself without the need for further ideological argumentation or foundation. Such discourse is in itself an ongoing invitation to participate in the discourse. Indeed, according to the Jewish understanding of learning proposed by E. Wiesel, this is its ultimate *raison d'être*[52].

Religious education is thus a substantial support for identity building of young people and is aiming at the establishment of a *communio,* a learning community of committed people sharing the same context of communication on ideologies, fundamental life options and religions. Once again, this task cannot be realised without it being embedded in the focus of the entire school on moral and ideological learning complexes and aspects of formation. It is frequently the case that the only class in which the name of God is mentioned is the religion education class. Images of God, humanity and the world, however, are implied by

---

49. M. CRAWFORD & G. ROSSITER, *The Secular Spirituality of Youth: Implications for Religious Educations*, in *British Journal of Religious Education* 18 (1996) 133-143, p. 137.
    50. H. LOMBAERTS, B. ROEBBEN, G. GINNEBERGE, *Godinet* (n. 7).
    51. J.A. VAN DER VEN & H.-G. ZIEBERTZ, *Jugendliche in multikulturellem und multireligiösem Kontext*, in *Religionspädagogische Beiträge* 35 (1995) 151-167, esp. p. 167. See for this positon also B. ROEBBEN, *Interreligieus leren op school. Een tussentijdse godsdienstpedagogische balans*, in ID. (ed.), *Religieus opvoeden in een multiculturele samenleving*, Leuven, Davidsfonds, 2000, 85-101.
    52. Quoted in R. BOSCHKI, *Dialogisch-kreative Religionsdidaktik* (n. 8), p. 18.

every aspect of the curriculum[53]. Adequate education at school consists precisely in the unfolding of the presuppositions of the curriculum in and through the learning process. It is evident, furthermore, that the time young people spend at school is an essential element of their biography and is a source of material for their education in fundamental life issues[54]. It is clearly necessary, therefore, that a multi-dimensional space be created in which competence with respect to religion and fundamental life options can be practised. This space might be located in a variety of courses as well as in other spaces and times within the school[55]. The question remains, however, as to the educational potential of the religious education class itself. Authors such as R. Englert[56] and N. Mette[57] are convinced that religious education should and does offer leadership in this arena. They argue that new religio-pedagogical and religio-didactic insights have already contributed to the revitalisation of theories and concepts of general pedagogics and didactics.

5. Towards a New Concept of Religious Education for Secondary Schools

Modernisation demands a degree of "mental discipline" in the environment in which young people live and move. The educational vision encapsulated in the school subject "religious education" is focused on the acquisition of religious competence. We now have to face the question as to whether religious education has a contribution to make, bearing in mind that Christian faith is in a state of crisis and schools are experiencing a high degree of uncertainty. In other words, what shape should the religious seed-bed – thematised in objective learning material – ultimately take in order to enable pupils to ask fundamental questions related to their lives and their futures and to ensure that the

53. C. Th. SCHEILKE, *Zukunft der Bildung – Schule der Zukunft*, in R. EHMANN *et al.* (eds.), *Religionsunterricht der Zukunft. Aspekte eine notwendigen Wandels*, Freiburg – Basel – Wien, Herder, 1998, 189-202.

54. F. SCHWEITZER, *Die Suche nach eigenem Glauben* (n. 12), pp. 165-166.

55. W. TZSCHEETZSCH, *Religionslehrer sein – Herausforderungen und Kompetenzen*, in *Theologische Quartalschrift* 179 (1999) 100-109.

56. R. ENGLERT, *Religionsunterricht in Deutschland. Situation und Prognose*, in J. BULCKENS & H. LOMBAERTS (eds.), *L'enseignement de la religion catholique à l'école secondaire. Enjeux pour la nouvelle Europe* (BETL, 109), Leuven, University Press – Peeters, 1993, 71-88, esp. pp. 87-88.

57. N. Mette, quoted in *Schulentwicklung und religiöse Bildung*, in *Katechetische Blätter* 124 (1999) 156-161, p. 157.

learning process takes place in a context of informed freedom? The following three paragraphs will endeavour to describe the process itself, while the fourth will focus on an important boundary condition.

Getting Down to Basics

Religious education offers objective material which is intended to reveal the internal logic of religions and fundamental life options. Such material points to the referential significance of the cultural system of signs related to religions and fundamental life options with a view to their ultimate "use" by pupils[58]. Religious education thus fulfils a "deictic" function[59]: if it works well, it can reveal pathways which can lead to insight in a person's life history because it is recognisable or at least non-alienating. The most important thing is not an informative presentation of knowledge but rather a theme oriented deepening of pupils' (personal and communal) foundational experiences based on well-selected teaching material[60]. Objective information and subjective integration are complementary. According to R. Englert this dialectic should be understood as follows: pupils first show themselves prepared to look closely at life's secrets and to explain them for themselves in a sensible and intelligent way; they then learn to understand religious traditions as responses to human longing; after some discussion they proceed by adopting a personal standpoint and thus move towards the establishment of a religious identity[61].

One must continue to ask, however, whether and to what extent the personal convictions of the teacher should be allowed to make their mark in the process. Religious educational researchers agree that with a view to learning the internal force of inquiry exhibited by the religious, teachers should not endeavour to hide or obscure their personal confession of faith[62]. The reason for this is that no one is capable of working or indeed teaching without a tradition. One important element in this

---

58. B. DRESSLER, *Bildende Religion – gebildeter Glaube. Religionsunterricht in Schnittfeld von Außensicht und Binnenperspektive*, in *Zeitschrift für Pädagogik und Theologie* 50 (1998) 395-409.

59. E. Weniger, quoted *ibid*.

60. D. ZILLESSEN, *Konfessioneller Religionsunterricht in multikultureller Lebenswelt?*, in J. LOTT (ed.), *Religion – warum und wozu in der Schule?* (n. 35), 301-320.

61. R. ENGLERT, *Der Religionsunterricht nach der Emigration des Glaubens-Lernens* (n. 41).

62. H. Luther, quoted in N. METTE, *Religionspädagogik* (n. 40), pp. 279-280; F. SCHWEITZER, *Zwischen Theologie und Praxis – Unterrichtsvorbereitung und das Problem der Lehrbarkeit von Religion*, in *Jahrbuch für Religionspädagogik* 7 (1991) 3-42.

regard is the fact that by refusing to hide his/her own attitude, the teacher has the potential to reveal what it is that inspires people to be religious. A purely detached presentation of religions and the religious motivations of those who subscribe to them would be counterproductive from the perspective of religious education. A purely confessional presentation would likewise do an injustice to those young men and women who are engaged in the process of religious learning. The creative and transformational potential of the tradition – which goes beyond historical-institutional and ecclesial-confessional representations thereof – would otherwise be concealed[63].

According to Englert, the objective representation of elementary curricular content can be enriching for the subjective religion of young people in three distinct ways: the tradition can help them to relativise the subjectivism and romanticism of direct access to God; the confessional element can form a challenge to pupils to examine and reflect upon the confessional character of their own convictions; the institutional element makes a communion visible which is endeavouring to live in relationship with the *ultimate reality* and to organise its life on the basis of this relationship[64]. In this respect, the religious educator presents by his "intelligible" association with a particular faith tradition (i.c. the Christian) a permanent invitation to young people to not be too easily satisfied, to not run with the pack, to keep watch on their own identity and its growth[65].

Mutually Critical Correlation

The tradition crisis affecting contemporary faith has resulted in the fact that the modern correlation didactic (elaborated in line with Vatican II by, among others, Edward Schillebeeckx, Paul Tillich and Karl Rahner) is no longer bearing fruit. At a time in which religious socialisation and interpretation of reality is absent, vital points of reference to faith as such are missing and it has become impossible in the context of

63. D. ZILLESSEN, *Konfessioneller Religionsunterricht in multikultureller Lebenswelt?* (n. 60), p. 316.

64. R. ENGLERT, *Der Religionsunterricht nach der Emigration des Glauben-Lernens* (n. 61); B. DRESSLER, *Bildende Religion – gebildeter Glaube* (n. 58), p. 404, argues similarly in this way: "Religiöse Bildung geschieht aus einem Glauben heraus – und sie legt diese Tatsache offen. Sie kann deshalb nur bekenntnisgebunden sein, gerade um für die Lernenden bekenntnisoffen bleiben zu können".

65. W. TZSCHEETZSCH, *Selbstkundgabe des Menschen. Grundprinzip einer personalen Religionsdidaktik*, in *Stimmen der Zeit* 121 (1996) 611-620.

religious education to take a spontaneous learning process moving from experience to revelation as an evident point of departure. It would appear, therefore, that the "traditional" correlation didactic understood as such has reached its end[66]. According to the evaluation offered by G. Bitter a great deal of effort in this direction was probably dependent on an incorrect use of induction in the religious education classroom[67].

Correlation as a basic principle of learning to live with fundamental life options, however, is far from dead and buried. The fact that the correlation didactic itself has become a source of difficulties does not mean that it is no longer possible to establish any links between faith and life. It might be more accurate to speak of a "correlation weakness", like we did before with R. Boschki: the obviousness of the connection between life and faith has become a problem and we are thus obliged to examine each situation anew in order to determine how we can relate faith to life in a plausible way. *Korrelatieren-Lernen als Fragen-Lernen* (correlational learning as learning to raise appropriate questions) remains crucial[68]. It is a hermeneutic-didactic principle which seeks to challenge pupils to tighten the knot between the familiar and the unfamiliar, between the everyday and the unusual, between the means and the end, between opinionated slogans and the unheard of, all in the context of a mutual and critical exchange. This is clearly an important element within the framework of formation in religious competence: young people are challenged to confront their subjective religious experience with that which remains unfamiliar and unknown, namely the elements of tradition, precisely with a view to sharpening their interpretation of their own religious biography.

A double response can be offered with respect to the problems associate with dealing with this didactic. Some people are of the opinion that the individualisation of (religious) experience has made a communal actualisation of the faith tradition well-nigh impossible. On top of this, they maintain, the connection with the local faith community has been severed. It boils down to a situation in which the school itself has to do something about religious tradition and religious practice by

---

66. R. ENGLERT, *Die Korrelationsdidaktik am Ausgang ihrer Epoche: Plädoyer für einen "ehrenhaften" Abgang*, in G. HILGER & G. REILLY (eds.), *Religionsunterricht im Abseits? Das Spannungsfeld Jugend-Schule-Religion*, München, Kösel, 1993, 97-110.

67. G. BITTER, *Plädoyer für eine zeitgemäße Korrelationsdidaktik*, in *Lebendige Katechese* 18 (1996) 1-8.

68. E. FEIFEL, *Didaktische Ansätze der Religionspädagogik*, in H.-G. ZIEBERTZ & W. SIMON (eds.), *Bilanz der Religionspädagogik*, Düsseldorf, Patmos, 1995, 56-110, p. 100.

engaging in a process of *learning by doing*, such as learning to pray, learning to celebrate liturgy, learning to experience symbols, learning to act as a servant *(diakonia)*, learning about religious aesthetics, etc[69]. Others are convinced that there are still enough elements with spiritual authority to be found in religious traditions which can help young people to think about and reflect upon their own identity[70]. The interrogative potential of religion in general and of the Christian faith in particular remains healthy. In other words, the question: "What questions do religiously inspired men and women consider worthy of a meaningful answer?" cannot be dismissed as meaningless.

It is probable that we are dealing here with a dialectic: affective-dynamic "playing" with religion also implies the cognitive capacity to derive lines of learning from existing religious practices and vice versa. A person's subjective religion as understood by young people implies the possibility of an objective religious dimension. In this sense religious education must be seen as a hermeneutical learning process, one which seeks out the junctures at which young people in the process of identity formation confront themselves with differences of interpretation in their environment (friends, parents, institutions) and one which seeks to establish a learning process around such junctures[71]. Many different angles of approach are possible in such a dialectic field.

Authentic Learning

Correlative learning as basic principle of human knowing is thus central to our. With respect to religious faith this means that teachers must be able to recontextualise: they must pay particular attention to the contemporary character of the initial situation in the classroom, they must get in touch with the primary questions young people are asking about life in general, they must help young people to make the subjective elements of their fundamental life options explicit. *Gelebte Religion* (actually lived religion), with its clarity and obscurity, its liberating and restraining aspects, must be the actual point of departure of such an

69. F. SCHWEITZER, *Die Suche nach eigenem Glauben* (n. 12), p. 170; A. BIESINGER in *Den religiösen Hunger stillen – in der Schule?* (Streitgespräch zwischen Albert Biesinger und Jürgen Lott), in *Publik Forum*, 10 April 1998, pp. 26-29.

70. G. BITTER, *Plädoyer für eine zeitgemäße Korrelationsdidaktik* (n. 67).

71. H. LOMBAERTS, B. ROEBBEN, G. GINNEBERGE, *Godinet* (n. 7).

approach to religious education[72]. While this might appear to be rather facile, it is probably the most important task facing the religious education teacher at the present moment, *in the heart of modernity*, in a context of moral and religious complexity and of the demise of answers "set in concrete". This constitutes the hermeneutical awareness of the postmodern person[73]. In this framework, which continues to exhibit the need for new points of reference at the level of meaning, there is also a clear need to work on qualitative religious education.

It is important in this regard that the young person as searching individual becomes central and not the young person as pupil[74]. Education must be oriented towards the human person as such, not as representative of the school system. It is at this level that theology and education encounter one another in the context of a critical-utopic religious didactic[75]. With a view to the authentic teaching of the person him/herself and inspired by the idea that every fundamental life option is a learning process, the didactic process takes on the complexion of a "hermeneutic didactic"[76]. What young people need for the fostering of their religious competence, what "successful learning" is, can ultimately be revealed by young people themselves. The areas of concern which they themselves consider important constitute the material source and point of departure of the searching process. Didactics should focus on the search to which young people themselves are committed to; and it should challenge them to start such a search. In their construction of knowledge and insight, young people allow their preconceptions and their (still provisional) interpretation of the context to play a role, to serve as a point of departure. Even where this would appear to be something of a void (for example because of the complete lack of religious socialisation

---

72. F. SCHWEITZER, *Gelehrte, gelernte, gelebte Religion. Zum Verhältnis von Religion, Leben und Lernen*, in A. GRÖZINGER & J. LOTT (eds.), *Gelebte Religion. Im Brennpunkt praktisch-theologische Denkens und Handelns* (Hermeneutica, 6), Rheinbach-Merzbach, CMZ, 1997, 142-156.

73. U. SCHWAB, *Geschlossene Konzeptionen und permanenter Wandel – Religiosität in der Moderne zwischen institutioneller Bindung und individueller Konstruktion*, in A. GRÖZINGER & J. LOTT (eds.), *Gelebte Religion* (n. 72), 130-141.

74. F. SCHWEITZER, *Gelehrte, gelernte, gelebte Religion* (n. 72), pp. 154-155.

75. C. BAKKER, *De modernisering van onderwijs en godsdienstonderwijs. Naar een constructivistisch georiënteerd vak levensbeschouwelijke vorming*, in C. BAKKER & H.-G. ZIEBERTZ (eds.), *Imaginatie en de constructie van identiteit. Visies op religieuze vorming*, Tilburg, TUP, 1998, 99-120.

76. F. SCHWEITZER, *Theologische Lehre und das Subjekt des Lernens. Der Beitrag der Allgemeinen Didaktik zur Praktisch-theologischen Hermeneutik*, in D. ZILLESSEN, S. ALKIER, R. KOERRENZ, H. SCHROETER (eds.), *Praktisch-theologische Hermeneutik. Ansätze, Anregungen, Aufgaben*, Rheinbach-Merzbach, CMZ, 1991, 87-98.

at home), the learning process can and must be commenced. In such circumstances, teachers will be obliged to kick start the event and endeavour to fill the vacuum in an appropriate way.

A great deal is asked and expected of the teacher in the context of such a hermeneutical learning process. Teachers need to know what they are about, what their own vision of things is, where they can find confrontational conceptual patterns. The teacher is a source of reference, a knowledge broker, a hermeneut – just to mention a few of Herman Lombaerts' concepts to address the difficult position of the teacher in the religious education class[77]. He or she must be capable of bringing different visions into dialogue with one another, of organising a pluralistic theology of religions in the classroom, of inviting those in their charge to continually change their perspective. This "total experience" has a formational character and young people quickly learn that they are involved parties. he Australian practical theologian T. Veling describes this process of discovering truth in the classroom situation from the perspective of the teacher as follows: "In my own teaching practice, I find myself constantly trying to read the class of which both myself and the students are members. I always come away from a class as if I have just come away from reading yet another intriguing chapter in an intriguing book. Every class is different, and I am continually surprised at the novel twists and turns, questions and responses, stories and reflections that emerge in a time of educational conversation. Each class bears all the marks of a complex and compelling text, one that I am constantly trying to read, feeling for the pulse and beat of the questions, issues and themes that are circulating among us"[78]. For Veling this constitutes the material resource for practical theology. In the present contribution on might likewise say that authentic learning in the religious education class is a source for contemporary practical theology.

Religious Education Teachers and the Christian Faith Community

Given the fundamental yet extremely demanding task of religious education – to confront the narrative experience of young people with the reflexive potential of the "internal rationality" of the Christian faith

---

77. See especially the remarkable essays of H. LOMBAERTS, *De klas als leergroep. De leerkracht als hermeneut* and *Godsdienstonderricht als communicatieve gebeurtenis*, both in H. LOMBAERTS & B. ROEBBEN (eds.), *Godsdienst op school in de branding* (n. 1), resp. 67-80 and 81-107.

78. T. VELING, *"Practical Theology": a New Sensibility for Theological Education*, in *Pacifica* 11 (1998) 195-210, p. 204.

and recontextualise it in their lives –, the religious education teacher deserves the support of society school and Church alike. In order to prevent him/her from running away from this task, it is of vital importance that he or she has the capacity and is at liberty to be a "correlating" person in many senses of the word: a person who is able to withstand the tension between context and tradition, who struggles with the confessional dimension of his/her convictions, who continues to enjoy a dynamic and affective relationship with his/her profession.

This raises significant questions, of course, which have a bearing on the training of religious education teachers: Does it have the capacity to assist young people to observe their own subjective religion? Does it have the conceptual apparatus to interpret this arena and to reveal its value to new teachers and teachers in training, including, among other things, ethical reflection, philosophical reference, a vision of *Alltagsreligion* (daily lived religiosity), sects and world religions[79]? Is it able to form new teachers to engage in self-driven meta-reflection, to analyse and transform their own faith both at the level of content and of disposition in a critical yet concerned manner?

Perhaps the most significant support a teacher might expect should come from the Church. Indeed, religious education teachers stand in fact at the boundary between Church and world. They are the primary interpreters of the tensions with which Christian faith confronts the communities. They are at the front line where faith and fundamental convictions are under attack and are being forced to be authentic and be prepared to accept responsibility. According to Bishop Wanke of the German Diocese of Erfurt, the faith community is the teacher's place of retreat, a place in which he/she should enjoy the explicit solidarity of the community at large[80]. Any endeavour to lay the blame for the tradition crisis at the feet of religious educators would clearly do a great injustice to reality which is evidently much more complex.

6. (Practical) Theology Challenged by Religious Education

Practical theology studies the religious practices of contemporary men and women (material object) on the basis of an empirical and/or

---

79. J. HEUMANN, *Kann man heute noch Religionslehrer sein?*, in *Religion Heute* 36 (1998) 216-217.

80. J. WANKE, *Chancen und Grenzen des schulischen Religionsunterrichts in einer säkularen Gesellschaft*, in *Christlich-Pädagogische Blätter* 111 (1998) 110-116.

hermeneutical religio-analytic range of instruments (formal object). Religious education is an excellent and fitting location for such research. It might be possible, for example, to ask whether and in what way the contemporary concept of religious education outlined in paragraphs 4 and 5 above can offer a real response to the religious questions being asked by young people today. Are the communication of fundamental life options and the development of identity as the concept presents them actually desirable and appropriate in the milieu in which young people live? Interesting empirical-analytic, hermeneutic and ideological-critical research is clearly an option in this regard[81], indeed such research is already in full swing[82]. Practical theological research in the field of religious education tends, moreover, to constitute a significant catalyst for the development of theology itself. Rooted in their doubts, protests and stubborn silences, young people can challenge both school and Church to clarify and improve their self-definition and the way in which they understand their relationship with their experience. In the same way, theologians who engage in practical theology on the basis of their experience of religious education can challenge the established theological discourse.

As conclusion, a brief practical report should serve to clarify what I mean here. I have been involved in the teacher training of young theologians in Flanders (K.U. Leuven) and I continue to do so in the Netherlands (K.U. Brabant in Tilburg). In their contacts with secondary school classes and in their interaction with their contemporaries, many such students are confronted with questions which often form the jumping off point of a hermeneutical process at the level of the class group for which they are responsible or at the level of their peer group outside the theological faculty. "What do you mean when you say you believe in the resurrection? You can't see God so who is God for you? What value is there in living according to the convictions of the Church?" and so forth. This process of inquiry goes on to become more intense and more chal-

---

81. For these distinctions, see H.-G. ZIEBERTZ, *Methodologische Multiperspektivität angesichts religiöser Umbrüche. Herausforderungen für die empirische Forschung in der Praktischen Theologie*, in B. PORZELT & R. GÜTH (eds.), *Empirische Religionspädagogik. Grundlagen – Zugänge – Aktuelle Projekte*, Münster – Hamburg – London, Lit-Verlag, 2000, 29-44, esp. pp. 33-34.

82. A. BUCHER, *Der Religionsunterricht: Besser als sein Ruf? Empirische Einblicke in ein umstrittenes Fach*, Innsbruck – Wien, Tyrolia, 1996; B. PORZELT & R. GÜTH (eds.), *Empirische Religionspädagogik* (see previous note); J.A. VAN DER VEN, *God Reinvented? A Theological Search in Texts and Tables* (Empiricial Studies in Theology, 1), Leiden, Brill, 1999.

lenging in the personal lives of the theology students themselves. They sense that their identity as religious leaders and as theologians is being called into question. On more than one occasion I have had the privilege to witness that the religious practices and the questions which such students bring into the university setting and which emerge in the context of seminars and classroom discussions on an academic level have a tendency to turn traditional theology on its head. It is not unusual for such students to find that what they have learned in the classroom is of little use when they are at home among their peers or in one or other practical context. This became quite evident to me in the Flemish situation in the context of a drawn out discussion on the significance of the resurrection during an intensive seminar in the teacher training programme. The sense of doubt with respect to this central point of Christian faith interpretation was paralysing for some. Academic tools would appear to have been insufficient. Fortunately enough there were a number of students who saw this sense of doubt as a challenge to look for a new interpretation of the resurrection and to search for contemporary basic human experiences which respond thereto. The same students were also able to make use of a few shreds of religious socialisation (for example "Jesus died and rose from the dead out of love for all humanity – This same love must be realised and universalised with great urgency in our ruthless world") which they were capable of activating in a creative manner.

In the Netherlands, by contrast, this substratum of religious socialisation is often absent, even among theology students. The priority in this context is to make the fundamental and traditional theological concepts their own once again. The days of what they call "cut-and-paste" theology are long gone. They refuse to let themselves be inspired by some obscure theological language game no matter how gently it is proposed. They are no longer interested in the sinking ship approach and its endeavours to calculate just how serious the damage is and just how much longer we are likely to stay afloat. What they are looking for are new points of contact with the Christian religious tradition as a basis for the clarification of their own important questions and those of their contemporaries. To continue the sinking ship image: they are restlessly in search of pieces of wreckage which they can hold on to in the troubled ocean of religious practices, meanings and meaning giving systems. They don't want to sink in these turbulent waters. They want to float with the aid of small-scale and narrative life belts, which are both transparent to them and to their immediate environment. They reject every form of religious domination exploitation of power.

What both groups of young people are doing, both from their own perspectives and their actual experience of secularisation, is engaging in the re-contextualisation of the Christian tradition[83]. Their experiences in the context of teaching practice at the secondary school level and their discussions with their contemporaries on difficult yet fundamental questions serve as the teaching material for their practical-theological formation. Their experience of religious education (at school and among friends) challenges them to re-situate themselves with respect to theology, a process which is essential if the tradition is to have a future. Where the return to sources is impeded, the tradition grinds to a standstill and begins to repeat and cultivate its own self-justification. Living tradition is an ongoing process of *Resubjektivierung objektivierter Erfahrung* (re-subjectivation of objectivated experiences)[84], a constant process of re-plausibilisation of her most fundamental visions and practices in new cultural and societal contexts. Religious education with young people today provides significant and substantial content to this process[85].

This vision of tradition, theological reflection and education has its roots in an optimistic theology of creation: God reveals Godself through and in human persons who want to understand and change their daily existence. The fact remains, however, that the model elaborated in paragraphs 4 and 5 above requires a substantial intellectual effort on the part of religion and theology. This is even more important at a time when the temptations of fideism are great and people are vulnerable in their dependence on one another, in their mutual search for truth in a postmodern context – a context "with a double soil and without safety nets"[86]. The challenge however is there: theology and the debate surrounding religious education can create an open and ongoing spiritual space which can help to prevent any overemphasis on pedagogics, didactics or even ethics[87]. The strength of Christian religious education lies

---

83. L. BOEVE, *Onderbroken traditie* (n. 5).

84. H. Fend, quoted in H.-J. FRAAS, *Gemeinschaft – Geschichte – Persönlichkeit. Dt 6,20 als Grundmodell religiöser Sozialisation*, in W. HOMOLKA & O. ZIEGELMEIER (eds.), *Von Wittenberg nach Memphis. FS R. Schwarz*, Göttingen, Vandenhoeck und Ruprecht, 1989, 21-37, here p. 23.

85. Cfr. B. ROEBBEN, *De decaloog in catechismus en catechese. Historische en systematische overwegingen*, in K.-W. MERKS & F. VOSMAN (eds.), *Een lichte last? De tien geboden in de katechismus van de katholiek kerk. Uitleg en commentaar*, Baarn, Gooi en Sticht, 1998, 87-112; ID., *Shaping a Playground for Transcendence* (n. 11), esp. pp. 344-346.

86. H. KEUPP, *Subjektsein heute: zwischen postmoderner Diffusion und der Suche nach neue Fundamenten*, in A. GRÖZINGER & J. LOTT (eds.), *Gelebte Religion* (n. 45), 99-129, esp. pp. 124-129.

87. F. SCHWEITZER, *Die Suche nach eigenem Glauben* (n. 12), p. 177.

perhaps in the fact that it can make a contribution to the de-systematisation of all systems. If it is able to do so in a responsible way then it has earned its right to speak. Only then will it also be in a position to adopt new approaches to the tradition crisis and to the broad social crisis in the realm of meaning giving of which it is a part.

Disciplined Conversations, Faithful Practices
Practical Theology and the Theological Education of Lay Ecclesial Ministers

Maureen O'Brien

It is by now commonplace to acknowledge the "explosion of ministries" sparked by the teachings of Vatican II and their implementation over the past thirty-five years. In the United States, the last two decades of the second millennium CE were marked by the rise of a variety of "new" ministries, particularly those pursued under the auspices of parish faith communities by nonordained women and men. Beyond specific functions such as distribution of the Eucharist, proclamation of Scripture, and so on, growing numbers of nonordained persons have also received training and authority to exercise both broader and more highly specialized ministerial leadership roles. The educational and formational needs of these "new ministers," now officially termed "lay ecclesial ministers," pose a new challenge for practical theology.

Congruent with the intent of this *Festschrift,* this essay aims to examine the situation of lay ecclesial ministers of the Roman Catholic church in the United States with a focus on education of these persons according to a practical theology model. Herman Lombaerts's distinguished work in catechetics and his attention to the formation of catechists help to influence my thinking on the complex issues raised as we consider the formation of these ministers[1].

In discussing and advocating the development of a practical theology paradigm for the education of ministers, I aim to present an exercise, in itself, in practical theology. To help promote effective modes of learning and meaning making, we need a deeper understanding of the identity and context of these ministers, to be explored in Section 1. Next, contemporary literature on professional socialization and adult learning theory will be probed for congruence and dissonance with the issues faced by lay ecclesial ministers. In the third section, I will develop an understanding of practical theology as "disciplined conversation" leading to "faithful practices" by

---

1. See especially H. LOMBAERTS, *Catechetics and the Formation of Catechists*, in M. WARREN (ed.), *Sourcebook for Modern Catechetics*, Vol. 2, Winona MN, Saint Mary's Press, 1997, 178-192.

these ministers, with some points derived from practical theological reflection on this group. Then, in Section 4, some key implications for ministerial education in a practical theological model will be presented.

1. Lay Ecclesial Ministry in the United States Today

There is currently a significant degree of attention focused on the growth in numbers and importance of the so-called "lay ecclesial ministers" in the United States. A multi-year project of the Subcommittee on Lay Ministry of the National Conference of Catholic Bishops has yielded an important empirical study with comparisons from 1992 to 1997: Murnion and DeLambo's *Parishes and Parish Ministers*[2]. The Subcommittee also has published *Lay Ecclesial Ministry: The State of the Questions*, a report on the project and its working conclusions[3]. Other scholarly research includes a comprehensive treatment of the phenomenon by Z. Fox[4].

All the studies acknowledge that clear definitions are not possible at this stage in the development of lay ecclesial ministry[5]. Fox speaks of "a not yet clearly differentiated group of people who are not ordained, but who are engaged in ministry with stability and specificity, which is different from the general Church ministry of the lay faithful"[6]. The Subcommittee report notes the flexibility and "permeability" of lay minister roles, and lists a "highly desirable" set of characteristics for a minister that includes: a lay Christian responding to the Spirit's call to ministry, who has been prepared through prayerful discernment and appropriate education, who brings competencies to ministry with community and hierarchical recognition, who commits to stability in the ministerial role, and who is either paid or volunteers with responsibility and necessary authority to lead in a particular ministry area[7]. "Lay" in these definitions includes nonordained members of religious orders.

---

2. P.J. MURNION & D. DeLAMBO, *Parishes and Parish Ministers*, New York, National Pastoral Life Center, 1999.

3. SUBCOMMITTEE ON LAY MINISTRY OF THE COMMITTEE ON THE LAITY, NATIONAL CONFERENCE OF CATHOLIC BISHOPS, *Lay Ecclesial Ministry. The State of the Questions*, Washington DC, United States Catholic Conference, 1999.

4. Z. FOX, *New Ecclesial Ministry. Lay Professionals Serving the Church*, Kansas City, Sheed and Ward, 1997. All these studies focus primarily on lay ecclesial ministers employed in parish settings.

5. I am using the designation "lay ecclesial minister" as the most recent and the term adopted by the Lay Ministry Subcommittee for their report.

6. Z. FOX, *New Ecclesial Ministry* (n. 4), p. xii.

7. SUBCOMMITTEE ON LAY MINISTRY, *Lay Ecclesial Ministry* (n. 3), pp. 2 and 8.

Murnion and DeLambo's empirical research uses the following definition for its subjects: "religious and lay in pastoral [parish] roles (not
including either school staffs or support staffs) and paid for at least 20
hours a week"[8]. In comparing their initial 1992 study with a follow-up
in 1997, some significant changes are evident. Most notably, the extrap-
olated total number of ministers in this category has grown by 35%,
from 21,569 to 29,146, employed in 63% of US parishes. The percentage
of religious community members vis-à-vis lay ministers has shifted:
from 1992-97, religious decreased from 42% to 28.9%, and laity
increased from 59% to 71% of the total. The new ministers continue to
be largely female – 82% in 1997 – and white – 93.6% in 1997[9]. Two-
thirds of the laypersons are married.

Why these shifts and increases? Murnion and DeLambo present their
own understanding succinctly.

> This growth results from the convergence of four factors:
> - the growing number of educated laypersons who wish to serve in
>   church ministry but do not wish to be ordained or join a religious
>   order
> - the declining number of priests in parish ministry, from 30,955 in
>   1992 to 27,154 in 1997, a decline of 12 percent
> - the increasing number of mothers in the workplace
> - the recognition of more ministry specialties which call for focused
>   experience and perhaps professional training.
>
> All of this has developed in the context of increased appreciation of
> the right and responsibility of laypersons to share in the mission and
> ministry of the church and the obverse, reduction in what might be
> called clericalism in the sense of excessive assignment of responsibili-
> ties in church life to the ordained[10].

Behind these brief observations is an extensive theological and eccle-
sial development of the mission and ministry of the whole church as
People of God – brought to new emphasis in the documents of Vatican
II and subsequent magisterial statements, and the work of contempo-
rary theologians. The emergence of lay ecclesial ministers in the United
States is both unprecedented and a return to Christian roots[11]. And as

---

8. P.J. MURNION & D. DeLAMBO, *Parishes and Parish Ministers* (n. 2), p. iii.
9. *Ibid.*
10. *Ibid.*, p. 22.
11. See, for example, the extensive treatments by K. OSBORNE, *Ministry: Lay Ministry
in the Roman Catholic Church. Its History and Theology*, New York – Mahwah NJ, Paulist
Press, 1993, and P. BERNIER, *Ministry in the Church. A Historical and Pastoral Approach*,
Mystic CT, Twenty-Third Publications, 1992.

Murnion and DeLambo imply, larger institutional and societal influences are also at work.

What do the new ministers do? The question can be addressed both by naming their titles and by listing their leadership responsibilities. For the titles, Murnion and DeLambo found that the following categories were most frequently used: Director or Coordinator of Religious Education, General Pastoral Minister, Youth Minister, and Music Minister[12]. Regarding the responsibilities for which these ministers exercise a leadership role, however, the authors note a lack of unanimity; indeed, these are "practically idiosyncratic"[13]. At the same time, there have emerged primary areas of leadership responsibility for each: religious educators are focused on religious education of youth, administration, sacramental preparation, and – to a lesser extent – the religious education of adults; general pastoral ministers work in administration, the catechumenate, religious education of adults, sacramental preparation, home visiting, small community development, care of the sick, and ministry to the elderly; liturgists are responsible for planning and leading liturgies; music ministers plan and lead the community's liturgical music; and youth ministers work in general ministry to youth and young adults, along with administration, religious education of youth, and sacramental preparation[14].

How are they prepared to minister? Lay ecclesial ministers generally have undergone, or are engaged in, specific preparation for their ministry. Programs available include: multi-year diocesan formation programs; diocesan programs affiliated with a college, university or seminary, typically offering degrees and certificates; degree and certificate academic programs at colleges, universities and seminaries; and non-degree programs offered by independent Catholic organizations. In 1998, there were 29,137 persons enrolled in these programs[15]. The programs typically include attention to major areas of theological disciplines, skill areas such as counseling, catechesis and liturgical planning, and spiritual formation; the institutions, however, vary greatly in the proportion of time spent on each area, with diocesan programs

---

12. P.J. MURNION & D. DELAMBO, *Parishes and Parish Ministers* (n. 2), p. 45. While there is growing attention devoted to the development of the role of lay "pastoral coordinator", i.e., a person serving as pastor in a parish with no resident priest, this presently describes only 2.1% of lay parish ministers in the US (*ibid.*).

13. *Ibid.*, p. 46.

14. *Ibid.*, pp. 48-49.

15. SUBCOMMITTEE ON LAY MINISTRY, *Lay Ecclesial Ministry* (n. 3), p. 29.

generally devoting more time to spiritual formation than academic programs[16].

How is the institutional church involved? As already noted, the National Conference of Catholic Bishops has shown a significant commitment to exploring the emergence of lay ecclesial ministers through its sponsorship of the recent studies. The concern for official oversight of the ministers is evident in the subcommittee's report, as well as in evolving institutional practice. Murnion and DeLambo report significant increases from 1992 to 1997 in the numbers of ministers who reported that they were trained (21.5%), screened (35.4%), or certified (39.8%) by their diocese, and the number of dioceses providing continuing education for them (75.7%)[17].

Along with the increasing numbers and responsibilities of lay ecclesial ministers, the post-Vatican II era has witnessed a concurrent attention to the professionalization of lay ecclesial ministers. I will discuss issues of professional socialization more thoroughly in the next section. At this point, it is worthwhile to note the development of formal lists of competency standards for catechetical leaders, parish ministers and youth ministers by their professional associations, and the recent convergence of these in a proposed set of "common competency goals" to contextualize the "specialized competencies" for each ministry and to serve as a guide for ministers themselves as well as the directors of their education and formation programs[18].

Regarding recognition and commissioning for ministry: as trenchantly discussed by Fox, disparity is evident between the socialization and formal recognition of ordained and nonordained ministers. The former group, whether priests or permanent deacons, undergo a prescribed formation culminating in a ritual of ordination that sets them apart from the rest of the faithful. They tend to have strong ties to one another and to their priestly or diaconal identity. They are easily identified and listed in official directories. The latter are hired by pastor-supervisors and can be removed at will; their roles and their authority are often not clearly defined; their ties to peers are often weak; and their

16. SUBCOMMITTEE ON LAY MINISTRY, *Lay Ecclesial Ministry* (n. 3), pp. 28-29.

17. P.J. MURNION & D. DeLAMBO, *Parishes and Parish Ministers* (n. 2), p. 65.

18. J.T. MERKT (ed.), *Common Formation Goals for Ministry*, National Association for Lay Ministry, National Conference of Catechetical Leadership, National Federation of Catholic Youth Ministers, 2000.

role is often not publicly recognized beyond their local parish[19]. As a result, there is increasing discussion of the need for more formal and widely used modes of commissioning for lay ecclesial ministers[20].

According to Murnion and DeLambo, satisfaction levels for lay parish ministers are "extraordinary," with over 90% stating that their present working situation could be described most of the time as good, creative, respected, challenging, spiritually rewarding, meaningful, and life giving[21]. Fox concurs, but notes that ministers express a high need for visible expressions of appreciation from those whom they serve, as well as greater role clarification[22]. Since the experience of longtime ministers and ministry educators points to dissatisfaction and problems as common, the highly positive data is open to question, and further investigation seems to be necessary.

Beyond this brief overview, then, how are we to understand the situation of lay ecclesial ministers at this time, in order to explore more deeply the ways that practical theology can enhance their readiness to engage in ministry? In my approach, I attempt to draw on both empirical evidence and the many impressions gained from ministry education and association with these ministers as they struggle to articulate their identity, needs and visions. This view takes seriously the minister as human subject, working to be effective in ministry and to grow in both self-understanding and communal recognition of her/his role. It assumes that such growth will depend on successful negotiation of conversations among multiple educative influences such as those represented below.

A number of "institutions" deeply affect the identity and functions of lay ecclesial ministers. Such institutions, in the sociological sense, are not necessarily formal organizations or defined with an educational purpose, but nevertheless constitute patterns of expected behavior with moral dimensions[23] and thus are profoundly educational. For, as stated by the

19. Z. FOX, *New Ecclesial Ministry* (n. 4), pp. 36-37. For a helpful discussion of the nature of "formal" and "informal" authority in relation to ministry, see B.O. McDERMOTT, *The Relationship Among Authority, Leadership, and Spirituality in Ministry*, in R.J. WICKS (ed.), *Handbook of Spirituality for Ministers*, New York – Mahwah NJ, Paulist Press, 1995, 381-390.

20. See the discussion in Z. FOX, *New Ecclesial Ministry* (n. 4), pp. 242-254, in which she argues for canonically defining the new ministers, establishing a formal relationship with their bishop, and ritually celebrating their assuming of ministerial roles and identities.

21. P.J. MURNION & D. DeLAMBO, *Parishes and Parish Ministers* (n. 2), pp. 61-63.

22. Z. FOX, *New Ecclesial Ministry* (n. 4), p. 45.

23. R.N. BELLAH, R. MADSEN, W.H. SULLIVAN, A. SWIDLER, S. TIPTON, *The Good Society*, New York, Alfred A. Knopf, 1991, p. 10.

editors of the present collection, learning happens "by perceiving and reinterpreting the strong learning environment in which one is involved in everyday life"[24]. Key elements of this "ecology of education" include:

The parish or local faith community: many ministers are first hired in their home parish after a period of volunteering there. Thus their understanding of church, of the role of nonordained ministers vis-à-vis clergy, of collaboration and the building up of the faith community, is notably shaped by the understandings present in the parish and its staff. The pastor exercises significant influence, both in his role as supervisor-employer and as the one who frequently has approached the parish volunteer with a job offer. The diocese, as noted above, is requiring a growing accountability from lay ecclesial ministers. The regional or national church and the universal magisterium have less day-to-day influence, but through their official teachings (or lack thereof) they shape the ministers' self-understanding.

Family and other close relational networks: since the majority of lay ecclesial ministers are married and female, the concerns of family often loom large for them. Murnion and DeLambo note how the emergence of mothers in the workplace has paralleled the rise of the "new ministers". At the same time, many ministers discover that the demands of their work place significant time pressures on family life, and push them into intense reflection on their identity as wife, mother, minister and other roles[25].

White and middle class status: the overwhelming majority of lay ecclesial ministers are white, and their educational backgrounds, interpersonal networks, places of residence and parishes of employment (i.e., those with budgets high enough to afford a staff) place them as well as those to whom they minister within the dominant middle class ethos of American life. It is frequently noted that this preponderance shapes the articulation of ministers' needs and interests in crucial ways. For example, national associations work to bring ethnic diversity to their representation, yet acknowledge that the goals of professionalization often are at odds with the needs of poorer and more ethnically diverse populations[26].

---

24. See the introduction of B. Roebben and M. Warren in this book.

25. Ministers are thoughtfully addressing their issues of vocational call in the midst of multiple pressures. A good example of such reflection from a student minister in the program I direct is B. BIAMONTE, *Who Am I? Employee or Minister?*, in *The Theologian* (Duquesne University Theology Department Newsletter), July 1999, pp. 18-20.

26. For example, the theme of the 2000 Conference of the National Association for Lay Ministry in the United States was *Celebrating Lay Ministry in the 21st Century. New Faces, New Opportunities, New Challenges*, and the presenters were chosen to represent diverse ethnicities and cultures. These presentations, however, often revealed the different viewpoints of white, middle class ministers, for whom professional standards such as education credentials were important, and ministers of color, who often could not hope to achieve these.

Gender and clerical culture: most lay ministers are female; all priests and permanent deacons are male. Besides the effects of differing gender socialization into characteristic traits and roles, the formal division between laity and clergy profoundly affects the self-understanding of lay ecclesial ministers. Fox gives anecdotes that reveal how the assumptions that priests make about ministry, including accepted mores of conduct in relation to one's bishop, liturgical protocols, communication styles, and so on, are either unknown to or challenged by lay ecclesial ministers[27].

Professional associations: such groups, particularly in their national and regional meetings, often provide invaluable support to members, both through educational opportunities and the sharing of developing wisdom on ministerial practice. As previously mentioned, a drive toward establishment of competency standards is currently integral to the work of associations representing lay ministers. Such standards, however, can be a mixed blessing, as they may overwhelm ministers by their sheer number and breadth of expectation, and seemingly present an impossible level of achievement in a still emerging profession with relatively little financial support for advanced training.

Ministry education and formation programs: while necessary for the preparation of qualified ministers, these programs vary so widely in their expectations that ministers may emerge from them with radically different levels of knowledge and skill. A number of programs may coexist in the same region, sometimes with little cooperation among them and even with engagement in competition for students.

American professional culture: the term "professional," despite its long history, carries a variety of meanings and associations today. Expectations regarding level of professional training (and commensurate salary), expertise, structures of authority, codes of ethics, self-regulation and so on among "secular" professions influence ministers' understanding of their own professionalism.

American culture as a whole: some of the key adjectives used in recent analyses to describe the culture of the United States are secular, privatized, pluralistic, individualistic, voluntaristic, fragmented, and anti-institutional[28]. While most Americans continue both to claim belief in a personal God and to attend religious services regularly, the lay

27. Z. Fox, *New Ecclesial Ministry* (n. 4), pp. 40-41.
28. See the influential analysis by R.N. Bellah, R. Madsen, W.H. Sullivan, A. Swidler, S. Tipton, *Habits of the Heart. Individualism and Commitment in American Life*, New York, Harper and Row, 1985.

ecclesial minister is a foreign entity to many. When commitment to participation in a faith community is seen as voluntary and easily abandoned or changed to suit the personal needs of the individual, the commitment of a lay ecclesial minister can seem at least highly inconvenient and ill-advised, if not absurd.

This complex set of institutional relationships creates unique issues and opportunities for lay ecclesial ministers, as they work to understand themselves and their vocation in the midst of sometimes dissonant understandings, expectations and practices. I will argue in Section 3 that a model of practical theological reflection is most suited to helping ministers engage the dissonances in meaningful and life giving ways.

Before doing so, however, let us turn to an examination of prominent themes in professional socialization and adult education as resources for our analysis.

2. Themes in Professional Socialization and Adult Education

As will become clearer in Section 3, I contend that ministry educators committed to the mode of practical theology must center on the dynamic of *formation and transformation* to be true to both the mission of the Christian community and to the education of ministers as human subjects. We can characterize "formation" as a process of shaping individual participants into a particular identity and mission through structured activities and the creation of a distinctive culture. In discussing the literature of professional socialization, I will use "formation" and "socialization" interchangeably[29]. "Transformation" is about conversion and change – for the individual participant, it may well include the fundamental change in identity experienced in the very process of formation. Most importantly, though, it describes the goal, often articulated in adult and higher education, of a deepening and enlarging of one's ability to make meaning in a complex, multifaceted world, particularly in those spheres of most concern for daily life, such as work, family, and community.

---

29. A standard definition of organizational socialization is "the process through which newcomers acquire the knowledge, skills, behaviors, and attitudes required for effective participation in an organization", from T.D. ALLEN, S.E. McMANUS, J.E.A. RUSSELL, *Newcomer Socialization and Stress. Formal Peer Relationships as a Source of Support*, in *Journal of Vocational Behavior* 54 (1999) 453-470, p. 456. They draw on J. VAN MAANEN & E.H. SCHEIN, *Toward a Theory of Organizational Socialization*, in *Research in Organizational Behavior*, Vol. 1, Greenwich CT, JAI Press, 1979, 209-264.

In this examination of literature on professional socialization, I propose that while its emphasis is formation, it carries within it the seeds of and a necessary drive for transformation. For adult education approaches, the reverse is true: while transformation is placed in the foreground, especially through the use of critical thinking, formation is a necessary element. Section 3, on practical theology, will place the discussion of formation and transformation in a theological, educational and ministerial context.

Professional Socialization

R. Yunker, whose work on professional socialization has received much attention from ministry educators, states that it must be studied wholistically, as an "inter-related system with a deep structure"[30]. Thus, while the goals of a specific socialization program may be the focus of study, they must be seen in the context of the other elements of the "ecology of education" to which participants belong, and which shape their professional socialization to a greater or lesser extent. The unique way in which they experience and participate in their own socialization will clearly depend heavily on the structure of the program; yet as active participants in meaning making they will formulate their own responses to the process[31].

To call someone a "professional" evokes certain standard expectations. Yunker lists aspects such as high levels of learning and prestige; the use of expertise to do things for other people; membership in organizations validating professionals' role and expertise; the use of formal institutional means to solve problems; exclusive control – a "quasi-monopoly" – over a set of skills; and prerogatives such as the right to control the admission of candidates, structure their training, induct them into the

---

30. R. YUNKER, *Professional Socialization Programs. Texts and Subtexts*, in *Ministry Educators in Conversation: What Kind of Future?*, Proceedings of the Invitational Conference, Association of Graduate Programs in Ministry (1993) 22-33, p. 23.

31. In an extensive study of the socialization of groups of aspiring psychiatrists, doctors and biochemists, Bucher and Stelling found in the "symbolic interactionist" school exemplified by Blumer a construct for explaining both the power of the "programming effect" of socialization and the trainees' own active role in the process. Key tenets of symbolic interactionism include: 1) the meanings that humans hold in relation to things shape how they act toward those things; 2) such meaning is derived through interaction with others; and 3) meaning is modified through an interpretive process. From R. BUCHER & J.F. STELLING, *Becoming Professional* (Sage Library of Social Research, 46), Beverly Hills CA, Sage Publications, 1977, pp. 275-277. They draw on H. BLUMER, *Symbolic Interactionism*, Englewood Cliffs NJ, Prentice-Hall, 1969, p. 2.

profession, set standards and monitor members' performance[32]. Gula and Sullivan both highlight the ethical and vocational dimensions of profession: the professional is one committed to service of others according to agreed upon codes of moral behavior and motivated by dedication to the community, conceiving of the profession as a personal calling, and thus worthy of public trust and admiration[33].

The task of professional socialization is initiation into an organizational culture, and includes multi-faceted aspects of technique, etiquette and attitude as well as technical knowledge. These include "long-standing rules of thumb, a somewhat special language, an ideology that helps edit a member's everyday experience, shared standards of relevance as to the critical aspects of the work that is being accomplished, unexamined prejudices, models for social etiquette and demeanor, certain customs and rituals suggestive of how members are to relate to colleagues, subordinates, superiors, and outsiders, and a sort of residual category of some rather plain 'horse' sense regarding what is appropriate and 'smart' behavior within the organization and what is not"[34]. Again, other authors highlight the shaping of values within socialization; Haynes, for example, discusses the preparation of social workers as addressing personal, social, political and professional values dimensions through both infusion and integration[35].

A holistic analysis of professional socialization is enhanced by attention to the "texts" and "subtexts" of a formation program. The "text" or "programming effect" includes both the overall design and goals of the program and the unintended messages built into this design[36]. The "subtext" is the group response of the trainees to the program. Yunker maintains that text and subtext are equally important in shaping professional socialization[37].

An important aspect of socialization is its relative "strength" or "weakness" in forming a distinctive professional identity. This characterization

32. R. YUNKER, *Professional Socialization Programs* (n. 30), pp. 22 and 25.

33. R.M. GULA, *Ethics in Pastoral Ministry*, New York – Mahwah NJ, Paulist Press, 1996, p. 13; W.M. SULLIVAN, *Work and Integrity, The Crisis and Promise of Professionalism in America*, New York, HarperBusiness, 1995, pp. 1-28.

34. R. YUNKER, *Professional Socialization Programs* (n. 30), p. 23, quoting J. VAN MAANEN & E.H. SCHEIN, *Toward a Theory of Organizational Socialization* (n. 29).

35. D.T. HAYNES, *A Theoretical Integrative Framework for Teaching Professional Social Work Values*, in *Journal of Social Work Education* 35 (1999) 39-50.

36. R. Yunker uses the terms *texts and subtexts*, while Bucher and Stelling refer to the *programming effect*.

37. R. YUNKER, *Professional Socialization Programs* (n. 30), p. 24. See note 31, above, for Bucher and Stelling's attempt to balance the influence of the programming effect with the trainees' responses.

depends in large part on aspects of the formation program such as its duration, the distinctive reputation of particular programs or their sponsoring institutions, the strength and prestige of the profession itself, the firmness of the program "text" across training settings and over time, the sequencing of program elements, the clarity of agreed upon professional techniques being taught, and the degree of peer contact and interdependence in training and post-training support. Yunker contrasts the socialization of medical and law enforcement professionals, for example, with that of elementary and secondary level teachers. She names the latter as a much weaker and more diffuse form of socialization than the former, noting that teacher technique is "relatively unrationalized" and thus allows for great variety in the structure of training programs. Also, subtexts for teachers are "essentially private (…) developed by individuals and restricted in their influence", and after one begins teaching as a full professional there is little occasion to receive ongoing peer consultation[38].

Looking briefly at connections between this overview and the socialization of lay ecclesial ministers, we can make some observations. 1) The development of competency standards by professional organizations represents a significant step in professionalization, as they work toward wider acceptance of a set of professional techniques, assumptions, behaviors, and attitudes. Yet many ministries are performed by persons who lack professional qualifications, implicitly calling into question the professional identity of those formally credentialed. Since there is far from the "quasi-monopoly" named by Yunker for the ministerial profession, and given the limited financial resources of many parishes, lay ecclesial ministers are not encouraged to develop a strongly guarded set of professional prerogatives. The ambiguity here works against a strong professional socialization. 2) Ministry formation/education programs are so varied that professional socialization is highly "diffuse". Some programs, notably those that require a sequenced schedule, cohort enrollments, intensive time commitment and frequent group formational activities such as retreats, are likely to build a stronger sense of ministerial identity. Many of these "strong" formation programs, however, are diocesan based and not primarily geared to the preparation of paid professionals. Academic ministry education programs, while more apt to provide advanced theological training for ministers with significant leadership responsibilities, are typically weaker in socialization due to

---

38. R. YUNKER, *Professional Socialization Programs* (n. 30), pp. 31-32.

their part-time, non-sequenced character, with less time spent on spiritual formation and communal activities[39]. The ongoing involvement of students in major life commitments beyond their ministerial education – ministry itself, family, and community obligations – further weakens their socialization. 3) There are few mechanisms available in lay ecclesial ministry (or ordained ministry, for that matter) for ongoing evaluation and supervision/mentoring. Virtually all formation programs strive to provide and require some type of supervised ministry for participants. But once engaged in professional ministry, people find themselves without any common expectations regarding performance review, consultation on difficult cases, peer support, and other vital opportunities to grow and to assess one's professional growth. Pastors are often content to set out a list of responsibilities and then give their staff "free rein" in ministry, asking only to be kept informed, with any evaluation coming either in the midst of problems that arise or in the yearly contract negotiation. Dioceses are seeking to provide more formal mechanisms for feedback and networking, but this is still nascent.

The external and internal sources of ambiguity and tension, then, not only make professional socialization more diffuse but also point to the ways in which its formation invites transformation. We see "conversion" occurring in any profession, primarily, in the process of changing from outsider to insider[40]. External critiques that force the reexamination of professional identity, however, may also impel both initiates and veterans of a profession to critical examination of both self and profession in potentially transformative ways.

Adult Education and "Critical Thinking"

The United States Catholic Conference Commission on Certification and Accreditation requires that ministry formation programs seeking accreditation show attention to "principles of adult learning"[41]. A well regarded list of such principles is elaborated by Jane Vella in *Learning to Listen, Learning to Teach*:

39. Also note in Z. FOX, *New Ecclesial Ministry* (n. 4), p. 30, that directors of graduate level ministry education programs are far from united on the necessity of providing or requiring spiritual formation in their programs.
40. R. BUCHER & J.F. STELLING, *Becoming Professional* (n. 31), p. 25; R. YUNKER, *Professional Socialization Programs* (n. 30), p. 23.
41. UNITED STATES CATHOLIC CONFERENCE COMMISSION ON CERTIFICATION AND ACCREDITATION, *Accreditation Handbook For Ministry Formation Programs*, Milwaukee WI, USCC Commission on Certification and Accreditation, 1999, Standard 4.1, p. 9.

– Needs assessment to discover what the adults believe is important to learn
– Creating a "safe" environment for learning
– Developing sound and respectful relationships
– Providing sequence and reinforcement for learning tasks
– Combining action with reflection
– Honoring learners as the subjects of their own learning
– Learning with attention to ideas, feelings and actions
– Teaching with "immediacy", i.e., teaching what is useful
– Mutuality in teacher-learner dialogue
– Fostering teamwork
– Highlighting the active process of learning through engagement
– Incorporating learner accountability for what is learned[42].

Drawing on these and highlighting in particular the prominence of "critical thinking" in adult education, this section will discuss key aspects from the literature that support the goal of "transformation" and thus have relevance for the education of a particular adult population: lay ecclesial ministers.

Underlying much of contemporary adult education theory is the assumption that, as adults are the subjects of their own learning, so they are engaged in the "construction" of knowledge. If we understand ourselves as the ones responsible for the determination and accomplishment of the learning that we need, then we also come to see that learning is an active and unique process for each individual. Brookfield states that "every adult's stock of prior learning and experience coheres into a unique, idiosyncratic mediatory mechanism through which new experiences and knowledges are filtered"[43]. Learning that is of value, then, will occur with the consent and the full participation of the adult learner, and will involve his/her whole self: as Vella notes in her seventh principle, feelings and actions are equally significant to cognitive dimensions in the learning process.

Much of the literature insists on the collaborative nature of such knowledge construction. Garrison maintains that "it should be clear that meaning is ultimately the responsibility of each individual but knowledge is created in collaboration with others. (...) Knowledge is

---

42. J. VELLA, *Learning to Listen, Learning to Teach. The Power of Dialogue in Educating Adults*, San Francisco, Jossey-Bass Publishers, 1994. The principles are used as a framework for the book.

43. S.D. BROOKFIELD, *Understanding and Facilitating Adult Learning*, San Francisco, Jossey-Bass Publishers, 1986, p. 2.

gained through interacting with the external world through direct experience and critical dialogue; therefore, this process must inherently be collaborative"[44]. Bruffee has put forth a strong argument for the social construction of all knowledge through the discourse of "knowledge communities". Each one of us is part of many such communities, which include family, ethnicity, neighborhood, political affiliation, nationality, prior educational settings, and others – some overlapping, some "nesting" inside one another, some opposed. Through collaborative processes in education, a new conversation is joined at the "boundaries" of the knowledge communities to which we are already affiliated, and a transformative "reacculturation" becomes possible which brings us into "a larger, more inclusive community of knowledgeable peers", but requires overcoming "resistance to change that evidences itself as ambivalence about engaging in conversation at the boundaries" of our familiar knowledge communities[45].

What is the nature of this collaborative discourse, and how does it lead to transformation? Leading theorists such as Brookfield and Mezirow emphasize the role of critical thinking within a reflection-action or praxis oriented process as essential. Brookfield observes that adults are continually engaging in activity, reflecting on it, analyzing it collaboratively, and trying out new activity based on the reflection and analysis, which leads to further reflection. Thus, effective facilitation of adult learning will capitalize on this praxis[46]. As adults engage in it in disciplined ways, their capacity for critical thinking is recognized and deepened, particularly in relation to significant experiences in their lives (whether positive or negative). Brookfield names the identification and challenging of assumptions and the imagining of new possibilities as the central dimensions of critical thinking, and summarizes its "phases" as: 1) a trigger event, which can be positive or negative; 2) appraisal: self-examination following the event; 3) exploration: looking for new ways of explaining or living with the discrepancies occasioned by appraisal of the event, and testing these new ways to look for congruence with our perception of what is happening to us; 4) developing alternative perspectives: using new ways of

44. D.R. GARRISON, *Critical Thinking and Self-Directed Learning in Adult Education. An Analysis of Responsibility and Control Issues*, in *Adult Education Quarterly* 42 (1992) 136-148, p. 144.

45. K.A. BRUFFEE, *Collaborative Learning: Higher Education, Interdependence, and the Authority of Knowledge*, Baltimore, Johns Hopkins University Press, 1999, p. 12.

46. S.D. BROOKFIELD, *Understanding and Facilitating Adult Learning* (n. 43), p. 16. See also J. MEZIROW & Associates, *Fostering Critical Thinking in Adulthood*, San Francisco, Jossey-Bass Publishers, 1990.

thinking and acting that make sense in our new situation; 5) integration of these new ways into our life[47].

From this perspective, what is the desired result of adult education; how is the nature of the "transformation" specified? The authors acknowledge the importance of acquiring technical skills and knowledge as an adult need and an important motivation for formal education. However, they insist that such technical gains take place within the prior and present contexts of participants' lives – within the ongoing shaping of "knowledge communities" – and therefore the educator lacks final control over the precise form of appropriation of knowledge by learners. Further, given the complexities of today's world and the ongoing nature of change in the workplace and other spheres of adult life, the learners' needs go beyond the acquisition of skills to the cultivation of "practical wisdom". The most successful and fulfilled adults in contemporary society will be those who situate their technical "training" within a framework in which they become "reflective practitioners", drawing on internalized values and intuitions to make valid and ethical decisions in concrete circumstances. Engaged in "a continuous recreation of their personal relationships, work worlds, and social circumstances"[48], they are active subjects and creators of useful knowledge – of what Schon calls "theories-in-use," the assumptions tested in practice and retained for use in new situations, but subject to ongoing re-evaluation[49].

To stress this critical and transformative perspective in education is to invite disequilibrium for the learners. While proponents such as Bruffee stress doing this in a collaborative environment and deemphasizing conflict, the challenge of radical disturbance to one's most closely held assumptions nevertheless remains. As Vella's "safety" principle reminds us, a learning process with humans as their own subjects cannot occur in an atmosphere in which they fear condemnation of their ideas or a destructive challenge to their assumptions. This does not mean that

47. S.D. BROOKFIELD, *Developing Critical Thinkers. Challenging Adults to Explore Alternative Ways of Thinking and Acting*, San Francisco, Jossey-Bass Publishers, 1988, pp. 25-29.
48. S.D. BROOKFIELD, *Understanding and Facilitating Adult Learning* (n. 43), p. 11.
49. See Brookfield's discussion of Schon in S.D. BROOKFIELD, *Developing Critical Thinkers* (n. 47), pp. 143ff. Also see Sullivan's use of Schon to argue against the influence of positivism and technical rationality in professionalism, and to advocate the model of reflective practitioner as one who has mastered the techniques of a field but who exercises these using a values based practical wisdom. W.M. SULLIVAN, *Work and Integrity* (n. 33), especially pp. 171-173, 200. References to Schon are from D.A. SCHON, *The Reflective Practitioner. How Professionals Think in Action*, New York, Basic Books, 1983.

learning will always be painless and joyful, but it does require that educators themselves understand, and appropriately caution learners to, the probable dissonances evoked by enlarging our knowledge communities. As Meyers puts it: "Teaching students new thinking processes involves gauging very sensitively the amount of disequilibrium that will do the most good. Too much can overload students and be dysfunctional, while too little can result in warm, wonderful classes where no learning takes place"[50]. This gauging process also must include attention to possible gender issues. Belenky, Clinchy, Goldberger, and Tarule discuss at length the ways that women frequently perceive education as adversarial and intimidating, and raise questions about the prevalence of a "doubting model" implied in some approaches to critical thinking, arguing instead for practices of "connected teaching" in which women's ability to learn is explicitly and frequently affirmed[51].

Adult education with a critical thinking focus is clearly concerned with transformation of the learners, in ways that will help them live and work in more fulfilled ways. Its practitioners hold Mezirow's conviction that "Meaning perspectives that permit us to deal with a broader range of experience, to be more discriminating, to be more open to other perspectives, and to better integrate our experiences are superior perspectives"[52]. At the same time, the more educators attempt to create the conditions in which to develop such transformed "meaning perspectives", the more apparent it becomes that "formation" is also necessary. To create truly collaborative learning communities, to invite trust and respect in a safe atmosphere, to introduce the new sources of knowledge required to broaden one's perspective beyond narrowness and bias – all this requires the conscious and deliberate setting of learning conditions and dispositions in a formative environment. A community of adult learners, engaged in critical and imaginative conversation, must be intentionally cultivated; learners must be "socialized" into full engagement in it.

Let us bring now bring these themes into explicit dialogue with the educational goals and methods of practical theology, focusing on how

50. C. MEYERS, *Teaching Students to Think Critically. A Guide for Faculty in All Disciplines*, San Francisco, Jossey-Bass, 1986, p. 15; quoted in S.D. BROOKFIELD, *Developing Critical Thinkers* (n. 47), p. 74.

51. M.F. BELENKY, B.M. CLINCHY, N.R. GOLDBERGER, J.M. TARULE, *Women's Ways of Knowing. The Development of Self, Voice, and Mind*, New York, Basic Books, 1986, especially pp. 214-229.

52. J. MEZIROW & Associates, *Fostering Critical Thinking in Adulthood* (n. 46), p. 14.

this interdisciplinary conversation can illuminate the "formation" and "transformation" of lay ecclesial ministers.

3. Practical Theology for Ministry Education

"If transformation depends so fundamentally on formation, then the Church's job is to form the Church *for* transformation. And that means to form *the world* for transformation. (…) The business of the Church, as people-who-know-they-are-the-Church, is to provide (within the limits imposed by the limits of the influence of her actual members) the type of formation that is suited to transformation. (…) Transformation is something that happens, and nobody can lay it on to order. We can only create opportunities for it"[53].

Rosemary Haughton's classic statement shapes my articulation of the purpose and goal of practical theology as an educational paradigm for lay ecclesial ministers. In what follows, I will briefly present some common understandings of practical theology in the United States context. Then, drawing on the insights from the literature of professional socialization and adult education, I will offer my understanding of practical theology as promoting *formation* into an owned ministerial identity for learning subjects through the *transformative* activity of disciplined conversation, leading in turn to more faithful practices in multiple contexts in church and society.

Theological Reflection

Facility in "theological reflection" is increasingly regarded as a key competency for ministry. As with "principles of adult learning", theological reflection is named as a requirement for ministry formation programs in the standards of the United States Catholic Conference Commission on Certification and Accreditation[54]. It can, however, connote many different things to different people. In its most elementary form, it may mean any prayerful reflection on the relation of one's faith to one's life experience. As used in ministry education, theological reflec-

---

53. R. HAUGHTON, *The Transformation of Man. A Study of Conversion and Community,* Paramus NJ, Paulist Press Deus Books, 1967, p. 252.
54. UNITED STATES CATHOLIC CONFERENCE COMMISSION ON CERTIFICATION AND ACCREDITATION, *Accreditation Handbook For Ministry Formation Programs* (n. 41), Standard 3.4, p. 8.

tion most commonly involves a process, usually in a group, through which a current, specific, personal, and important experience[55] from one's life and/or ministry is chosen and probed to discover how God may be encountered in its midst. Bringing the resources of Christian tradition and the contemporary experience of Christians together in this reflection is meant to lead to new insight and pastoral action. R.L. Kinast and J.D. and E.E. Whitehead have developed "portable" and widely used models for use in ministry[56].

This sort of experience-based theological reflection bears strong similarities to the praxis oriented work of religious education, rooted in the pedagogy of Paulo Freire and brought to preeminent expression in the United States by Thomas Groome. The "shared Christian praxis" approach developed by Groome proposes five basic movements:
– naming/expressing a present action as experienced by the community
– engaging in critical reflection on this action
– bringing forth the Christian "Story" (expressed in Scripture, tradition, ritual and other forms) and "Vision" (mandates arising from the Story to empower the praxis of Christians) appropriate to the present action
– bringing the critical insights on present action into hermeneutical dialogue with the Christian Story and Vision
– making decisions for Christian living as shaped by the critical conversation of the preceding movements[57].

Practical Theology

In recent years, several key developments have helped to bring the power and potential of theological reflection into sharper focus and to explore its congruence with religious education. One has been the new attention to "practical" or "pastoral" theology[58]. As elaborated preeminently by Farley[59], theological education has too sharply divided the

55. R.L. KINAST, *Let Ministry Teach. A Guide to Theological Reflection*, Collegeville MN, Liturgical Press, 1996, pp. 2-4.

56. See *ibid.* and J.D. WHITEHEAD & E.E. WHITEHEAD, *Method in Ministry. Theological Reflection and Christian Ministry*, Kansas City, Sheed and Ward, 1995.

57. T.H. GROOME, *Sharing Faith. A Comprehensive Approach to Religious Education and Pastoral Ministry*, San Francisco, Harper, 1991, pp. 146-148.

58. I prefer "practical theology" because it more effectively connotes a praxis oriented process as well as a broadening of the church's concerns to the experiences of the world rather than remaining concentrated on intra-ecclesial, "pastoral" matters.

59. E. FARLEY, *Theologia. The Fragmentation and Unity of Theological Education*, Philadelphia, Fortress Press, 1983.

academic study of Bible, church history and systematic theology from their "application" in the traditional practical theological disciplines such as pastoral care, religious education, liturgical leadership, and preaching. In an alternative framework, practical theology has been presented as the overarching sensibility for all theological endeavors. Instead of one-way transmission of truth to ministerial practitioners and the Christian faithful from scholarly experts, a practical theology scheme envisions the enrichment of all discourse about God – in academy, church, family, work and world – through the following commitments:

– By drawing on the experience of "ordinary" Christians in the particularity of their culture and historical situation, theology is necessarily contextualized.
– By contextualized and ongoing reflection in a variety of Christian communities, theology is challenged to rethink supposedly universal assumptions and to wrestle with tensions in ways that lead to new insights[60].
– All Christians are encouraged to understand themselves as "doing theology" when they engage in theological reflection.
– Some persons (ministers and/or academicians) will assume roles as "practical theologians" in mediating between the ongoing reflection and ministry of Christian communities and the academy[61].
– The processes used in the traditionally "practical" (particularly religious education) and the traditionally "scholarly" disciplines of theology will be rethought for their congruence with this model.
– Thus the theological enterprise as a whole will be reconceived[62].

Don Browning's "fundamental" formulation of practical theology as a reconception of the entire theological enterprise situates the traditional theological disciplines within the practical framework. In the phase of *descriptive theology*, we attempt to arrive at a "thick" description of a

60. Herman Lombaerts names one of the three dimensions of catechetics as "the endless probing of the symbolic character of the Judeo-Christian tradition. This symbol system reflects the dynamic and shifting interaction between an unchanging core of divine revelation and the actual social contexts of particular times and places", in H. LOMBAERTS, *Catechetics and the Formation of Catechists* (n. 1), p. 179, and acknowledges the difficulty of this task in a pluralistic world.
61. R.P. IMBELLI & T.H. GROOME, *Signposts Towards a Pastoral Theology*, in *Theological Studies* 53 (1992) 127-137, pp. 136-137.
62. As Lombaerts notes in discussing catechetics, in such an understanding the catechist and the theologian will be speaking the same message. H. LOMBAERTS, *Catechetics and the Formation of Catechists* (n. 1), p. 190.

concrete situation by examining the prevailing understandings of the community's (faith-based) vision, obligational norms, human tendencies and needs, environmental-social constraints, and specific rules and roles, with extensive use of the social sciences as integral to this descriptive process. Through *historical theology*, the questions arising from practice are brought to the foundational texts of Christian tradition to surface insights from our past in relation to our present dilemmas. Then, in the moment of *systematic theology*, there is a hermeneutical "fusion of horizons between the vision implicit in contemporary practices and the vision implied in the practices of the normative Christian texts"[63], creating new meanings for our situation. Finally, *strategic practical theology* brings the insights of the previous three movements – always understood as part of the overall practical enterprise – together in the attempt to frame faithful and effective responses to our concrete situations today[64].

Browning names this as a critical correlational process, indebted to the work of David Tracy, and draws on Tracy's definition of practical theology as "the mutually critical correlation of the interpreted theory and praxis of the Christian faith with the interpreted theory and praxis of the contemporary situation"[65]. With this emphasis on hermeneutics and critical thinking, Browning thus points us squarely toward the promise and potential of practical theology to change our perspectives, as individuals and as churches, and thus to change our practices. Parallels with critical thinking and transformation in adult education are evident; see, for example, Brookfield's phases of critical thinking described in Section 2.

A key question for educators, then, is how does one gain facility in practical theological reflection? Drawing on the components implied in the schemes of Groome, Browning and Tracy, we can infer that those who wish to gain proficiency will need:
– a personal and spiritual disposition characterized by self-awareness, prayerfulness, openness, and the ability to reconstruct one's practices in light of new evidence
– ongoing engagement in practices that yield rich experiences where God may be encountered

63. D.S. BROWNING, *A Fundamental Practical Theology. Descriptive and Strategic Proposals*, Minneapolis MN, Fortress Press, 1991, p. 51.
64. *Ibid.*, especially pp. 47-58.
65. D. TRACY, *Foundations of Practical Theology*, in D. BROWNING (ed.), *Practical Theology*, San Francisco, Harper and Row, 1983, 61-82, p. 76.

– ability to choose appropriately evocative experiences for reflection
– sufficient knowledge of contemporary experience and culture to be
 able to interpret one's experience, guided by accurate information as
 well as awareness of diverse experiences beyond one's own (requiring
 familiarity with social sciences)
– facility in interpretation of experience in light of social sciences and
 diversity of contemporary insights
– sufficient knowledge of the prominent "facts" of the Christian
 "Story" – as known through Scripture, sacraments, ritual, images,
 bodily experience and other sources – and the diversity of interpretations which have shaped that Story
– facility in interpretation of the Christian Story by drawing on understandings of contemporary experience and culture in dialogue with it
– facility in holding this interpretive process in tension with present
 realities in order to imagine new possibilities for faithful practice
– sufficient skills training to engage in specific areas of ministry to
 which one is called, while situating the creative performance of ministerial practices within a creative reworking of these practices in line
 with the new interpretive insights gained through reflection
– facility in sustaining dialogue with multiple partners and texts for the
 sake of action[66].

The desired "competency" for practical theologians – including
Christian ministers – can be summed up as "practical wisdom" or
phronesis. Through acquiring the abilities listed above, persons become
skilled in an ongoing process of reflection-in-action that derives its
moral vision from the Christian tradition/Story – particularly, as maintained by Groome, from the values embedded in Jesus' vision of the
Reign of God[67] – and engages in a dynamic reinterpretation of that tradition in ways that will advance the Reign of God for the world in
which we live. It is a process that is necessarily critical in that it brings
the evidence of new experience to challenge our prevailing assumptions,
and continually pushes us toward imagining new alternatives. And as
Lombaerts puts it, such wisdom is "a quality proper to faith in itself
(…) sustained by the action of the Spirit"[68].

---

66. Cf. this list with the four interpretive skills needed by catechists, by H. LOM-
BAERTS, *Catechetics and the Formation of Catechists* (n. 1), p. 187: "to discern the influence
of the context; to listen to what Christians are saying; to foresee the skills that will be
needed; to evaluate".
67. T.H. GROOME, *Sharing Faith* (n. 57), especially pp. 14-18.
68. H. LOMBAERTS, *Catechetics and the Formation of Catechists* (n. 1), p. 181.

Commitment to practical theology, then, is both profoundly formative and transformative. Its participants are practicing its approach in order to be formed in a disposition, or *habitus*, for ongoing practice that is characterized by practical wisdom. Explicit within the formation, however, is the commitment to transformation: the very nature of critical correlation leads to changed perspectives and, most proponents would insist, such change is not valid unless it also results in changed practices. As Haughton's words remind us, however, we cannot command transformation; thus the importance of a formation that is most conducive to the possibility of transformation.

Using practical theology as both a tool and a goal, then, let us bring together the insights of professional socialization and adult education with the situation of lay ecclesial ministers to discover the possibilities and limitations for this group's development in practical wisdom.

Highlights from a "Fusion of Horizons"

1. The *professional* socialization of lay ecclesial ministers in their particular "knowledge community" must be understood and fostered within their *primary* socialization as Christian disciples in the "knowledge community" of the church.

All Christian ministry is to serve the mission of the church and flows from initiation into that community. "All of the faithful, including the laity, by virtue of their baptism and confirmation, are given a share in Christ's priestly ministry. Such ministry is appropriate in its own right and should not be seen as a way of participating in the ministry of the ordained"[69]. The Holy Spirit bestows gifts and charisms in the Christian community for its building up and for service to the world. Drawing on the Body of Christ image, Christian ministry is the exercise of each individual part for the good of the whole body, as called through inner conviction and through communal recognition and shaped by, and toward, the practices or "institutions" of that body. As Sullivan observes in his discussion of self-directed, ethical professionals: "Meaning arises not simply out of activity, but out of relationship with human others who already embody in their lives and characters the pattern of a meaningful life built up in community"[70].

---

69. SUBCOMMITTEE ON LAY MINISTRY, *Lay Ecclesial Ministry* (n. 3) p. 15.
70. W.M. SULLIVAN, *Work and Integrity* (n. 33), p. 204.

Lay ecclesial ministers, then, discover their gifts and the nature of their particular call through participation in the gathered community that follows Jesus. Such discernment requires formation in the *habitus* of discipleship; through belonging to a group that strives to live according to the way of the Lord, some individuals find a vocation that brings leadership responsibilities while keeping them firmly embedded within the Body of Christ. Baptism, not ordination or lay commissioning, is the sacrament of ministry.

Bruffee's understanding of various "knowledge communities" as "nested" one within the other is especially helpful as an image for the identity of the lay ecclesial minister. The formation of the community of lay ecclesial ministers – attending, per socialization theory, to the desired technical knowledge and skills, values, attitudes and behaviors – is nested within their ongoing formation as Christian disciples[71]. We might name its desired outcome as the cultivation of practical wisdom for ministerial leadership, but always exercised in mutuality within the faith community.

Thus primary socialization of lay ecclesial ministers is in the community of disciples – a larger community than that of lay ecclesial ministers as a whole, and yet primarily experienced through membership in a particular gathering of Christians. As noted in Murnion and DeLambo, the "local" character of lay ministry is empirically verified[72]; this contemporary reality also resonates with the early church's practice of a local calling forth of the gifts within each community for ministry. The ministerial socialization process for lay ecclesial ministers, then, must be continually examined for how it supports their particular, "professional" identity and their primary identity. As McCarthy states in emphasizing the importance of the discernment of identity, "Ministry then is never 'just' a profession. It is always a way of life, a way of being in the world"[73]. The primary formation is not to be contradicted or superseded by the professional one.

It is clear from the articulation by lay ecclesial ministers of their vocation that they have a strong desire to serve; indeed, Murnion and

---

71. At the most specialized levels of lay ecclesial ministry – for example, the parish Director of Religious Education – a relatively strong professional socialization may exist. We can conceive of this knowledge community as "nested" within the more general community of lay ecclesial ministers.

72. P.J. MURNION & D. DELAMBO, *Parishes and Parish Ministers* (n. 2), pp. 23-24.

73. M. MCCARTHY, *Response to Dr. Rose Yunker's Presentation*, in *Ministry Educators in Conversation: What Kind of Future?*, Proceedings of the Invitational Conference, Association of Graduate Programs in Ministry (1993) 34-39, p. 35.

DeLambo claim that "for the most part, the emergence and evolution of lay pastoral ministry (...), is the result of a practical pastoral style that is determined to provide service and build community"[74]. Their motivation for ministry education, then, is likely to be grounded to a significant degree in the desire to receive adequate preparation for the type of service to which they feel called. And, as with school teachers whose own education is formative to their understanding of how to teach[75], their understanding of how to serve is likely to be shaped significantly by the ministry styles with which they have grown up.

At the same time, formation for professional ministry in a pluralistic culture will expose ministers to the larger questions and contradictions of the society in which they live. A practical theology approach, as presented in Browning and Groome's work, will necessarily widen the conversation beyond intra-church concerns. Such a perspective is integral to the model of servant church advocated in *Gaudium et Spes* and the social teachings of the church. The Christian disciple, and even more so the Christian ecclesial minister, cannot neglect the needs of the world in discerning appropriate pastoral actions. Thus practical theological reflection enlarges both consciousness and commitment.

2. As a result of the nested identities of lay ecclesial ministers, and for both theological and cultural reasons, their socialization will necessarily be *paradoxical and marginal*. This is particularly true because:

a. They are simultaneously differentiating from *and* identifying with other professionals and with the Christian faithful. Professional socialization assumes a process of gradually inducting neophytes into a specialized realm, replete with professional "prerogatives". They are being equipped to do things that others are not qualified to do. However, while the formation of lay ecclesial ministers, including earning academic degrees and obtaining diocesan certification, is meant to provide them with the necessary skills and qualifications to be professionals, it is at the same time intended to anchor them more fully in the universal mission of the church and all its members.

b. They are simultaneously seeking to empower all the faithful *and* to exercise their particular competencies as these arise from personal charism and training. A key competency of lay ecclesial ministry is the ability to collaborate with others and, especially, to empower others to claim and develop their own gifts for ministry. Ministers working in

---

74. P.J. MURNION & D. DELAMBO, *Parishes and Parish Ministers* (n. 2), p. 67.
75. R. YUNKER, *Professional Socialization Programs* (n. 30), p. 31.

isolation are seen as both in danger of "burnout" and as not adequately fulfilling their mission. The adage is sometimes used that ministers should be "working themselves out of a job" – i.e., equipping others so well that those others will eventually assume leadership responsibilities. The paradox here is evident, as few other professions are so consciously focused on blurring the differentiation between themselves and other people by sharing responsibilities and, indeed, prerogatives.

c. The "marginal" character of the lay ministers' profession can be assessed from several angles. At an obvious level, there are difficulties in the very newness of the profession and the lack of models for it. As Fox asks, are clergy and lay ministers being socialized into the same profession[76]? As nonordained persons, lay ecclesial ministers frequently experience themselves on the periphery of a central clerical culture with enormous prerogatives and privileges. At the same time, they are marginal within the Christian community, where others may not understand or accept their role. And within the society as a whole, they are clearly anomalous. Furthermore, even if others outside the church come to understand the profession, it will usually be experienced as counter cultural.

3. A practical theological approach will be optimal for lay ecclesial ministers in negotiating – not necessarily resolving – the dissonances that arise from the realities named above, and fostering life giving, collaborative ministry within the community of disciples.

a. Experts on professional socialization point to the experience of the "shared ordeal"[77] as important in forming strong professional identification with others in one's field. The variety of ways that lay ecclesial ministers are prepared has worked against this sense of a shared experience. At the most basic level of fostering it, practical theological reflection within a disciplined community of reflection can create a common experience of critical interpretation. Simply making the commitment to gathering regularly for conversation can constitute a sufficient "ordeal" in the lives of ministers so as to strengthen their identification with the profession[78]. At

76. Z. FOX, *New Ecclesial Ministry* (n. 4), p. 40.

77. R. YUNKER, *Professional Socialization Programs* (n. 30), pp. 28 and 32. Examples in the medical profession of "shared ordeal" include a common set of intensive courses and examinations and the physical ordeal of spending sleep deprived days and nights on call in medical centers.

78. I previously belonged to a small group of professional lay ministers who for several years committed to weekly meetings, plus additional preparation time, to engage in a structured process of theological reflection. Sustaining that commitment in the midst of many work and family demands was difficult and frequently commented upon by the

the deeper level of practical theological conversation, also, lay ecclesial ministers can come to a critical interpretation of their paradoxical and marginal ministry that opens the possibility of claiming these aspects as gifts, resulting in deeper commitments. Daloz, Keen, Keen, and Parks, in their study of adults committed to the common good, speak of how a number of these people experienced what the authors call "vulnerability-based marginality", especially as members of racial minorities and/or economically or educationally deprived groups. For others, their upbringing promoted a sense of "value-based marginality", in belonging to families and communities that consciously chose a counter cultural stance in order to address others' needs and work for the common good. The authors posit that "Even when it carries a price, marginality can also bear certain gifts: greater self-knowledge, greater awareness of others, and a kind of comfort with life at the edge. The central gift of marginality, however, is its power to promote both empathy with the other and a critical perspective on one's own tribe"[79]. Lay ecclesial ministers, through the pain of marginality, may begin both to claim their right to just treatment within the church and also become more attuned to the injustices suffered by others, in church and world. They may come to see the "gift" of their unique position within the knowledge communities related to ministry as providing an angle of vision that will bring the whole church more into more faithful fulfillment of its mission. Groome articulates the universal scope of the mission by stating that the specific emphasis of the Christian minister is "the empowerment of people as agent-subjects, humanly and in faith – whatever their faith may be – that people may come to act and be actors in humanizing and faith-filled ways"[80].

b. A central source to enrich critical interpretation of marginality is Scripture. Practical theology will encourage the serious study of the message of the prophets and the treatment of the "stranger" in the Hebrew Bible; and most centrally, participants will be drawn to reflection on the marginal yet transforming witness of Jesus of Nazareth, who welcomed those most despised and preached a Reign in which margins and center would be reversed. Lay ecclesial ministers who experience

---

participants – yet the very difficulty and "cost" of the gatherings increased their value to us, and our regard for one another.

79. L.A.P. DALOZ, C.H. KEEN, J.P. KEEN, S.D. PARKS, *Common Fire: Lives of Commitment in a Complex World*, Boston, Beacon Press, 1996, p. 76. Also see T.A. VELING, *Living in the Margins. Intentional Communities and the Art of Interpretation*, New York, Crossroad, 1996, for a sophisticated analysis of marginality, hermeneutics and intentional Christian communities.

80. T.H. GROOME, *Sharing Faith* (n. 57), p. 334.

their leadership as unrecognized may also find in Jesus the model of exercising a charismatic "informal authority", flowing from his relationship with God and proving to be uniquely transformative in his ability to reach people's innermost desires, as distinguished from a "formal authority" that can be distant and uninspired[81].

c. Groome and Rebecca Chopp point to the centrality of personal and communal story in practical theology and theological education. From a feminist perspective, Chopp notes the many dimensions of marginality experienced by women. She observes that for those who seek theological education, there is a strong drive toward narrativity, a practice of "writing one's life" through education in order to understand the dynamics of that life more fully and to become committed to personal and social transformation. "Narrativity allows the most credible description of the 'I' of identity – an ongoing process shaped by and shaping other agents, traditions, and institutions"[82]. To tell a story of marginality is to understand the consequences of one's formation in multiple knowledge communities and to take responsibility for writing a new story of liberation, for oneself and others – while coping with the ambiguity inherent in "on the one hand, the necessity for constructing new forms of narrativity and, on the other hand, the lack of models, forms, and shapes for these to take"[83] – that lack certainly contributing to a tension for lay ecclesial ministers.

d. To take seriously the model of practical theology is to be constantly on the lookout for transformation. Lay ecclesial ministers, through engagement in the process and through faith in the Christian belief in redemption, in life beyond death, will be able to identify the small transformations that are occasioned by their ministry. And, per Haughton's perspective, they will seek to create formative opportunities for others to grow in discipleship with the ongoing disposition to open doors that the Spirit may enter to bring transformation. In the end, perhaps, they will find a degree of integration among the paradoxical elements of their identity through living these commitments rather than through a differentiating process of socialization. Their integration, while provisional, can be grounded in the values of the Reign of God and thus open to ongoing renewal.

---

81. B.O. McDermott, *The Relationship Among Authority, Leadership, and Spirituality in Ministry* (n. 19), especially pp. 382-386.

82. R.S. Chopp, *Saving Work. Feminist Practices of Theological Education*, Louisville KY, Westminster John Knox Press, 1995, p. 32.

83. *Ibid.*, p. 42.

Let us turn, then, to some recommendations for ministry education programs in promoting practical theological reflection for lay ecclesial ministers.

4. Ministry Education and Practical Theology

1. *The activity of practical theology is "disciplined conversation" leading to "faithful practices".*

In another essay, I stressed four key elements for such conversation: 1) an attitude of spiritual discernment that assumes God's word and work in the reflective process and adopts conversational "ground rules" establishing openness to that word; 2) viewing discipline as guided by discipleship: Christian faith as committed to keeping the Christian tradition as a privileged partner in the conversation; 3) keeping all necessary partners in the conversation: human participants with a "stake" in the outcome, prior and conflicting interpretations of the situation, experiences of the participants and others, understandings of the contextual situatedness of all participants, and so on; and 4) taking regular "pauses" to account for the voices not heard in the conversation – the "null curriculum" – and to critically think about our own thinking processes. At the same time that it is disciplined, however, such conversation will also be fluid and even playful, engaging imagination and intuition along with cognition to allow the breaking through of new possibilities[84].

This conversation is meant to result in faithful practices. As Browning notes, our practices remain relatively given and unreflected upon until they are found to be wanting. What Schon calls "espoused theories", the conventional wisdom on how professionals accomplish their work, are unchallenged until they are ineffective in solving problems. Practical theology assumes that ministerial practices may also develop a quality of givenness, and educators may come to teach techniques unreflectively.

---

84. M.R. O'BRIEN, *Theology That Is Practical. The Model for the Next Millennium*, in *Theological Explorations* [Electronic Journal of the Theology Department of Duquesne University, Pittbsburgh PA], 18 June 2001 [http://www.duq.edu/liberalarts/gradtheology/theo_explorations/volume1/obrien2.html]. An important missing "voice" throughout the present essay is that of diverse cultures; I must acknowledge my own embeddedness in the white, middle class, North American piece of the ministry conversation, and invite collaborative discourse with a larger and more diverse group in order to honor my own commitment to the model advocated here. On "playfulness" in practical theology, see T.A. VELING, *"Practical Theology". A New Sensibility for Theological Education*, in *Pacifica* 11 (1998) 195-210, especially p. 205.

Through disciplined conversation, inadequacies and un-faithfulness are brought to the surface and the practices are reinterpreted to allow for new practices, more attuned to the mission of Christian disciples as they face the particular issues of their various communities. As Chopp names it, theological education is not merely professional training, but the involvement of subjects in doing theology: "about 'saving work,' the emancipatory praxis of God and of Christian community in the world"[85].

2. *Ministry educators should strive for a thematic and methodological continuity between their own educational practices, the approach of practical theology, and the ministerial practices of their students.*

Practical theology, a praxis oriented education, and authentic practices in ministry itself are congruent in aim and approach. Groome's work provides a notable example of a praxis approach originally conceived for the particular work of religious educators, then explicitly translated into a comprehensive approach to all of pastoral ministry and a thought system appropriate to the entire theological enterprise[86]. In their program design, ministry educators should continually incorporate "texts" in which their own teaching and the reflective practices they encourage in student ministers have the same contours as the ministerial styles they expect those ministers to incorporate[87]. Further, they should evaluate their own effectiveness with such continuity in mind.

3. *Ministry educators can encourage critical thinking in a practical theological mode with lay ecclesial ministers by fostering increased self-awareness.*

One aspect of this awareness, per Brookfield, is helping people to see how they learn to be critical thinkers: reflecting on their own learning style and looking at ways to adapt it in changed circumstances; understanding their motivations in learning activities and how they integrate new learning into existing analytical frameworks; discerning how they

85. R.S. CHOPP, *Saving Work* (n. 82), p. 77.
86. T.H. GROOME, *Sharing Faith* (n. 57) is a preeminent example of this congruence. Browning comments that his and Groome's approaches both hold that "the structure of theological reflection and the dynamics of Christian education should be the same", in D.S. BROWNING, *A Fundamental Practical Theology* (n. 63), p. 218.
87. Besides drawing on practical theological reflection models, ministry education can profitably use similar approaches from adult education and higher education literature, notably sources such as those cited in this essay.

work alone and with others, how they adjust for their weaknesses and emphasize their strengths in learning[88].

A related concern is the ministers' own perception of what they "need" to become effective, and of their own areas of greatest potential growth. Ministry educators can use frequent pedagogical exercises to encourage the articulation of pre-understandings, uncovering of assumptions, identification of the most significant images, stories, metaphors, and experiences that shape ministers' self-understanding, and introduction of new alternatives in each of these areas.

4. *Ministry education must create specific contexts for disciplined conversation while empowering ministers to similar creations in their diverse contexts.*

Bucher and Stelling conclude from their research on socialization that "role-playing" – the concrete practice of the role that trainees will play upon completion of their training – is by far the most important of the "situational variables" in professional training. When trainees perceive that they are doing things that real professionals do, and are given responsibility in doing them, such activities help trainees gain a sense of mastery in the field[89]. Thus the "role-playing" of practical theological reflection should receive attention throughout a ministry education program.

However, due to the diversity of ministries and of ministers' own circumstances, it is foolhardy for ministry educators to assume that they are sponsoring the most meaningful and highly valued knowledge communities for student ministers. Recognizing, as per the wisdom of professional socialization literature, that they play only one part in the formation of ministers, they should offer a "portable" paradigm for practical theological reflection and challenge student ministers to find the most appropriate venue to practice it in their own, various contexts. Since many lay ecclesial ministers study part-time while continuing with ministry and other life commitments, educators should draw upon this situation as advantageous for ongoing role-playing in practical theological reflection. Consistent with the wisdom of Christian spirituality that disciples need spiritual "disciplines" – regular prayer and opportunities for ascetic practices – in order to foster the *habitus* of prayer throughout daily activities, ministry educators can advocate the discipline of doing practical theolog-

88. D.S. BROOKFIELD, *Developing Critical Thinkers* (n. 47), pp. 82-85.
89. R. BUCHER & J.F. STELLING, *Becoming Professional* (n. 31), pp. 266-268.

ical conversation in a committed and "substantive"[90] community in order that ministers acquire it as a daily disposition. The value of the practical theology approach will be tested in its implementation, not only in graduate seminars, but in adult Bible study groups, peer networking of lay ecclesial ministers, liturgical preaching, one-to-one pastoral encounters – the many formal and informal opportunities that ministers have to invite growth in those they serve and to seek growth themselves[91].

At the same time, ministry educators must be sensitive to "safety" issues for ministers as they seek to bring a practical theological perspective to their ministry. The kind of critically interpretive and correlational thinking and conversation being encouraged by educators may threaten established practices in the faith communities served by the ministers. As Schon notes, workers often will not voice a critique of official "espoused theories" even though they are actually using their own internal constructions, called "theories-in-use," to address problems effectively[92]. The pressures of church authorities to conform to official "espoused theories" may push practical theological reflection underground or make it impossible to sustain in some contexts. Thus an important aspect of practical wisdom for ministry will be the prudential judgments necessary about the appropriate balance of equilibrium and disequilibrium – of attention to formation and to transformation – that is most appropriate for the communities in which one ministers as well as for one's own flourishing in ministry.

5. *Ministry educators should consciously seek to "enlarge"[93] ministers' perspectives beyond the ecclesial through practical theological reflection.*

By incorporating the perspectives of various disciplines besides Christian theological tradition, ministry educators acknowledge their own assumption that ministers need more inclusive, permeable perspectives because:

---

90. R.S. CHOPP, *Saving Work* (n. 82), pp. 65-66, draws on Sandel's valuable distinction between the desirable "substantive" community and the "sentimental" and "associational" types, which do not sponsor members toward critical reflection and transformation. From M.J. SANDEL, *Liberalism and the Limits of Justice*, Cambridge, Cambridge University Press, 1982, pp. 140-148. See also my article, M.R. O'BRIEN, *How We Are Together. Educating for Group Self-Understanding in the Congregation*, in *Religious Education* 92 (1997) 315-331, on the characteristics of "community" as distinguished from "primary group" and "association".

91. See L.M. ENGLISH, *Informal and Incidental Teaching Strategies in Lay-Led Parishes*, in *Religious Education* 94 (1999) 300-312.

92. Schon as cited in S.D. BROOKFIELD, *Developing Critical Thinkers* (n. 47), pp. 151-157.

93. L.A.P. DALOZ, C.H. KEEN, J.P. KEEN, S.D. PARKS, *Common Fire* (n. 79), speak of "a constructive, enlarging engagement with the other" – with those not part of our own community or tribe – as "the single most important pattern we have found in the lives of people committed to the common good", p. 63.

- Christian tradition insists that God is found in all things, not only in the church, and so expertise and enthusiasm to search for God in all things is necessary;
- ministers and all humans are subjects worthy of full development, and such development implies ever more complex understandings of inter-relationships among the many institutions shaping our existence. As Brookfield puts it: "we believe that out of such experiences come self-insight and more satisfactory lives. We regard those adults who exhibit contextual awareness, reflective skepticism, and imaginative specula-tion, and who can identify and analyze the assumptions by which they are living, as somehow more developed, mature, or adult"[94];
- they minister in a pluralistic world;
- such a perspective is essential for commitment to the common good.

6. *Ministry educators from all contexts – seminaries, universities, diocesan and other formation programs – and involved in the education of all ministers – lay, ordained, and religious – must themselves engage in practical theological dialogue.*

A frequently voiced tension in the United States is the difficulty that lay ecclesial ministers and clergy experience in collaborating, given that their formation for ministry has been so different and separately con-ducted. Further, lay ecclesial ministers find that others not only have varied perceptions of who the lay minister is, but also of what they should know and do. Pastors, diocesan agencies, parishioners, and pro-fessional associations form diverse judgments on "how much" theology, spiritual formation, and training in technical skills the minister should have. Ministry formation programs have their own strengths and weak-nesses in what they are able to provide. The Lay Ministry Subcommit-tee states that "dialogue among the various agencies ... would be help-ful to ensure the best use of resources and the provision of quality programs for prospective lay ministers"[95]. Critical and imaginative con-versation in the mode of practical theology would help educators to

---

94. S.D. BROOKFIELD, *Developing Critical Thinkers* (n. 47), p. 113.
95. SUBCOMMITTEE ON LAY MINISTRY, *Lay Ecclesial Ministry* (n. 3), p. 26. As the fol-low-up to a conference among ministry educators sponsored by the Association of Grad-uate Programs in Ministry (AGPIM), an instrument to foster such dialogue within dio-ceses and regions was developed: *The Socialization of Professional Ministers. A Structured Dialogue for Leaders of Professional Ministry Training and Formation Programs, Based on a Presentation by Dr. Rose Yunker,* n.d.

clarify and openly acknowledge some of the texts and subtexts relevant
to their vision of formation for their group of ministers. And the process
of clarification could then invite change and reacculturation – as adult
educators remind us, a process fraught with discomfort and even pain,
but ultimately open to more faithful practices.

Ministry educators in dialogue also should find non-threatening ways
to surface the "subtexts" of student ministers' responses to the education
programs in order to identify congruities and contradictions with their
own intent. As McCarthy reminds ministry educators about themselves:
"We already have fully developed assumptive worlds which will impact
what we see, hear, and think, and what we fail to see, hear, or think.
These multiple histories which we bring to every endeavor shape our
engagements and are the source of the 'old myths that continue to whis-
per' to us"[96].

The emergence of lay ecclesial ministry is an occasion of grassroots
transformation of the practices of the Roman Catholic church. The
resulting formation, of the ministers and of the church as a whole, is
still at a very early stage. As the exciting work of practical theology continues in response to this phenomenon, we do well to heed the reminder
of Lombaerts: "The start of the ecclesial tradition shows circumstances
that highlight the revealing power of the person of Christ. Throughout
its history, all sorts of circumstances have led the church to turn toward
the area of uncertainty as part of the historical character of a mystery
focused on the radically "other". This turn to mystery actually accompanied the work of defining, in a disciplined and authoritative manner,
both correct teaching and the code of right living"[97]. As we live in
uncertainty, yet we contemplate mystery and move, through disciplined
conversation, to practices more faithful to the Reign of God and the
One who proclaims it to us.

96. M. McCarthy, Response to Dr. Rose Yunker's Presentation (n. 73), p. 37.
97. H. Lombaerts, Catechetics and the Formation of Catechists (n. 1), p. 184.

Competence for Spiritual Guidance in Pastoral Ministry: A Theological Educational Programme

Tjeu van Knippenberg

In their meetings pastors regularly deal with the definition of their identity. Pastoral identity proves not to be a self-evident effect of ordination and appointment, or experience and recognition. The dynamics of pastoral self-conception are analogous to the way in which contemporary people collectively conceive their identity. The latter is not closed, grafted onto the general and the timeless. Rather, it is open, changeable and contextual. It is in this context that I will deal with the issue of competence in pastoral ministry. The question here is: what has to be learned? By choosing "spiritual guidance" in the title of my contribution, I want to make clear what I consider as the center of pastoral ministry and, accordingly, the center of the required pastoral competence. This choice is contextual. It has to do with the perceived *kairos* nowadays. In different times and cultures the center of pastoral competence can be placed elsewhere. Even nowadays one can, with good arguments, interpret culture in such a way that the center has to be canon law or moral theology or dogmatics. All these choices have their own reasons: the need for structure in the church, the loss of a base for values and norms, or doctrinal uncertainty. Change of personal and collective identity goes together with change of religious identity. It matches the question Herman Lombaerts deals with: what does it mean to intentionally aim for the continuity of the Christian tradition?[1] Investigating this question, Herman Lombaerts is always mindful of the cultural and social context of the subject under research. In view of the subject of my contribution the question of contextuality cannot be neglected. The meaning of both competence and pastoral ministry has changed during the last half of the twentieth century. In accordance with this change, I am placing "spiritual guidance" as a keyword between "competence" and "pastoral ministry". Doing so, I hope to

---

1. See for example H. LOMBAERTS, *Van generatie tot generatie*, in L. LEIJSSEN, H. LOMBAERTS, B. ROEBBEN (eds.), *Geloven als toekomst. Godsdienstpedagogische visies en bijdragen aangeboden aan Professor Jozef Bulckens bij zijn emeritaat*, Leuven – Amersfoort, Acco, 1995, 213-230.

highlight what, in our cultural context, is important in the education of future ministers, priests, deacons and pastoral workers and to promote an education which may lead to an effective pastoral practice. Our question is then: what is the key task in pastoral ministry and which competencies are required to perform this ministry? In order to answer this question, I shall first concentrate on pastoral ministry: its domain (1), its perspective (2) and its general task of discovering meaning (3). Next I will describe the permanent goal (4) and the key function of ministers (5). Finally I shall discuss briefly the issue of the competence necessary for this work (6).

Pastoral Domain

The ancient name for pastoral ministry is *cura animarum*. According to this designation, pastoral ministry is *cura*, the loving attention to *anima*, human's breath of life. From this point of view the soul is the specific pastoral domain. Soul however, is neither visible nor tangible. For that matter, I will, after a brief review on the soul itself, concentrate on life cycle and life history as vehicles of the soul and as the factual domain of pastoral ministry.

How can the concept of soul be understood from the notion of *cura animarum*? In general, soul refers to what animates man, a source, or the breath of life: "Then the Lord formed man from the dust of the ground and breathed into his nostrils the breath of life: and the man became a living being" (Gen 2,7). I conceive soul as the capacity by which man can be put in touch with the larger tissue within which existence is embraced. In philosophical terms it can be called the tissue of being, in religious terms the tissue of creation. Our senses make it possible, to a certain extent, to perceive what happens in time and space: we can look back and ahead, we can explore our environment. The soul, on the other hand, is the ability to come in contact with the transcendent, what goes beyond time and space. The biblical term for soul is "life" or "breath". This describes what makes the body alive. Man does not "have" life nor soul. Soul does not indicate his individuality, but rather his being in relation. It is a unique sign which connects a person with his origin and with other men – dead, living and the not yet born. In theological terms soul is God's image in man. It is the principle from which man can say "I am a part of the whole". It is also the principle by which my name is connected with the Name, "I am" is connected with

Yahweh, that is I AM. Without soul the meaning of life is in danger to be reduced to momentary feelings and motivation. The "other" is in danger of disappearing from sight.

The capacity of the soul is always present, whether we are sleeping or awake, saints or sinners, angry or happy, mad or brilliant. This capacity can work via a dream while asleep, via candor in a child, or via ideas in a poet. Seeing reality from the perspective of the soul presupposes, however, an intensive contact with what is factually present here and now. In the gospel according to St. Thomas we find written: "Recognize what is under your eyes, then what is hidden will be revealed to you". We do not need to seek far away, but rather nearby and open-mindedly, all senses opening to what is with us in time and space.

What does it mean to conceive the soul as the domain of pastoral ministry? Soul cannot be directly perceived. We come to learn what it is only through phenomena in the visible world. These phenomena manifest themselves in the individual and the collective course of life. Human reality takes place collectively in the course of history, as well as individually in the life cycle. In a way life cycle is fixed, beginning at birth and ending at death. Between these two moments, development of growth, adulthood and old age takes its course. This is a linear sequence of life stages. Life cycle has, in its cultural modification, something steering and forcing: a boy of fourteen is not allowed to leave the home and a twenty-year-old has to look for a new environment. The objectivity of the life cycle seems to point to an ordered development of a plan of life present in every man. Life cycle begins at a fixed point and comes to an end at a fixed point: this is the conditioned outline of human development. Attention to regularity in the phases of life is therefore a step towards understanding and mapping meaning, direction, goal or destination of man's way. According to Josef Müller, perceiving the reality of life is the point of departure in pastoral praxis. A ministry of perception is about realistically considering and accepting concrete data[2].

Is the content of this life cycle then a puzzle to solve, a novel drafted in advance or a garden in planning? In this regard, man's life story serves to discover the meaning of important events and experiences; it forms the thread in one's own life. In their stories men report to themselves and to others on events and experiences in their lives. Contrary to life cycle, this life story can begin at every moment. A story of life does not

---

2. J. MÜLLER, *Pastoraltheologie. Ein Handbuch für Studium und Seelsorge,* Graz – Wien – Köln, Styria, 1993, pp. 15-33.

go on uninterrupted like a timetable from birth to future death. In their spontaneous life stories people place the beginning at different points and moments. Often it is a recent event which evokes many emotions: "yesterday in the school yard John's jealous look stung me", "as long as my parents are alive I may not die". These are the various starting points of (fragments of) life stories. The perspective on reality is also determined by "now that I feel that jealousy", or "my parents being alive". In short, the meaning of things is connected with both circumstances in the environment and the course of time. While the concept of life cycle suggests continuity and direction, man experiences irregularities, breaks and accelerations on the way. We need stories to discover our personal meanings in all this. If life cycle should follow from step to step a causal course, we would not need stories. If it should be told, it would run dry for want of plot and dénouement.

Even in the collective life the state of affairs is not causally fixed. There is always new development. History also begins regularly anew: "since the beginning of the Gulf war" or "since the computer era". Such events can change the meaning of what is self evident until now. Events in the future, on the other hand, can be a subject of hopeful expectation or anxious anticipation. Determining which direction to take, one has the choice between several trajectories. By choosing a trajectory for their story, people create connections between events seemingly unconnected until now. In a story these events are constructed as separate elements. Ricoeur uses the term "configuration" for this art of composition[3]: it is a mediation between concordance and discordance. Characteristic for this narrative composition is the synthesis of what was heterogeneous. Configuration directs the sequence of seemingly contrary events and makes those understandable. This happens provisionally, such that the story can be altered by a new configuration.

There is a relationship between life cycle and life story: events happening in the life cycle are material for the story. These events manifest themselves in a stream. Their sequence and mutual influence causes a process of change[4]. The meaning of someone's life cycle can only be examined and understood by telling and re-telling stories. In telling, one rearranges experiences and configurations of events to construct their meanings and senses, until one reaches a satisfactory scenario. The con-

3. P. RICOEUR, *Soi-même comme un autre*, Paris, Éd. du Seuil, 1990, pp. 168-169.
4. H. HERMANS & H. KEMPEN, *The Dialogical Self. Meaning as Movement*, San Diego, Academic Press, 1993.

figurating activity connects the ever-changing and -surprising events in the course of life. This connection structures the story and is the thread as being seen at this moment. The story, however, is in principle open and can be revised or regauged. This is also the meaning of telling life story, to a pastor for instance. The teller wonders how to evaluate changes in her life and how the thread of continuity takes shape. In this way a person looks for development, regauging or strengthening of identity. Paul Ricoeur uses the term "narrative identity". Identical has a double meaning: one can distinguish between *idem-* and *ipse*-identity. Idem-identity *(mêmeté)*, refers to the unchangeable core of personality, a permanence in time[5]. Here is permanence, continuity: uninterruptedness between the first and the last phase of development. This continuity is there, but is threatened by the conditions of life. Time is such a condition. It brings about *dissemblance, écart, différence*[6]. Ipse-identity *(Ipséité)*, differs from the permanent core of personality. It stems from the hermeneutical process of reflection and self-insight. It belongs to a life as a tissue of told stories. It belongs also in the tissue of the different and the others. One could say that, moving along the axes of time and space, ipse-identity is developing itself by telling and thereby creating a narrative identity. The care of souls attends therefore to the soul as the breath in human's history and in the story of the individual. In this sense life story is the pastoral domain.

Perspective

How we perceive events and construct configurations and which meanings we give, are influenced by the perspective we adopt. To identify pastoral ministry it is a matter of major importance to be aware of its own perspective(s). What is a perspective? The perspective people take at a certain moment substantially determines what they will see in themselves, in others and in the world. One's perspective can be seen as a network of cognitions, affects and intentions through which reality is perceived and ordered[7]. It is shaped by biographical events and the social, cultural and environmental context in which we find ourselves. Someone who is hungry but can not afford a meal sees the most appeal-

---

5. P. RICOEUR, *Soi-même comme un autre* (n. 3), p. 12.

6. *Ibid.*, p. 142.

7. J.M. CHARON, *Symbolic Interactionism. An Introduction, an Interpretation, an Integration*, New York, Englewood Cliffs, 1979.

ing dishes everywhere, someone who is lonely sees talkative and loving people on every corner of the street, someone with an aching thumb sees and envies all other people living without pain. Our perspective may be seen as the current, more or less stable, point of orientation from which we seek a route on our chart of life and follow it. To explicit the pastoral perspective, I will first distinguish and stress the religious and Christian dimensions in it.

The perspective which influences our powers of observation may have a religious character. The Dutch author Abel Herzberg writes from this perspective: "Everything we are, what we see, experience, say, undergo and do is fragmentary. But there is no fragment in which the soul of everything alive has not found expression. There is no moment without eternity, no mortal being, however deformed or well-shaped it may be, in which not the immortal creation is revealed"[8]. We talk about a religious perspective when the discrepancies and even absurdities of everything we experience find a point of connection in the end. Simple happenings and experiences enter into a relationship with a larger whole. With Abel Herzberg, this happens essentially from a point of connection which he calls "the immortal creation". Out of this core his religious perspective is formed, a perspective that is characterized by the point of departure that the life an individual leads is a fragment in a larger whole which has its roots in Creation. Belonging to Creation puts the person in a fabric, a network in which contradictions find their place. It is from this perspective that Abel Herzberg sees what he sees.

We find with the psalmist the experience of wonder about his own existence in time and space in the midst of the infinite: "When I see Thine heavens – the work of Thine fingers, moon and stars Thou placed there. What then is man that Thou payest heed to him, the son of man that Thou lookest at him?" (Ps 8,4-5). Wherever this religious perspective is active, the world and place we occupy become qualified in a certain way. Thus, on seeing the wheat fields, a woman from the Middle Ages would exclaim: "This world is pregnant of God!". Whoever is accessible to this perspective may have the same experience today. For the devout, the history of God with God's people is active in the course of events. All partial histories come in contact with its proper connection here. In the experience of the conditions of existence, here and now resounds the horizon of a more comprehensive whole[9]. Where this is

---

8. A.J. HERZBERG, *Drie rode rozen*, Amsterdam, Querido, 1978, pp. 114-115.

not the case, a religious answer becomes impossible. Whenever in such a situation an encoded religious answer is given, it has the character of a bolt from the blue.

In pastoral theological literature a question that has been raised is whether the pastor can use the typical stock-in-trade of a theologian. In general, this question stems from the observation that theology does not play the role that could be expected from a science which for centuries has systematically gathered human insights and experiences *sub ratione Dei*. A theologian may ask: what inspires us? What is our ultimate drive? In that question the pneumatic or spiritual dimension comes under discussion. This perspective can be operationalized in the following threefold question: where in a person's situation do signs appear which refer to the ultimate meaning of his moral action, to the foundation of the whole of meaning where he belongs to and to his experience of the holy?[10] It cannot be taken for granted that the parishioner in general is consciously dealing with these questions. The pastor is concerned with these questions, because of the nature of his professional background, since they probe the presence of the Holy Spirit in terms of the ultimate drive behind our behavior, the basic trust which is the foundation of the spatio-temporal setting and the values which are considered as inviolable. The pastor knows that these questions are important for the person, irrespective of whether the person attributes a religious meaning to them. At the very least these questions can function as a diagnostic instrument. They form a background for the meaning of certain words, silences and gestures. They are based on the belief that the person is not located in the anonymity of time and space, but in the divine time and space manifesting itself in the presence of the Holy Spirit.

Paul Pruyser, psychologist of religion, states that pastors have at their disposal a unique perspective and adequate concepts to understand human reality in a specific way[11]. They have knowledge of creation and providence, of the evil and the holy, of grace and merit and of the ultimate goal. This perspective is called the *Kingdom of God* and can be perceived, according to the gospel, in all kinds of phenomena of every-

9. H. CLINEBELL, *Ecotherapy. Healing Ourselves, Healing the Earth*, New York – London, The Howard Press, 1996.

10. The questions have been derived from P. TILLICH, *Systematic Theology. Volume III*, Chicago, University of Chicago Press, 1963, p. 107. He calls the Spirit "not a separated being, but the presence of the Divine Life within creaturely life". This Spiritual Presence becomes evident in the content of the threefold question.

11. P. PRUYSER, *The Minister as Diagnostician*, Philadelphia, Westminster Press, 1976.

day life: in the joy of finding something which was thought to be lost, in the frankness of a child and in the growing of a seed. These concepts and images are probably not immediately suitable for use in a conversation. They can, however, serve to a certain extent as a framework which clarifies events, thoughts and feelings. Such a theological set of instruments can be useful to determine what is holy to someone and what motives a person. Twenty years after Pruyser, Howard W. Stone designed an eight-question model from a theological perspective. He considers the eight questions as constitutive elements of a theological template, a structure which enables us to process information in a certain way[12]. According to Stone, this template enables the pastor to use his own theological perspective as a primary frame of reference.

In the tradition of pastoral ministry we are familiar with the encouragement to change our old perspective. This has to do with activating the soul: "look with the eyes of your soul". It is interesting that often a change of perspective is brought about by going beyond the borders of the common life cycle. In the *martyrologium* the day the saint died is called birthday. Here we find the age-old meditation on death. In this exercise the starting point for the life story is the contemplation on one's own death. One meditates on one's own ambitions, anxieties and longings from the moment that the conditions of life are to be lost. The basic assumption is that confrontation with this situation provides a good impetus for coming into contact with reality. Other cultures trace the starting point of the life story to the ancestors. People have a house-altar in honor of their parents and ancestors. The latter are involved in the communication about important life events. People who celebrate rituals on such an altar, realize that life fabric consists of more than the people living here and now. One's own life story extends before birth. In life story one explores the double value in all spatio-temporality: border and connection. Time as it is now comes into relation with a more embracing time. Environment as it is here comes into relation with a more embracing community. It is in this way that Jesus tells parables. The perspective is again the kingdom of God, where history is removed from its seeming conditionedness. The power of religion lies thus in its changing of perspectives. According to J. Assmann, from this power life gets two-dimensionality or two-temporality *(Zweizeitigkeit)*. The timeless structure of religion gives one the opportunity to live at the same

---

12. H.W. STONE, *Theological Context for Pastoral Caregiving. Word in Deed*, New York – London, The Howard Pastoral Press, 1996.

time in two times and by that to keep a critical distance to the absolutism of commonness[13].

Reality as we experience it in our daily lives, layered with all its nuances, is too complex to be perceived and understood from one perspective. So perspectives need to be changed: one looks at the same object from a different point of view. Depending on the token perspective, there are different ways to represent what has been seen – for instance, in a religious, a Christian or a pastoral way. The stratification of reality explains why we need different approaches so as to constantly perceive new fragments of reality. I will come back to this point when considering hermeneutical competence.

Meaning

Perspective implies coherence. One may call it coherence, because all kinds of often contradictory experiences come together in the person as a center. In general, this coherence will remain more or less implicit. More or less, for, to a certain extent, it is possible to make explicit important experiences and the connection between them and through this to obtain a view of the point of orientation we occupy. The perspective that has taken shape within us, which is repeatedly nascent, influences the way in which we observe situations, matters and people. This observation in turn influences our actions.

One continually encounters the question of how things are connected, whether while puzzling, reading a novel or gardening. In dealing with a puzzle-piece, a paragraph or a plant, the puzzler, reader and gardener alike use their intelligence and their creativity to locate a place for it that is adequate in the larger whole. The meaning of a fragment becomes clear when its right time and place in the whole have been found.

For the time being I like to define the broader whole which people belong to as time and space. These are the conditions of life. They form the puzzle board's or the garden's contours within which someone's life history takes place. Following on from this image, a person is like a puzzle piece or a plant which finds its destination by locating its place in time and space. What does it mean to be in the here and now? What is

---

13. J. ASSMANN, *Das kulturelle Gedächtnis. Schrift, Erinnerung und politische Identität in frühen Hochkulturen*, München, Beck, 1999, p. 57.

my and our place? The question concerning meaning arises whenever there is a confrontation with time and space as conditions of existence. We are continually in touch with time and space, like a fish with water, but we are not continuously conscious of it. This behavior is not always easy nor should it be taken for granted. Time and space simultaneously facilitate and restrict our conduct. We are continually conditioned by these pillars of existence, but the relationship we build up with them is variable. This raises a question concerning the meaning of this relationship, a question concerning meaning in general.

In life stories landmarks of time and space play an important role: "when I was a child", "before I got married", "in my birth town", etc. Questions of meaning originate from the experience of time and space. A woman, pregnant from her first child, says: "I realize that I shall be nevermore alone". A homeless person: "now I am sleeping in the open air, but at the end of this month I will receive my social security bene- fit". A well-known artist: "it would be wonderful to be anonymous in town". The background question is always: what is the meaning of time and space for these people as they experience it or would like to experi- ence it?

Meaning and the experience or validation of it: these are notions which become vital only if and when contact with time and space – the conditions of existence – changes into a confrontation with existence itself. At such moments, the question concerning the meaning and the very ground of what we are and what we experience thrusts itself for- ward. Broadly speaking, this is expressed in the question: "what is the meaning of life?" This may be interpreted as "what is life?" and "how is life?". It is also a question about the reason for existence: what is the purpose of life, and what is the nature and the value of it? Those ques- tions arise against the background of the concrete experience of the con- tours of human existence.

All mortals exist in time and space. If and when the question of the meaning of life occurs to someone, it is not a purely individual question. Nor is there a fortuitous answer conceived by the individual concerned or any other person for that matter. The question and its subsequent val- idation are the products of a shared existence. They arise and are cher- ished in primary relationships. Meaning is a social category. Since the earliest of time, the question and the answer have been developing within communities. The questions which are asked and the subsequent answers people search for and give reveal something of the culture, the collective identity of a particular group. This leads, over and over, in different times and places, to the symbolization of life's conceptions. People exchange these symbols with one another and in this way an outline comes into being within which life's manifestations may be understood. We call such a validation outline a view of life. In a view of life, notions about the nature and value of life are gathered in a consistent body of symbols which point to what, in the final analysis, matters in life.

Each culture has its explicit and implicit life conceptions. These conceptions create a framework for meaning. If "time is money" is the rule, it is not difficult to imagine what has to be seen as the measure for meaningful human action. A person who departs from "you only live once" will go all out to make the best of this moment. Everyone has some rules of thumb, shaped by the culture one belongs to, which serve as guidelines for the person in determining what has more or less meaning. In this orientation faith plays a role.

Christianity is a particular view of life. Like other views of life, it manifests itself in a consistent body of symbols. Particular to Christian belief is the reference to a transcendent reality to which we are allowed entrance through Jesus Christ. Connecting with this transcendent reality forms the basis of our existence and ultimately gives meaning to it. This is expressed concisely in the answer to the first question of the old Roman Catholic Catechism: "Why are we on earth?" – "We are on earth to serve God and through this to be happy here and in the hereafter". This is typical of a question concerning meaning and an answer offered from faith. The answers in the catechism represent the pledge of faith of the Church. They contain the building blocks from which one's personal answer in faith is erected. It is clear, certainly for this era, that the creation of a personal answer in faith does not happen in close connection with an answer from the catechism. Why?

In the answer to the first question of the Catechism, the time of our own course of life naturally flows into the stream of eternal time. Our space of existence becomes connected naturally with the space of the universe. There is the unshaken presence of a certain religious perspective. In the Western world questions about human existence have been viewed for ages from such a perspective as a matter of course; and from that perspective they were connected with Christian answers. Those answers had so much authority and influence that they tended to anticipate the questions. The encompassing question concerning the meaning of existence – "Why are we on earth?" – seemed, in the old Catechism, begging for the answer, given once and for all.

The religious point of view became so focused on the answers about the meaning of the deeper layers of existence that the vital experience became subordinate to it. Over the centuries the meaning of our thinking, acting and feeling, including the consequences for our eternal salvation, has been included, worked out and systematized in watertight systems. The road has been set; in principle, anybody may come to know it in time. There is a pre-formed point by which all individual history of meaning is gauged. Even today, people living in groups where such a system is accepted generally or universally can easily support each other in finding or regauging the right answer to questions about the meaning of existence.

Many contemporary people, however, resist such an all-embracing history about the meaning of life. To a large extent, they feel restricted by such perspective in working within their own experience. After all, is a systematic answer possible and desirable in the midst of the absurdities in which life manifests itself? Where validation of existence is concerned, there is a huge pitfall for the ministers of a religion. They take care of the religious content as it is formulated in a certain tradition, such that the premeditated answer becomes the gauge for true or false, for eternal salvation or perdition. The question about the meaning of life is to be answered in a certain way. Such faithful reproduction of that answer has consequences for the devotees of that religion in the personal and the collective dimension of their existence. In such a situation it is not surprising that people try to shake off the oppressive validation of the official religions.

However, the existential question remains delicate, and soothing answers are required. Such a question is, therefore, readily and easily kept in tutelage. Since people want to give meaning to their existence, the temptation to offer a carefully-reasoned answer is great. Currently, there are all kinds of institutions of an economic, social, political and religious character active on the world market, which are aware of and pander to this need. In glowing terms, they sing praises of what is of ultimate importance to us and to which we should give our hearts. According to the law of supply and demand, this cumulates in those who rummage, try out and engage provisionally with what suits them most. The experience of meaning has become largely individual.

The situation in the validation market and the natural longing to satisfy our desire for coherence produce the danger that we search too readily in the Christian faith for the validation answers it gives. We therefore find ourselves on thin ice when we theoretically associate validation and

Christian faith. The question "does Christian faith offer meaning?" and further, "can Christian faith have a function for contemporary people in their search for meaning?" exert a kind of pressure on that belief itself: the pressure of topicality or relevance and of usefulness. If we look at faith in this way, we run the risk of finding in it what we put in it ourselves, from above or below. Christian faith is not meant to provide the surplus problems of our society with meaning. Faith does not restrict itself to the taking away of unintelligible, painful disillusions and it cannot be reduced to the function of neutralizing unknown fears[14].

Nevertheless, meaning and faith are closely connected. Christian faith offers a context, a content and a concrete form to existential experiences. The core of this faith was established in the Councils of Nicea and Constantinople and were laid down in the Creed. Creed, "Credo" in Latin, has to do with "Cor-do" – with "I believe" as much as with "I give my heart". That which people consider important from their innermost hearts shapes the outline of the meaning they look for in life. The history of the Creed shows that the personal meaning one finds in faith is always connected with the faith of the community. It is not a personal concoction, but a heritage. For centuries this heritage has been offered to help people understand and furnish their lives. It has not only taken shape in a balanced doctrine on the meaning of human life, but it has created also symbols which fill the concrete time and space.

In accordance with its character, faith plays an important role in managing the span of our lives. Faith looks at concrete reality, as experienced here and now, from the viewpoint of final reality. That final reality – God – is to be trusted and therefore time is to be trusted: "life with God is stronger than death". From this perspective, life's road can be trod with a certain measure of self-loss. The practical side of this is clearly seen in Roman Catholic practice, which offers a structure for the course of life in the sacraments, which endow the nodal points of life with meaning. Between celebrating birth (baptism) and the end of this time (the last sacraments), there are the celebrations of growing up (confirmation), community (the Eucharist), the celebrating of conversion (confession), the personal covenant (marriage) and/or being sent upon a mission in the Church (ordination).

In the final analysis, all of these sacraments have to do with the possible experience of continuity as embodied in the death and resurrection

14. J.B. METZ, *Glaube in Geschichte und Gesellschaft. Studien zu einer praktischen Fundamentaltheologie*, Mainz, Matthias-Grünewald, 1977, p. 134.

of Jesus Christ. In all its manifestations – in birth and growing up, in sin and faithfulness – life offers the possibility to participate in a life-in-fullness. This is not only expressed in these sacraments, which have their place at the nodal points of the life cycle, but also throughout the course of the year. There are advent and birth, suffering and death and resurrection and the gift of the Spirit. That is the year cycle which is, liturgically enacted in rituals. C.G. Jung called the ecclesiastical year a "therapeutic system"[15]. Just as the Ecclesiastical year gives a temporal context to the course of human existence as it is laid down in birth, death and resurrection, so the consecration of the house makes the house a part of the divine environment. Such symbols are reminders: they place time and space in a certain perspective, which connects synchronically and diachronically both at the current moment and in the long run – that is, at least if we have the right organs of sense and cognitions for it.

The objectivity of granting meaning to the life cycle and living space does not usurp the place of subjective experience. It lends structure to time and space, but does not take away the oppression of it and does not offer a cut and dried answer to the meaning of every personal moment of life. For that purpose, there are prayer and meditation in which a person may experience ongoing time. In the history of Christian spirituality, we find many worked-out examples of this, such as the already mentioned meditation upon death. In the course of centuries, this meditation has been the very instrument to come to know oneself and, subsequently, to know God. Knowledge of God means that God is our Creator and that we are His creatures. In the perspective of death, the quality of life, as it is lived here and now, is sharply brought to light[16]. An old pastoral image is that of a guard, supposed to know the signs of time, night and day and those of space, rest and threat. As a guard, the pastor is also an advocate of meaning.

Permanent Goal

Working on a life story, pastoral ministry aims at different goals which lie at the heart of concrete actions such as liturgy, catechesis and home-visit. In this section however, I like to concentrate on the permanent

---

15. Cfr. A. GRÜN, *Verwandlung. Eine vergessene Dimension geistlichen Lebens*, Mainz, Matthias-Grünewald, 1993, p. 76.

16. M. VAN KNIPPENBERG, *Communicative Self-investigation in Pastoral Group Work on Death*, in *Journal of Empirical Theology* 2 (1988) 64-88.

goal, referring to a goal that should always be kept in mind. In an explicit pastoral interaction, there needs to be continuity between the concrete goals that are striven after in that interaction and the permanent goal, which can be described as the regauging of religious identity. What, then, is religious identity? It is the answer which may be given to the question "who am I as a religious person?". The answer to this question is not a formula established for all time, but is given instead in a dynamic process that is enacted in the interaction of the individual with his or her symbolic and social environment. It is the crystallization point of the symbolic and social position assumed at any given moment. It draws in general traits the development which may be realized by pastoral ministry. In the scheme below, the permanent goal is indicated in the intersection between the social dimension (*horizontal*) and the symbolic dimension (*vertical*).

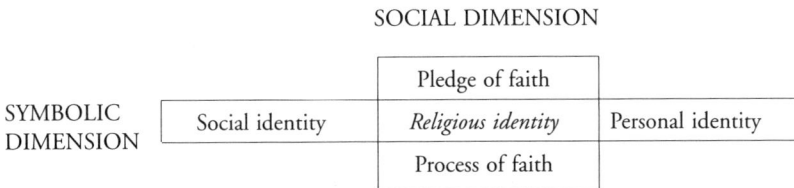

SOCIAL DIMENSION

		Pledge of faith	
SYMBOLIC DIMENSION	Social identity	*Religious identity*	Personal identity
		Process of faith	

The symbolic dimension of Christian religious identity is represented by the vertical axis. Religious identity is poised on the symbolic axis, between the extreme poles of *pledge of faith* and *process of faith*. By pledge of faith I mean the content of faith as handed over by the Christian tradition; process of faith denotes the interpreting response of a person. Our response to Christian revelation is always enacted in current interpretative experiences. People's belief cannot be developed apart from religious tradition or from what people consider as important at a given moment in their lives.

The social dimension on the horizontal axis is anchored by social identity on the one end, and personal identity on the other. These categories are adopted from Krappmann, who employs this distinction, following E. Goffman[17]. The notion of *social identity* relates to the social standards with which a person stands face to face in the prevailing process of interaction. The notion of *personal identity*, on the other

17. L. KRAPPMANN, *Soziologische Dimensionen der Identität*, Stuttgart, Klett, 1978.

hand, relates to the individuality and innateness attributed to a person. Both poles emanate from the expectations and standards of others. Identity in this context is the competence of a person to simultaneously acquiesce in the expectations of others and, with regard to these expectations, profile himself as an individual. It is the social location of a person, that is, the place where one shows to others and to oneself one's own place. It is not a permanent asset. Rather, since it forms part of the interaction process, it has to be formulated continually against changing expectations and a changing life history.

Within this scheme, religious identity is built up from the positions one occupies on the horizontal and the vertical axis. They form two perspectives from which the question "who am I as a religious person" takes its tangible form; the perspective of social connections and the perspective of configurations of meaning. The answer to this question is subject to ongoing fluctuations, which are bound up with one's personal, cultural and social situation. The regauging of religious identity is therefore necessarily a permanent goal of pastoral ministry. Truly pastoral ministry keeps in sight the tension within the two dimensions of religious identity. With regard to the symbolic dimension, this takes shape when the religious tradition and the personal life history are considered together. As regards the social dimension, this takes form when a person's interaction with himself and with others – the intra-personal and the interpersonal communication – are continuously related to each other.

In modern times everyone has to attribute an identity to himself or herself. This is related to changes which are above all about individualizing and pluralizing processes. No longer is one totally dependent on one's origin and social context for determining the shape of one's own life and the norms that direct it. As people became aware of this, they revolted against a ministry which founds its authority on a framework of a priori values and norms. Such ministry has as its point of departure a set biblical and/or ecclesiastical pledge of faith; the message is delivered in a given biblical or ecclesiastical language. In this way, believers are urged to take decisions and restore their religious identity. From the 1960s onward, however, forms of pastoral ministry emerge which take as their starting point that which goes on in the mind of the person seeking guidance. This anthropological paradigm highlights a non-directive way of working with the biographical qualities of the person seeking spiritual guidance. This new orientation has been the subject of a turbulent development, considered a wind of change as opposed to the first type of ministry. Its language is derived from experience and psychology. The values and criteria for decisions it adopts are taken from the story of a person's life. What matters is, in the light of the Gospel, to aim at the recovery of an individual's fundamental wholeness as a road to religious identity.

Self-experience, personal meaning and identity are mediated. Through confrontation with beyond-individual patterns of interpretation and behavior, individuals are provided the opportunity to build up their personal meaning. This happens in primary relationships and social contexts they live in. All people live from founding histories "from which they obtain the orientation and direction of their acting"[18]. In this context, identity is the awareness to be someone recognizable by oneself and by others, a subject of a history as it takes shape in life story until now. This life story is about realizing ourselves in time and space. It is about succeeding and failing in the past, and expectation and distrust towards the future. It is about the teller who is connected in a framework with other people. The "I" tells about these others and the way they look at oneself, in a connected tale about time and space.

While the story is structured by connection, it remains for the rest open. Narrative identity is temporary. It is a mixture between imagination and living experience *(un mixte instable entre fabulation et expérience vive)*[19]. Typical of this temporarity is the try-out character and the fallibility of identity. The experimental character of identity is connected with the fact that the self is plural. More identities are possible: the tissue of identity consists of more threads. Personal life history is therefore multidimensional. Autobiography is never complete. The temporary character of identity is also connected with the fact that while we formulate the end of the story, we ourselves shall not have the opportunity to retell the real end. Autobiography is thus never complete. Henning Luther's concept of identity has to be understood in this sense[20]. He emphasizes its fragmented character. Too glibly, identity can be characterized by completeness, harmony and consistency. It is important to include experiences of negativity and conflict. Identity, according to Ricoeur, is dependent on telling. It is not in the way of immediate intuition. We understand ourselves only via the detour of human signs.

18. J. ASSMANN, *Das kulturelle Gedächtnis* (n. 18), p. 296.
19. P. RICOEUR, *Soi-même comme un autre* (n. 3), p. 191.
20. H. LUTHER, *Religion und Alltag. Bausteine zu einer Praktischen Theologie des Subjektes*, Stuttgart, Radius Verlag, 1993, pp. 155ff.

How should we know, love and hate, if not put in words by stories? Without the story of its history in time and space, identity should be lost for want of description.

Even religious identity depends on telling, and on the narrative which constitutes the continuity of the self within the factuality of interruption and discontinuity. Here, the basis of the story is in the tradition of faith. The religious identity line develops along the detour of bible and tradition. Human origin and direction have been set down in the biblical narrative and in subsequent articulations within which has been put in words who the human person is.

Understanding oneself and regauging religious identity are connected with the interpretation of texts. Symbols and stories of our culture belong to these texts, including belief symbols and texts, encounter with other people and the text of one's very own life story as it takes shape in time and space. Working with these texts, religious identity may be regauged via the detour of time and space. Time-identity is in God as the Eternal One: "My times are in your hand" (Ps 31,15). It is the fixed point that gives continuity to the story one can tell from and about one's own history. It is the anchor point for autobiographical identity. Similarly, space-identity is in God as the Present One: "Even though I walk through the darkest valley, I fear no evil; for you are with me" (Ps 23,4). It is the fixed point that gives connectedness to being in the network of other people. It is the anchor point for relational identity. Religious identity takes shape thus via the detour of autobiographical and relational identity.

Key Functions

Up to this point I have sketched the contours of pastoral ministry as a helping profession about discovering meaning in the process towards regauging religious identity; it does so specifically via the perspective of transcendence in the domain of individual and collective life history. This description of the pastoral domain, perspective, focus and goal gives an indication to our choice of the pastoral key function. It needs to be a function concerning the central pastoral mission: promoting consciousness of the fabric of creation. The human life cycle in its own spatio-temporal condition is transcended by one who presents oneself in a dynamic creative way. The human person is the image of God, oriented to this transcendence. This orientation demands continuous practice. It is only the experience of being in tune with this transcendence which reveals the connection and meaning of things, events and experiences in the human life cycle. Pastoral ministry is about assisting in this area.

How does a pastor perform this task? Pointing out specific pastoral activities is not difficult. One might think of actions such as administering the sacraments, blessing people, preaching, leading a burial, assisting in the public debate on ethics, teaching religious education and counselling the bereaved. But pastors have also business-like meetings, they chat with volunteers, organize parish feasts, gather with organizations and meet with people in daily life. In doing so, they are also working as a pastor. It is clear that pastoral activities can be more ecclesial or more secular, more ritual or more personal, depending on ordination or skills, and on whether they are performed by clergy or laity. Amidst such diversity, the question remains: what are the pastoral functions and how are they related with each other by a key task? In pastoral theological literature there are different answers to this question, generally depending on the classical division of kerygma, liturgia, diaconia and koinonia. I will follow here the division of specific pastoral functions as formulated by J.A. van der Ven in his study on reflective ministry. He distinguishes seven specific functions, corresponding to the work pastors perform in the sectors of liturgy, catechesis, practical ecclesiology, diaconia, mission, pastoral counseling and spiritual guidance[21]. He further designates hermeneutic communication as a general function, the common denominator of the seven specific functions. Here the question remains: what is the key task of pastoral ministry?

The capacity for hermeneutic communication is indeed a quality required in all these functions. It is central to pastoral competence and as such a formal quality. Nonetheless, I do not consider it as a general function, because in my view a general function needs to be a key task, playing a substantial role and being integral to all other functions. Such is the way Karl Rahner defined the mission of the Church in two mutually-related epitomes: worship of God and mediation of salvation[22], the latter being realized in the classical functions of *kerygma, diaconia, liturgia* and *koinonia*. Rahner's notions appear in the everyday work of today's pastors. Indeed, in order to trace the pastoral key task, it is vital not to lose sight of the combined notions of worship of God

21. J.A. VAN DER VEN, *Education for Reflective Ministry* (Louvain Theological and Pastoral Monographs, 24), Leuven, Peeters Press, 1998.
22. K. RAHNER (ed.), *Handbuch der Pastoraltheologie. Praktische Theologie der Kirche in der Gegenwart*, Freiburg – Basel – Wien, Herder, 1964-1972.

and mediation of salvation as ecclesiastical terms of reference for pastoral work. The very combination of these terms of reference implies that the pastor's key task is, in fact, the representation of the transcendent and the creation of conditions for the parishioner's encounter with God. In other words, pastoral work is essentially in service of people, in order that they may link their individual, socially related reality with eschatological reality.

Indications for the pastoral key task can also be found in the context as I have sketched it in broad outlines of individualism and pluralism. This context evokes tensions between fundamentalism and liberalism, a rigid ecclesiastical discipline and freedom of faith, an ideological emphasis on political problem solving (war, environment, health) and private enterprise. Christians nowadays find it very difficult to name the things that unite. Even pastoral functions are in danger of being practiced each in their own moment and place, out of this wider context. The complexity of biographical direction taxes the energies of individuals in a pluralistic society. Being thrown upon one's own resources, being forced to make decisions and the connected requirement of *Dauerreflektion,* highlights the need to promote life guidance as a central focus in pastoral ministry.

Another indication for the pastoral key function can be found in culture. Ten leading American psychologists of culture and religion have written a book *On Losing the Soul*[23]. It is about something that has been lost, not only in North-American culture, but also in Europe: the soul[24]. Soul is not only the innermost point of individuals but also of culture. This diagnosis helps to explain the increasing emphasis on the care for the soul in pastoral theological literature in the past few years. I. Baumgartner formulated the hypothesis that modern people suffer from the inability to accept themselves or their own borders and finiteness, a problem which can be healed only in a religious framework. According to him salvation and healing go together. In our time the primacy is *cura animarum specialis,* the individual care of souls[25]. According to Baumgartner *cura animarum specialis* is therefore the key task.

Spiritual guidance seems to be the *kairological* key function of pastoral ministry. Spiritual guidance, as operationalised in Eucharist and

23. R.K. FENN & D. CAPPS (eds.), *On Losing the Soul. Essays in the Social Psychology of Religion*, Albany, State University of New York Press, 1995.

24. H. DE DIJN, *De herontdekking van de ziel. Voor een volwaardige kwaliteitszorg,* Nijmegen, Valkhof Pers, 1999, pp. 69-70.

25. I. BAUMGARTNER, *Heilende Seelsorge in Lebenskrisen,* Düsseldorf, Patmos, 1992.

confession, and in pastoral encounter and retreats, may be wanted as a key function, but can no longer be considered a matter of course nowadays. In recent years, questions regarding spiritual guidance have increased in number and urgency. What exactly is the spiritual aspect of the complex psychological processes within human nature and human culture? In which way and to what extent does the spiritual relate to everyday life? Is it a relevant factor in the development of the self and that of the society? How is spiritual guidance carried out? Questions of this kind become increasingly urgent as the connection with the transcendent has proportionally lost its ground as an accepted phenomenon, as can be seen in public debate on this matter, at least in the Western culture. Also, professional care is becoming more and more of a secular matter. It is, however, in the relationship with the transcendent that the essential and distinguishing factor of spiritual guidance lies.

The foundation of spiritual guidance is the conviction that persons can only grow to full stature through developing their awareness of being connected with the transpersonal and the transcendent. The Bible narrates the history of humanity and its estrangement from God and the attempt at reunion. Struggle is a common factor in this and similar cases. There is a strained relationship between the transcendent and the immanent. Heteronomy is opposed to autonomy, and surrender has its counterpart in control. Life is more or less constructed of these and similarly opposing pairs. Among other things, the ambivalence that springs from this fact is expressed in the theological and psychological languages, in the visible and invisible world, in the tangible and the intangible. This ambivalence is of great value, and it more or less "engineers" spiritual guidance.

Spiritual guidance helps people discover meaning in their spatio-temporal conditions by not being locked up in it. To that end the soul is activated as a detector of meaning. Contact with the soul comes into existence through attention, reflection and the experience of creaturely relationship: lending and accepting hospitality, being each other's fellow traveller. Communication from the soul occurs through respectfully exploring the life cycle, and taking seriously the contours of history and environment, in order that the inside breaks through. The soul is present in the spatio-temporal limitation of the body, sometimes restricted, sometimes transparent. Accordingly, the care of souls goes through the everyday things of life, via the detour of time and space.

At times people reveal their animation, their soul. They discern in their life anchor points as well as irregularities. They manage parts and create connections between seemingly dissociated events. In their life story they look for connections, for the ground in their history and constellation. Pastors are there to excavate old wells which are present in everyone. This is symbolised in Moses who beats the rock with the vision: the steppe will flourish. Managers of a well know that water must stream; standing still it becomes poisonous. Pastors are therefore advocates of the soul, of continuity. Pastoral ministry contributes to the working of the soul in life history, especially in spiritual guidance as a key task in a variety of functions.

Competence

Herman Lombaerts sees two simultaneous movements in processes of change. The one is mourning: one has to leave behind certain familiar frames of reference. The other is discovering: through a new freedom of mind one can come to establish uncommon connections between almost unknown factors[26]. This is specially true in regard to pastoral ministry. Amidst this tension of mourning and discovering we situated the question: which is the key task of this ministry? What qualifications or competencies are required for pastoral ministry, in particular for spiritual guidance as its key task? Competence is essentially a matter of knowledge, insight, skills and attitudes, necessary to perform the tasks belonging to the office of pastor. Enhancing this competence engenders tension between the developing of technical skills and of the spiritual disposition of the (future) pastor.

In my description of the nature and content of the pastoral profession and my indication of a key function, I have tried to provide a base for the required competence. Herman Lombaerts states in his description of the competence of religion teachers that the main competence is not a good knowledge of the different theological and social disciplines, but the competence to communicate with the religious and ethical consciousness of young people[27]. In my view this corresponds to what a parish expects from a new incumbent, as reflected from the results of an analysis of function profiles such as the one presented in 1997 by the

26. H. LOMBAERTS, *Religion – Société et enseignement religieux à l'école*, in J. BULCKENS & H. LOMBAERTS (eds.), *L'enseignement de la religion catholique à l'école secondaire. Enjeux pour la nouvelle Europe* (BETL, 109), Leuven, University Press – Peeters, 1993, 3-30, p. 19.
27. *Ibid.*, p. 30.

Vrije Universiteit Amsterdam. The results of this analysis may be summarized in four aspects which constitute the core of the required competence.
- The importance of contemporary preaching in keeping with the multiformity of a congregation
- The importance of pastoral empathy
- The importance of skilful operation of the construct of planned change
- The importance of personal commitment and concomitant communicative competency.

All these notions have to do with what goes on in today's society. Preaching not only demands theological skills but also, very strongly, pastoral empathy, skills in planned change and personal commitment[28]. What comes under discussion is the relationship between theological content and communicative skills. No matter how we consider the possibilities of academic knowledge, we must, in any event, admit that theology has built up capital through thinking systematically about human destination over a long period of time. This statement seems justified given that this period of systematizing has produced some sound insights into what a human being fundamentally is and into the way his particular nature can develop into the full measure of the human person. This heritage is a valuable tool for practice. The history of spiritual guidance shows that through the ages theological insights have been explicitly used[29]. It seems, however, that in spite of recent initiatives (see Pruyser and Stone), the willingness to work from a theological viewpoint has not returned. Compared to the instrumentarium of a medical doctor or a psychotherapist, the theological tools are not as sharply outlined and they cannot boast general approval. The system of theological concepts has been tested less scientifically and is therefore considered less reliable by many people. Since the Enlightenment, this system has lost a great deal of its former intellectual credibility.

It is evident that there is a strong challenge to hermeneutics and communication. Pastoral ministry, as based on spiritual guidance, has in its central focus the relationship between the ultimate and the pre-ultimate, transcendence and immanence, faith and experience. The exchange on these matters is paralinguistic and non-verbal, but takes place in the end

28. Cfr. the articles by W.F VAN STEGEREN and G. VAN DAM in *Praktische Theologie* 25 (1998) no. 5.
29. Cfr. *Dictionnaire de la Spiritualité*. Vol. III, Paris, Beauchesne, 1957, 1002-1214.

by means of the spoken word. Language is more than using a vocabulary: "language is the body of our spirit", as Gerhard Ebeling has stated[30]. It embodies that which lives within us. It externalises our inner life: we are as proud and shy of it as with our own bodies. It is a social barometer: others may derive from it the state of our minds, the place we occupy. This means that, within the context of the present ambivalent attitude toward the spiritual dimension of existence, it is not simple to communicate about God. Embarrassment is rife, especially in spiritual guidance, for there our human and religious individuality is tried for authenticity: this is enacted on a plane which does not coincide with Sunday services, funerals, or divinity lessons. Of old the latter are places where communicating about God was less fraught with problems. Nowadays, there may even be the risk of the language that is common to such places developing into a ghetto-language. Outside these "reservations", religious communication requires a large measure of freedom, both as regards oneself and the other. It demands a language in which we may express that which has been confided to us, for these two polarities always present themselves: giving thought to the heritage acquired and granting oneself an individual position within it.

---

30. G. EBELING, *Gott und Wort,* Tübingen, J.C.B. Mohr, 1966, p. 12.

Epilogue
Christ in the Desert

Herman Lombaerts *

Gustave van de Woestyne belongs to the first generation of painters who established themselves in Saint-Martens-Latem, a small rural village in Belgium. Reacting against Impressionism, they identified themselves as the School of Latem. Most of van de Woestyne's work is situated at the boundaries of Symbolism and Expressionism. Although his style suggests links with contemporaries such as Renoir, Monet, Khnopff, Dix and Magritte, or older traditions like the Flemish primitives (Breughel), the Burgundy miniaturists, or Byzantine paintings, he recreates with his own depth what was explored already by other artists.

Latem means a place where the humble, the poor, the lonely and the blind establish themselves. Van de Woestyne's work demonstrates his preference for portrayal of ordinary people whose innermost feelings he seemed to understand. His work relates to his personal experience of unrest and anxiety, of the ineluctable loneliness, separation and isolation of human existence. He often pictures himself at the centre of the emotional struggle of his paintings.

In *Christ in the desert* (1939), van de Woestyne probably began, characteristically, by painting the eyes with an amazingly clear and detailed figurative shape; and then building around this central focus.

The Christ figure, slightly to the left of the middle of the canvas, expresses an immobile inner stillness, similar to the eternal sameness of the surrounding desert. There is no symmetry in the composition of the body. The two eyes seem to be lost in different worlds, with a different content, a different degree of involvement. One eye gazes as though what is seen evokes clarity, purity, strength, hope and security; the other suggests vagueness, lacks sharpness, is lost in confusion and sadness, looks in a different direction. The eyes communicate different messages.

---

* This text has been reproduced with permission of the publisher, from R. CRUMLIN (ed.) *Beyond Belief: Modern Art and the Religious Imagination*, Melbourne, National Gallery of Victoria, 1998. The exact reference in the exposition catalogue is: H. LOMBAERTS, *Gustave van de Woestyne's Christ in the Desert*, pp. 68-69. This text refers to the image on the front cover of this book.

One eye sees things at the horizon – inaccessible in this world but absolutely essential for the meaning of life. The other eye represents the inner experience of van de Woestyne himself, the probing and inescapable loneliness.

The face is marked by the ascetic discipline of withdrawal into the inner world and confrontation with the inherent split of human nature, recognizable in the strange composition of the hands. The mouth is shut and mute, receptive but controlling carefully what is to be exchanged with the outside world.

The hands express a decisive struggle: the immersion in a painstaking dialogue about a fatal paradox, life and death. One hand is slightly closed, pointing upwards and to the body, as if protecting an inner treasure, a subtle thought. The colour is similar to the vibrant and lively expression of the face. Details are carefully articulated, bespeaking the probing time of their being painted – reminiscent of the time of the transforming process of being lost in a desert. The other hand is half open, painted in a lively colour, ready to let go, to die, but still part of the body, still echoing a threatening inner voice.

Christ's dress evokes the image of a seamless garment, without decoration or relief[1]. One piece of undisturbed sameness, this, clearly separated from the burning desert, unchangeably the same beyond time.

There are three main coloured spaces: Christ's head with the unspoiled black hair, and one hand; the pale dress; and the desert. These three spaces suggest a clear separation, dimensions of life which cannot be mixed. Fusion and confusion are to be transcended.

The figure of Christ expresses the bare and emptying experience of entering one's own loneliness as the only access to the contemplation of an unexpected reality. In this Christ figure, the painter reveals his personal story. Christ's desert experience reflects that of the artist and of the spectator, within the mystery of ordinary human struggle.

---

1. The infant Jesus is often depicted as wrapped in bands of continuous cloth ('swaddling bands'); and the great Passion altars of the late Middle Ages contrast the plain, unsewn tunic, the *chiton*, worn by Jesus with the garb of his taunters and of the soldiers who cast lots for this garment. R.E. BROWN, *The Death of the Messiah: From Gethsemane to the Grave*, Vol. 2, London, Geoffrey Chapman, 1994, pp. 955-958, notes the reference in John (19,23-24) to this tunic, 'without seam from the top [to the bottom] woven throughout', pointing out that the evangelist attaches considerable importance to this garment. Rich in symbolic associations, the *chiton*, worn next to the skin, says Brown, recalls the special coat of Joseph (Gen 37,3), the garment of the high priest (Lev 21,10), and the clothing worn by the Galilean poor. It is also a symbol of unity.

Bibliography of Herman Lombaerts

1. *Beluister het Concilie.* Gent, HIGRO, 1962, 32 pp.
2. De invloed van de optische controle op de spelling. – *Tijdschrift voor Opvoedkunde* 8 (1962-63) 91-114.
3. Het Oude Verbond in het nieuw godsdienstleerplan van het lager onderwijs. – *Vernieuwde Catechese*, Brussel, Diocesane Dienst voor Catechese, 1965, 37-58.
4. & C. JEZIERSKI, Pour une présentation catéchétique de la résurrection du Christ. – *La résurrection du Christ. Événement, mystère, catéchèse*, Bruxelles, Lumen Vitae, 1967, 116-124. [→ 9]
5. Une Église des pauvres, servante de l'humanité. – *Lumen Vitae* 22 (1967) 491-523.
6. *Het brood breken, de kelk rondgeven ... Wat beoogt een catechese over de eucharistie?* Brussel, De Procure, [1969], 32 pp. [= 7]
7. Rompre le pain ... faire passer la coupe. Visées pour une catéchèse de l'eucharistie. – *Lumen Vitae* 24 (1969) 261-278. [→ 6]
8. Vers un programme d'enseignement religieux dans les écoles secondaires de Belgique. – *Lumen Vitae* 24 (1969) 619-639. [→ 9]
9. & C. JEZIERSKI, Per une presentazione catechetica della risurrezione di Cristo. – *La resurrezione di Cristo*. Bologna, Edizioni Dehoniane, 1970, 175-187. [= 4]
10. La coopération des sous-groupes. Son importance pour la catéchèse des adolescents. – *Lumen Vitae* 26 (1971) 33-52. [→ 12]
11. & J. VAN NIEUWENHOVE, Une formation pastorale latino-américaine en Europe? Réflexion à la suite d'un voyage. – *Lumen Vitae* 26 (1971) 611-652.
12. De samenwerking van subgroepen. Het belang ervan voor de catechese voor adolescenten. – *Aanzetten voor een schoolcatechetische didactiek. Verslagboek van de Vliebergh-Sencie-Leergang Afdeling Catechese, augustus 1971* (Theologische en pastorale publikaties Faculteit der Godgeleerdheid, Katholieke Universiteit te Leuven). Antwerpen – Utrecht, Patmos, 1972, 135-162. [= 10]
13. De impliciete structuren onder controle krijgen. – *Tijdschrift voor Catechese* 2 (1972) 106-112.
14. *Dossier à soumettre au XIème Chapitre Général. Approches d'analyse critique d'une pratique catéchétique.* Rome, Maison Généralice, 1975, 53 pp. + annexes.
15. Religieuse beleving en maatschappijkritische inzet. Een experiment. – *Jeugd en Samenleving* 6 (1976) 610-618.
16. Latijnsamerikaanse "bevrijdingscatechese" in Europa? – *Verbum* 45 (1976) 2-30.
17. Drie interviews inzake schoolcatechetisch groepswerk. – *Tijdschrift voor Catechese* 7 (1977) 251-274.

18. Catechese: een didactiek van het geloofsgetuigenis? – *Tijdschrift voor Catechese* 8 (1978) 153-160.

19. Expérience, Rite, Parole. – *Temps et Paroles* (1978) no. 17, 27-37; no. 18, 31-40; no. 19, 33-39; no. 20, 31-39; no. 21, 29-38.

20. Ervaringsgerichte Catechese. – *Korrel* 1 (1979) 139-149.

21. "Laissez venir les enfants", dit Jésus. La catéchèse dans les pays dits sous-développés. – *Vivant Univers* (1979) no. 320, 26-32.

22. The Reciprocal Relationships between Moral Commitment and Faith Expression in Worship. – C. BRUSSELMANS & J.A. O'DONOHOE (eds.), *Toward Moral and Religious Maturity. The First International Conference on Moral and Religious Development*, Morristown, NJ, Silver Burdett, 1980, 251-276.

23. Mgr Romero op het prikbord. Enkele didactische kanttekeningen. – *Korrel* 2 (1980) 289-295.
    = *School en Godsdienst* (1981) 117-120.
    = Archbishop Romero on the Bulletin Board: Some Teaching Notes. – *Word in Life* 29 (1981) no. 1, 46-48.

24. La symbolisation religieuse dans une messe de jeunes. – *Lumen Vitae* 35 (1980) 93-118.

25. Liberation and Committed Christians in Belgium. – *Towards a Dialogue with Third World Theologians*, Zeist – Nijmegen, K.U. Nijmegen, 1981, 29-31.

26. Leerkracht en leerlingen aan de arbeid. – *Korrel* 3 (1981) 19-22.

27. School en arbeid. – *Korrel* 3 (1981) 23-30.

28. De kerkelijkheid van de leerkracht godsdienst. – *Korrel* 3 (1981) 137-141.

29. Sociale rechtvaardigheid in het leerplan. – *Korrel* 3 (1981) 219-224.

30. Heropstanding in de Verenigde Staten. Ontwikkeling van het godsdienstonderwijs in de V.S. – *Verbum* 48 (1981) 171-183.

31. The Evangelisation of the Schoolmilieu. An Ecological Issue. – *Evangelisation and the Catholic School*, Dublin, Secretariat of Secondary Schools, 1982, 27-37.
    = *Word in Life* 30 (1982) no. 2, 55-64.
    = *The Sower* (1983) no. 2, 24-28; no. 3, 26-28; no. 4, 19-21.
    = *Bulletin* (Nov. 1982) 14-23.

32. Bestaan er gewelddadige koks? Voorstelling van een cahier over het geweld. – *Korrel* 4 (1982) 132-137.

33. Van "doorgeven" naar "omgaan met krachtenvelden"? – *Verbum* 49 (1982) 288-294.

34. Het waardenpatroon van de school. – *Waardenopvoeding in gelovig perspectief. Van zelfontplooiing naar solidariteit. Verslagboek van de Vliebergh-Sencie-Leergang – afdelingen catechese en bijbel, augustus 1982* (Nikè-reeks, 7), Leuven, Acco, 1983, ²1986, 23-35.

35. Sacramenten met jonge mensen. – *Korrel* 5 (1983) 191-197.

36. Christus Koning: een catechetische ontsluiting. – *Internationaal Katholiek Tijdschrift Communio* 9 (1984) 53-59.

37. Religious Education and the Catechism. – *Mount Oliver Review* 1 (1984) 3-15.
    = *Word in Life* 34 (1986) no. 1, 13-19.

38. Initiatieven in Vlaanderen. – J. KERKHOFS, K. DE TROYER, A. LIÉGEOIS, J.L. VANDERHOEVEN (eds.), *Creativiteit in de pastoraal. Verslag van een colloquium ingericht op 16-17-18 november 1984 te Leuven door de werkgroep pastoraal van de Faculteit der Godgeleerdheid*, Leuven – Amersfoort, Acco, 1985, 21-32.

39. Jongeren tot geloof brengen. Beschrijving van een (on)mogelijk proces. – J. VERCAMMEN (ed.), *Jeugd en geloof*, Leuven, Acco, 1985, 61-73.

40. & M. BONAMI, Bibliographie systématique et critique concernant la psychosociologie. – *C.F.I.P.-Bibliographie*, Bruxelles, C.F.I.P., 1985, 1-44.

41. Godsdienstonderricht in Franstalig Canada. – *Korrel* 7 (1985) 304-312.

42. Youth: Religious Education and Liturgy. – *Word in Life* 33 (1985) no. 2, 4-10.

43. Readers of a Century. – *The Living Light* 23 (1987) 158-173.

44. L'école chrétienne face à la société contemporaine. – *Lumen Vitae* 42 (1987) 367-379.

45. De klasdeur op een kier. Analyse en evaluatie van Bert de Reuvers "Schoolkatechese en communicatie". – *Verbum* 55 (1988) 70-74.

46. Geloofsontwikkeling en geloofscommunicatie. Het debat over een catechismus voor volwassenen. – J. BULCKENS & P. COOREMAN (eds.), *Kerkelijk leven in Vlaanderen anno 2000. Opstellen voor Prof. Dr. Jan Kerkhofs bij zijn emeritaat* (Nikè-reeks: Didachè), Leuven – Amersfoort, Acco, 1989, 229-243.

47. Methoden voor de jeugdpastoraal. – J. VERCAMMEN (ed.), *Jeugd en pastoraal*, Leuven, Acco, 1989, 65-85.

48. Wat baat ons de rest van gisteren? – *Jota* 4 (1989) 43-56.

49. La catéchétique et la formation des catéchètes. – *Lumen Vitae* 44 (1989) 401-412.

50. & J. BULCKENS (eds.), *Jeugd tussen religieuze aanspreekbaarheid en levensbeschouwelijke onverschilligheid. Verslagboek van de Vliebergh-Sencie-Leergang, afdeling Catechese, augustus 1989* (Nikè-reeks, 23). Leuven – Amersfoort, Acco, 1990, 221 pp.

51. Religieuze aanspreekbaarheid van jongeren vroeger en nu. – *Ibid.*, 11-50.

52. Wel en wee in de volwassenencatechese. – *Korrel* 12 (1990) 8-19.

53. Perspectieven en modellen in de volwassenencatechese. – *Korrel* 12 (1990) 20-33.

54. An International Perspective on Catechetics, With Special Emphasis on Europe and Latin America. – *The Living Light* 26 (1990) 304-323.

55. El pensamiento sistémico y la acción pastoral. – *Medellín* 63 (1990) 417-437.

56. Artiesten knipogen naar katecheten, maar merken zij het? – *Verbum* 57 (1990) 81-87.
= *Opstap* 10 (1990) 93-99.

57. Società europea, scuola, religione e insegnamento della religione. – F. PAJER (ed.), *L'insegnamento scolastico della religione nella nuova Europa*, Leumann (Torino), Elle Di Ci, 1991, 25-50.

58. Society, Culture and the Catholic School: Partnership for what Future? – N. BRENNAN, P. ARCHER, T. MCCORMACK (eds.), *The Catholic School in Contemporary Society*, Dublin, Conference of Major Religious Superiors, 1991, 101-121.

59. Under Northern Lights: A Report from the Second International Consultation on Adult Religious Education. – *Insight* (1991) 20-29.
60. Welk godsdienstonderwijs? Samenspraak met J. Bulckens en I. Verhack. – *Kultuurleven* 58 (1991) no. 2, 6-17.
61. Texture culturelle et quête de vérité. – *Lumen Vitae* 46 (1991) 261-275.
62. Het verborgen leerplan op school. – B. ROEBBEN & R. SNIJKERS (eds.), *Waarden in een vrije val? Over morele opvoeding vandaag* (Korrelcahier, 5), Averbode – Boxtel, Altiora – Katholieke Bijbelstichting, 1992, 81-87.
63. Licentiaatsverhandelingen Godsdienstwetenschappen. – M. LAMBERIGTS, L. GEVERS, B. PATTYN (eds.), *Hoger Instituut voor Godsdienstwetenschappen. Faculteit der Godgeleerdheid K.U. Leuven 1942-1992. Rondom catechese en godsdienstonderricht* (Documenta Libraria, 13), Leuven, Bibliotheek van de Faculteit der Godgeleerdheid, 1992, 59-87.
64. Op zoek naar de tweede mondigheid. Media als basismateriaal voor kunst. – *Verbum* 59 (1992) 95-98.
65. De zekerheid voorbij … Over het behoud van de christelijke traditie. – *Verbum* 59 (1992) 101-108.
66. & J. BULCKENS (eds.), *L'enseignement de la religion catholique à l'école secondaire. Enjeux pour la nouvelle Europe* (BETL, 109). Leuven, University Press – Peeters, 1993, XII-264 pp. [Avant-propos, VII-IX; Conclusions, 247-256]
67. Religion – Société et enseignement religieux à l'école. – *Ibid.*, 3-30. [→ 93]
68. Editor, *Lexicon Lasalliaans Schoolbeleid*. Groot-Bijgaarden, Lasalliaans Perspectief, 1993-1995, 470 pp.
69. Inleiding. – *Ibid.*, Rubr. 1.3, 1-4.
70. Terugblik op J.-B. De La Salle. – *Ibid.*, Rubr. 2.1, 1-13.
71. & S. DECOCK, Een gemeenschappelijke zending. Oriëntaties voor de 21ste eeuw. – *Ibid.*, Rubr. 2-3, 1-10.
72. Het systeem en zijn omgeving. – *Ibid.*, Rubr. 3.1, 1-10.
73. Systeemanalyse en (school-)organisatie. – *Ibid.*, Rubr. 3.2, 1-29.
74. Continuïteit en verandering. – *Ibid.*, Rubr. 3.3, 1-11.
75. Evaluatie en diagnose. – *Ibid.*, Rubr. 3.4, 1-19.
76. School in dienst van de moderne wereld. – *Ibid.*, Rubr. 4.1, 1-16.
77. School, cultuur en geloven. – *Ibid.*, Rubr. 4.3, 1-14.
78. Organisatiecultuur in Lasalliaanse scholen. – *Ibid.*, Rubr. 5.1, 1-24.
79. & D. MICHIELS, Klasseraad en evaluatie van leerresultaten. – *Ibid.*, Rubr. 5-3, 1-16.
80. Onderhandelingsethiek. – *Ibid.*, Rubr. 6.7, 1-19.
81. Instrumentele toerusting: inleiding – *Ibid.*, Rubr. 7.1., 1-2.
82. Beschrijving van de werking van een schoolinstelling. – *Ibid.*, Rubr. 7.3., 1-8.
83. De school en zingeving, waarden en godsdienst. – *Ibid.*, Rubr. 7.6., 1-9.
84. & L. LEIJSSEN, B. ROEBBEN (eds.), *Geloven als toekomst. Godsdienstpedagogische visies en bijdragen aangeboden aan Professor Jozef Bulckens bij zijn emeritaat*, Leuven – Amersfoort, Acco, 1995, 640 pp. [Ten geleide, 11-14]
85. Van generatie tot generatie. – *Ibid.*, 213-230.
86. Onderwijs en maatschappij – Wat brengt ons de toekomst? – *Impuls* 25 (1995) 4, 55-64.
= *Zilveren sporen. 25 jaar Onderwijsimpulsen*, Leuven – Amersfoort, Acco, 1995.

87. & L. BOEVE (eds.), *Traditie en initiatie. Perspectieven voor de toekomst. Verslagboek van de Vliebergh-Sencie-Leergang, Afdeling Catechese, 21 en 22 augustus 1995* (Nikè-reeks, 36), Leuven – Amersfoort, Acco, 1996, 221 pp. [Woord vooraf, 7-10]

88. Weerbaar of weerloos? Godsdienstige tradities in de hedendaagse maatschappij. – *Ibid.*, 79-108.

89. On the Double Borders of the *"New Europe". A Mirror of an Old Future?* – A. CAMPS, B. KLEIN GOLDEWIJK, J. VAN NIEUWENHOVE (eds.), *Cultural Identity in Latin America and in Europe*, Kampen, Kok, 1996, 38-57.

90. Editor, *Leadership and Management of Christian Schools. A Systemic Lasallian Viewpoint*, Rome – Groot-Bijgaarden, 1997, VIII-361 pp. [= partial translation of 68]

91. Catechetics and the Formation of Catechists. – M. WARREN (ed.), *Sourcebook for Modern Catechetics*, Vol. 2, Winona, Saint Mary's Press, 1997, 178-191.

92. Religious Education Today and the Catechism. – *Ibid.*, 243-257.

93. Religion, Society, and the Teaching of Religion in Schools. – *Ibid.*, 306-329 [= 67]

94. & J. DE TAVERNIER (eds.), *De smalle grens tussen assertiviteit en agressiviteit. Over de leerbaarheid van geweldloosheid en verzoening* (Nikè-reeks, 43), Leuven – Amersfoort, Acco, 1998, 216 pp. [Ten geleide, 7-9]

95. & B. ROEBBEN (eds.), *Gods Website. Mediacultuur en godsdienstige vorming* (Nikè-reeks, 44), Leuven – Amersfoort, Acco, 1998, 212 pp. [Woord vooraf, 7-13]

96. & B. ROEBBEN, G. GINNEBERGE, Godsdienstdidactiek op het Internet (GODINET). – *Ibid.*, 193-209.

97. De 'Missies' van de katholieke hogescholen. Een globaal profiel. – *H-oge Lijn* 6 (1998) 3, 3-6.

98. Geloofscommunicatie. Van overdracht naar communicatie. – *Tijdschrift voor Geestelijk Leven* 54 (1998) 633-645.

99. Het gewetensonderzoek van een Internationaal Instituut: uitdagingen en beleidsstrategieën (Den Haan, 13 november 1998). – *Lasalliaanse Vormingssessie VII. 'Schoolhouden binnen het nieuwe decreet: is een participatief schoolbeleid nog haalbaar?'*, Groot-Bijgaarden, Lasalliaans Perspectief, 1998, 33-38.

100. Gustave van de Woestyne's Christ in the Desert. – R. CRUMLIN (ed.), *Beyond Belief: Modern Art and the Religious Imagination*, Melbourne, National Gallery of Victoria, 1998, 68-69.

101. Systematisch. – *Nova et Vetera* 76 (1998-99) 28-48.

102. & B. ROEBBEN, G. GINNEBERGE, GODINET. Een flexibel werkinstrument voor een vak in beweging. – *Verbum* 66 (1999) 1, 11-20. [→ 103]

103. & B. ROEBBEN, G. GINNEBERGE, GODINET. Ein flexibles Arbeitsinstrumentum für ein Fach in Bewegung. – *Religionspädagogische Beiträge* (1999) no. 42, 167-178 [= 102]

104. Factores que apoyan y garantizan la educación. Análisis deontológico. – J.-M. QUINTANA CABANAS, H. LOMBAERTS, P.-M. GIL LARRAÑAGA, R. ARTACHO LÓPEZ, *La difícil tarea de educar (Cátedra de Educación Cristiana, Madrid, 10 noviembre 1998)*, Madrid, San Juan Bautista De La Salle, 1999, 33-54.

105. La situación de la enseñanza de la religión en Bélgica y Holanda. – COMISIÓN EPISCOPAL DE ENSEÑANZA, *La enseñanza de la religión, una propuesta de vida (I Congreso Nacional de Profesores de Religión Madrid, 12-14 noviembre de 1999)*, Madrid, 1999, 189-201.
106. Young People Owning Their Religious Formation: Changing Roles of Catholic Schools (The Damien Lundy Lecture 1999). – *Mentor: Magazine for Headteachers and Staff* 4 (1999) no. 5, 8-12.
107. & B. ROEBBEN (eds.), *Godsdienst op school in de branding. Een tussentijdse balans* (Cahiers voor Didactiek, 7), Deurne, Wolters Plantyn, 2000, 121 pp. [Woord vooraf, 7-12]
108. De klas als leergroep. De leraar als hermeneut. – *Ibid.,* 67-80.
109. Het godsdienstonderricht als communicatieve gebeurtenis. – *Ibid.,* 81-107.

[Bibliography closed October 1, 2000 – compiled by Leo Kenis and Bert Roebben]

List of Contributors

Anton BUCHER

Studied theology and educational sciences in Fribourg, was research assistent in Mainz und Fribourg, received in 1990 the *Habilitation* in pedagogics of religion. He is since 1993 Professor of Religious Education at the University of Salzburg. In 2000 he obtained the *Habilitation* in educational sciences. His main fields of interest are: empirical research in religious education, research on happiness in the life world of children. His latest publications include: *Braucht Mutter Kirche brave Kinder? Religiöse Reifung kontra kirchliche Infantilisierung*, München, Kösel, 1997; *Religionsunterricht zwischen Lernfach und Lebenshilfe. Eine empirische Untersuchung zum katholischen Religionsunterricht in der Bundesrepublik Deutschland*, Stuttgart, 2000; *Was macht Kinder glücklich? Historische, theoretische und empirische Annäherungen an eine Sehnsucht, die nicht altert*, München, 2001 (forthcoming). – Address: Institut für Religionspädagogik, Universität Salzburg, Universitätsplatz 1, A-5020 Salzburg, Austria.

Roland CAMPICHE

Licentiate in theology and doctor in sociology at the University of Lausanne. Completed his education in Göttingen, Strasbourg, Chicago and Köln. He has been teaching sociology of religion at the University of Lausanne since 1970. In 1971 he was appointed as Director of the Bureau Romand de l'Institut d'Éthique Sociale de la Fédération des Églises protestantes de la Suisse (domain of social politics). Since december 1999, he is Director of the "Observatoire des religions en Suisse". For his latest publications one could refer to: *Croire en Suisse(s)*, Lausanne, L'Age d'Homme, 1992 (ed., with A. DUBACH *et al.*; translation in German, 1993: *Jeder ein Sonderfall*); *Entretiens avec Cyril Dépraz, Quand les sectes affolent. Ordre du Temple Solaire, médias et fin de millénaire*, Lausanne – Genève, Institut d'éthique sociale Labor et Fides, 1995; *Cultures jeunes et religions en Europe*, Paris, Cerf, 1997 (ed.). – Address: Departement d'histoire et sciences des religions, Faculté de Theologie, Université de Lausanne, rue des Terreaux 10, CH-1003 Lausanne, Switzerland.

Rosemary CRUMLIN, rsm

Art curator and art historian with a special interest in modern art and spirituality. She was responsible for the exhibitions and books *Aboriginal Art and Spirituality: Images of Religion in Australian Art* and *Beyond Belief: Modern Art and the Religious Imagination*. She is working at present on curating the exhibition *O Soul O Spirit O Fire: Celebrating Fifty Years of the Blake Prize for Religious*

Art, and its accompanying book, *Changing Icons*. Between 1973 and 1986 she was a staff member and then Director of the National Pastoral Institute of Religious Education (Australia). She has academic qualifications in religious education, adult education, art and art history and honorary doctorates in theology (STD) and education, respectively from the Melbourne College of Divinity and the Australian Catholic University. – Address: 138 Glenhuntly Road, Elwood 3184, Melbourne 03, Victoria, Australia.

Catherine DOOLEY, op

Associate Professor in the Department of Religion and Religious Education at The Catholic University of America, Washington, D.C. She holds master's degrees from The Catholic University of America, Harvard Divinity School, and a M.A. and Ph.D. from the K.U. Leuven. She has published widely in catechetical and liturgical journals and has written a number of texts and resources for religious education. Her latest publications include: *The Echo Within: Emerging Issues in Religious Education. A Tribute to Berard L. Marthaler*, Thomas More, Allen TX, 1997 (ed., with M. COLLINS); *Ecclesial Mediation of Grace: Essays in Sacramental and Liturgical Theology* [ed., special issue of *Louvain Studies* 23 (1998) no. 2]. – Address: The Catholic University of America, 4610 Guilford Road, College Park, MA 20740, USA.

Norbert METTE

Studied theology and social sciences. Since 1984 he is Professor of Practical Theology at the University of Paderborn. He has published and edited widely on questions of pastoral theology, religious education and social ethics – e.g. *Religionspädagogik*, Patmos, Düsseldorf, 1994; *Praktisch-theologische Erkundungen* (Theologie und Praxis, 1), Münster, Lit-Verlag, 1998; *Orientierung Theologie*, Reinbek, Rowohlt, 2000 (with H.-M. GUTMANN); *Lexikon der Religionspädagogik*, Neukirchen-Vluyn, Neukirchener Verlag, 2001 (ed., with F. RICKERS). – Address: Universität-Gesamthochschule Paderborn, Fachbereich 1, Katholische Theologie / Praktische Theologie, Warburger Straße 100, D-33098 Paderborn, Germany.

Maureen O'BRIEN

Assistant Professor of Theology and Director of Pastoral Ministry at Duquesne University, Pittsburgh, Pennsylvania, USA. She earned the Ph.D. in Religion and Education at Boston College. Her fields of interests include the intersection of religious education and practical theology, religious education for the public church, and the education of lay ecclesial ministers. She has published a number of articles on these and related topics. Recent publications include: *Practical Theology and Postmodern Religious Education*, in *Religious Education* 94 (1999) 313-328; *Interprofessional Education in Theology and Social Work:*

Postmodern and Practical Theological Dimensions, in *Teaching Theology and Religion* 3 (2000) 20-32. – Address: Duquesne University, Fisher Hall, 600 Forbes Avenue, Pittsburgh, PA 15282, USA.

Flavio PAJER

Licentiate in education and doctor in theology. He is Professor of Pedagogics and Didactics of Religion in two international Faculties of Educational Sciences in Rome. In the last decennium he was visiting professor at the Higher Institute of Educational Sciences affiliated with the ICAO, in Abidjan (Ivory Coast). He works particularly in the field of permanent education of secondary school teachers of religion in Italy. As a member of the Curatorium of the European Forum for Religious Education at Schools, he has published in the field of religious education and pastoral care. His latest publications include: *L'insegnamento scolastico della religione nella nuova Europa*, Torino, Elle Di Ci, 1991 (ed.); *Religio. Enciclopedia tematica dell'educazione religiosa*, Casale Monferrata, Piemme, 1998 (ed., with Z. TRENTI, L. PRENNA, G. MORANTE, L. GALLO, M. GIUSEPPE); *L'insegnamento delle scienze religiose in Europa*, Napoli, 2000 (ed.). – Address: Via Aurelia 476, I-00100 Roma, Italy.

Bert ROEBBEN
Studied theology, educational sciences and canon law at the K.U. Leuven. He received the STD degree in Leuven in 1994, with a dissertation on moral education in Christian perspective. During the period 1995-2000, he lectured in the department of Pastoral Theology and in the teacher training department of the Faculty of Theology of the K.U. Leuven, and in the Faculty of Theology of Tilburg University. He was a guest lecturer at the KTU in Utrecht. Since October 2000 he is appointed as Associate Professor of Practical Theology/Religious Education at the Faculty of Theology of Tilburg University. His research interests are: religious education, moral education, fundamental practical theology, the intersection between youth cultures and theology and adult formation and theology. His latest publications include: *Een tijd van opvoeden. Moraalpedagogiek in christelijk perspectief*, Leuven – Amersfoort, Acco, 1995; *Gods Website. Mediacultuur en godsdienstige vorming*, Leuven – Amersfoort, Acco, 1998 (ed., with H. LOMBAERTS); *Religieus opvoeden in een multiculturele samenleving*, Leuven, Davidsfonds, 2000 (ed.). – Address: Faculty of Theology, K.U. Brabant, PO Box 9130, NL-5000 HC Tilburg, The Netherlands.

Graham ROSSITER

Associate Professor of Religious and Moral Education, and Head of the School of Religious Education at Australian Catholic University in Sydney (Australia). He is also Director of the Cardinal Clancy Centre for Research in the Spiritual, Moral, Religious and Pastoral Dimensions of Education. His study interests are in the spirituality of youth, the spiritual and moral influence of film and television, and school religious education curricula. A number of his recent publications have appeared in the Australian Journal of Religious Education. Remarkable is his study on *The Shaping Influence of Film and Television on Young People's Spirituality* in *International Journal of Children's Spirituality* 1 (1996) 52-67; 2 (1997) 21-35; 4 (1999) 207-224. – Address: Cardinal Clancy Center for Research in the Spiritual, Moral, Religious and Pastoral Dimensions of Education, Australian Catholic University, 179 Albert Road, Strathfield NSW 2135, Australia.

Kieran SCOTT

Associate Professor of Religious Education in the Graduate School of Religion and Religious Education at Fordham University, New York. He pursued doctoral studies at Columbia University and Union Theological Seminary in New York. His current research interests engage the areas of adult education, critical ecclesiology, youth ministry and the inter-play between practical theology and religious education. His most recent publications include: *Perspectives on Marriage*, New York, Oxford University Press, ²2000 (ed., with M. WARREN). – Address: Graduate School of Religion and Religious Education, Fordham University, 115 Cornell Avenue, Hawthorne, NY 07506, USA.

Tjeu VAN KNIPPENBERG

Studied ecumenical theology at the University of Nijmegen and group work at colleges for social-educational training in Nijmegen. He has worked in the seminary of his congregation (the Lazarists in Zundert), in ecumenical organisations and health care ministry in Zutphen, at the Interuniversity Institute for Missiological and Ecumenical Research in Utrecht, in campus ministry in Nijmegen and at the Department of Pastoral Theology of Nijmegen University. Since January 1988 he is Professor of Pastoral Theology at the Faculty of Theology of Tilburg University. His fields of interest are: fundamental practical theology, poimenics and pastoral care. His latest publications include: *Between two Languages. Spiritual Guidance and the Communication of Christian Faith*, Tilburg, Tilburg University Press, 1998; *Tussen Naam en Identiteit. Ontwerp van een model voor geestelijke begeleiding*, Kampen, Kok, 1998. – Address: Faculty of Theology, K.U. Brabant, PO Box 9130, NL-5000 HC Tilburg, The Netherlands.

Michael WARREN

Has a doctorate in religious education from The Catholic University of America. He has taught in the Department of Theology at St. John's University, New York City, since 1975. His latest books are: *Sourcebook for Modern Catechetics*, Vol. 2, Winona, Saint Mary's Press, 1997 (ed.); *Seeing Through the Media: A Religious View of Communications and Cultural Analysis*, Harrisburg, Trinity Press International, 1997; *At This Time, in This Place: The Spirit Embodied in the Local Assembly,* Harrisburg, Trinity Press International, 1999. – Address: Department of Theology and Religious Studies, St. John's University, 186-16 Abigail Adams Ave., Jamaica, NY 11432-1909, USA.

Hans-Georg ZIEBERTZ

Studied theology, sociology and educational sciences in Münster. He received a Ph.D in theology (Nijmegen), in educational sciences (Tübingen) and the *Habilitation* in pedagogics of religion (Mainz). After a period of teaching in the Netherlands (Nijmegen and Utrecht) he was appointed in 1998 as Professor of Practical Theology/Religious Education at the University of Würzburg (Germany). Fields of interest are religious socialisation, religion and post-modernity, identity formation. His latest publications include: *Religion, Christentum und Moderne. Veränderte Religionspräsenz als Herausforderung,* Stuttgart – Köln, Kohlhammer, 1999; *The Human Image of God,* Leiden – Boston – Köln, Brill, 2001 (ed., with F. SCHWEITZER, H. HÄRING, D. BROWNING); *Religious Individualization and Christian Religious Semantics,* Münster – Hamburg – London, Lit-Verlag, 2001 (ed.). – Address: Institut für Praktische Theologie, Lehrstuhl für Religionspädagogik und Didaktik des Religionsunterrichts, Universität Würzburg, Wittelsbacher Platz 1, D-97404 Würzburg, Germany.

PRINTED ON PERMANENT PAPER • IMPRIME SUR PAPIER PERMANENT • GEDRUKT OP DUURZAAM PAPIER - ISO 9706

N.V. PEETERS S.A., KLEIN DALENSTRAAT 42, B-3020 HERENT